Fort Worth from World War II to 1960

Harold Rich

Number 11 in the Texas Local Series

University of North Texas Press
Denton, Texas

Printed in the United States of America.

10 9 8 7 6 5 4 3 2 1

Permissions:
University of North Texas Press
1155 Union Circle #311336
Denton, TX 76203-5017

The paper used in this book meets the minimum requirements of the American National Standard for Permanence of Paper for Printed Library Materials, z39.48.1984. Binding materials have been chosen for durability.

Library of Congress Cataloging-in-Publication Data is available from the Library of Congress.

ISBN 978-1-57441-984-9 (cloth)
ISBN 978-1-57441-992-4 (ebook)

Fort Worth from World War II to 1960 is Number 11 in the Texas Local Series.

The electronic edition of this book was made possible by the support of the Vick Family Foundation.

Typeset by vPrompt eServices.

"Our deeds still travel with us from afar
And what we have been makes us what we are."
Middlemarch by George Eliot

"For the wind passeth over it, and it is gone;
And the place thereof shall know it no more."

Psalms 103:16 (King James Version)

Contents

List of Charts and Graphs

List of Abbreviations

CAA	Civil Aeronautics Authority
CCGFW	Citizens' Committee for a Greater Fort Worth
DWI	driving while intoxicated
FHA	Federal Housing Administration
FPHA	Federal Public Housing Agency
FWVL	Fort Worth Voters League
GM	General Motors
GMA	General Ministers Association
HBPL	Home & Business Protective League
IAM	International Association of Machinists
JPS	John Peter Smith Hospital
MP	military police
NAACP	National Association for the Advancement of Colored People
NYU	New York University
OPA	Office of Price Administration
POA	Police Officers Association
PPL	People's Protective League
RMHOA	Riverside Merchants and Home-Owners Association
ROTC	Reserve Officer Training Corps
SESCL	Southeast Side Civic League
STI	sexually transmitted infection
SWCIAN	Southwestern College of Industrial Arts for Negroes
TBA	Texas Barber Association
TCIC	Texas Commission on Interracial Cooperation
TCU	Texas Christian University
UCLA	University of California at Los Angeles
UGM	Union Gospel Mission
USES	United States Employment Service Office
USO	United Service Organization
USPHSH	United States Public Health Service Hospital
UT	University of Texas at Austin
WPA	Works Project Administration
WPB	War Production Board

Preface

Fort Worth from World War II to 1960 covers Fort Worth history from America's entry into World War II through the first years of the Cold War and into 1960. The story begins with the attack on Pearl Harbor on December 7, 1941, where *Fort Worth Between the World Wars* (Texas A&M University Press, 2020) ended, and closes with the end of the second Eisenhower administration. Along with *Fort Worth: Outpost, Cowtown, Boomtown* (University of Oklahoma Press, 2014), the three volumes provide a broad historical survey of Fort Worth from 1880 to 1960, eighty-one eventful years. Throughout, the intent was to be as inclusive as possible while maintaining foci on vice and crime, race relations, policing, and economic development. Whenever possible, names have been named and places identified to aid future scholars in extending and deepening the history.

Every city is both unique and the same. Fort Worth shared many common issues with thousands of other cities at the same time it developed its own distinctive and colorful story. That past was not always kind or fair or pretty, but it was, and is, fascinating.

I would like, once again, to thank Dr. Todd Kerstetter and Dr. Ben Proctor, two multifaceted scholars and caring individuals, as well as many other members of Texas Christian University's History Department.

I also want to commend the staff at the Fort Worth Library History Center for their pleasant assistance. Generous thanks to the University of Texas at Arlington Library's Special Collections, represented by Sara Pezzoni, for their support in providing photographs.

Previously, I recognized my parents, my son, and my granddaughters. I am very glad to have had such a devoted mother and father in my life and three wonderful progenies. Scott, Elizabeth, and Emily, you three are my best work.

In closing, a personal, somewhat cryptic thought: Two beings outside my family were important to me, one long ago and far away and one with a wet nose and the sweetest disposition that remained by my side for over sixteen years (my Sadie). I still think of both every day.

Harold Rich, January 2025

Part 1

Fort Worth in World War II and the Postwar, 1942–1950

Chapter 1

The War and Fort Worth

The European war that began in September 1939 had far-reaching effects on the United States and Texas. The cruelest impacts arrived even before the Pearl Harbor attack, December 7, 1941, brought the United States into the fray. In November 1941 the British Air Ministry reported Pilot Officer Roger Atkinson of Fort Worth was one of nine Americans killed in action while serving in the Eagle Squadron of the Canadian Air Force.[1] Officer Atkinson would be just one of 15,764 Texans who made the ultimate sacrifice in World War II; thousands of others would suffer major injuries and 785,063 Texans would serve in the nation's military between 1941 and 1945, a higher service rate than Texas's 4.85 percent of the population in 1940. Their sacrifices left indelible marks on them and their families, but those who remained on the home front also endured radical changes to their lives and the world in which they lived. One of the starkest forces rearranging society came from a mass migration that significantly altered demographics. That mass movement between 1941 and 1947 created the greatest population shift in Texas history as 500,000 Texans relocated, most leaving farms and small communities for high-paying defense jobs in cities where the burgeoning defense industry clamored for workers.[2]

The rural to urban shift was reflected in the 1950 Census, which showed two hundred rural Texas counties with population declines while fifty-four urban counties added significant population. The effect was so dramatic that, for the first time ever, more Texans lived in urban than in rural settings. At the same time, Texas's African American population declined 4.5 percent, an effect of Blacks leaving the state for defense jobs and better living conditions in the North and West. The war also forever changed the Texas economy, stimulating industrialization at an unprecedented pace and expanding oil production to become Texas's most important industry. The rise in oil production was fortuitous, occurring as wartime demand spiked, making oil a critical national defense commodity. In 1941 Texas produced just over 36 percent of the nation's petroleum; by 1947 the state's production had grown 50 percent, increasing Texas's production to almost 44 percent of total American oil output.[3]

The war's impact on Fort Worth and Tarrant County mirrored that of the nation and the state in its immediacy and intensity. A sailor and a Marine from Tarrant County (home to Fort Worth) were among the 2,403 Americans killed at Pearl Harbor, and Lieutenant Commander Stanley P. Mosely of Fort Worth was one of four submarine commanders awarded a Navy Cross by Admiral Chester Nimitz for bravery following the attack.[4] In the course of the war, approximately 30,000 Tarrant County residents would serve in the military and 530 (some reports counted 566) would lose their lives. The war's massive economic impact began quickly as large defense spending ended the Great Depression while expanding the military's local footprint. Much of that early effect came from military aviation–related construction developing Hicks and Tarrant airfields, the Eagle Mountain Marine Air Base, and the Army Air Force Training Command. Fort Worth was no stranger to military aviation; in 1917 the War Department built three training airfields within a fourteen-mile radius of downtown, as well as the Camp Bowie base just west of downtown where up to 100,000 doughboys trained. All were major economic boosts to the local economy. In contrast, the local economic effect in World War II came not from large military bases but from massive defense contracts that stimulated Fort Worth's industrial sector, expanding existing businesses like American Cyanamid and Chemical Corporation

Texas Recruits at Fort Worth Recruiting Office before leaving for duty in the Air Corps, August 12, 1941. Courtesy *Fort Worth Star Telegram* Collection, Special Collections, University of Texas at Arlington Libraries.

and Williamson-Dickie (uniform supplier) and bringing a massive Convair bomber plant. The influx of defense dollars created thousands of jobs, drawing workers and causing a population boom that significantly impacted Fort Worth in the war and postwar periods. Fort Worth businessmen recognized the war's economic potential early on. In 1940 the chamber of commerce predicted Fort Worth would be a center for 65,000 military personnel and defense workers. Their estimate proved to be conservative: 35,000 soldiers would train in Brownwood and 18,000 in Mineral Wells; Convair alone employed 30,000, while thousands more toiled at various local industries with defense contracts.[5]

The before and after economic effects were dramatically reflected in statistics. Immediately before the war Fort Worth still struggled with high unemployment. The 1940 United States Census counted 66,866 employed workers in Fort Worth, plus another 4,237 on public emergency work, for a total workforce of 71,103, while 8,489 remained unemployed, suggesting an unemployment rate of 10.7 percent—clear evidence that the Depression lingered despite sizable New Deal relief and work programs. Between 1935 and 1942 the Federal Emergency Relief Appropriations Act allocated $486.1 million for Texas projects, the majority ($273.6 million) through the Works Project Administration (WPA).[6] The WPA was a massive effort, employing 3.3 million workers nationally at its height in November 1938. After fighting broke out in Europe in September 1939, the agency's funding dwindled, but as late as January 2, 1943, the WPA still employed 253,981 workers. The end came soon afterward; WPA offices closed on May 1, 1943, signaling that defense spending had replaced and surpassed relief programs.[7] Texas was an early entrant in commanding a share of the defense appropriations bonanza, receiving $23 million in defense contracts in the first months after Pearl Harbor, a substantial 11 percent of $209.5 million appropriated. From that point, national defense expenditures grew exponentially, reaching $2.5 billion in May 1941 and increasing at even faster rates afterward. Texas's share of the pie grew. By August 1942 Texas companies held $2.34 billion in defense contracts, an impressive figure, but only eleventh nationally, far behind California, the leader with $6.39 billion, and second-place New York, $6.12 billion.[8] The sharp influx of federal spending had a tremendous economic impact on the nation. The number of Americans reporting an annual income of $50,000 or more had declined from 43,184 in 1928 (just before the Depression) to just 7,738 in 1932; by 1942 their number had more than tripled to 25,106. As incomes rose, so did income taxes. The tax due on a single person earning a $5,000 annual wage increased from $110 in 1940 to $746 in 1942.[9]

Fort Worth had received a fair share of defense contracts and industry before 1941, but its share of appropriations would increase significantly after Pearl Harbor. In the harried days following December 7, the Fort Worth Police Department, already scrambling to set up twenty-two aircraft observations stations and develop blackout protocols to defend against air attacks, was ordered to protect the 240 local defense contractors, an impossible task. That Fort Worth had 240 firms with defense contracts that early was impressive, although most were small operations that would pale in comparison to the huge facilities that would be built. In 1941 construction had already

Firefighter H. K. Pitts and Lieutenant J. P. Pettyjohn in one of twenty-one fire trucks sounding alarms in a blackout drill, January 19, 1942. Courtesy *Fort Worth Star Telegram* Collection, Special Collections, University of Texas at Arlington Libraries.

begun on several sizable projects, including the Army Quartermaster Depot on the city's south side, Globe Aircraft where trainers would be built for the Army Air Corps and, the jewel in the crown overwhelming everything else, Consolidated Vultree Aircraft Corporation (soon known as Convair). The construction of Convair began September 24, 1941, on 526 acres near

Lake Worth that Fort Worth purchased for $99,750 and donated. Convair was not one of the 240 plants assigned police protection since it had its own security force.[10]

Convair by itself was huge, both in its contribution to the war effort and in its importance to the Fort Worth economy. In May 1941 Convair Fort Worth received $163.6 million, almost half of the $327.9 million appropriated for three aircraft manufacturers. In comparison, total federal payments to all three companies amounted to only $80 million in all of 1939.[11] The building alone was a major project, costing $22.4 million plus another $10.5 million spent on machinery and equipment, all thrown together in just six months so that 15,000 workers could be on the job producing B-24 bombers by March 1942.[12] The plant officially opened in April 1942, two months ahead of schedule, an event commemorated by the *Star Telegram* with a 188-page edition on April 19, 1942, largely consisting of business ads welcoming the plant and boasting of each company's contribution to the construction. For example, Fort Worth's Acme Brick reported it had supplied 4.6 million bricks for the plant's construction. Employment quickly spiraled to 30,000, creating commercial numbers that would have seemed impossible in the 1930s. The first B-24 rolled out April 18, 1942 (some sources claim April 17), only seven months after the start of construction, an engineering and production miracle. By the end of production on November 27, 1944, when the last bomber rolled out, Convair had built 3,000 B-24s.[13]

The plant drew supporting industries that augmented the existing aviation infrastructure. Tarrant Airfield (which would become Carswell Air Force Base, now the Joint Reserve Base), was built adjacent to Convair as one of seven new Midwestern and Southwestern Air Force bases. Tarrant Airfield served as home base for thousands of airmen, as well as the Army Air Corps Flying Training Command, 100 officers and staff transferred from Washington, DC, to Fort Worth in June 1942.[14] Convair and the Air Force base joined an already sizable aviation industry supporting 1,200 workers. Civilian airlines became an established transportation mode in the 1930s, creating a sustained surge in Fort Worth's commercial traffic that increased from 20,080 passengers in 1930 to 159,591 in 1941, an almost 700 percent increase. That expansion helped to make Fort Worth the Southern Base

Headquarters for American Airlines, a sizable operation employing 330 local staff, including 100 pilots, and to lure Braniff and Delta to open local offices and shops. Hicks Field—a World War I training base north of Fort Worth with hangars, shops, and administrative offices from the Great War—was rejuvenated prior to Pearl Harbor to provide initial civilian pilot training (interesting side note: 43 World War I pilots lived in Fort Worth at the time). Graduating cadets moved directly into military training at Randolph Army Air Base in San Antonio.[15]

The economic rising tide spread widely, bringing prosperity to many businesses that had struggled in the 1920s and 1930s. Texas Steel was a good example of a long-term Fort Worth industry that barely survived after peace broke out in 1918. The company founder, George Armstrong, avoided bankruptcy post–World War I by selling to John Kirby of Houston, who converted the bolt works into a steel mill but lost so much money that the business was saved from bankruptcy and closure in 1926 only because employees agreed to a 50 percent pay cut. Even then, Kirby could not turn a profit and returned the business to Armstrong. By 1943 Texas Steel hummed with defense contracts, running seven days a week, twenty-four hours a day, and was still unable to meet demand.[16]

The war's economic effect meshed with and accelerated an upward trend that had slowly begun bringing Texas out of the industrial depths it had occupied since the Civil War and Reconstruction. From 1880 to 1940, Texas's industrial production experienced steady expansion, growing from the nation's twenty-seventh largest in value of manufacturing goods to fourteenth, from twenty-seventh to eleventh in value added by manufacturing, and from twenty-ninth to sixteenth in number of workers employed in manufacturing. Texas even did relatively well in the Depression years of the 1930s, leading the nation with a 3.4 percentage increase in manufacturing plants (California was second with 2.4 percent), a result all the more impressive considering the national total declined 12.7 percent.[17]

The huge economic inputs took time to trickle down to become visible in economic indicators. Fort Worth bank clearings were some of the first to record substantial upswings, rising to $199 million in the first six months of 1941, up $29 million, or 17 percent, from the same period in 1940, but retail sales lagged slightly behind, recording only a 12 percent increase in February 1941 compared to 1940, the second lowest of forty cities, besting only Oakland, California, which rose a scant 2 percent. In comparison, retail sales rose 17 percent in Dallas and 24 percent in Houston. The relative poorer outcomes for Fort Worth began to change in January 1942, when local sales increased 19 percent over January 1940 (better than Dallas's 16 percent), followed by a 36 percent rise in February 1943 compared to February 1942 (substantially better than Dallas's 27 percent or Houston's 26 percent). From that point the numbers took off, rising 75 percent in a two-week period ending April 17, 1943, followed by a 122 percent increase the next fortnight, far more than the 78 percent for Dallas or 50 percent for Houston.[18]

The general business upswing eventually spread to city finances that had tottered on the edge of bankruptcy throughout most of the Depression. City coffers swelled so dramatically that Fort Worth entered the 1942/1943 fiscal year with a $500,000 surplus, a bonanza that enabled the council to maintain a property tax rate of $1.83 per $100 valuation (the rate included school funding) and still fund, along with other revenue sources, a $5.5 million budget—a significant increase. In October 1943 the improved financial situation allowed Fort Worth to resume paying wages in cash, ending the practice of issuing warrants—essentially promises to pay at a later date that banks redeemed at a discounted rate, varying from 1 to 3 percent, the loss absorbed by employees.[19] Fort Worth had often resorted to warrants in its cash-strapped history, most notably during the Panic of 1893 and its aftermath, and had resumed the practice on October 15, 1933, during the depths of the Depression. The era of good times for the municipal budget continued in 1944 when the city entered the fiscal year with a $1.2 million surplus, although ongoing commodity shortages that slowed cash outgo contributed to the positive balance. The 1944/1945 budget, $6,952,775—the largest ever to that point—included a 5 percent raise for all employees below department head; funding for 123 new employees, including 100 firefighters to staff four new fire stations; and the initial contribution for an employee pension plan. Support for a pension solidified into action in February 1944 after City Manager Sam Bothwell appointed a special committee to study hospitalization and retirement plans for the 1,500 city employees not covered by Social

Security. Their proposal was impressive for its time, providing retirement income regardless of length of service for workers disabled in the line of duty and for employees regardless of tenure at age 65 or at age 60 with twenty-five years of service. The pensions were funded by both the city and employee contributing 7.5 percent of wages, later reduced to 4 percent.[20]

Defense expenditures stimulated Fort Worth's building trades, bringing unprecedented construction. In 1941 city building permits totaled $6,540,476, approximately $2 million more than in 1940, but the actual construction for the area was much larger. Federal projects like Convair ($14 million), Tarrant Airfield ($10 million), the Marine Corps Air Base at Eagle Mountain Lake ($4.7 million), and the Quartermaster Depot ($5 million) did not require city permits (the latter two were also outside Fort Worth city limits, as was the $3 million Liberator Village).[21] In 1942, the last year before wartime restrictions eliminated most non-defense building, city building permits registered $11 million, almost doubling the amount in 1941. Construction that year included 1,347 single-family homes valued at $3.6 million, plus twenty-seven duplexes and four apartment houses in addition to a new 12,000 square-foot A&P (the largest in the region) that opened in May at 1608 Hemphill Street to coincide with the paving of Hemphill Street from Magnolia Avenue to Biddison Street. Also in 1942 Pennsylvania Avenue Hospital, closed for four years, reopened with seventy-five beds to help meet rising medical demands accompanying Fort Worth's rapid population growth. Fort Worth Mayor T. J. Harrell credited the industrial boom for driving Fort Worth's population from 207,667 in 1940 to 259,102 in 1945, an increase of almost 25 percent in five years. The mayor's figures may have been too conservative; the 1940 United States Census showed a population of 177,662, far less than the over 200,000 Harrell claimed, which would have meant the population surged almost 46 percent. In any case, Fort Worth's rapid population increase strained housing, transportation, and city services throughout the war and afterward.[22]

The massive infusion of federal dollars creating thousands of jobs abruptly ended the unemployment problem that had endured through the Depression, replacing it almost overnight with severe labor shortages. Social agencies at first feared the opposite condition would prevail, that the defense economy would attract more workers than jobs, creating "extremely serious" problems. Those fears were supported by a national study that found defense jobs attracted twice the number of workers actually needed. The study attempted a separate focus on the impact of defense work on Blacks, but dismissed the effort after concluding that Black concerns were "essentially the same" as white concerns.[23] Any concerns about idle, unemployed workers were quickly replaced with complaints of worker shortages. As early as summer 1942, Fort Worth hotel and restaurant trades reported problems finding staff, blaming the situation on men leaving for the military and both men and women taking better paying defense jobs. They were right. In 1943 almost one-third of Fort Worth's workforce, 35,000, worked at Convair, which did not exist until 1942. With no real hope of competing for those workers, businesses like restaurants and hotels had little choice but to ask for the public's patience. Estimates predicted that Fort Worth's workforce would almost double from 64,157 in 1940 to 122,211 by the end of 1942, but the actual result fell short, reaching just 102,000 in 1943, the total held back because the supply of workers was insufficient to fill thousands of vacancies. USES predicted that all 300,000 unemployed in Texas would be on the job by the end of the year of 1942, a radical transition from the depths of the Depression just ten years earlier when 13 million Americans languished unemployed.[24]

The Fort Worth experience was part of a national recovery. Unemployment in the United States remained as high as 8.8 million in 1940, then began a precipitous decline to 3.5 million in April 1942, dropping to only 1 million one year later. A corresponding drop in unemployment benefits followed, declining from $9.9 million in 1940 to only $5.5 million in 1941, and to only $119,500 in the first quarter in 1942, less than one-tenth the $1,619,420 in the same period in 1941. The change was so dramatic and so sudden that the *Star Telegram* termed the first ten months of 1942 the greatest economic success since the "boom days" of 1929. The article lamented that good defense jobs starting at $0.60 an hour languished unfilled, waiting for applicants, while classes in occupational training at the Fort Worth War Industries Training School, 108 Commerce Street, struggled to fill 500 empty seats.[25]

Christmas Lights on Seventh Street in Downtown Fort Worth, November 16, 1941. Courtesy *Fort Worth Star Telegram* Collection, Special Collections, University of Texas at Arlington Libraries.

The excess of demand over supply opened opportunities for many workers previously considered unemployable or less employable. In 1943 the Fort Worth office of USES placed 67,138 out of 69,288 applicants, an amazing 96 percent success rate. Perhaps more startling was that more than half of the new hires belonged to groups traditionally ignored by employers, including 26,055 "white women," 10,075 "Negro women," and 3,263 persons described as physically "handicapped." The presence of women, Blacks, and challenged workers in such high numbers was a clear effect of a dwindling labor reserve that had declined 90 percent in one year, from 33,000 in 1943 to just 3,300 by 1944. The WMC estimated that, even with full utilization, the Fort Worth–Dallas area would face a 60,000-worker shortfall in November 1943.[26] Various efforts were tried to alleviate the crisis, but to little avail. The Salvation Army set up the Civilian Replacement Service in October 1942 to recruit older workers back into the workforce, but it attracted only fifty women and eighty-six men, hardly a dent in demand. Another plan instituted the same month offered habitual offenders in local jails—most often men charged with public order infractions like intoxication, the option of doing railroad sectional work for $0.43 an hour in lieu of confinement. The first day six of twelve detainees took the work option. Police Chief T. G. Curry termed the program a success and a "noble successor" to World War I, when police gave men found in pool rooms and bars a choice between being jailed for vagrancy or going to work. The Labor Stabilization Plan of 1943 attempted to reduce workdays lost to job changes by requiring workers in critical industries or classifications to obtain clearances before leaving one job for another. All may have provided marginal relief, but nothing could stretch supply to meet demand. In June 1944 a serious discussion considered working German POWs in area grain elevators, but the idea was rejected over sabotage fears.[27]

Unquestionably, World War II ushered in radical changes, ending the Depression and replacing it with general prosperity and a national labor shortage, but the war had many other consequences. The national emergency also changed the nature of labor strikes, reducing their number and shortening their length so that the few strikes during the war tended to be minor disruptions of short tenure. In 1941 the United States experienced 4,285 work stoppages; in 1942 their number declined dramatically to 2,968, then rose to 3,750 in 1943—a level still 12 percent below 1941. The bigger effect may have been in duration. The average walkout in 1942 and 1943 lasted only 7.1 days, but even that number was inflated by four coal strikes responsible for 63 percent of all lost workdays. Without those four, the average lost time was a mere three days, indicating that management and labor tended to settle differences quickly.[28]

A rapidly expanding population combined with limited to nonexistent residential construction produced severe housing shortages. Convair workers, especially couples with children, were especially hard-pressed to find lodging. On May 12, 1942, the federal government announced the construction of 500 apartment units restricted to Convair workers. Liberator Village, as the development became known, opened 104 apartments on February 1, 1943, the first of eventually 1,500 housing units that would be home to

6,000 people. The Village offered a real community, with schools through the ninth grade, a library, barber and beauty shops, a clinic, and a grocery, plus a nursery providing childcare for working parents—a major benefit for women, who made up 23 percent of Convair workers. Higher wages accompanying defense work had an unintended consequence of putting many rent-assisted residents above mandated maximum income levels. Soaring wages raised the average annual income at Ripley Arnold Housing Project from $874 to $1,275 and at Butler Place (reserved for Blacks) from $785 to $1,050, incomes that exceeded the maximum allowable, threatening evictions at a time when few to no housing options existed. Fortunately, the Federal Housing Administration (FHA) pressured local officials to ignore evictions until the housing crisis subsided.[29]

Statistics indicate Fort Worth did very well economically during the war years 1941–1945. Retail sales surged 36.7 percent in the first quarter of 1943, exceeding the national percentage rate of 21.2 percent and 22 percent for Texas. Fort Worth's sales growth ranked fourth nationally behind Detroit, Michigan (number 1), Akron, Ohio, and Portland, Oregon. Houston, the only other Texas city listed in the top ten, ranked eighth with a 19.8 percent rise. In the third quarter of 1943, Fort Worth led all Texas cities in payroll gains with a 106.7 percentage increase, far surpassing a 39 percent rise for all of Texas, and Fort Worth's 42 percent increase in department store sales tied Houston for the state's largest percentage increase. Tarrant County also outperformed the other three Texas urban counties in percentage growth in most commercial and industrial statistics. In 1942 Tarrant County's spendable income rose 63 percent compared to 1941, the highest increase of the four large Texas counties and significantly larger than the 47 percent in Harris County or 45 percent for both Bexar and Dallas Counties. Tarrant's total income in 1942, $323,879,000, raised its national ranking from sixty-third to fifty-fourth, moving it ahead of Bexar County at fifty-ninth with $312,707,000, but behind Harris County, ranked thirty-fourth with $510,285,000, and Dallas County at thirty-fifth with $493,664,000.[30]

Fort Worth also performed better than Dallas, Houston, and San Antonio in several banking-related statistics. Fort Worth bank clearings rose substantially every year from 1940 through 1943, from $355 million in 1940 to $468 million in 1941, surging 22 percent in 1942 to $571.5 million, 15.6 percent to $660.8 million in 1943 (the largest since 1929), then hit $735.4 million in 1944. Deposits rose perhaps even more dramatically, increasing $27 million to $146 million in 1942, almost doubling to $257 million in 1943, and adding $65 million to $322.1 million in 1944—almost three times that of 1941. Payments by checks increased 30.2 percent in the first quarter of 1942 (all percentages based on comparison to same period, previous year), the highest percentage increase in the United States (Houston was fourth nationally with 26.7 percent), considerably better than the state's 25.3 percent rise and twice the 14.7 percent national average.[31]

Chapter 2

Crime, Criminals, and Vice in Wartime

Law enforcement changed dramatically after 1933 when the end of Prohibition significantly reduced the concentration on alcohol violations. After Prohibition most alcohol enforcement involved clandestinely produced and untaxed spirits or distribution of commercial liquor in dry political subdivisions where alcohol fetched twice to three times its going value. Few resources were devoted to policing illegal operators, and the few who were prosecuted tended to get off with light fines or sentences. The Fort Worth office of the Texas Liquor Control Board covered a four-county region, a vast area of approximately 3,000 square miles. The agents did what they could, but the sheer size overwhelmed them. In a three-month stretch of 1943, the Fort Worth office seized 123 cases of liquor and made numerous arrests, but most convictions carried only a $500 fine plus court costs. The bigger disincentive may have been loss of the liquor, which the state either destroyed or, in the case of name brands, sold.[1]

World War II, which had wide-ranging influences on the home front, scarcely affected vice operations in Fort Worth. The two most prevalent forms, gambling and prostitution, received only sporadic police attention, allowing both to continue largely unabated and unchanged. Gamblers arrived with the first settlers and prospered, becoming a significant and enduring part of Fort Worth's history. In the 1940s and 1950s gambling was ubiquitous, available at corner stores and bars, as well as at larger operations such as hotels and upscale casinos. Small wagers could be made at most taverns, diners, and shops using counter punchboards, slot machines, or marble boards. In February 1942 police estimated fifty marble boards were in use within the city, but they expected the number to grow following a district court ruling prohibiting the seizure of machines unless officers actually observed gambling. Slot machines were also common and openly displayed in many venues. Uniformed officers reported they often saw the machines on café counters during breaks and meals.[2]

A few large gambling operations, including upscale venues, served the more serious and wealthier gamblers. They received little press or police attention except for an occasional raid that was well-choregraphed to garner publicity while causing the least operational disturbance. In contrast, low-end gambling was everywhere, despite frequent enforcement efforts that carried light punishments, usually $10 to $25 bonds often forfeited as fines. For example, in March 1942 a 21-year-old woman was arrested three times in three consecutive days while running the same dice game at the same locale. After each arrest she was released on a $25 bond and simply resumed her trade.

Fort Worth's gambling problem was certainly not unique in Texas. In November 1944 a Galveston, Texas, grand jury described gambling as prevalent with little enforcement efforts other than the occasional raid netting standard fines, identical to the situation in Fort Worth. The somewhat casual attitudes ignored serious social costs associated with gambling. In 1944 Lon Weatherly, a former Fort Worth Police identification expert who became a railway mail clerk, was sentenced to five years in prison for mail theft that he blamed on his gambling addiction, claiming that he began stealing to cover debts owed to Fort Worth gambling houses.[3]

Occasionally complaints would reach a critical mass, resulting in highly publicized raids that were played up impressively in the press but achieved little. In November 1944 sixty-four Lake Como residents petitioned the city council to do something about a beer tavern and gambling joint plaguing

Fort Worth Police Detectives Lon Crane and Ray Neston, May 21, 1942. Courtesy *Fort Worth Star Telegram* Collection, Special Collections, University of Texas at Arlington Libraries.

their neighborhood. City Councilman Marks supported the neighbors, adding that gambling had become "too rampant" and was "getting out of hand." Police responded with an aggressive sweep of known gambling spots, making several arrests, although most were street-level players, not operators, and certainly not customers frequenting elite, high-end spots. The dragnet caught ten Black men shooting dice at 300 East Thirteenth Street and 300 Jones Street, two white men playing cards, six undescribed men shooting dice at 600 West Magnolia Avenue, and a policy board (a version of a numbers game) operator at 3500 West Vickery Boulevard—a rare arrest for that form. Arrests of low-level miscreants were relatively easy in a period when police could detain persons for investigation on mere suspicion without specifying a crime. In August 1943 Fort Worth Police made 488 custodial arrests, charging 133 with gambling, 13 with vagrancy, and 342 with investigation, with another 13 facing unspecified charges.[4]

Large-scale gamblers involved in more complex operations usually avoided arrest, although they sometimes faced other threats. Louis C. Tindall was an ex-rodeo trick rider known to associate with Tiffin Hall and George Wilderspin, both known gamblers. According to his former wife, Tindall ran the biggest policy game in town. She may not have been an objective witness; at the time Louis was serving a prison sentence for assaulting to murder her mother, his ex–mother-in-law. In November 1944 Louis received emergency leave to care for a daughter stricken with polio. Perhaps he provided some care, but he also found time to be indicted for running a gambling place and to receive death threats, reputedly from a bounty offered by Benny Binion, a Dallas gambler who later opened a Las Vegas casino. On November 12, 1944, around 1:00 a.m., Tindall and his current wife, Opal, both armed with pistols because of the threats, pulled into their driveway at 5417 Byers Avenue. Louis, waiting in the car while Opal went inside to check the house (a seeming reversal of roles), was struck with a shotgun blast and three pistol shots from unknown assailants. He and Opal emptied their weapons in returning fire, but the men escaped apparently unscathed. Louis died of his wounds two weeks later, on November 26.[5]

Gauging from arrest reports, dice games seemed to be the most common game for the serious gambler. Dice games operated twenty-four hours a day in many downtown hotels, taverns, and other joints spread throughout the city. The futility of enforcement is evident in police reports of raid after raid hitting the same locations, indicating business continued unabated and unfazed. In one week in November 1944, police hit dice games in the 1000, 1100, and 1200 blocks of Main Street, as well as at 2400 North Main Street, 100 East Exchange Avenue, and 3500 West Vickery Boulevard. The game at 1200 Main Street must have been especially prominent; officers raided it twice in one day, making seven arrests at 12:30 p.m. and nine more at 5:00 p.m. The following week officers again found dice games again at 1000 and 1100 Main Street and 100 East Exchange Avenue. The Court Hotel, 111 East Sixth Street, was perhaps the best-known and most frequently raided of the downtown spots. In six months between June 1, 1945, and November 1, 1945, police officers made twenty-seven visits to the Court, making 100 arrests. The repeat raids confirmed that gambling was common and that police enforcement by fine collection had little to no deterrent effect.[6]

The Court Hotel was the scene of a curious incident involving Tarrant County Sheriff Dusty Rhodes. The evening of October 31, 1945, Sheriff Rhodes was robbed and beaten in the hotel's lobby by two men, one of whom Rhodes recognized as a known hoodlum. The sheriff and Mrs. Rhodes had left the sheriff's office around 11:00 p.m., then stopped on Sixth Street, where the wife waited in the car while Sheriff Rhodes checked the Halloween crowd on Main Street (it is questionable why a county sheriff would be monitoring a crowd within the city). During the walk Sheriff Rhodes stopped to say hello to an acquaintance at the Court Hotel desk (again, a strange choice with his wife alone late at night) and was attacked. Jess Hill and Leonard Stokes later confessed that they had just robbed thirty people at the dice game on the fourth floor and were going through the hotel safe when Rhodes walked in. Jess Hill was convicted and sentenced to over 100 years but escaped from the Wynne State Prison Farm in 1946. Interestingly, police had raided the Court the previous night, arresting ten gamblers.[7]

Fort Worth had a historical link with prostitution from its early beginnings, but the sex trade reached new heights during both world wars. In World War I rampant sex for hire and a soaring sexually transmitted infection (STI) rate among soldiers, one of the highest in the nation, caused the War Department to threaten the relocation of Camp Bowie. The base was saved by a unified civilian-military campaign of strenuous vice enforcement that, for the first time, dealt a sustained blow to Hell's Half Acre, although prostitution and other vice forms survived. In the 1920s novelist Jim Thompson worked as a bellboy at the Hotel Texas, one of the nicer hotels in town that lasted through the decades (in November 1963 President John F. Kennedy would spend his last night at the hotel before traveling to Dallas). Thompson earned $15 a week as a bellboy but made up to $300 weekly on the side from supplying guests with liquor, women, and drugs.

In World War II Fort Worth was without a major military training installation but drew thousands of servicemen from Tarrant Airfield or from nearby bases, especially Camp Wolters, just one hour west, where 25,000 Army recruits and training staff were housed or Camp Bowie in Brownwood,

120 miles southwest. Camp Wolters, just outside the Mineral Wells city limits, overwhelmed the small town of 6,303 (1940 Census) that was without a sizable vice infrastructure. In July 1942 the local newspaper boasted that the town did not have professional gamblers or slot machines and enjoyed a low level of drunkenness, averaging only ten drunk arrests each week (one-third were soldiers). They added that the incidence of STIs had actually declined compared to 1941, the previous year. What Mineral Wells lacked Fort Worth had in abundance. The Health Division of the Council on Social Agencies, a Fort Worth health oversight organization, warned that prostitution-related STI was the number one social issue threatening the nation's war economy. They suggested Fort Worth adopt the successful prostitution abatement efforts used in other cities, including opening prophylactic stations providing free condoms. The council spread its warning to the general public, screening films on STI at area theaters and airing STI prevention broadcasts over local radio stations, although it had to overcome serious objections that the broadcasts violated public decency standards.[8]

In a repetition of World War I, federal authorities in January 1942, just five weeks after Pearl Harbor, warned Fort Worth that failure to curtail prostitution would bring dire consequences. Paul McNutt of the Office of Defense Health and Fred Kearney of the Federal Security Board reported that a high percentage of Fort Worth draftees were diagnosed with STIs and that many infected soldiers reported their exposure occurred while in Fort Worth. Brigadier General E. F. Reinhardt, commander of Fort Wolters Army Base, sent military investigators to Fort Worth. They reported prostitution was rampant in small, inexpensive downtown hotels and brothels and was also readily available in many larger and nicer hotels and bars. General Reinhardt threatened to declare Fort Worth off-limits if the problem was not alleviated—a potentially serious blow to local businesses. The council directed City Manager Bothwell to ensure rigid enforcement of vice laws, an order City Health Director Dr. H. M. Williams welcomed as a tool to close brothels. Fort Worth Police reacted dramatically, ordering all prostitutes to leave town, a step Houston and San Antonio had already taken. Initial reports were positive; officers checking known brothels the following Saturday night found most closed and only one active prostitute. That did not hold for long.

Suspected prostitutes held after a Fort Worth Police Vice raid, January 22, 1942. Courtesy *Fort Worth Star Telegram* Collection, Special Collections, University of Texas at Arlington Libraries.

The next week 60 officers making overnight raids arrested 320 men and women, including 85 known or suspected prostitutes, many who had come to Fort Worth after being run out of other cities. Most were released the next day on $10 bonds for vagrancy, but 45 remained jailed.[9]

Despite the poor follow up, Surgeon General Thomas Parran praised the effort, claiming that Fort Worth's segregated vice district covering most of the southeast downtown was essentially closed, an important step in reducing STIs. The next month Parran testified before Congress in support of a $2.5 million appropriation funding the war on "social diseases," telling the committee that STIs were the number one factor degrading the Army's effectiveness and the second greatest hindrance for the Navy (unfortunately, the report did not identify the Navy's primary threat). He pointed to statistics that 47,000 of every 1 million men examined by the Selective Service System (the military draft) were found to have syphilis, an infection rate similar to an Army study that reported 40 out of 1,000 soldiers had some form of STI.

For context, both rates, while high, were one-half the rate experienced at Camp Bowie during World War I. Parran blamed the problem on economic prosperity created by military spending (assuming disposable income led to prostitution) but noted that while Houston, San Antonio, and Corpus Christi had controlled their problem, Fort Worth and Dallas had not. Surgeon General Parran would be involved in an unsavory incident as supervisor of the Tuskegee Syphilis experiment, a program that left infected Mississippi Blacks untreated in order to study the disease's progression.[10]

Prostitution survived but spread out of the cheap downtown hotels, becoming less centralized as it moved into bars and more remote areas. In the first large, concerted action since the January 21 raids, police officers in March 1942 arrested twenty-five men and thirty-five women at several "joints," although most arrests were for liquor violations, especially for serving underage children and employing girls under 18. At one Main Street bar officers found four juvenile girls drinking at a table with three soldiers and a sailor. The transition of the sex trade away from hotels to bars was a nationwide phenomenon that grew out of the anti-prostitution campaigns targeting traditional brothels. The program successfully closed many houses, but many of the working women simply relocated to taverns. In December 1942 the National Advisory Police Committee on Social Protection reported the campaign against STIs had virtually eliminated vice district brothels only to see them replaced by mobile call girls and streetwalkers as well as noncommercial but promiscuous women. The committee report suggested police switch their tactics to meet new threats, which they called more dangerous than a mad dog. It appeared clear that enforcement drives designed to reduce STI transmission rates had relocated prostitution but had not done much to reduce its presence. In February 1943 the Army reported an alarming rise in draftees rejected due to STIs, sparking renewed calls from Texas health providers for measures to reduce exposures. The statistics were not promising. In six months between July 1, 1943, and December 31, 1943, Texas health clinics reported 6,906 new gonorrhea cases and 15,870 new syphilis cases added to an existing patient load of 156,924.[11]

Many authorities blamed promiscuous juvenile girls for increases in STI rates. In February 1943 local authorities sentenced three girls, ages 10, 11, and 12, to the state reformatory after the girls admitted stealing merchandise valued at $75 from Leonard's Brothers Department Store and having "improper relations" with four men ranging in age from 47 to 88. Three of the men were charged with contributing to the delinquency of a minor and the fourth with receiving and concealing stolen property. Such salacious reports added support to calls from medical professionals for corrective actions. Dr. Harold Williams, the city health officer, warned that failure to curtail STI would result in Fort Worth being placed off-limits or under the May Act, making the Justice Department responsible for controlling prostitution. Local military brass seconded Dr. Williams's warning. A joint city-county initiative established a "health ward" at the county jail to test promiscuous women and treat the infected. Some insight appeared in an April 1944 District Court case of a 16-year-old girl suing to be released from the ward. The petitioner had twice been committed and released on promises to quarantine at home and seek STI treatment and twice rearrested after failing to do either. Dr. Williams testified that the girl was "sulfa resistant" and would have to be committed to the United States Public Health Service rapid treatment center recently established at Mineral Wells.[12]

A desire to leave the treatment ward was understandable given the harsh conditions confronting women and girls. As the only facility in the county testing promiscuous women, as well as women criminally charged, the cells were often overcrowded, a problem made worse by frequent lengthy delays in testing and diagnosis. Medical examinations were performed only on Mondays and Thursdays, forcing a woman committed on Friday to wait until at least Monday to see a doctor, followed by several more days waiting for test results while being held in a setting with few amenities. Extended incarcerations came under public scrutiny when a married woman was held for five days without an examination before being released on a writ of habeas corpus. The resulting uproar led to a plan to convert the downtown City-County Hospital building, left in disuse since 1939, into a rapid treatment center for infectious STIs. Unfortunately, opponents killed the idea, arguing that dedicating the structure would leave Fort Worth and Tarrant County without expansion space in the event of a medical emergency. That left a 150-bed hospital in Waco, funded by the Federal Works Agency and operated by the Texas Department of Health and the Waco Health Department, as the nearest nonmilitary rapid treatment center for women with STI. The only relief granted was the addition of two more jail matrons for the health ward at a cost of $4.40 per day, the addition approved by county commissioners in February 1944.[13]

In July 1943 Captain Harry Roberson arrived from Wichita Falls to take over as provost marshal for the Fort Worth area. Roberson vowed to run promiscuous women out of town and end the threat from two of Hitler's "greatest friends," syphilis and gonorrhea. His vow seemed wildly ambitious given the situation he left in Wichita Falls. A Wichita Falls Police study reported 64 percent of the thirty-four women arrested in an average week carried a sexually transmitted infection. To be fair, the situations in Wichita Falls and Fort Worth were not unique; many cities were in the same condition and some had worse problems. STI was so common that a 1943 survey of eighty-one cities ranked Fort Worth thirtieth in cases among military personnel—not anything to boast about but better than San Antonio, the highest ranked Texas city at fourth, Dallas at fifteenth, and Houston at sixteenth. In comparison, New Orleans ranked eleventh. City Health Director Williams downplayed the numbers, claiming they were dated and that new cases had declined 25 percent.[14]

Roberson focused on enforcement rather than treatment or prevention through public service announcements. Soon after arriving he ordered aggressive enforcement of military curfews set at 11:30 p.m. on weekdays and 2:30 a.m. on weekends, as well as increased monitoring of taxi stands, restaurants, and hotels where women were known to solicit. In October 1943 Roberson declared much of the east side of downtown off-limits to military personnel, an area stretching east from Calhoun Street to Riverside Drive, north to Third Street and south to Lancaster Avenue, a largely African American section of town. The order came after several soldiers reported losing money to Black women, including one case in which the victim refused to prosecute despite claiming he lost $400 (highly suggestive that more was involved than just a simple theft). Despite all the efforts and associated pitfalls, men continued to be involved in shady circumstances. In April 1944 police took a soldier to a hospital after they found him downtown at 4:00 a.m., apparently drugged and clad only in pants and underwear.[15]

In November 1943 Roberson arranged meetings between city and military authorities and tavern owners, hotel staff, and taxi drivers to discuss steps to reduce prostitution. He proposed banning unescorted women in restaurants, a measure opposed by Hugh Marshall, president of the Fort Worth Restaurant Association, who warned the ban would penalize working women and reduce restaurant sales. A few café owners opted to voluntarily comply by putting up placards reading "Couples Only" or "No Unescorted Women." Eventually, the military did the obvious and addressed the culpability of the men involved. The existing procedure following prostitution arrests was to hold the woman for up to ten days while verifying the presence or absence of STI, but to simply send the soldier to a prophylactic station for instruction in condom use. Under new guidelines issued in 1944, miscreant soldiers were booked for misconduct and put on restricted privileges and/or confined four weeks to monitor for infections.[16]

The association of promiscuity and STIs as a threat to the war effort helped create an environment that opened the door to radical solutions that would not normally be considered. Such was the case in 1943 and 1944 when Fort Worth and Tarrant County sanctioned forced sterilizations of several youths. Tarrant County District Attorney Marvin Brown broke the story on April 18, 1944, when he asked district judges to convene a special grand jury charged with investigating the legality of five forced sterilizations recently performed on juveniles. The procedures were conducted under the auspices of county officers with the approval and advice of physicians and the consents of parents or guardians, but without patient input. Brown urged haste, warning that eleven more sterilizations were already scheduled. He quickly met with members of the Tarrant County Juvenile Board, made up of Tarrant County District judges, the Juvenile Office, and County Judge Clarence Kraft. Judge Kraft had come to Fort Worth to play for the Fort Worth Panthers after having played first base in 1914 for the Boston Braves. He left the Panthers in 1924 and opened a downtown Ford dealership before being elected county judge in 1943, serving until 1948. At the meeting District Court Judge Walter Morris criticized sterilizations as a cruel and inhumane, but District Judge Powell was open to the idea, suggesting the operations were necessary and acceptable if done with extreme caution. Powell added that all five completed sterilizations and the eleven scheduled were all legal, citing the 1927 US Supreme Court case of *Buck v. Bell* that upheld a Virginia law legalizing forced sterilizations to promote the "health of the patient and the welfare of society."[17]

The grand jury, led by Foreman W. P. Robertson, opened hearings. District Attorney Brown appeared first, telling the panel he had found no applicable criminal violations in the procedures. Mrs. Esthyr Harris and Mrs. Maxine Burlingame, deputy probation officers with the Tarrant County Juvenile Office, followed, appearing in support of sterilizations. They stated they had become familiar with mentally challenged youths (not their terminology) in the course of their office work and while transporting youths to various institutions. In February 1943 Mrs. Harris had driven three boys to the School for Feeble Minded Children in Austin, and in April she and Mrs. Burlingame took a child to a youth care facility in San Antonio. They confirmed that the sterilizations that had begun in May 1943 were all authorized either by Judge Kraft and/or Tarrant County District Attorney Brown for four girls and one boy, and that each had been with the consent of a parent or parental authority. The respective mothers signed for a 17-year-old (who worked as a domestic) and a 19-year-old, a grandmother signed for an 18-year-old with two illegitimate children, and a maternal aunt signed for her 16-year-old nephew in the Texas School for the Feeble Minded. The lone exception, a 20-year-old wife of a serviceman, authorized her own sterilization. The two probation officers added that the woman's husband had joined the Army while on parole from the Texas Training School for Boys (that relevancy was left unexplained) and that the "younger girls" were all "feeble minded" (it is unknown to whom "younger" referred but probably the 17-, 18-, and 19-year-olds). Further, they revealed that two families funded their children's operations, the Veteran's Bureau loaned money to a veteran for his child's surgery, and the other two were performed at the City-County Hospital, presumably as charity cases since the other three were self-paid.[18]

A rather spirited discussion developed between the two case workers and Brown over the district attorney's knowledge and involvement in the process.

Throughout the hearing, Brown tried to distance himself and his office from the matter while the women insisted that he was directly involved and instrumental. Mrs. Harris was certain that Brown was well aware of all five procedures, recalling that his staff had directed the Juvenile Office to list sterilizations as physical examinations in their Summary of Activities to hide the truth from Catholic voters due to fears Brown would lose votes if his involvement became public (the district attorney was an elected position). Brown did not directly address the allegations, choosing instead to evade personal responsibility while suggesting that his office may have participated without his knowledge. Brown asked the two women if they had any correspondence in which he requested sterilizations. Mrs. Burlingame produced an unsigned letter to a doctor she claimed was from Brown that recommended a sterilization if the physician agreed it would be in the girl's and public's best interests. Brown denied the letter was from him. When questioned directly, Mrs. Harris admitted she did not have written documentation to support the charge that Brown feared losing the Catholic vote, but that she had heard him say it. Brown steadfastly maintained that he and his office had routinely refused to get involved in the sterilization process, and that two weeks earlier he had refused Mrs. Harris's request to sterilize a 14-year-old girl known to have had "improper relations with boys" and to have written a lewd poem. He reported Mrs. Harris promoted sterilization as necessary to prevent the young girl from becoming a prostitute (how sterilization would prevent prostitution was unexplained). Harris denied recommending sterilization in that case, saying it was not justified since the girl had only copied the poem, not written it, and was already in care at a Waco home. She suggested Brown had confused her with a woman not affiliated with the county whom she had referred to the district attorney when asked about having a girl sterilized.[19]

Mrs. Harris discussed the eleven people slated for sterilization. All the necessary paperwork had been completed for three: a mother who was committed to an institution in Austin (presumably the school for the "feeble-minded"), a daughter of a World War I veteran hospitalized with tuberculous and unable to oversee the girl, and a girl the Shore Patrol referred after several cases of syphilis were traced to her. All three fell within Juvenile Office standards condoning sterilization of any person held to be "feeble minded" and/or with "revolting sex habits or inability to stay away from the other sex." Mrs. Harris added that there was a real and growing need for sterilizations and that all potential candidates were examined and approved by a United States Public Health Service Hospital (USPHSH) doctor, the county judge or district attorney, and the parents or guardians or, in cases where the person was an adult, by the person themselves.[20]

Judge Young, chair of the Tarrant County Juvenile Board, took the initiative, ordering the juvenile department to cease direct or indirect involvement in any future sterilizations, apart from exceptional circumstances, and to delay any scheduled operations until the grand jury report, due out in a week. He added that the right to sterilize "feeble-minded" youths was open to debate, but there was no question that the Juvenile Board had no right to order sterilizations of adults, likely referring to the 20-year-old who signed for herself. Despite all his misgivings and desire to distance himself from the issue, District Attorney Marvin Brown supported the legality of all five completed sterilizations, perhaps playing defense in case of further legal scrutiny. Mrs. Harris continued to support sterilizations, arguing that the five persons already sterilized were approved by Judge Kraft as persons whose sexual and mental behavior "constituted a social menace to the community." She added that all five had been declared "feeble-minded" and institutionalized and were part of a growing problem that could not be solved via ordinary means.[21]

Afterward, most tried to disassociate themselves from the scandal and place all the blame on Judge Kraft. District Judge McGregor ordered that no public agency, including the Juvenile Office, have anything to do with sterilization. District Attorney Brown continued to maintain that neither he nor his office had or would approve or authorize sterilizations. District Judge Young made the rather shaky assertion that the County Juvenile Board had nothing to do with sterilization of the "feeble minded," adding that neither he nor the board knew anything about the five operations and that Kraft was only person handling cases involving the feeble minded. Mrs. Harris and Mrs. Burlingame, the two women deputy probation officers, agreed that Kraft was the chief force behind sterilizations. They were probably right in that Kraft, as county judge, was the presiding figure in adjudicating mental status cases. His annual report for 1943 listed 192 lunacy hearings in which 127 persons were deemed insane and 124 were committed to state hospitals. He also determined that nine patients had regained their sanity and eleven persons had been committed to the State Colony for the Feebleminded in Austin. The record indicates that Kraft had the primary responsibility and authority in adjudicating mental cases and that Kraft strongly supported sterilizations. When the public outcry effectively ended the practice as an option under local auspices, Kraft tried to drum up support at the state level, proposing that the Juvenile Board go on record supporting state legislation that sanctioned forced sterilizations. Fortunately, the board voted down the proposal, some members adding that governments did not have the legal right to forcefully sterilize people. Judge Kraft still exercised considerable power over the plight of the unfortunate. In 1944 he conducted a hearing on the fate of one of the five sterilized persons, the 20-year-old woman who had spent time at three mental institutions and was married to a patient committed to the State Colony for the Feebleminded. Judge Kraft committed her to the same school that held her husband, a fate already shared by some of the other four sterilized victims.[22]

Illegal narcotics were around in the war years but received scant public notice. Part of the reason may have been that the Pacific war temporarily disrupted the marijuana supply chain. The Japanese occupation of the Philippines ended the trade in hemp used for ropemaking. Hemp was a cannabis plant containing the active psychotropic ingredient found in marijuana. To replace a critical commodity, the federal government launched an agricultural program to stimulate hemp production in six states, but no reports tied those products to the illegal drug market. Rather, Mexico emerged as the primary marijuana source. Either because of degraded supply or other reasons, marijuana, which had been available locally for some time, appeared only occasionally in the local press. In March 1944 federal narcotics agents arrested George Everett Scott, a 24-year-old Convair planning engineer, for selling "marihuana reefers" to coworkers. A search of his garage apartment, 4625 Lafayette Avenue, found almost two ounces of the raw product in a trunk and four "reefers," rolled marijuana cigarettes, in his coat. Scott, released on a $1,500 bond, was a native of Minneapolis who came to

Fort Worth six months earlier from California to work at Convair, where he earned $90 a week—a solid middle-class wage. He was an aberration in that most marijuana incidents involved Hispanics or African Americans. In 1945 police charged John Williams and Dorsey Lee Reddicks, both African American men, with possession of illegal narcotics after police officers stopping them for speeding found twelve marijuana cigarettes in their car.[23]

Pharmacies were a source for drug dealers and users who used authentic or forged prescriptions or committed outright thefts. In 1943 detectives investigating a burglary at Kilman's Pharmacy, 1730 College Avenue, discovered several forged prescriptions. Through descriptions and mug shots, the pharmacy staff identified a 25-year-old Riverside man and his accomplice, a known woman drug addict who had recently died. On October 8, 1943, two men held up the Renfro Drug general offices, 1601 North Ballinger Street, taking some cash, but making off with $17,000 worth of narcotics: 6,500 grains of morphine, 6,000 grains of codeine, 4,000 Dilaudid tablets, and two ounces of cocaine. In one night in April 1944, three pharmacy burglaries netted the culprits drugs and little else.[24]

Cocaine appeared sporadically in news reports. A particularly unsavory incident in 1944 involved a "white powder" that may have been cocaine. In April Cedric Louks, blaming his rage on a white powder that cost him $3.50 a dose, viciously assaulted Mrs. Joyce Swinford, a 21-year-old waitress at a Main Street café. Louks met Mrs. Swinford, the wife of a serviceman, at the café, and took her to his home, 3411 Oscar Avenue, where Louks's 18-year-old wife, Bonnie Lee, joined them in three-person sex "perversions." When Mrs. Swinford tried to leave, Louks became enraged and struck her with a hammer, then dragged her across the street to an open lot where he violated her with a broomstick. Mrs. Swinford played dead until Louks left, then summoned help from a neighbor.[25]

Morphine was perhaps the most commonly abused narcotic, or at least it appeared most often in news reports. In 1943 news broke of a scandalous affair featuring bigamy and morphine abuse involving Fort Worth elites. Winfield Scott, who came to Fort Worth with almost nothing and became one of the city's wealthiest men, died in 1911, leaving his fortune to his then 10-year-old son, Winfield Scott Jr. The younger Scott lived a dissolute life as an alcoholic and morphine addict who went through multiple marriages. In 1933, at the age of 31, he made Ruth Ann Crow the seventh Mrs. Scott. Their marriage lasted ten years, a record for him, before Ruth Ann filed for a Mexican divorce in February 1943, charging Scott was addicted to narcotics. Despite the divorce and allegations, the two remained cordial, agreeing to keep the split quiet to protect their joint business interests. That decision would cause problems five months later in July 1943 when Ruth married Dr. David Cameron in Marietta, Oklahoma. The local district attorney in Oklahoma, unaware of the secret divorce, filed bigamy charges against the new Mrs. Cameron, but Texas Governor Coke Stevenson refused to extradite after he learned of the Mexican divorce. Ruth Ann returned to Fort Worth to 75 Westover Terrace in Westover Hills, a ritzy Fort Worth suburb. A reporter arriving for an interview was greeted by Winfield, who affirmed his support for his ex-wife in every way. Winfield admitted that he was under an eighteen-month suspended sentence for smuggling forty grains of morphine across the Mexican border at Laredo, Texas. The suspension ran five years, contingent on his good behavior, a condition he began in good faith by committing himself for treatment at the USPHSH in Lexington, Kentucky. Mrs. Cameron, in good spirits despite her new husband's absence as an Army doctor in England, planned to remain at her Westover Hills home until his return when the couple would settle in El Paso, his home.[26]

The following year things really went south for the junior Scott. In 1944 Charlotte Morgan Scott O'Neil, Winfield's fourth wife (1925 to 1929) and the mother of his daughter, filed three lawsuits seeking $400,000. The suits alleged Scott transferred the deeds for eight Fort Worth properties and an 11,000-acre ranch in Tarrant and Johnson Counties to his mother in order to hide his ownership, thereby excluding them as community property. Scott faced more problems. In April 1944 United States marshals arrested him under a warrant for violating the court's probation conditions by consuming alcohol and using narcotics. At the revocation hearing, Scott denied using narcotics but admitted drinking alcohol, an act his attorney blamed on pressure stemming from the three lawsuits filed so soon after he left treatment in Kentucky. The presiding judge revoked Scott's suspended sentence, committing him to federal prison for eighteen months. Scott did not let the sentence

Mrs. Ruth Ann Cameron, November 10, 1943. Courtesy *Fort Worth Star Telegram* Collection, Special Collections, University of Texas at Arlington Libraries.

deter him from announcing plans to remarry wife number seven, Ruth Scott Cameron, who was in El Paso arranging a divorce with her husband's father, who acted as a proxy while Captain Cameron was still stationed overseas. The suits brought by Mrs. Scott number four were settled by mutual agreements that increased support payments for Scott's daughter and extended them until she was 21, at which point a trust would kick in. Not surprisingly, Scott died at the young age of 54 in November 1956 after being fifteen months bed-ridden. He was survived by his seventh wife, who became his eighth, and his daughter, both living in California.[27]

In 1944 prosecutors were able to close the file on the notorious Green Dragon drug case of 1940, a bust of a major national drug ring centered in the Randol Mill area east of Fort Worth that resulted in the conviction of at least twenty-nine persons, including some law enforcement officials on the take. The end came with the March 1944 execution of Emanuel Weiss in New York for offenses related to his involvement with Murder Inc. Weiss was one of the original Texas indictments, but Texas postponed his prosecution in favor of the New York charges. His death finally closed that case file, ending the Green Dragon story.[28]

Chapter 3

Wartime Policing

The war years did not bring great changes or advances in either the police department or the fire department but did present staffing challenges as both departments dealt with personnel shortages they could not fill. Several police officers and firefighters left for the military or better paying jobs in defense plants, creating vacancies at a time when the labor pool stood depleted. A few efforts to expand the applicant pool provided some relief, but none offered a complete solution. Fortunately, the available statistics suggest that crime rates declined, probably an effect of so many young men of criminogenic age leaving for military service. On the other hand, juvenile delinquency rose, reaching a level that highlighted the need for improved youth detention facilities.

In the months after Pearl Harbor, both the police department and the fire department experienced considerable internal upheaval. On the last day of 1941, Chief of Detectives Tom Jackson and Detective Joe Y. Defee retired, ending careers both had begun in 1909. An illness had confined Defee to desk duty for several years, but he had adjusted well, becoming known for his prodigious memory and as an expert on "Negro crimes." Howard Grant replaced Jackson as detective chief with a salary of $230 monthly, considerably more than the $60 monthly pension Jackson received or the $50 going to Defee. Chief of Police Karl N. Howard, who had replaced Chief A. E. Dowdell in 1939, took a leave of absence in June to attend midshipman school at Northwestern University prior to entering the Navy Reserve as a second lieutenant. Howard, only 39 years old, may have been influenced by domestic instability. On October 9, 1942, only four months after leaving the city, he divorced his wife and six weeks later married his former secretary, Mary Nell Forbes, 3019 Yucca Avenue. The marriage lasted barely five months before Howard, citing harsh and cruel treatment, filed for a divorce in Corpus Christi, Texas, and quickly remarried his first wife in time for the couple to leave for a duty assignment in Portland, Maine. Howard returned to the police after being discharged in 1946 as a captain in the patrol division under Chief R. E. "Bob" Dysart. At the start of the war the city council had guaranteed reinstatement without demotion for employees leaving for military service, but the city attorney decreed the rule did not apply to department heads.[1]

The fire department also went through an imposed major personnel change that pushed veterans out the door in favor of younger staff. In January 1942 the fire chief, without prior notice, involuntarily retired five senior staff, replacing them with junior personnel. The action came as a surprise to those forced out; one veteran learned he was retired from a newspaper article listing his $50 monthly pension. All the affected personnel were veterans with years of service. M. A. Jameson captained the first company to arrive at the great 1909 fire that destroyed much of the near south side, and William O. Kimble, a battalion chief, had served as a Fort Worth firefighter for forty-eight years. Kimble compared his forced retirement to the shock of the Pearl Harbor attack. The curt treatment of veteran firefighters and their replacement with junior personnel promoted over more senior members created internal grumblings. In September 1942 two private citizens, J. B. Burkhart, a grocer at 1700 Vickery Boulevard, and H. L. McKinney, 4213 Meadowbrook Boulevard, reported twelve firemen had told them that the department suffered from dissension in the ranks and of low morale. City Manager Bothwell defended the forced retirements as legal under civil service rules (equating legal with correctness) but admitted they had created resentment and that the subsequent promotions had given too little consideration to seniority. Bothwell did not recommend any corrective action.[2]

Other personnel matters arose, indicating a struggling department. Ben Bell, a tenured firefighter, was left incapacitated after a heart attack in 1937 but had continued on the payroll for ninety-nine weeks thanks to fellow firemen working his shift. That ended on March 1, 1939, when the fire chief dismissed Bell, the termination canceling his pension. Bell died just a short time later, leaving a destitute wife who sued the city for back pay, alleging that from 1937 until the termination, Bell was paid just $125 monthly, less than the state mandated $150 minimum. The court ruled against the claim in 1943, enraging many firefighters upset that the fire department had left a widow penniless. City Manager Bothwell stirred more controversy by prohibiting firemen from working off-duty jobs, ending a long-standing practice in which many worked off days as bellhops and taximen. Morale and the work environment did not begin to improve until 1945, when the city manager demoted the chief to captain and promoted Charlie Ligon to chief. Ligon, a city firefighter since 1905, proved to be popular with the rank and file.[3]

Throughout all its personnel troubles, the fire department remained engaged and on the job. In 1941 firemen responded to fires causing $331,870 in damages and answered 3,119 alarm calls, almost nine per day. Some days were far from average. On January 22, 1943, they received ninety-six fire alarm calls that were largely grass or trash fires, but a few involved structures, including a downtown Griddle System Café that burned. A massive grain elevator explosion in February 1943 at Burrus Mills in Saginaw, Texas (a suburb just north of Fort Worth noted for its large storage elevators), brought about a policy change regarding use of personnel and equipment outside the city limits. The blast, heard as far as thirty miles away in Dallas, injured five men and caused $5 million in damages, a huge event that overwhelmed the local fire department, bringing several Fort Worth Fire vehicles and staff to assist. In a post-incident review the city council tightened rules, restricting future assistance to cases where lives were in danger or Fort Worth property was threatened. The next month, April 1943, both the fire chief and City Manager Bothwell cited the new criteria in refusing to send firefighters to Globe Aircraft before Mayor I. N. McCrary overruled them based on Globe President Joe B. Hogsett's promise to reimburse the city. The process went so smoothly that two Fort Worth fire companies arrived on scene within an hour after the first alarm, their quick response helping limit damages to only $65,000. The city billed Globe $500.[4]

The war caused a serious drain on fire and police personnel as men left for the military or to take better paying defense jobs. In the spring of 1942, just months after Pearl Harbor, the police department reported 7 unfilled vacancies, while the fire department held a full staff of 270 despite having lost 12 firefighters to military service. The situation deteriorated from that point forward. In 1943 the police department struggled with a 30-man shortage with no relief in sight. Both departments widened their nets, dropping requirements for a preemployment medical examination and extending the maximum recruitment age from 36 to 50 for police and from 33 to 46 for firefighters, tapping into older applicants not subject to the draft while the fire department looked into hiring 17-year-olds. To get around civil service regulations, new hires younger or older than the age limits were listed as temporary and rehired every ninety days, putting them on the payroll but leaving them without pensions or benefits, a liability the city promised to correct once the war was over. Evasions became moot after July 1, 1942, when civil service rules were suspended for the duration of the war, removing most employment standards until civil service was reinstated in 1946. At reinstatement, eight police officers older than 36 (the civil service maximum for recruits) when they were hired between 1942 and 1945 were dismissed, and all officers who were under 35 when hired had to take and pass the entry examination or be dismissed.[5]

Chief Curry instituted changes to put more officers on the streets. In March 1942 he ended the longstanding "police taxi service" in which oncoming patrol officers drove relieved staff home, effectively putting on-duty officers out of service for the first part of their shift, sometimes for extended periods while the men stopped for coffee. The end came after a police captain reported seeing nine men in one patrol car, one on duty and eight being driven home in a seriously overcrowded vehicle. The new rules required officers to provide their own transportation and dispatchers to log coffee breaks for command review.[6]

The changes helped but could not fully relieve shortages, forcing the police to consider other personnel sources. In November 1943 Police Chief Curry, faced with eight vacancies he could not fill, hired ten women to serve as unarmed traffic officers to direct traffic, check parking meters, and monitor traffic conditions. Applicants had to be younger than 40 and able to work fifty-four-hour weeks for an annual salary of $1,447.50 ($27.83 weekly). The experiment seemed to work out well; no adverse notices appeared. Eighteen months later, six of the original ten were still employed and the department was recruiting four replacements. Hiring women helped, but personnel losses continued unabated. In the last half of 1943 nine patrolmen took induction physicals. Bereft of untapped resources, Chief Curry called in the Army, convincing the provost marshal to assign a military police (MP) officer to each of the six patrol cars on the 11:00 p.m. to 7:00 a.m. shift. The move came at a cost, leaving only six MPs for downtown foot patrol.[7]

Chief Curry also instituted continuous training under the direction of Captain R. R. Howerton. On October 4, 1943, Howerton began a 100-hour program conducted in 2-hour classes held immediately before or after work shifts. The training had no effect on staffing since all classes were conducted on the officers' own time and without compensation. In January 1945 the department mandated three classes per week, also during off-duty hours. A big advance in communications came in April 1945 when the department began using a two-way radio system built by two city technicians out of confiscated marble boards (electronic gambling devices). The radios eventually replaced call boxes.[8]

Given staffing problems, it was fortunate that the war years were accompanied by an overall crime reduction. The drop occasioned a slight decline in arrests, from 20,448 in 1940 to 20,421 in 1941 (traffic citations were included in the total). In July 1942 Fort Worth Police credited a sustained downward crime trend to the removal of large numbers of young men into the military or defense jobs where they earned good wages. Available statistics after 1942 are spotty and reflect mixed results. In the first six months of 1944 automobile thefts were on the rise, with 328 reported compared to only 538 in all of 1943, but burglaries were slightly lower, with 436 recorded versus 952 in all

Miss Lois Rylander, applicant to be a Fort Worth policewoman, November 2, 1943. Courtesy *Fort Worth Star Telegram* Collection, Special Collections, University of Texas at Arlington Libraries.

of 1943. No local figures were available on suicides, but the national rate rose dramatically from 10.2 per 100,000 in 1900 to 17.4 in 1932 (likely an effect of the start of the Depression), then declined to 14.4 in 1940. Homicides followed a similar trajectory, soaring in the first years of the Depression, then declining in the 1940s. Fort Worth experienced a then all-time high of 54 homicides in 1931, followed by 51 in 1932, then began a steady decline while still averaging over 40 per year between 1930 and 1937, a remarkably high rate of 23.5 per 100,000, based on a population of 170,000 (in comparison, Fort Worth's homicide rate in 2016 was 8.02 per 100,000). In 1940 murders dropped to only 22, then rose slightly through 1943 while continuing at a low rate, averaging only 30 per year, a reduction of 25 percent compared to the 1930s. The only later figures found showed 14 homicides in the first six months of 1944, the total inflated by 5 in the month of June (the report noted that 12 of the victims were African Americans).[9]

Chart 3.1 Homicides in Fort Worth by Year, 1930–1937 and 1940–1943

Year	No. of Homicides
1930	33
1931	54
1932	51
1933	44
1934	33
1935	38
1936	35
1937	37
1940	22
1941	28
1942	33
1943	37

Source: For the years 1930–1937, see *Fort Worth Star Telegram*, December 31, 1942, p. 7. For the years 1940–1943, see *Fort Worth Star Telegram*, July 2, 1944, p. 13.

Statistics provide a sense of the magnitude of the carnage, but not the profound horror associated in many of the deaths. In 1941 four homicides were committed in one spree that almost took the life of a police officer. On August 31, 1941, a Sunday evening, G. D. Driskill shot and killed his wife, her sister, and her niece at their mutual home, 2514 Columbus Avenue, before he was killed in a shootout with responding police. Driskill cut down one of the first officers to arrive, John L. Nash, with a shotgun blast to the stomach from only twelve feet away. Two years later, in September 1943, Nash, 58 years old, returned to work, a remarkable survival and recovery for a man who lost most of his intestines. A poignant and tragic mistake took the life of John Clark Jr., a 15-year-old *Star Telegram* paperboy and student at Paschal High School. Clark became one of thirty-three homicides in 1942 while delivering a newspaper to 3253 Odessa Avenue, just few blocks from his home, 3016 Greene Avenue, and his high school. F. R. White, awakened by his daughter, who heard someone on their front porch, fired two shots through a glass screen, killing the young man.[10]

Two other incidents stood out. In 1943 Mrs. Mava R. Hanks was indicted twice for murder after performing two abortions, one on Mrs. Laura Holland and another on an unnamed woman. The prosecutor admitted the charges might not stand up to legal review. In November 1944 two police officers barely escaped mortal injury while responding to a shooting at 5412 Kilpatrick Avenue in the Lake Como neighborhood. Officers Snow and Stevenson arrived to find ambulance attendants loading Mrs. Laura Richardson, shot twice in the abdomen, and neighbors pointing to her husband, Vernon Richardson, as the assailant. As the officers approached, Mr. Richardson pulled a pistol and fired, striking Stevenson in the hand and Snow in the ankle. They returned fire, hitting him three times and killing him.[11]

Few police brutality reports surfaced during the war, perhaps a byproduct of wartime patriotism uniting all in a common cause. Assault charges were filed against Fort Worth Police jailers Reece Davis and H. S. Windle in the beating of a prisoner on October 12, 1941, but the district attorney dismissed the case after being unable to locate the complaining party, Grogan Paul White, who had left for the army. In October 1942 two officers were accused of assaulting Mrs. M. C. Maginnis at her home, 1121 East Belknap

Street, during a disturbance call involving an argument with her son-in-law. The officers admitted that she suffered two black eyes, a bruised hip, and a skinned knee but insisted the injuries were the result of her resisting arrest. A witness initially said Mrs. Maginnis was drunk but later recanted, saying he made the statement because he feared the police. In 1945 Police Officer Frank Farrar was suspended after admitting he clubbed a Black woman known to solicit on the streets and steal from servicemen. The incident came to light only because the woman, claiming she acted in self-defense, stabbed the officer. The wound was minor but served to increase public attention and scrutiny. Police officers also had fans committed to their support. A prime example was Mrs. Mae Carleton, a 69-year-old former downtown café waitress who bought a twenty-room hotel at 1606½ Main Street. Mrs. Carleton, affectionately called Mom by officers for her dedication to their welfare, frequently brought pies and cakes to police headquarters.[12]

Juvenile delinquency, a steadily increasing problem for years, soared during the war. The Council of Social Agencies, an oversight committee for local social welfare agencies, studied the problem and suggested, but did not document, that the upward trend in juvenile delinquency began in the 1930s due to a significant increase in the number of children born out of wedlock. The study found that Tarrant County juvenile authorities handled 2,049 delinquents in three years, 1931, 1933 and 1935 (it is unknown why they skipped 1932 and 1934 or omitted other years), an annual average of 683. The available statistics indicate that juvenile delinquency rose substantially during World War II, likely as a product of parental absences caused by military service or work. In 1943 Fort Worth Police detained 1,153 persons younger than 17, almost twice the annual average for the county in the 1930s. In the first half of 1944 the number held rose to 822, suggesting a 42 percent increase if the trend held. The local experience matched national statistics of a general upward trend. J. Edgar Hoover, director of the FBI, released crime statistics for the first six months of 1944 in which persons under 21 years of age were responsible for 23 percent of all arrests. The young were most noticeably involved in property crimes, accounting for 36.3 percent of all theft arrests, 25.8 percent of robberies, 53.3 percent of burglaries, and 64.5 of automobile thefts. Fort Worth Police statistics mirrored the national trend. Between February and July 1943, juveniles were responsible for twenty-five car thefts and were reported to be heavily involved in thefts of tires and gasoline, items strictly rationed and in short supply that were difficult to secure or prosecute due to the absence of unique identifiers. Police encouraged owners to record tire serial numbers but had so little success that they switched focus to increasing penalties. The Tarrant County District Attorney's Office supported that initiative, upping its recommended bail from $300 to $500 for related thefts and the state legislature increased thefts of tires, gas caps, and batteries from misdemeanors to felonies.[13]

Youth gangs, present from almost the beginning of Fort Worth's existence, experienced a resurgence during the war. No public reports appeared regarding African American gangs and only one surfaced involving Hispanic gangs, but it is likely both existed without receiving much notice from the mainstream media. The only reported incident involving Hispanics appeared in October 1944 when Assistant District Attorney Drew S. Coleman announced a 16-year-old was in custody after a gang of nine youths of "Mexican descent" entered the home of Rosie Reyan, 913 Peach Street, and "shot up the place." The most notorious Anglo group, the Cue Rack Gang, was known for various offenses and for their remarkable escape skills. One member, Billy Joe Ellis, ran away in 1943 from an Ellis County farm (about sixty miles southeast of Fort Worth) where he had been paroled from the Youth Correctional Facility at Gatesville, Texas. Ellis remained free for three days before being arrested on June 18 in Fort Worth in a stolen car and returned to Gatesville. Another Cue Racker, Bert Mullins, all of 13 years old, escaped from Gatesville, making it all the way to Hugo, Oklahoma, before he was captured on June 15, 1943, along with two other boys and two girls, all from Fort Worth, in a car stolen in Fort Worth. The Hugo Oklahoma jail held Mullins only three days before he dug his way out using a spoon. Rearrested three days later in Fort Worth, Mullins announced he would abandon his life of crime, marry, and settle down. His conversion came too late to prevent a federal court judge from sentencing him and the other two boys found in the stolen car, James Lloyd Clement and Billy Gene Bridges, both 16 and both Cue Rack members, to three years in a federal reformatory, the three earning the federal charge by taking a stolen car across state lines. In 1947 Mullins, now all of 17 years old and the leader of the Cue Rack Gang, was rearrested along with Roscoe Garrett of Cleburne in California in a stolen car. District Attorney Marvin Brown cited Mullins's misadventures and those of Billy Joe Ellis in an argument for a harsh punishment for Dickie E. Howell, a 17-year-old convicted of burglary. The jury was swayed, assessing Howell five years in state prison.[14]

The surging juvenile crime rate raised awareness of a critical need for more appropriate institutional facilities to house youthful offenders. The existing practice had been to hold arrested or detained juveniles at the Tarrant County Jail in a separate cell adjacent to adult prisoners. A soaring juvenile crime rate created overcrowding problems that aggravated inherent issues with the arrangement. In 1943 the courts committed 236 children to extended stays, overwhelming cell space and forcing the county to place many underage offenders in private homes at an exorbitant cost. The upward trend continued into the first eleven months of 1944 when 243 children were taken to the county lockup, an average of 22 per month. While most detainees were kept only a day or two, a few court-committed cases remained in custody much longer, including one child held forty-five days and five others detained from twenty-one to thirty-nine days. Housing youths for so long in in jail cells alongside adults was particularly egregious considering that many were not charged with crimes but had simply left home. At least 50 of the 243 committed in 1944 had run away or been abandoned and were held pending disposition hearings. Many would become permanent wards of the county, further stretching resources. In 1944 the Council on Social Agencies concluded that condemning juveniles to cells alongside adult prisoners was injurious to their welfare. The report struck home. Tarrant County paid $3,800 for an eight-room house at 4809 Collinwood Avenue that it adapted to house thirty children under 4 years old under the care of staff from the Lena Pope Home, a childcare center already caring for sixty-five children committed by the county and another fifty-five committed by district courts. The new space on Collinwood allowed for the conversion of the Tarrant County Children's Home on Kimbo Road into a detention center for juvenile delinquents, replacing the county jail.[15]

Jails, plagued by fights between inmates and minimal staffing, were not safe places for juveniles or adults. In February 1942 a 32-year-old inmate fatally beat Dallas Boyd Watson, 56 years old, from Dallas, after Watson asked him to be quiet so he could sleep. Both were in jail for drunkenness. In March 1942 a turnkey named Henderson received a three-day suspension for failing to promptly report an altercation that sent a prisoner to a local hospital. A worse incident in 1944 resulting in the death of a Burleson, Texas, stockman brought a major grand jury investigation that lasted months and heard from seventeen witnesses. William F. Dunn, 62 years old, was arrested for drunkenness the evening of October 12, 1944, after officers found him unconscious in his car at Drew Street and Wayside Avenue. Dunn remained unconscious for twelve hours in jail before police sent him by police vehicle (not an ambulance) to a hospital, where he died from natural causes. A physician testified Dunn was a known teetotaler who suffered from hypertension and fainting spells, which probably explained his unconsciousness. The final report absolved the police of criminal liability but faulted them for taking Dunn to the jail and waiting so long before sending him to a hospital.[16]

Four inmates broke out of the Tarrant County Jail on March 26, 1943. The escape began with prisoner Wilmer McCart subduing Jailer C. W. Brown and using his keys to release Harold McMurray, Frank James, and William Carter. The four took the elevator to the ground floor, where they overpowered the staff and took two revolvers before running outside and commandeering a car. The escape began to come undone when Motorcycle Officer L. E. Woods saw the vehicle cut across a corner and began a short pursuit that ended with a crash at Commerce and Bluff Streets. All escapees except Carter were immediately recaptured. Sheriff Dusty Rhodes fired Brown over the incident.[17]

The cost, quality, and quantity of jail food service became a thorny issue for both the county and the city. The standard Fort Worth City Jail menu consisted of a cup of coffee and two sandwiches, each with half an egg and one slice of bacon, served morning and evening (no lunch service). In August 1942 the meal service changed to only one sandwich with one egg and two slices of bacon (an extra slice of bread available on request) each morning and evening, a potential savings of two slices of bread per prisoner, per day.

In March 1943 Tarrant County began releasing drunks after only a few hours (the standard detention had been three days), thereby saving the cost of meals for three days. The change, along with other cost-cutting moves, reduced daily food expenditures from $53 to $22 but caused the Fort Worth Police to suspend taking drunk arrests to the county jail. Instead, intoxication arrestees were retained at the city jail for three days, the extra food costs recovered by not having to pay $2.50 court costs to the justice of the peace and $2.25 in constable fees per prisoner. The change made economic sense, but it aggravated problems with jail overcrowding and associated health risks for prisoners forced to survive for up to twenty days on an inadequate diet of one sandwich with coffee twice daily. In 1945 Corporation Court Judge W. H. Gilmartin called for improvements to the city jail's food service and for elimination of its chronic lice infestation. Jail problems were directly related to chronic alcoholics, who made up a large portion of the jail population. Many alcoholics were serial offenders; one man had been arrested over 500 times and a woman had more than 600 arrests. Gilmartin suggested the city establish a farm where prisoners serving long-term sentences could work off their time in healthier conditions. The proposal would become a reality, but it would take a few years.[18]

Traffic enforcement, a rather recent police responsibility, had expanded in the 1940s to be a major drain on police resources. As the number of vehicles on the street increased, traffic collisions exploded, averaging 5.7 million a year, although 85 percent were minor collisions without physical injuries. In 1941 Tarrant County reported 5,412 traffic accidents and 69 traffic fatalities (up from 62 in 1940). Fort Worth accounted for 31 of the deaths, including 18 pedestrians, down from 21 in 1940. In 1942 Fort Worth traffic fatalities declined dramatically to 21 (13 pedestrians), representing a fatality rate of 11.8 per 100,000 population, worse than Dallas (9.8) but better than Houston (12.0) and San Antonio (15.0). In 1943 traffic deaths dropped to just 15 (12 pedestrians). The rather stark declines during the war years were likely the product of fewer vehicles on the road and slower speeds due to gasoline and tire rationing.[19]

The police dealt with several notorious criminals in the 1940s. In 1943 Fort Worth Police officers and FBI agents arrested two nationally known bandits, Thomas Nathan "Pete" Norris and his brother, Gene Paul Norris. Pete, then age 31, began his life of crime in the 1930s with the Sonny Lamb Gang based in Hot Springs, Arkansas, that operated across a wide region, using machine guns to rob banks, groceries, department stores, bars, and gamblers. Hot Springs became the gang's safe haven thanks to Herbert Ackers, chief of detectives of Hot Springs Police, who provided protection in exchange for regular payoffs. The cozy arrangement ended in dramatic style in a shootout with Hot Springs Police on August 14, 1936, in which Sonny Lamb was slain. The ensuing cleanup campaign led to Ackers's conviction in 1938 and a four-year sentence in federal prison. Two days after Lamb's death, Fort Worth Detective Captain H. E. Chappie assisted in the arrest of Pete Norris in Rogers, Arkansas, on several outstanding warrants, including one for a Fort Worth robbery. Texas sentenced Pete to 436 years for robbery and murder but Gene Paul Norris, Pete's younger brother, along with Marshall Wichard, engineered his escape from the Ferguson Unit on March 16, 1942. The brothers and their associates resumed their criminal enterprises, robbing numerous local groceries and three J. C. Penney's Department Stores, becoming so active that Pete became the FBI's Public Enemy No. 1, all while the brothers bought a streetcar diner on Fort Worth's north side for $350. Acting on an informant's tip, Fort Worth Police staked out a grocery the gang had targeted as well as the brothers' reported residence, a farm outside Kennedale, Texas (a suburb southeast of Fort Worth). The farmhouse made a great hideaway, being well-placed in a secluded area that made undercover surveillance difficult. Unable to approach on the ground without being seen, the FBI used an airplane to identify cars on the property known to be associated with the brothers. On February 23, 1943, a contingent of FBI agents and officers from the Fort Worth Police and other agencies quickly moved in, capturing Pete Norris as he plowed a field. Gene Paul Norris and Jeanette Lyle, 16 years old, of Houston, Gene's sweetheart, fled in a vehicle but were captured after their car overturned. Subsequently, witnesses identified both Norris brothers and Nick Cascio out of a lineup as responsible for the December 17, 1942, robbery of Worth Foods General Office, 1111 West Vickery Boulevard, in which $11,500 was taken.[20]

Gene Paul Norris, Jeanette Lyle, and Thomas Nathan "Pete" Norris, February 24, 1943. Courtesy *Fort Worth Star Telegram* Collection, Special Collections, University of Texas at Arlington Libraries.

Gene Paul Norris fought his charges, calling in major legal assistance from lawyer Percy Foreman (they conducted their meetings in the Fort Worth Police Detective office). The cost in lawyer fees proved to be money well spent. Foreman convinced the jury that Gene Paul was too incapacitated by an injury suffered at the brothers' Oklahoma machine shop to have participated in the Worth Foods robbery. The victory was hollow, though, as Gene Paul received eight years for aiding Pete's escape and was transferred to Montgomery County, where he faced several other charges. On May 30, while awaiting trial, he and a cellmate, L. C. Gilham, overpowered a jailer and fled, only to be recaptured a few days later in Harris County, standing in Cypress Creek trying to throw off bloodhounds. Gene Paul testified in November 1943 that he bribed Montgomery County Sheriff Rodney Chambless and Jailer Henry Montgomery with $900 to allow him and Gillham to escape. The evidence against the two lawmen, including FBI recordings of Sheriff

Chambless and Norris's sister discussing the payment, seemed overwhelming, but both were acquitted, the jury accepting Sheriff Chambless's claim that he took the money as a ruse to discover where Norris secreted cash from the Fort Worth robberies. It was true that Sheriff Chambless was very interested in the loot; he grilled Norris repeatedly about the money, promising favors if given the location. Gene eventually gave the sheriff a spot where he supposedly hid the cash, but a search turned up nothing.[21]

Pete Norris pled guilty on March 29, 1943, avoiding the state's option of the death penalty in exchange for two life sentences. Pete and three other inmates escaped in February 1945 from Retrieve Prison Farm in Brazoria County by overpowering a guard, but Pete was quickly recaptured. A few months later, in December, Pete was shot while using a smuggled gun to escape from the Wharton County Jail. Either jails became more secure or Pete gave up; after the Wharton County misadventure he remained in prison until paroled in December 1960, at which time he announced plans to return to Oklahoma to farm or open a business.[22]

Ray Sellers was another well-known gangster active in the war years. Sellers, the ex-husband of Marie Barrow, sister of Clyde Barrow of Bonnie and Clyde infamy, was a burglar, safe cracker, and general thief with convictions for Dyer Act violations (transporting stolen cars across state lines) and for burglaries in Dallas and four surrounding counties. On October 3, 1943, he escaped during a rodeo at an Oklahoma prison where he was serving ten years for burglary. Just five days later, two men held up the Renfro Drug general offices, 1601 North Ballinger Street, making off with cash and 6,500 grains of morphine, 6,000 grains of codeine, 4,000 Dilaudid tablets, and 2 ounces of cocaine, the narcotics estimated to be worth $17,000. Police were without leads until three 10-year-old girls gave them a vehicle plate number they had scratched into the sidewalk using a rock. The girls, playing outside the day before the robbery, became suspicious after seeing the car and its occupants hanging around Jarvis and Summit Streets. The license led police to Ray Sellers, whom thirteen witnesses picked out of a photographic lineup as one of the Renfro robbers. Sellers remained a fugitive until December 2, when he appeared at a Dallas dairy with a .45-caliber bullet wound to his chest. He survived several days at Dallas's Parkland Hospital but refused to tell detectives anything about how he had been shot or who shot him. Fort Worth detectives took two witnesses to the hospital who confirmed their earlier identification, leading to a grand jury indictment, but Sellers died the next day. A second person charged in the Renfro robbery, James B. "Red" Kavanaugh, an associate of Lois Green, reputed to be the kingpin of Dallas crime, disappeared about the same time that Sellers was shot. Fort Worth detectives believed that a skeleton found near Arlington in March 1950 was Kavanaugh, but the forensics of the period was unable to make a positive identification. Police suspected that both Sellers and Kavanaugh had been killed on the orders of Green.[23]

Ernest Harris owned a tavern at 2500 East Belknap Street, as well as Northside Amusements, which supplied marble board games to bars, but was also known to deal in stolen property and be involved in several questionable enterprises. In April 1944 Harris received a two-year suspended sentence for possessing stolen tires; two months later he killed Horace Jones, a 38-year-old man Harris found in the company of Ernest Harris's estranged wife, Edith. Edith, who had filed for divorce on May 31, and another woman had collected Jones and a second man when the men finished their midnight shifts at American Manufacturing. The foursome drove to the second man's home where the men changed from their work clothes and were leaving when Harris pulled up and opened fire, killing Jones and wounding Edith. Ernest turned himself in on June 7, 1944, and was out on bond in November when he was arrested for assault to murder Sergeant J. Baetzel, a soldier stationed at Camp Bowie in Brownwood, Texas. Baetzel suffered a fractured skull, broken jaw, and several missing teeth during a disturbance at Harris's East Belknap Street tavern. Days later Harris was convicted of Jones's homicide and sentenced to five years, but the conviction was squashed and a new trial ordered after the judge learned the jurors had been told about the Baetzel assault during deliberations.[24]

Fort Worth Police also dealt with the bizarre and unusual. One such incident began at 7:30 a.m. on October 27, 1944, when a man grabbed Miss Virginia Fleming, 20 years old, at Jennings and Cannon Streets as she walked to work. Miss Fleming telephoned police after breaking away. Responding officers located and detained Curtis Dashmer, 33 years old, at 310 West Terrell Avenue. Their quick police work was made easier by the suspect's distinctive appearance, a man wearing a woman's dress with open-toed high heels and sporting "vivid red" lipstick. During the search at the jail, officers discovered Dashmer also wore a silk slip and rayon panties. An assistant district attorney reported that Dashmer was known to parade about in his wife's clothes and was a suspect in another assault committed that same morning. Just three hours after the incident and arrest, Dashmer was sentenced to a year in jail for aggravated assault.[25]

Interactions with alcoholics was (and is) a regular part of police work, but one incident in 1944 proved anything but routine. On October 27, 1944, Dewey Ward Jenkins, a 53-year-old man with 289 arrests in 19 years, was killed at a small downtown hotel that catered to the dispossessed, renting beds in an open dormitory setting. Claude Lyles, 38, surrendered at the police station, telling officers that Jenkins had beaten him until he passed out or blacked out and that when he awoke, he retaliated by striking Jenkins with a tire tool as he slept.[26]

Fort Worth had long had a sizable presence of a traveling group with historical ties to Ireland that were commonly referred to as "gypsies." Members worked circuses and carnivals during spring and summers and spent winters in warmer climes like Fort Worth, where they carried an unsavory reputation and were associated with dodgy schemes. In the 1940s many of the community lived in a camp near East Lancaster Avenue and Riverside Drive, the men working various odd jobs and the women, often dressed in brightly colored skirts and sport shirts and coats, running fortune-telling parlors where they conned customers through promises to cure back pain or through phony predictions, as well as through outright thefts. In 1945 police arrested three such "gypsy" women fortune-tellers, charging them with taking cash under the pretense of "blessing" the money in their customers' wallets or taking the wallet to insert a charm, then returning with instructions not to open the wallet until the next day, at which time the victims would find their cash gone.[27]

Some sensational incidents came from inside the broader community, including those in law and politics. Judge Gus Brown came close to losing an eye during an altercation with his barber that began as an argument about the treatment of disabled veterans. On February 5, 1944, Judge Brown, a World War I veteran who lost a leg in the war, was in the chair of barber R. M. McMillan at Elam's Barber Shop, 113 West Weatherford Street. Brown mentioned he was writing a book about crippled war veterans, which somehow led to a heated exchange, so incensing Brown that he had another barber finish the haircut. Brown left but later returned, striking McMillan, who fought back, causing the injury to Brown's eye. On July 14, 1944, Marvin Beaty, a candidate for the Texas legislature, stabbed his political opponent, Marvin B. Simpson Jr., and Simpson's father, Marvin B. Simpson Sr. The incident, occurring during a political rally at Morningside School, began when Simpson the younger charged Beaty had been indicted while serving as justice of the peace—a true statement in that Beaty was charged with three counts of assessing illegal fees and twenty-one counts of misapplying county funds—but Simpson failed to mention all but one charge was dismissed and that Beaty was acquitted in the lone case that went to trial. As Simpson Jr. left the podium, Beaty challenged him, threatening to drag Simpson's divorce into the political muck. Simpson Jr. contended he was justified in bringing up the indictments because Beaty had downplayed Simpson's military service. Eventually, Simpson Sr. joined the fray, which turned physical. No clear picture emerged as to who turned the dispute into a physical altercation that became a brawl, but all agreed that Beaty slashed the older Simpson's chest and abdomen and the younger Simpson's chest and arm. Simpson Sr. was hospitalized in serious condition, but Junior was treated and sent home to recuperate. Beaty regretted the incident, sending his apologies to both men, but continued campaigning that evening, after he bonded out of jail on two counts of assault to murder. In the Democratic primary for state representative just five days later, Simpson defeated Beaty 9,348 to 5,668.[28]

One of the more sensational criminal incidents involving Fort Worth elites occurred in Tulsa, Oklahoma, where Mrs. Elia Howard, 2436 Winton Terrace, a 44-year-old described as a "gray-haired divorcee of Fort Worth," shot and killed Mrs. Blanche S. Simmons. The incident began on March 25, 1943, in a hotel lobby when Mrs. Howard confronted Mrs. Simmons, the 55-year-old wife of oil wildcatter T. Karl Simmons with whom Howard was romantically involved. Perhaps wanting to avoid a public display, the two agreed to take their dispute to Mrs. Howard's room, but once there, the argument became physical and fatal. According to Mrs. Howard, the only surviving witness, Mrs. Simmons pulled a pistol that discharged as the two fought over it, killing Mrs. Simmons. During the trial, Karl Simmons admitted that he began a relationship with Mrs. Howard during a visit to Fort Worth in 1935 and gave her $20,000 in 1942, but subsequently borrowed $5,000, giving her a note of indebtedness. Soon after the loan, Mr. Simmons confessed the affair to his wife and began to distance himself from Howard. In June 1943 a jury acquitted Mrs. Howard of manslaughter. Just months later, in October 1943, T. Karl Simmons died of natural causes at 60 years of age and Mrs. Howard sued the Simmons estate for $19,380, claiming the oilman had promised to marry her and pay her legal bills.[29]

Chapter 4

African Americans and Hispanics in the War

According to the 1940 Census, Fort Worth was home to 20,288 African Americans, almost 12 percent of the total population (177,662). Blacks were among the first Americans to enter military service; the initial group of Fort Worth draftees reporting for induction in November 1941 included fifteen African Americans, another forty-two would follow on June 23, 1942. Unfortunately, putting on the uniform did little to ward off racism. The American military remained segregated, as did many military support organizations. The United Service Organization (USO), operating clubs reserved for military personnel, maintained segregated facilities in most of the South and in some other regions. Brownwood, Texas, 125 miles southwest of Fort Worth and home to the Camp Bowie training base, had a large Black USO club, while downtown Fort Worth had a smaller USO at the African American YMCA, 1600 Jones Street, and a USO for whites at the Hotel Texas. Segregation was most frequently and blatantly associated with the South, but other regions displayed clear racist views. Radio station WTIC in Hartford, Connecticut, canceled a news program in which a Yale University professor criticized the Red Cross for segregating blood by the donor's race. Despite widespread inequities at home and in the military, many

African Americans served with distinction. In January 1945 Mount Zion Baptist Church honored Captain Leonard Jackson, 1200 Missouri Avenue, one of at least five Tuskegee Airmen from Fort Worth. Jackson was awarded the Distinguished Flying Cross and an Air Medal for piloting Mustang fighter airplanes escorting bombers during the Italian campaign.[1]

In most cases Black soldiers were relegated to menial jobs, although time and circumstances sometimes altered their career paths. In March 1942 the *Star Telegram* reported "Borrie" Miller (actual name, Doris Miller) of Waco, a sailor assigned to kitchen duty, received the Navy Cross for manning a machine gun during the December 7, 1941, Pearl Harbor attack. Miller was the first Black man to receive the award. In December 1943 Miller was killed in action in the Pacific theater when Japanese torpedoes sank his ship. Upward mobility for Blacks, though limited, was possible in the military. In 1942 the Texas Selective Service Board, lamenting a lack of Black officers, solicited eligible applicants with a high school education to apply for Officer Candidate School. Surprisingly, the highest-paid MP stationed in Fort Worth was a Black sergeant. In 1944 Tech Sergeant Tulley B. Bond of Kansas earned $468 monthly, a very high wage that was due, in part, to his large family. Bond received $114 in base pay, $94 in subsistence pay, and $260 for his wife and their ten children still living at home (he also had two adult sons in the military). Sergeant Bond, 52 years old, joined the Army at 18, saw service in Vera Cruz, Mexico, in 1912 and spent fourteen months in France during World War I, receiving the Distinguished Service Medal. At Fort Worth Sergeant Bond was in charge of the "Negro prophylactic station," part of the Army's campaign to eradicate STIs.[2]

Confrontations between Black and white servicemen were a regrettable reality. In 1942 a fight between one white and one Black soldier at a bowling alley across from Fort Dix, New Jersey, turned deadly when MPs fired at a fleeing Black soldier, precipitating an exchange of gunfire with Black barracks that killed two African Americans and one white and injured five others, race unspecified. Peace was restored only after white and Black officers courageously intervened, ordering both sides to cease firing. In November 1942 MPs in Phoenix shot a Black soldier during an arrest, setting off a three-hour gun battle between Blacks and police, both military and civilian, that killed two Black soldiers and injured twelve persons of both races. In June 1943 23 persons were killed and 700 injured during a major race confrontation in Detroit and riots broke out in four other American cities, including Beaumont, Texas. Fort Worth escaped any comparable racial incidents, perhaps because the nearest large training camp lay sixty miles away, but that remoteness did not save Dallas. On January 3, 1943, two Black soldiers found without passes at a Black café in northeast Dallas fought MPs trying to arrest them, setting off a melee that drew in others who surrounded the two MPs and the first responding Dallas Police officers. Order was restored only after reinforcements from several agencies, civilian and military, subdued the crowd and removed seventy Black servicemen to a stockade. Afterward the Army declared Dallas off-limits to Black soldiers.[3]

The prevalence of racism at every level of local life seemed to all but ensure confrontations. Racial insensitivity was on display everywhere. On June 3, 1944, Fort Worth banks closed to commemorate the birthday of Jefferson Davis, the only president of the Confederacy. Racial epithets were common in Southern newspapers, although by the 1940s reporters had dropped the vulgarism that had been prevalent in favor of "Negro" or "colored" to refer to African Americans. Reporters were so consistent in identifying Black persons that the lack of a racial identifier could be assumed to mean that the subject was white. A 1943 newspaper article described Martha Thomas, a murder victim, as a "Negress," and a summary of Fort Worth crime in the first six months of 1944 noted that June had been deadly, with five homicides, including three "Negroes." The report described the prior months as relatively quiet with only the wounding of two Hispanics at Danceland, 603 West Magnolia Avenue, deemed a "major shooting," although nine "Negroes" had been killed in that span, apparently insufficient to rank as "major."[4]

Almost every aspect of life in Fort Worth operated under strict racial codes mandating segregated schools, cafés, toilets, and drinking fountains, to name some of the more obvious manifestations. Racial divisions permeated society to such an incredible degree that war bond drives were racially divided; a bond drive in the summer of 1944 set a separate $175,000 goal for Fort Worth Blacks. Reverend W. S. Brentzin, chair of the separate appeal, organized a launch rally at Mount Gilead Baptist Church, 600 Grove Street, on July 23. The list of racial divides went from the ridiculous to the absurd, including divisions that placed humans in jeopardy. From 1945 to 1953, the Southwestern Exposition and Fat Stock Show held separate livestock competitions for white and Black participants with unequal prize money, $645 for Blacks and $2,040 for whites. In 1945 the Fort Worth Negro 4-H Club won the ribbon for best Negro Boys Show participants. Black cowboys were not allowed to compete in the rodeo until 1956. Separate medical facilities treated Black and white patients. In November 1944 Fort Worth Police officers responding to the shooting of a Black woman reported "Negro ambulance attendants" were loading the victim into an ambulance as they arrived. The injured woman would have been taken to either a Black-operated hospital or to Black wards at John Peter Smith Hospital, St. Joseph's Hospital, Harris Hospital, or All Saints Hospital. In 1940 Fort Worth had fifteen hospitals with 1,148 beds for whites, but only 55 for Blacks. Peter Smith was the most likely destination for Black patients, but major private white hospitals reserved a few beds for Blacks; Harris and All Saints had 2 each and St. Joseph's had 10. The two hospitals designated for Blacks, ERMH and Fort Worth Community Hospital, had 25 and 10 beds, respectively. A Negro Health Week celebrated April 4–11, 1943, was sponsored by the Voluntary Health League with the cooperation of health departments throughout Tarrant County. Even in death segregation prevailed. In 1944 Tarrant County paid Ed Brown $15 to dig graves for "Negro" paupers.[5]

Psychological costs associated with military service combined with rampant racism to create a heavy burden for returning servicemen. Ollie Brown, 909 Luella Street, came home in 1944 after two years of overseas Army service suffering from "spells" and "fits," symptoms that would now probably be diagnosed as PTSD. His condition worsened, leading to an arrest in June 1945 for burglarizing the home of a white woman, a crime for which he was sentenced to twenty-five years in Leavenworth Penitentiary. Brown's mother, Irma Brown, started a letter-writing campaign to Walter White, executive director of the National Association for the Advancement of Colored People (NAACP), seeking her son's release. Mrs. Brown lamented that African Americans "have no help in Texas at all. They are so down on us.

Fear Nigers [*sic*] [unreadable] they treat us most anyway." The NAACP legal team, including Thurgood Marshall, later a United States Supreme Court justice, appealed Brown's court martial, arguing that he did not receive a fair hearing due to his race.[6]

Race was a major factor in the disposition of crimes, especially crimes perpetuated by a Black man against a white woman. Lynchings declined precipitously in the 1940s, perhaps an effect of millions of young Black men being removed from the South either by military service or by the Great Migration to the North and West. The Tuskegee Institute reported five lynchings in 1940, four in 1941, five in 1942, three in 1943, and two in 1944. One of the 1942 lynching victims, Willie Vinson, was a 23-year-old Black man in Texarkana, Texas, who was chased and shot by neighbors after a white woman reported he had sexually assaulted her. The captors turned Vinson over to authorities, but the next day, July 13, 1942, a mob took him from a hospital bed and lynched him, afterward dragging his dead body through the streets. Most of the town witnessed the execution, but no one came forward to identify the perpetrators. The two 1944 victims were both Black men, one from Mississippi and one from Tennessee, one of whom was a 65-year-old minister taken from his home and shot after he refused to relinquish his farm where oil had been found.[7]

Fort Worth had progressed beyond lynching but still treated Black on white crimes differently, employing inflammatory language in reporting and rushing the accused through a legal process where they faced harsh sentences. A lurid frontpage headline in 1944 exclaiming "Negro Terrorist Attacks Glenwood Woman in Home" involved an incident in which Mrs. Gladys Williams, 710 West Leuda Street, fought off an intruder who escaped with her purse. In 1943 Clarence Richardson, a 19-year-old Black youth, received a life sentence for striking Jane Hatfield, described as a "blonde," in her driveway, 916 Galveston Avenue, and running away with her purse containing $8. The blow was serious, requiring eighteen stiches to Miss Hatfield's head, and Richardson had a previous conviction for burglary as well as other charges, but a life sentence for a 19-year-old in an $8 robbery is hard to reconcile. On June 15, 1945, Mrs. Lydia McBride, a 56-year-old white woman, was sexually assaulted and beaten to death. One month later, on July 12, Richard Gamble, a 31-year-old Black man nicknamed "Gotch Eye" for an eye injury, was convicted and sentenced to die. Gamble steadfastly maintained his innocence through his trial, but confessed just moments before being executed on June 28, 1946, barely a year after the crime.[8]

Most African Americans lived their lives quietly while enduring oppressive racism, but a few reached their limit and fought back. Fort Worth city transit buses, rigidly segregated, were the scene of several confrontations. In 1943 Miss Opal Pelton, a white woman of 508 Seamon Avenue, gave up her seat in the front section (reserved for whites) to a woman with a child in her arms and, left without seating in the white section, moved to the rear cross seat, an area reserved for Blacks. Subsequently, an African American couple, Clarence Fletcher, 22 years old, and his 17-year-old wife, Earline, sat next to Miss Pelton in the only available seats. Miss Pelton objected to Mrs. Fletcher sitting beside her and rose to leave, but, according to her complaint, Earline bit her arm and Mr. Fletcher pushed her into an open window. Both husband and wife were arrested. Mrs. Fletcher pled guilty and was sentenced to a year in jail (a year in jail for what?), but Mr. Fletcher pled not guilty and waited trial. In July 1944 M. O. Mosley Jr., 1326 Hemphill Street, boarded a crowded downtown city bus with several whites standing in the aisle. Mosley was attacked after she asked a young Black woman seated in the front of the Black section to move to the rear where several seats were vacant. The woman was arrested for disturbing the peace but quickly released thanks to Attorney Jack Carter who made her bond, a rare outcome. Problems related to seating on buses multiplied as ridership soared, driven by wartime rationing that limited automobile usage and the expansion of demand accompanying the surge in defense workers. In September 1943 the Morningside Civic League asked the bus company to do something about Blacks crowding into buses, although what they thought management could do was a mystery.[9]

Fort Worth schools remained rigidly segregated with no pretensions to equality. In 1943 the district spent $0.49 per day per student to educate white students, but only $0.35 per Black student, almost 30 percent less. The school board also showed little empathy for the plight of its lowest-paid employees, who were predominantly Black. On October 29, 1843, the board dismissed thirty-eight Black maids who had sought a pay raise from $50 to $75 monthly, claiming the terminations were done to alleviate worker shortages, an improbable spin. The school board was slightly less hostile to a 1944 request from the local branch of the Texas Commission on Interracial Cooperation (TCIC) for a Reserve Officer Training Corps (ROTC) chapter at I. M. Terrell High School, the designated Black high school. TCIC pointed out that every white high school and some junior high schools already had ROTC units. The board agreed, with the stipulation that the military, which supplied the equipment, sign off on the chapter. Faced with daily struggles to provide a quality education, a few dedicated school staff did the best they could. One dedicated local couple devoted all their lives to educating Black children. Mrs. Emma J. Guinn retired in the 1940s after forty-five years as a FWISD teacher. Mrs. Guinn was the widow of James E. Guinn, also a long-time FWISD teacher and principal for whom an elementary school was named. Mrs. Guinn was a local product, having graduated from I. M. Terrell High School.[10]

Faced with strict segregation that was violently enforced, Blacks turned inward to create and celebrate their own culture. African Americans celebrated Juneteenth to commemorate the announced end of slavery in Texas on June 19, 1865. In 1942 Fort Worth Blacks gathered at local parks for picnics, foot races, and water events, but without fireworks, eliminated to preserve explosives for the war. Juneteenth offered Blacks their once annual access to the baseball diamonds, tennis courts, and swimming pool at Forest Park, as well as the Botanic Gardens and zoo with full concessions. Many workers took the day off, causing some upscale housewives to complain of being left "maidless," although defense plants reported most Black workers reported as scheduled. The party continued that evening at 7:00 p.m. with a hayride from the Black USO, 1600 Jones Street, to Greenway Park, where a joint USO-YMCA program honored Blacks in the military. Lieutenant Jack Drake of the 72nd Aviation Squadron, stationed at Fort Worth Army Airfield, addressed the crowd, followed by dancing in the Recreation Building to the music of the Red Calhoun Orchestra.[11]

The rest of the year Blacks did what they could to make their lives better. The USO and numerous clubs offered socializing opportunities, primarily dances. In 1944 New Year's Eve fell on a Sunday, forcing schedule adjustments. On Friday twenty-one hostesses from the "Negro Service Men's Center" (USO) on Jones Street visited Black servicemen at the USPHSH, offering companionship and dancing. The next day, Saturday, December 30, the USO held a big New Year's Eve dance, followed by a matinee dance on Monday, January 1, 1945, at 6:00 p.m.

Baseball was the major professional sport in town. Blacks watched the minor league Cats from segregated seating but also supported local Black teams as well as teams from the Negro Baseball League playing exhibition games at LaGrave Field. On May 27, 1944, the St. Louis Stars met the Atlanta Black Crackers (a separate seating section reserved for whites), and in 1945 the Kansas City Monarchs faced the Chicago American Giants. The Monarchs' roster included Vance Smith, a local product, and two future Major League Hall of Famers, Satchel Paige pitching and Jackie Robinson playing shortstop. Fort Worth's own Black baseball team, the Fort Worth Black Giants, played at LaGrave (admission seventy-five cents for adults, forty cents for children and servicemen) against teams like the Houston Ship Yard Tigers, Dallas Monarchs, Hubbard City Nine, Greer's Cuban All-Stars, and the Midnight Fliers from Tarrant Airfield.

Amateur athletic facilities for African American youths were limited. The Crime Prevention and Prison Reform Society, also headquartered at 1600 South Jones Street along with the YMCA and USO, solicited funding for a recreation center at Mount Gilead Baptist Church, 600 Grove Street, to provide wholesome activities and religious education for youths to help divert them from juvenile delinquency. The Black YWCA, opened in 1941 at 1913 North Crump Street, was one of the few options for African American girls.[12]

The great labor shortage created by the war unleashed an unplanned consequence, opening previously closed employment opportunities for Blacks and other ignored groups. The effect was huge in scope, doubling the number of Blacks in the industrial workforce. In October 1942, less than a year into the war, the unavailability of white staff led one downtown department store to hire "Negro girls" as elevator operators (elevators at the time were not automatic but had operators), and City Ice Delivery,

913 East Ninth Street, hired its first two Black women as ice pullers, promising to add five more as soon as they could be found. Those were important early steps, but the major payoff came when African Americans moved into high-paying jobs in war industries, starting a trend that would transform the American workforce. In April 1942 Blacks were 10 percent of the American population, but only 5.8 percent of the 12 million war industry workers; by the summer of 1943 their numbers had risen to account for 6.7 percent of over 14 million defense workers—better but still not proportional to population. The War Manpower Commission (WMC) suggested that the lingering disparity of Black workers in defense industries could be explained by the concentration of two-thirds of the Black population in fourteen largely agricultural southern states where job training and occupational opportunities remained limited. What began in the 1940s represented the start of a process that would take much longer. During the Korean War between 1950 and 1953, Fort Worth's Convair plant employed 30,000 workers, but only 1,200, or 4 percent, were African Americans, and even that figure may well have overstated the degree of progress. Most industries that hired Blacks, including defense plants, tended to concentrate Black workers in low-skilled laboring and janitorial positions, but even those menial jobs paid better than many skilled positions in nondefense companies.[13]

Federal government programs and agencies assisted in advancing employment opportunities for Blacks and other excluded groups. Federal appropriations funded seven nurseries in Fort Worth for the children of war workers, including three designated for Black children: Lake Como, Butler Place, and North Side. The United States Employment Service Office (USES) successfully found jobs for substantial numbers of Blacks in defense work, perhaps due more to need than choice, but the effect was the same for those hired. In March 1944 the local USES referred 5,966 applicants, 2,488 of whom were hired, including 54 described as "handicapped," 925 nonwhites, 973 women, and 590 white males. The jobs represented real and important advances, but racial divisions still existed in the workplace. In 1942 Thelma Pages, a Black teacher at Lincoln High School of Dallas, sued in federal court over unequal conditions in which white teachers with the same qualifications earned $1,800 annually compared to only $1,260 for her.[14]

Labor activism, which might have been a force to redress grievances, took a backseat to patriotism and the need to sustain production to win the war. Still, many unions were able to maintain a presence in the Black community. In 1944 local Black union members meeting at Mount Pisgah Baptist Church heard Theodore Scott, an American Federation of Labor (AFL) organizer from Dallas, and Phillip Weightman, the Congress of Industrial Organization (CIO) vice president from Chicago, call for unionization of all laborers. Also attending were J. Pittman, the local CIO representative, and several officers of the Negro Welfare Council, including Council President Reverend S. R. Prince, Secretary Almita Robinson, and member G. W. Williams. Union recruitment and activity were made more difficult by extreme views that questioned the patriotism of union workers seeking better conditions. That effect was especially true for African Americans. In 1944 Texas Democrats fighting civil rights legislation campaigned against what they termed federal interference promoted by the CIO with its "negro-white equality" agenda. The Southern Baptist Convention's Committee on Negro Ministerial Education meeting in Atlanta warned that poor educational backgrounds left Blacks vulnerable to subversive groups that tended to target them. The committee, noting that only 100 of 3,999 Black Baptist ministers held college degrees, recommended endowing $5,000 scholarships at thirteen Black colleges to draw more Black students into formal theological training.[15]

Another artifact of the war economy, scarce housing, had a racial dimension that relegated Blacks to worse living conditions than whites. Housing was tight for everyone; a 1943 War Housing Center survey reported Fort Worth had a rental vacancy rate of just .4 percent, indicating virtually no available rental housing. Still, racial disparities clearly appeared in statistics on housing utilization. The report deemed only 6.9 percent of Fort Worth's 50,000 "white dwelling units" overcrowded and found that 44.5 percent, almost half, were below optimum capacity of 1.5 persons per room, figures suggesting that the existing white housing could accommodate 25,000 more renters. The same study found 17.6 percent of "Negro housing units" were overcrowded and only 30 percent were underutilized, clear evidence that Blacks lived in more crowded conditions. In December 1944 the

National Housing Administration tacitly recognized the racial divide by designating 200 "stop-gap" temporary housing units bound for Fort Worth as "Negro" and only fifty as "white." The problem persisted through the war and beyond. In 1946 the National Urban League, a civil rights organization founded in 1910, reported that 80 percent of Black Americans lived in substandard housing.[16]

During the war African Americans won major court decisions supporting their fight for political rights. In November 1942 the United States Fifth Circuit Court of Appeals agreed to hear the case of Lonnie E. Smith, a Black man from Houston, Texas, challenging the exclusion of Black voters from the Democratic primary. Despite opposition from Texas Attorney General Grover Sellers and two Houston election judges, the United States Supreme Court ruled for Smith in *Smith v. Allwright*, ending exclusively white primaries in 1944. The effect was significant. The number of African Americans registered to vote in the South quadrupled from 200,000 in 1940 to 800,000 in 1948. The Tarrant County Democratic Party acknowledged the court order but remained recalcitrant, barring Blacks from precinct conventions, a step supported by District Attorney Marvin Brown, who criticized the court's ruling as a threat to states' rights. Under pressure, A. H. Sanders, chair of the Tarrant County Democratic Party, relented, ordering precinct chairmen to allow Black voters on condition that they acted "gentlemanly and ladylike" and vowed to support the Democratic slate in the general election. Many rank-and-file white Democrats refused to accept the court's decision and organized as the Regular Democrats of Texas to discourage Black voting participation and increase white turnout. The group ran newspaper ads urging white voters to flood precinct meetings, ensuring the selection of convention delegates committed to states' rights and opposed to federal interference in support of "negro-white equality." Intimidation worked; only 187 African Americans voted in the July 1944 Democratic primary (the first after the court ruling), a pittance of the 33,130 Black population of Tarrant County. The ballot box at 1013 East Hattie Street turned in the largest number of Black votes, 32, but 1601 New York Avenue was close behind with 30. Still, opening primaries was an important step in the lengthy process that would finally grant African Americans the basic political rights due every

American. The movement also likely aided other advances in local politics, such as formation in 1945 of the Southside Civic League by Black property owners. Under Chairman F. C. Thurman, the league became the voice of Black residents, effectively promoting grassroots improvements like the paving of New York Avenue, East Leuda Street and East Cannon Avenue, the first agenda items.[17]

Rigid lines of segregation remained unchanged in most areas, including social mixing, where only minor and transitory exceptions occurred. One isolated, limited effort at coexistence occurred when Fort Worth's Methodist Churches declared February 8, 1945, Race Relations Day. That Sunday Reverend J. H. Smith, pastor of Allen Chapel African Methodist Church (Black), spoke and his church choir sang at Riverside Methodist Church (white); the First Methodist Church (white) collected an offering in support of "negro Methodists"; and Reverend F. Rivers Barnwell, described as a "negro boy soprano," sang at Meadowbrook Methodist Church (white). In 1945 Fort Worth was also the first Texas city to open an office of the National Urban League.[18]

Hispanics also faced blatant discrimination in their daily lives, often considered foreigners simply on the basis of their brown skin and different surnames regardless of place of origin. In 1943 a downtown café refused service to James Reza and his Uncle Joe, telling them they did not serve "Mexicans"—an ironic statement considering Uncle Joe was in an American Army uniform. In 1944 Jack Danciger, a Fort Worth Jew who served as honorary Mexican consul, complained to Charles Keith, owner of The Skateland, 541 North Main Street, that Blanca and Azencena Tamez (daughters of a former Mexican consul at Eagle Pass, Texas) and Dolores and Virginia Garcia (whose father was an American soldier stationed in the Pacific) had been turned away from the rink because they were "Mexicans." Keith admitted denying them entry but claimed he had no personal objection and refused because he feared Anglo patrons would leave if he admitted "Mexicans." The problem existed across Texas. In 1945 Staff Sergeant Marcario Garcia of Sugarland, Texas, holder of the Congressional Medal of Honor, faced assault charges after being involved in a fight at a Richmond, Texas, café after the manager refused to serve him a cup of coffee, saying he did not serve "Mexicans." Two sailors came to Garcia's aid after he was hit with a baseball bat.[19]

Like Blacks, Hispanics united around their own community to celebrate holidays like Mexican Independence Day, September 16. In 1944 the holiday fell on a Saturday, but the party started Friday evening at Guerrero Park (Twenty-First Street and Grove Avenue) with the crowning of Queen Magdalena Rangel and continued at the City Recreation Building where Fort Worth's "Mexican colony" celebrated with songs, dances, and speeches emceed by Pedro Cepeda with musical entertainment by the Claudio Mata Orchestra. The *Star Telegram* displayed racial and geographical ineptness, writing that invitations were sent to "citizens of this country" and that many "North Americans" attended the celebrations. Mexican Americans attended mainstream schools with Anglos, although many opted for parochial schools like San Jose Mission School, a Catholic school for Mexican Americans established by the Sisters of St. Mary of Namur in 1926 at Fourteenth and Commerce Streets.[20]

The economic doors the war forced open to African Americans and women also admitted Mexican Americans. On June 7, 1943, Superintendent J. J. Pendergast of the Texas and Pacific Railway announced the hiring of twelve "Mexican girls" at the railroad's Stove Foundry Road shops. The twelve were the first Hispanic women and some of the first women employed in a mechanic's shop. The company installed a separate dressing room and shower for the women who ranged in age from 18 to 49. Pendergast admitted that some of the male employees remained skeptical but that he knew women could do the jobs from his experiences with women workers during World War I. The new hires began with menial, unskilled tasks like cleaning and oiling the machinery, but they quickly earned respect for performing unpleasant jobs, such as filling lubricators during a pouring rain. As they gained experience, they moved into more demanding jobs requiring more skill. The trial proved so successful that by the end of 1943 Texas and Pacific hired sixty-two more women. However, all distinctions were not erased in one sweep. "Mexican women" in the railroad shops were more likely to be assigned "he-man," physically demanding jobs like washing and refueling engines and operating "ponderous" turntables, while Anglo women, often

Miss Madalaine Rangel, queen of Mexican Independence Day at Vicente Guerrero Park, September 16, 1944. Courtesy *Fort Worth Star Telegram* Collection, Special Collections, University of Texas at Arlington Libraries.

described as "attractive" and "blond," tended to get easier and cleaner tasks like baggage handlers, although mail bags were ponderous, weighing from 35 to 125 pounds, which must have presented quite a challenge for one woman weighing just 101 pounds.[21]

No records appeared concerning American Indians in Fort Worth, but the national record reflects that they entered the military in significant numbers. In the 1940s Native Americans were, for the first time, subject to the draft, but most entering the military did so as volunteers. At the start of World War II approximately 60,000 American Indians were draft age, between 21 and 44; less than a year later one in seven, or 8,800, were in uniform.[22]

Chapter 5

Women in the War and Postwar

World War II changed women's lives in myriad ways. Nearly 350,000 American women volunteered for military service, 543 died in that service, and many others were wounded or returned with physical and emotional scars. In 1947 36 women veterans were patients at the USPHSH, a small part of the institution's total patient load of 897, but a slightly higher percentage than of women serving in the military. Women on the home front also contributed in various ways: 120 Fort Worth women became Red Cross Corps drivers, others donated blood or served as air raid wardens, learned auto mechanics, or worked at defense plants. Many unable to perform factory work volunteered at the employment registry helping staff defense industries. Women were prominent in nursing and many health fields. Just seven months after Pearl Harbor, 4,961 Fort Worthians, the majority women, had completed Red Cross First Aid training, 752 women took home nursing training, and 634 finished nutrition classes. In August 1942 the Red Cross offered free eighty-hour courses leading to certification as nurse's aides, contingent solely on a pledge to donate 150 hours of service each year. The class attracted 350 women, including Mrs. Elliot Roosevelt, President Franklin Roosevelt and Eleanor Roosevelt's daughter-in-law, the former Ruth Googins

Eleanor Roosevelt with son Elliot Roosevelt and his wife, the former Ruth Googins at Dutch Branch Ranch, March 8, 1937. Courtesy *Fort Worth Star Telegram* Collection, Special Collections, University of Texas at Arlington Libraries.

of Fort Worth. Ruth and the president's son, married in 1933, settled on a ranch near Benbrook, Texas, just southwest of Fort Worth. In 1943 she cited her work as a rancher and as a Red Cross nurse's aide in a petition for an increased gasoline allotment sufficient to power each of her three automobiles 1,000 miles a month (36,000 miles per year, a rather large amount).

The board granted a preferred mileage book for only one car, leaving the other two with basic "A" books.[1]

World War II marked a major societal shift as women entered the general labor pool in large numbers, many taking jobs previously held only by men. It is likely that only the necessities of war could have spawned such a major transformation so quickly. There was no question the country needed women's labor. Planners knew in April 1942 that the available male labor pool, shrunken by military service, would be insufficient and that at least 1 million women workers would be needed to meet production quotas in 1943. Hollywood was one of the first industries to react, replacing men with women set workers and technicians in 1942. Other businesses quickly joined in. In March 1942 Winifred Wiley, age 21, 1021 South Henderson Street, became Fort Worth's first woman elevator operator; just months later several African American women joined her. More robust, outdoor work followed. May Loraine Crowell began work as a "front man," pumping gasoline at the Firestone Store, 1001 West Seventh Street, and 3 women (out of 160 applying) became meter readers for Texas Electric in December 1942. In the course of their workday, they walked eight to ten miles clad in uniform caps, long-sleeved shirts, and gaberdine slacks. The city of Fort Worth hired Mrs. Mary Fain and Mrs. H. V. Shank as sanitary inspectors in 1943. Women also made inroads into office work, expanding their presence in many previously male office positions. By 1943 the number of women employed in banking doubled compared to prewar, to 130,000, almost half the 280,000 total workforce.[2]

Women showed up everywhere, doing jobs previously reserved for men. In June 1943 Mrs. Myrtle Rose, 507 Loney Street, became Fort Worth's first woman taxicab driver, although police rules limited her to driving only between 7:00 a.m. and 6:00 p.m. and prohibited her from picking up drunks. Yellow Cab administrators promised to hire more women if Mrs. Rose performed well. Fort Worth's local bus service followed in 1943, hiring a woman as a conductor on its trailer-buses, semitrucks pulling enclosed trailers fitted for passengers that were used on high volume routes, especially those transporting Convair workers. The company planned to add nine more women conductors and to train women as drivers. Al Clyde, who took office

Eva Barnes, first woman to serve as Tarrant County assistant district attorney, December 14, 1944. Courtesy *Fort Worth Star Telegram* Collection, Special Collections, University of Texas at Arlington Libraries.

January 1, 1945, as Tarrant County district attorney, appointed the county's first woman assistant district attorney, Eva Barnes. Ms. Barnes, born in England, came to the United States in 1921 and graduated from law school in 1932. In addition, four women served in the Texas legislature in its forty-eighth session, the most in history to that point.[3]

For all the doors opening for women, it was Rosie the Riveter who became the public face of women in the World War II workforce. Women entered defense work in great numbers, doing many jobs that had traditionally been assigned to men. The need was critical. In 1942 W. R. Woolrich, dean of engineering at the University of Texas, predicted war production quotas for December 1943 would require 20 million defense workers, 12 million more than were then employed and far in excess of available manpower. The need was so critical that speakers at a 1942 Fort Worth Convention of the General Federation of Women's Clubs warned of a looming labor draft if women did not voluntarily enter defense industries. The good news was that women, once at work, proved capable of doing the jobs quite well; at least 40,000 rose to become supervisors and foremen in the nation's defense plants.[4] Others moved into traditionally male preserves in related industries. In 1942 thirty-two women trained at Meacham Airport to replace men in the Aircraft Communications Service of the Civil Aeronautics Authority (CAA) and several others attended classes at Tarrant Field in general aircraft mechanics to provide service, repair and maintenance. Texas Christian University (TCU) received funding from the federal government for classes in business office skills normally reserve for men, such as accounting, purchasing, and supervision.[27]

An expansive local training program developed specifically to meet Convair's needs, the area's largest employer poised to hire many women workers. The training process began with interviews at USES, 408 Taylor Street, where applicants were vetted for the essential requirements: a citizen in good health of "normal" height and weight (more leniency was given for being over- than underweight) with at least two years of high school (drafting and inspection jobs required a high school diploma) and between 20 and 30 years of age (later raised to 35). Convair foremen requested the maximum age limit, warning that older women tended to be "too bossy" and more likely to "get surly" about taking orders and to stir up friction among younger "girls." Successful applicants attended classes six hours a day for six to ten weeks, depending on position, at Technical High School where training ran twenty-four hours a day, seven days a week. Trainees referred by USES attended without charge, but private agency referrals paid tuition. The training programs became wildly popular; twenty-two classes of twenty-five students each were in session in July 1942. They also proved demanding; 17 percent of women either resigned or were dismissed during the initial ten-day trial period. In January 1943 the War Industries Board began intensive eight-hour a day classes in barns at Will Rogers Memorial Center training women already on the payroll at Convair and earning $125 monthly. Enrolled women beyond Convair's maximum age of 35 were transferred to North Texas Agricultural College at Arlington (now the University of Texas at Arlington) where they trained for other industries. Many women bound for Convair studied to become inspectors responsible for checking and signing off production work, a highly sought position that required a high school education and mechanical ability. In November 1942 twelve women completed the first inspector class and began earning $216 monthly, a middle-class wage, eight going to work at Convair and four at Globe Aircraft. All the effort paid off; by 1945 women made up 36 percent of Convair's total workforce.[6]

The great experiment created by necessity contributed significantly to the war effort while tearing down many gender-based stereotypes. Touring Convair in 1942, Lt. General Henry H. Arnold admitted women had proven they could do almost any job in production and that their success had written a new chapter in aircraft manufacturing. Vice President H. O. West of Boeing Aircraft confessed to some initial misgivings over whether or not women would take work and safety regulations seriously but changed his mind after they became half the Seattle plant's workforce. By December 1942, just one year after Pearl Harbor, 4.5 million women worked in war production and their number was predicted to rise to 6 million by the end of 1943. That success was repeated in the general workforce. By Labor Day 1943, 16 million, or 30 percent of the nation's 54.3 million total workforce, were women. Fort Worth mirrored those statistics in October 1943 with 30,000 women workers on the job—almost 30 percent of the city's 102,000 workforce.[7]

The war not only provided jobs to women in general but also opened opportunities for older women, a barrier seldom crossed before the war. In 1943 James Ellis, local director of the WMC, applauded Fort Worth companies for hiring older workers and urged others to follow their example. In November 1943 the Fort Worth Police complied, at least partially, by inviting women as old as 39 to apply for ten positions as unarmed women traffic officers, a first for the department. The new traffic officers began training November 22 at the Fort Worth Library after being welcomed by Chief Curry, who told them three-fourths of police work was traffic related.[8]

The great increase in women employed outside the home carried positive and negative consequences. Working broadened life for many women, exposing them to new challenges and experiences, but it also forced many to leave their children unattended at home or with strangers. The Unites States Children's Bureau called the absence of working mothers the greatest challenge facing children in the war. The issue was particularly difficult in the 1940s when birth control was not widely available, making family planning difficult. Some limited advances offering hope for the future were in development stages. Birth control clinics experienced exponential growth in the previous decade, spreading from just 15 cities nationwide in 1930 to 400 in 1942. A clinic opened in Fort Worth in 1938, but access was limited to Anglo women (a San Antonio clinic served all races). Still, one clinic could do little, making planned pregnancies difficult at a time when public financial support hardly existed. Many poor mothers were left with no option but to work despite the few resources available for childcare.[9]

Working mothers with family and friends able to care for their children were fortunate, but not all had that option, and many were left no option but to rely on hired childcare, usually outside the home. A few childcare centers existed before the war. The Day Nursery, 308 South Adams Street, had cared for the children of working mothers since 1930, taking in as many as 114 children ranging in age from 6 weeks to 12 years. It was one of a very few, leaving a great demand that so exceeded supply that the federal government stepped in, financing childcare centers through the Office of Civil Defense. In December 1942 day nurseries opened at Katy Lake, Ripley Arnold, Consolidated (Convair), Sycamore Park, Butler Place, Lake Como, and North Side, the latter three reserved for Black children. The centers tried their best and were better than many other options, but the supply of affordable childcare never approached demand, leaving many children unattended or inadequately supervised. The assault on family structure was often cited as a major factor in the concurrent rise of juvenile delinquency.[10]

Some mothers chose not to work, as did some women without children. A 1943 survey by the Office of Civil Defense found that 20 percent of childless women between 20 and 50 years old remained unemployed despite the serious need. The study also revealed that women workers were slightly more likely than men to quit; eight women resigned for every ten hired, compared to seven out of ten men, both seemingly high ratios. The researchers suggested improvements in transportation and increased housing and childcare options would reduce the "quit rate." Lack of childcare was one of several issues that limited the supply of women workers, making it impossible to close the gap between labor demand and supply. In December 1943 the local employment services had 579 jobs requiring no experience open for women, but only 200 women registered.[11]

World War II and World War I both brought large numbers of women into the workforce, but World War II differed in that more women remained employed after the war ended. In March 1951 Fort Worth businesses added 900 workers, 700 of whom were women, increasing the city's total workforce to 154,800 and the number of women workers to 50,200, 32 percent of the total workforce. Many of the 700 women went to work at Convair. In 1945 36 percent of Convair's workforce were women; in May 1951 the percentage had fallen to 15.4 percent (4,600 women employees) a significant number, but below the 32 percent of Fort Worth's total workforce occupied by women. The disparity between Convair's percentage of women employees and the overall percentage for the city's workforce did not necessarily imply Convair had underperformed in hiring women postwar. Rather, the higher percentage for the general workforce was a product of women holding large majorities in a few professions where they traditionally dominated, like teaching and nursing, while women at Convair tended to hold positions previously filled only by men and where they represented smaller percentages. It was true that the battle for employment equality had only begun, that opportunities remained gender-defined and limited by traditional assumptions. An example of traditional values defining new careers can be seen in airlines advertising for stewards as "women's job." An American Airlines advertisement for "stewardesses" asked, "Are You the All-American Type Girl?" To answer yes, applicants had to be single, between 20 and 28 years old, stand five feet two to five feet seven inches tall, and weigh 130 pounds or less. It was not just aviation; many in academia still held limited views regarding women's roles. Dr. V. H. Green, former president of the British Royal Society of Medicine, stated in a March 1950 article that no genius in history had been a woman, that God or Providence had given women but one creative genius, "to have babies."[12]

Despite obstacles, some remarkable firsts were achieved in the 1950s, although they remained exceptions to the existing norms rather than redefinitions. In 1953 Mrs. Joe (Clarice) Spurlock, a teacher and principal, became the first woman to sit on the Fort Worth City Council, and in November 1954 Mrs. Lucy Lee Jenkins, a former machinist and wrestler, became the first woman Tarrant County Deputy Sheriff. Sheriff Harlon Wright praised her appointment, saying women provided access to areas restricted to men but still limited Deputy Jenkins to serving papers and acting as a court bailiff. An amendment to the Texas Constitution allowing women to serve as jurors was part of a package presented to voters in April 1951, but the outlook was not bright for passage; Texans had rejected a similar amendment in 1949. In 1951 the amendment passed, becoming effective November 19, 1951. The 100 person Tarrant County jury pool called that month included two women, albeit by mistake, not as a result of the amendment (too soon after the change to be implemented). One, Don Moorman, made the roll because administrators assumed Don was a man, but no such confusion explained the second woman called, Miriam Cassell. Two months later the first two women intentionally called for jury service, Mrs. Simon W. Freese and Mrs. Grace Padgett, joined ten men in Criminal District Court No. 2 as part of the grand jury. Women still had far to go to escape the double standard and achieve equal justice under the law. An egregious example occurred In November 1951 when F. B. Parker, a 36-year-old man, 3018 North Hampton, received only a five-year sentence for raping his 18-year-old sister, the leniency explained by the victim's admission that she had had had sex with five or six men.[13]

Women with unwanted pregnancies found themselves in an untenable societal and legal position that often resulted in serious injuries and/or prosecution. Kathryn A. Stagg, a 25-year-old airline steward based in Dallas, died March 29, 1952, at a Fort Worth hospital after a botched abortion performed for $350 by James H. McClurkin, a local pharmacist. On a Wednesday Ms. Stagg rode a bus to Fort Worth to meet McClurkin, who took her to a tourist court where he performed the abortion. On Friday she seemed well enough that McClurkin took her to his home, 1100 Locust Street, to finish recuperating, but the next day he rushed her to a hospital after finding her unconscious. Ms. Stagg died from gangrene infection related to the botched abortion. Her body went home to Pompton Plains, New Jersey, for burial. McClurkin stood trial for murder, but the jury deadlocked eight to four for conviction, resulting in a mistrial. In December 1953 a 22-year-old woman paid Arnold Logan, a chiropractor, $100 for an abortion performed at his office, 1111 East Belknap Street, then returned to her rented room to recuperate. Her landlady, alarmed at her condition, phoned for a doctor, who sent her to a hospital. Police took a statement at the hospital, then arrested Logan, who was released on $2,500 bond. In 1954 a 40-year-old north side woman, the wife of an ex–Fort Worth police officer, was arrested along with another woman after trying and failing twice to perform an abortion on a 16-year-old waitress. After the second attempt, the girl went to the City-County Hospital where her baby was born only to die within two hours. Not all abortions involved young, single women. In 1958 relatives demanded an autopsy for Mrs. Ruby Ruth Wilbanks, a 35-year-old mother of two whose death had been ruled as natural causes. The examination determined Mrs. Wilbanks died from a botched abortion, throwing suspicion on her husband, who denied even knowing his wife was pregnant. Investigators determined that Mr. Wilbanks had lied, that he and Mrs. Ruth Lee Tumlinson, 50 years old, had performed the abortion using an unknown instrument. Both were charged with murder. Even pregnant married women endured some degree of ostracizing. In 1947 Law Sone, president of Texas Wesleyan College, asked Mrs. Alma Coats, the wife of an Air Force sergeant, to leave the school because of her pregnancy, stating it was an issue of propriety for the many "unmarried girls" on campus.

Mrs. Coats planned to continue her studies at a college in Brownwood, Texas, that accepted her and her condition.[14]

Despite all the mayhem, no discussions developed about providing women with a legal, safe alternative to backroom abortions. Even the national director of Planned Parenthood, William Vogt, could not or would not suggest legalization as an option. In a January 1953 speech at St. Andrews Episcopal Church, Director Vogt avoided sensitive issues like the risks associated with illegal abortions, choosing instead to advocate for cheaper and easier access to birth control. His argument focused not on confronting the human cost wrought by illegal operations but on using birth control to control population growth that he believed overburdened resources and forced lower living standards.[15]

Women attempted to make some important advances in politics and business, but not all were successful. A city charter amendment election in December 1946 was noteworthy for the fifty-seven women who served as poll judges (seventy poll judges total). The press noted that the position placed women in some traditionally all-male enclaves like fire halls. In July 1948 the National Federation of Business and Professional Women's Club meeting in Fort Worth to mark the centennial of the Seneca Falls Convention, the first women's rights convention in the United States, adopted a six-point program calling for equal pay for women. In the 1949 city council election, Mrs. Edahazell Smith ran for Place 6, the first woman to do so in the memory of city hall staff. Mrs. Smith did not win.[16]

A few women received a degree of notoriety, but often for less than praiseworthy endeavors. One couple employed gender bias as a publicity stunt to create press for the husband's 1944 campaign for the Twelfth Congressional District. In July 1944 O. A. Cole sued to enjoin Mrs. Glory (also listed as Clory) Fincher Cole, his wife, from opposing him in the election, arguing that her candidacy constituted a violation of her marriage vow to obey. Mrs. Cole, the owner and manager of Southern Business College, countered that she was not required to relinquish political rights as a consequence of marriage. The matter went to the Sixty-Seventh District Court, where Judge Morris responded reasonably, dismissing the suit for lack of merit, telling Mr. Cole, "You come in here as if this woman was a pawn or chattel." The matter, already farcical, turned ridiculous after the Gas Ration Board ruled both campaigns were publicity stunts and denied their requests for increased gasoline rations. Mr. Cole responded by parading through downtown in a car pulled by mules while Mrs. Cole filed for removal of her disabilities of marriage, the divorce hearing set for July 31, 1944. In any case, Mr. Cole lost badly, coming in fifth with 344 votes in a race Fritz Lanham won with 10,361 votes. No votes were recorded for Mrs. Cole.[17]

Postwar, most women making the news tended to be involved in social and cultural endeavors. In 1946 two local women who had been music students and performers in New York City, Mrs. F. L. Synder and Mrs. Betty B. Spain, along with Mrs. Jeanne Axtell, founded the Fort Worth Opera, the only civic opera company in the Southwest. The three convinced 200 sponsors to donate $50 each to fund the first season at Will Rogers Auditorium. The productions were praised by the *New York Times* as the envy of "more metropolitan centers." In 1947 Mrs. Louis Bonneli organized ninety local war brides into the Overseas Wives Club of Fort Worth. The group, chaired by Mrs. Bonneli, met at the YWCA. Many existing women's clubs resumed full operations after curtailing activities during the war. In 1948 the Women's Club Garden Department held a centennial celebration of the first 100 years of Fort Worth's growth and development. The keynote speaker, Mrs. J. W. Poindexter, discussed interviews with long-time women residents involved in the development of schools and other local institutions. The list included Mrs. C. E. Mitchell, born in Blue Mound (a town north of Fort Worth) before the "fort" was established; Mrs. Medora P. Turner; Mrs. John F. Swayne, an early leader in the women's movement; Mrs. Belle M. Burchill, the first woman postmaster (appointed by President Garfield); Mrs. James H. Polk; Mrs. Ida Van Zandt Jarvis; and Mrs. J. B. Young.[18]

Ruth Googins Roosevelt once again made national news, this time for divorcing Elliot, the president's son. By 1944 their marriage had soured to the extent that Ruth hired Fort Worth attorney Robert Hanger to file for divorce on June 24. The decision to split was mutual, coming after Elliot told Ruth he no longer had feelings for her and after both had others in waiting. Elliot, on duty in the European theater, signed a waiver of appearance granting

Ruth custody of their three children and deeding his claim on the Benbrook ranch to them. Neither grieved for long. Elliot married Faye Emerson, an actress, that November, but Ruth was quicker, marrying Lieutenant Harry T. Eidson just three months after she filed for divorce. Ruth and Lieutenant Eidson met in the summer of 1942 in Colorado Springs, Colorado, becoming romantically involved soon thereafter. Ironically, Eidson had served as Elliot's pilot in North Africa.[19]

Chapter 6

The War Winds Down

In January 1945, as World War II entered its last phases, Fort Worth citizens carried on as normally as possible. On New Year's Day TCU, with a record of 7–2–1, lost to Oklahoma A&M in the Cotton Bowl and the *Star Telegram* featured a column by Damon Runyon and comics with the latest adventures of *Terry and the Pirates*, *Little Orphan Annie*, and *Blondie*. Still, the trappings of everyday life could not hide the war's traumas, especially for the families of 548,381 Texans serving in the military at the end of 1944, the sixth highest total of all states, the same rank Texas held in population. Fierce battles raged as Allied forces advanced across a wide European front and retook most of the Pacific, inching closer to Japan. Victories came frequently, but so did grim reminders of their cost in human lives. On January 6, 1945, two Fort Worth men were confirmed killed in action and a third was reported missing. On April 10, 1945, the *Fort Worth Press* printed a map with stars indicating the homes of Fort Worth residents killed in the war, part of 556 fatalities from Tarrant County, and the *Star Telegram* ran the names of Tarrant County war dead on July 7, 1946. Many other returning soldiers and sailors dealt with serious wounds, some requiring extended time and treatment to heal and others that never healed.

Demand for home nursing care so exceeded supply that the Tarrant County Red Cross expanded training classes. Americans left at home continued sacrificing for the war effort, stretching resources through conservation, recycling, and sometimes just doing without. Fort Worthians gathered clothing for Europe's war-torn countries and saved 250,000 pounds of animal fat to supplement military and civilian supplies. Even tin cans went into the war effort. In 1945 Elton Hyder, local chair of the tin can drive, voiced optimism that Fort Worth would again exceed its quota. War funding, always a critical need, continued with a Seventh War Loan Drive in 1945.[1]

Rationing and price controls, a big part of life on the home front, began to subside as the war wound down, although many lingered into the immediate postwar and beyond. Scarcity of common items such as paper bags and clothes hangers developed soon after Pearl Harbor, followed by shortages in automobile tires and gasoline, critical commodities that were rationed beginning in 1942. Even rationing was not enough to ensure adequate inventories of some items. In January 1945 insufficient production forced cancelation of shoe ration stamps until the summer, and officials warned smokers that cigarette shortages were expected to last two more years. The situation for automobile tires was particularly bleak. In 1945 the Fort Worth Office of Price Administration (OPA) estimated the forty-nine-county region of North Texas would receive only 27,012 tires for its 254,120 registered automobiles, about 1 tire for every 10.7 cars, and only 4,603 tires for 35,355 trucks, about 1 for every 8 trucks. The outlook was so poor that no tires were allocated for A Class ration card holders and B and C Card holders received considerably fewer than in 1944. Even those estimates proved optimistic; in March the OPA cut the April quota for passenger car tires another 37 percent, dropping the allowance to 16,299. The good news was that the national gasoline allotment increased 132,000 barrels, rising to 1,276,000 barrels daily. The bad news was that estimates projected it would take at least a year after fighting ended for industries to convert from war production and into consumer goods like refrigerators, irons, and radios.[2]

Retailers generally opposed all price controls but especially fought those imposed by state mandates. Leonard's, the largest Fort Worth retailer, criticized the Texas Fair Trade Act, which empowered manufacturers to set maximum prices, arguing the bill forced retailers to raise many prices. Shops also had issues with federal edicts, which they saw as too pervasive and rigid, pointing to OPA regulations requiring agency approval for a one-cent increase in the cost of a loaf of bread to twelve cents. Many people upset with controls and rationing turned to evasion. Car dealers got around maximum pricing guidelines by requiring buyers to furnish a trade-in vehicle, allowing creative accounting to obscure the actual selling price, at least until the local OPA ordered dealers to display cash prices. The agency also cracked down on car repair overcharges, setting billable hours for fifty-four common repairs. Petty violations were widespread and usually dealt with by small fines. In March 1945 the local OPA fined seven restaurants, three grocers, and one liquor store for minor violations. One fined business, a restaurant at the Lake Worth Casino, had charged fifteen cents for coffee supposed to sell for a nickel and up-priced alcoholic drinks to thirty-two cents. A more serious case involving overcharges netted a $500 fine for Back Us Laundry. OPA executive level employees proved just as culpable as the general public; in March 1945 OPA District Director of Rationing J. Warner Zimmer and two staffers were suspended pending an investigation into an alleged fraudulent automobile transaction.[3]

Meat-packing, a major Fort Worth industry, struggled with wartime rationing and price controls that lingered for months after the war ended. The OPA used a two-prong approach, relying on rationing to preserve and fairly distribute commodities and price controls to combat price gouging, both carrying deleterious effects. In 1943 authorized meat prices were so low that ranchers held cattle off the market and packinghouses stored frozen carcasses, drying up supply and creating serious shortages. Cattlemen warned that without upward price adjustments, they would withhold 15.4 million surplus cattle, leaving consumers to search for beef that did not exist. The looming threat was so serious that in November 1943 the War Food Administration suspended price ceilings for cattle on the hoof, sparking a banner year in 1944 for ranchers and the Fort Worth Stockyards. The stockyards received the most cattle (1,029,333) since 1925, the most calves (480,061) since 1937, the most hogs (1,091,824), sheep, and lambs in its history, and the most horses and mules (28,756) since 1939. Prices also rose precipitously, raising concern that the lid had come off too far, that consumers would refuse to pay higher costs and leave packinghouses holding unsalable product. In January 1945 the OPA reinstated ceiling prices of \$17.25 to \$18.60 per hundredweight for cattle on the hoof, then dropped prices another \$0.50 on July 2. The president of Safeway Stores blamed the OPA for severe shortages that caused New York City butcher shops, besieged by long customer queues, to set a \$10 per customer maximum purchase limit.[4]

A black market in beef soon developed. In March 1945 Frank Taylor, chief OPA enforcement attorney in Dallas, reported under-the-counter sales in Fort Worth and Dallas had distributed 10 million pounds of meat. W. L. Pier, vice president of United Stockyards Corporation and general manager of the Fort Worth Stockyards, claimed that Fort Worth's black market, one of the nation's largest, had taken over the supply, leaving packinghouses bereft while unscrupulous operators paid above the maximum allowable prices. Pier reported that in one day's trading legitimate dealers bought only 592 cattle and local butchers another 847 while black marketeers took 4,136. A. A. Lund, general manager of Armour in Fort Worth, challenged the OPA to find cattle at the ceiling, saying his buyers were only able to buy 203 of 8,750 cattle traded in one week, the rest taken by buyers paying over set market prices.[5]

Although rationing continued on many commodities, consumers began to see some relief as early as 1944 when war production slowed, freeing workers and resources for civilian production. That year Senator Harry Truman of Missouri, chairman of the Committee on War Programs, urged companies to accelerate the shift to civilian production to absorb defense workers let go when \$8 billion in war contracts were canceled. Bomber production remained high as late as May 1944 when 8,902 four-engine heavy aircraft rolled off assembly lines, but by the end of 1944 even aircraft production had slackened. The B-24 Liberator program ended in June 1944, but Fort Worth's Convair facility survived quite well, winning a contract in May 1945 for a Navy version of the bomber and tooling up for the next generation bomber, the B-32. Military supplies so overwhelmed demand that in 1944 the Army and the Navy began auctioning 10,000 trucks and 4,600 motorcycles deemed surplus, as well as 1,000 small airplanes no longer needed for flight instructor training. The surpluses brought some relief to a market stressed by reduced civilian production of trucks and motorcycles and a complete ban on general aviation aircraft.[6]

The local WMC prematurely announced an end to worker shortages but quickly reversed its declaration. In 1944 workers flooded the local USES, many thrown out of work by production curtailments and cancelations. On February 2, 1945, the WMC reported heavy worker inflow had raised supply to meet demand, allowing employment priorities for nonessential business to remain unchanged. The rosy labor assessment was flawed. The majority of the workers flooding the USES in 1944, 58 percent, were draft-age men between 18 and 38 changing jobs before new regulations became effective requiring draft-age men to receive Selective Service Board approval before leaving a job under threat of reclassification to 1-A draft status, a major penalty. The regulations grew out of a study that found war production lost three days of work each time a worker switched jobs. At the start of 1945 the national WMC added a national midnight curfew for places of entertainment and/or alcohol consumption to conserve fuel, electricity, transportation resources, and labor (presumably by reducing hangovers). Local commissions were given authority to penalize violators by withholding or reducing their allotted electrical power, rationed food, and workers. In March the local WMC office synchronized with the national order, ordering cafés to close at midnight, excluding those catering to defense workers. All signs indicated that the local labor situation remained strained, even to the point of threatening to reclassify Fort Worth as a Group One Labor Shortage Area that would have banned further defense contracts, canceled some existing contracts, and placed industries on a mandatory forty-eight-hour work week. Many feared the final catalyst leading to that declaration would come with the expiration on March 31, 1945, of extended furloughs for draftees and servicemen working at local industries.[7] By May three local plants reported severe staff shortages that threatened production schedules. On May 14, 1945, the USES announced enhanced enforcement of a nationwide "work or else" program that assigned idle men to jobs. Police Chief T. G. Curry cooperated, beginning a "work or jail" program to force an estimated 2,000 slackers to work.[8]

Aircraft production may have slowed, releasing some workers, but defense production still hummed along as a major force driving the economy. Convair and other aircraft manufacturers were a big part of that economy, but other industries were also important. Fort Worth was the largest artillery rounds supplier west of the Mississippi River, and demand for ordnance actually increased after D-Day as the allied assault into the German homeland ran into hardened defenses requiring twenty to thirty times as much artillery firepower to breach. To encourage production, General Dwight D. Eisenhower sent twenty-seven artillerymen to munitions plants across the country, including a representative to Texas Steel, supplier of 5 million large rounds since the start of the war. Encouragement could help, but the real problem hindering production remained insufficient labor. James Ellis, local director of the WMC, estimated local industries needed 6,000 additional workers to meet expanding production demands, an impossible requirement given the exhaustion of the labor pool. Ellis suggested that greater utilization of women workers could add 3,500 to the workforce, still leaving a deficit of 2,500 with no known available resources. The only option Ellis offered was to cut employment allowances for nonessential jobs another 10 to 20 percent (the board set the ceiling or maximum number of workers allocated for nonessential jobs). The Fort Worth Chamber of Commerce called for in-migration of new workers, although they did not indicate from where that movement might originate.[9]

The city of Fort Worth, beset with labor and housing problems, was still able to accomplish some long overdue projects. In February 1945, while the war still raged, the city council accepted bids for construction of additional counter space at Meacham Airport, a joint project with Braniff Airways and American Airlines, the two airlines paying half the estimated $4,000 cost. That summer American Airlines began flights from Fort Worth to London, $315 one-way. Fort Worth government also addressed lingering issues of pay and retirement, areas in which the city lagged behind some state mandates. In January 1945 the Tarrant County district attorney chided Fort Worth for paying entering firefighters and police officers only $145 monthly, below the state mandated minimum $150. In February the council announced a revised retirement scheme, an issue that had been on and off the table for twelve years. The plan, adopted that autumn in one of the city's most progressive budgets, granted employees twelve days of sick leave and established an actuary pension plan with a maximum monthly benefit of $100 for employees retiring at 60 years of age with twenty-five years of service or at 65 with at least fifteen years. Pensions were funded by both the city and employees contributing 4 percent of salaries. On January 1, 1947, twenty-two of sixty-five eligible employees opted for retirement. The budget also granted a $10 raise for all employees earning less than $235 monthly, a condition that excluded only fifty-two staff.[10]

The city seemed to have a tendency to evade state regulations. During the 1945 city council election, a nonincumbent candidate charged that the city's tax rate of $1.56 per $100 valuation was deceptive because the rate excluded charges for garbage, water, and sewer services that pushed the tax rate over state limits. Citizens, seemingly unconcerned about the charges, returned all nine incumbents to office. The new council named Roscoe Carnrike mayor.[11]

Preparations for the coming peace began while the war still raged. The OPA implemented a national program granting veterans preferential treatment for civil service jobs and higher rationed food allocations for new businesses (no new, nondefense manufacturing or processing plants had been approved since March l, 1942). The Fort Worth mayor proposed improvements to the already overburdened water and sewage system to accommodate the population surge expected when discharged soldiers returned home. Many locals looked to the experience of Abilene, Texas, a city of 27,000 about 150 miles west of Fort Worth. Abilene had boomed with the 1940 construction of Camp Barkley, an Army training base for up to 50,000 soldiers. The huge human influx spilled over into the city, taking up all available habitations and sending rents soaring. When the base began downsizing after 1943, declining to only 4,000 personnel, the real estate market reversed direction, evidenced by for-rent signs appearing in yards and falling rents. The downturn benefited many residents who had scraped by in substandard housing, but it also cratered the local economy. Abilene attacked the problem by converting their one plentiful resource, abandoned military facilities, into private commercial and manufacturing properties, a process that took time but that offered some hope.[12]

Germany's surrender in May 1945 occasioned a restrained celebration, perhaps a reflection that the battle with Japan remained unfinished and of the high costs already paid and yet to be paid. Churches held special services and many shops closed, leaving downtown deserted, but schools remained open and most workers stayed on the job, opting to continue producing to speed the final victory. The end of the European war brought especially good news to one prominent Fort Worth family. Amon Carter Jr., son of the *Star Telegram* publisher, was reported missing February 13, 1943, while serving in the Army in North Africa. In May 1945 Carter was released from a German prisoner of war camp and reunited with his father and family. Germany's surrender changed the nature of defense production. The War Department immediately canceled contracts for 17,000 planes, including the B-24 and B-32 built in Fort Worth, in favor of longer-range transports and bombers like the B-29 needed in the Pacific theater. Gasoline rationing also eased as allotments increased from four to six gallons weekly for A Card–holders, and the mileage allowance for B Cards climbed from 475 to 650 before ending altogether in August. Some food items like poultry, eggs, sugar, and beef remained rationed and in short supply, forcing a few local restaurants to close one week a month. Things were worse in Amarillo, where some cafés closed temporarily, awaiting increased supplies.[13]

Japan's surrender brought sudden and massive cutbacks in defense production. Within days the Army and Navy canceled $4 billion in contracts, releasing over a million workers immediately and creating 6.2 million unemployed by December 1945. The WMC urged displaced workers to remain calm, that the rapid and dramatic rise in the unemployed would end as industries transitioned to civilian production. The Committee for Economic Development was less sanguine, predicting a slight overall decrease in national employment. Advances in retail sales and bank clearings supported the more optimistic view. National retail sales rose 18 percent in June 1946 over the same period in 1945, and Fort Worth bank clearings increased dramatically in 1945, rising almost 11 percent to $815.5 million, up $80 million from $735.3 million in 1944. Fort Worth did better than most cities, experiencing a short readjustment period before recovering to have 103,222 in the workforce at the end of 1945, 36 percent higher than in 1940.[14]

Housing conditions reached their lowest point in the early postwar period as returning veterans overwhelmed an already overstretched market. In February 1945 the Fort Worth Chamber of Commerce termed the local housing situation extreme, a problem shared by many communities; in December 1945 Chicago converted 250 streetcars into living quarters. That same year an average of 4.5 persons occupied each housing unit in Fort Worth, up substantially from 3.48 persons in 1940. There was literally no place to turn given an overall vacancy rate of a mere .5 percent. In 1945 Director R. L. Hunter of the chamber's housing committee reported 9,700 persons—30 percent the families of military men—lived in substandard housing in Fort Worth. Hunter estimated Fort Worth would need 13,000 additional housing units to meet its postwar needs, an impossible figure for the short-term. In the interim, on January 3, 1945, he petitioned the National Housing Agency for 2,000 temporary dwellings to supplement 250 house trailers and hutments requested earlier. The request lingered for a month without action, prompting the local War Production Board (WPB) to recommend building 300 houses solely for defense workers, selling one-third and renting the rest.[15]

The long-term solution lay in revitalizing civilian construction that had virtually disappeared. Construction's low ebb came in 1943, when Fort Worth building permits sank to the lowest level since 1934, during the depths of the Depression. The few permits issued in 1943 were small jobs involving remodels or additions rather than new construction; the largest project was a $50,000 expansion of Hobbs Manufacturing. Building increased slightly in 1944 to $3,335,090, then more than doubled to $8,353,776 in 1945, the most since 1942 and an impressive total given that 1942 benefited from defense plant construction that stimulated commercial building. In contrast, 1945 construction was driven by 1,495 new homes built at a total cost of $4,178,345 (the average was $2,790), accounting for more than half of all building. Industry insiders held optimistic outlooks for 1946 but warned looming material shortages could curtail construction.[16]

Chapter 7

The Postwar and Fort Worth

Fort Worth entered 1946 still struggling with critical housing shortages created by an influx of workers and the aftereffects of the wartime ban on residential construction. The Fort Worth Chamber of Commerce's Housing Committee warned that insufficient housing threatened Fort Worth's economic future. The local economy also reeled for a time under the loss of 17,000 jobs from massive defense cutbacks but recovered quite well thanks to renewed defense appropriations stimulated by the Cold War and a revitalized civilian market. The expansion of the 87th Air Corp and the 17th Bomb Wing added 10,000 base personnel at Fort Worth Airfield, renamed Carswell Air Force Base in February 1948 in honor of Major Horace S. Carswell, an Army pilot from Fort Worth who received the Medal of Honor for sacrificing himself to save others in the crash of a B-24. The added active-duty personnel and returning veterans gave Fort Worth a large military population. Many veterans took advantage of educational benefits granted under the GI Bill, overwhelming local schools. In November 1945 some 290 ex-servicemen, most taking accounting classes, enrolled in TCU, swelling enrollment to 2,200, a new record that was certain to be broken in the spring semester thanks to 700 new applications already received. The rush to campus was part of a national phenomenon in which 600,000 to 700,000 ex-GIs attended college in 1947, part of 7.8 million who would take advantage of the GI Bill's educational benefits. The new students aggravated the existing housing crisis. A November 1945 study found 1,700 veterans without proper housing in Fort Worth, forcing many to move in with families who were already underhoused and overcrowded. Others, without available family or other options, fared worse. One recently returned soldier found his wife and two children crammed into two unfurnished rooms without a kitchen.[1]

The city and the federal government through the Federal Public Housing Agency (FPHA) tried to offer relief. During the war the FPHA built Liberator Village, a $3.5 million complex of 1,500 apartments south of White Settlement Road at Cherry Lane and Clifford Street, to house Convair and Carswell workers. The first of four phases, fifteen barracks converted into apartments for 1,200 Convair workers, opened in 1942. Eventually, the Village's 1,500 apartments provided homes for 6,000 residents who paid $25 monthly for a one bedroom and $30 for a two bedroom. The FPHA hired three Tarrant County Sheriff's deputies, each earning $200 monthly, to patrol the complex. In the 1950s as the housing supply began to catch up to demand, occupancy rates began to fall and restrictions were lifted, opening the Village to all renters. In 1953 the city of White Settlement took over and began razing 1,000 frame apartments but refurbished 500 of the nicer tile units. By 1959 occupancy had fallen to the point that only 181 of 487 units were occupied, despite low $36 monthly rents for standard apartments and four-bedroom units going for $54. Eventually the few remaining apartments were demolished, leaving only one building standing.[2]

The FPHA established preferential guidelines that required vacancies be held fifteen days for veterans only before opening them to others. The regulation pretty much closed the early postwar housing market to nonveterans, sparking a local protest on November 29, 1946, with hundreds demanding Congress appropriate $150 million for housing relief. Congress actually had budgeted $190 million in January 1946 for emergency housing relief, much of the appropriations set aside for college students. When issues delayed implementation, the Fort Worth City Council sought 1,000 temporary dwellings from the federal government, placing the first 300 received on thirty acres adjacent to Trinity Park, part of a sixty-five-acre lot west of University Drive off Crestline

Road the city purchased from the Van Zandt estate. Veterans were given first refusal for the temporary units equipped with gas ranges, an "ice box," space heaters, a water heater, and window shades. The process went rather quickly; 250 lucky people began moving into the "homettes" in early 1946 even as another 270 units were on the way from Amarillo.[3]

Critics blamed price controls, another legacy of the war, for much of the housing shortage, although many others supported controls as necessary to prevent price gouging. Construction of new homes received a boost on October 15, 1945, when Fort Worth removed an $8,000 ceiling on new home construction, but critics still blamed remaining price controls on rents and construction materials for slowing building. Construction material manufacturers agreed, citing price controls as responsible for critical supply shortages that hampered home construction. Many landlords fought back by holding properties off the market in anticipation that rent controls would be removed. All the negative issues further reduced available dwellings, adding to the number of homeless and underhomed families. The OPA ordered a review of 6,000 local residential rental units that had gone on the market after rents had been frozen on March 1, 1942, to determine if landlords had withheld properties.[4]

The debate over price controls continued with reasonable arguments on both sides. The Fort Worth Chamber of Commerce argued price restrictions aggravated the housing crisis by making new home construction unprofitable. On February 19, 1946, the National Association of Manufacturers ran a full-page appeal in the *Star Telegram* claiming the end of price controls would unleash production, end shortages, and allow prices to fall, although they conceded the process would take time. Supporters who credited controls for counteracting inflationary pressures warned that prices would soar if pent-up demand set prices in a market of scarcity. Many area bankers agreed, predicting inflation could reach 12 to 15 percent in 1946, with 25 percent possible in 1947. They also joined builders in concerns that rising material costs would slow construction and derail the transition to civilian production. Material cost inflation was critical in the city of Fort Worth's decision to postpone all but the most essential parts of a recently approved bond package after initial bids came in 50 percent above estimates.[5]

It took a few more months for price controls to end and even longer for supporters to accept that they were gone for good. In April 1945 Congress restricted OPA operations in preparation for the agency's official expiration on July 1, 1946. On July 2 a group of Riverside landlords sent a funeral wreath to the local OPA director in mock sympathy at the agency's death. The flowers were premature; 150 employees were still at work prosecuting earlier violations. Others, far from celebrating the agency's demise, urged restraint to rein in the inflation they were sure was coming. The Fort Worth Apartment House and Property Owners Association called on landlords to follow the example of car dealers and grocers and voluntarily delay and mitigate price increases. Mayor Carnrike proposed a Fair Rent Committee to referee rent disputes, although the board had no legal authority. Those and other efforts at voluntary restraints were doomed to failure as rents and beef prices rose significantly even as supplies increased. After only a week President Harry Truman resurrected the OPA, but under new, more flexible regulations, allowing 3 to 12 percent increases on a variety of commodities from bicycles to mattresses to toasters.[6]

The newer, kinder OPA rolled back some food prices, creating resentment, evasion, and another round of severe meat shortages. In response the OPA ordered a return to price levels effective June 30, 1946, the day before cancelation, aggravating shortages and reinvigorating the black market. The severe negative reactions brought a quick 15 percent price increase, which helped, but some local restaurants, still struggling to find beef, began substituting fish, increasing sales at the Fort Worth fish market by 30 percent. Supply problems worsened as ranchers once again refused to sell for the ceiling price, ushering in another meat famine. The Fort Worth Stockyards admitted a vibrant black market remained a major market force, calling its existence a "known fact" and the only way to explain how cattle on the hoof regularly sold for $4 above the set maximum per hundredweight. In October 1946 the OPA granted a 30 percent price hike, but it was too little, too late. On October 14, 1946, the OPA canceled all meat price controls, setting off a supply deluge that swamped the Fort Worth Stockyards. In one twenty-four-hour period, 1,616 cattle trucks with 16,759 animals worth $1 million arrived, over twice the $400,000 daily average. The surge continued for days, bringing 43,224 animals to the Fort Worth market in just seventy-two hours as prices rose quickly, hitting $28.75 per hundredweight.[7]

Cattle trucks and trailers queuing outside Stockyards loading docks, July 8, 1946. Courtesy *Fort Worth Star Telegram* Collection, Special Collections, University of Texas at Arlington Libraries.

The removal of beef ceilings seemed to unlock the floodgates of OPA opposition and federal controls in general. By the final week of October 1946, only three percent of foods items (sugar, syrup, and rice) retained price ceilings, and 10 million workers were exempted from salary limits, signaling the approaching end of the OPA and the War Stabilization Board. On November 4, 1946, all 1,642 OPA offices closed, making the United States free of OPA ceilings for the first time since early 1942. On December 15, 1946, President Truman abolished remaining restrictions on rents, housing, and a few food items, a date often cited as the end the war for the home front.[8]

Housing remained an especially poignant problem for returning veterans for several more years. A 1946 Census Bureau study reported that 90 percent of the 18,000 veterans (2,000 were Black) in Fort Worth had an average weekly income of $52, sufficient to afford the $57 monthly mortgage on a $5,800 five-room house. The problem was not demand, but supply. The same study found that many veterans able and willing to buy homes were underhoused; one-third of white married veterans lived with either family or friends or were stuck in rented rooms, trailers, or tourist camps, while another one-sixth occupied homes needing major repair and lacking running water and/or private flush toilets and baths.[9]

Fort Worth's housing shortage began to improve after reaching a low point in January 1946 when 3,000 veterans were without adequate housing. That January the city issued $1,970,305 in building permits, followed by $3,512,765 in March, an all-time high and the fourth highest in the state after Houston ($15,268,250), Dallas ($5,690,224), and San Antonio ($4,413,030). Texas's residential construction boom was part of an ambitious national program President Truman announced in February 1946 to build 2.7 million homes in two years. The program accelerated construction by substantially raising salaries, attracting more workers, and concentrating construction resources while also expanding mortgage insurance coverage that stabilized costs, making home ownership more affordable.[10] From that point building reached incredible new heights, more than doubling Fort Worth's annual building permits from $8,446,000 in 1945 to $22,966,000 in 1946. In 1946 Fort Worth built 3,000 new homes at an average cost of $6,500. They were part of a great construction age between 1920 and 1950 in which Fort Worth added 52,433 domiciles (single-family, duplexes, and multifamily). The massive building program was even more remarkable considering very little was built during the Great Depression years of the 1930s, concentrating most construction in the 1920s and the 1940s, excepting the war years. Only 110 domiciles were built in 1934, the fewest of any year, and 7,000, the most (almost 14 percent of the total), were added in 1950. The explosion in postwar home construction was national; the United States built 15 million new homes between 1946 and the mid-1950s, bringing supply even with demand.[11]

The waning of the war also signaled the reappearance of labor turmoil as workers moved to address issues put on hold during the war. In January 1945 the local chamber of commerce boasted that not one hour of production had been lost to strikes or lockouts in 1944, a claim they would not be able to make about 1945. In July 1945, while the Pacific war still raged, 50,000 Americans walked picket lines; in August 80,000 did so, in September the number grew to 205,000, and 1 million Americans were on strike in December 1946. Work stoppages may have been overdue, but they came at a price, helping swell unemployment rolls to 3.5 million, delaying the conversion to civilian production and increasing inflationary pressures, all at a cost to the economy of over $2 billion. Despite the heavy costs, businesses generally eschewed Washington's mediation as unwanted interference in free enterprise, although they were not as averse to appealing to public opinion. In January 1945 General Motors (GM) ran a full-page statement in the *Star Telegram* condemning government intervention in labor relations, and General Electric asked why the company was beset by strikes when it paid wages above the national average. GE ran photographs of half-completed appliances sitting on assembly lines idled by strikes, an obvious appeal to pent-up consumer demand.[12] One of the first local work stoppages in June 1945 was a two-day spontaneous walkout by several hundred workers (reports vary from 200 to 1,000) at the local Armour Plant to protest the suspension of five and termination of two workers, all African-American, on the killing floor for missing work on Emancipation Day, June 19 (Juneteenth). The company eventually conceded, rehiring at least one of the terminated workers and withdrawing the suspensions. More strikes followed over bread-and-butter issues like pay raises. In October 1945 picketers marched outside Convair seeking pay raises but left after the company agreed to negotiate with union representatives. A national Greyhound Bus strike in November idled 100 local workers and stranded 150 passengers in Fort Worth.[13]

The first postwar major labor action began January 16, 1946, when some 2,500 packinghouse workers walked out at Armour as part of a national contract dispute over union demands for a $0.25 hourly pay increase when the company offered only $0.075. Armour's average hourly rate for union workers, $0.87, was inflated by well-paid skilled employees, obscuring that one-third of the workforce earned less than $0.80. After a few weeks, the union returned to work on assurances by the Truman administration that it would work toward a fair settlement. Armour eventually joined two other big four packers in signing off on hourly wages increases ranging from $0.07 to $0.23, with higher adjustments in the South to correct for the region's lower pay scales.[14]

A bitter strike at Convair in 1946 turned violent. An impromptu unauthorized walkout in 1945 had temporarily halted work, but a more serious stoppage that began on February 27, 1946, became a full walkout on March 1 as relations between the union and management degenerated into accusations and threats, then property damage and physical violence. Attitudes began to harden after some strikers placed a red circle cut from packages of Lucky Strike cigarettes on their work badges, making them appear to be foremen supporting the union (supervisors wore red badges). Confrontations escalated quickly from that point. On March 27, 1946, four members of the striking International Association of Machinists (IAM) charged that Convair Chief of Plant Security E. E. Barbe threatened them with a firearm as they walked the picket line. Management countercharged, claiming union men had overturned cars, blocking the plant entrance. Union representatives conceded cars had been overturned but claimed that it was the work of nonunion men and the company protective force scheming to block the plant entrance and blame the union. The main gate became the center of confrontations, often involving vehicles attempting to enter that were stoned and/or had their tires slashed. On April 17 strikers vandalized a delivery truck at the company's main gate, throwing sixty-three 100-pound sacks of plaster into the street.[15]

Things took a turn for the worse the morning of May l, 1946, when a bomb exploded outside 151 Roberts Cutoff Road where the F. W. Barton family lived in a garage apartment and O. A. Chowning and his family lived in the main house—two workers who regularly crossed Convair picket lines. The blast did little damage other than to Barton's car parked in the driveway. An unexploded stick of dynamite was found in the fuel port of Chowning's car, its presence betrayed by a hanging fuse. That same morning another bomb exploded outside 1514 Lincoln Avenue, the home of R. C. Kinzer, the secretary-treasurer of the Federal Independent Texas Union (FITU), a small union opposed to the strike that the IAM considered a company union. On October 18, 1946, the FITU lost a National Labor Relations Board election to replace the IAM as the representative for Convair's 5,500 maintenance and production hourly staff, but won representation for 374 salaried employees.[16]

The situation degenerated to a new low the next day, May 2, 1946, when an explosion at 2:55 a.m. destroyed a utility pole on Grant's Lane, one-quarter

Union members picketing outside Convair after an impromptu walkout, October 3, 1945. Courtesy *Fort Worth Star Telegram* Collection, Special Collections, University of Texas at Arlington Libraries.

of a mile from Convair's main gate. The blast decommissioned nineteen of the plant's twenty-one telephone circuits and convinced the Tarrant County district attorney and the Tarrant County sheriff to call for state assistance, bringing ten state officers who manned prominent positions outside the main gate. The plant itself was inside Fort Worth city limits, but the street outside the main gate where most confrontations occurred was Tarrant County's jurisdiction. The Fort Worth Police got involved to the extent of assigning guards to the homes of two nonunion workers receiving anonymous telephone threats, but it was impossible to guard every home. Several nonunion workers reported four men and a woman came to their homes, threatening and warning them not to work the next day. The evening of May 6 a fourth explosion at 814 Northwest Fourteenth Street, the home of Joe P. Henry, damaged a station wagon known as the "scab wagon" for its use to transport seven nonunion workers (all but one a World War II veteran) to Convair. The national IAM headquarters sent representatives to investigate the violence.[17]

Joe Earl Meadows inspecting bombed 1941 station wagon, May 7, 1946.
Courtesy *Fort Worth Star Telegram* Collection, Special Collections,
University of Texas at Arlington Libraries.

After the bombings local law enforcement, which had been constrained, adopted more of a hardline stance. On May 9, 1946, Fort Worth Police arrested thirty-one IAM picketers, including John F. Foster Jr., the IAM district president, at the Texas and Pacific Railroad yards, Lamar Street and Lancaster Avenue, near downtown and several miles from Convair. The union men were protesting the unloading of machinery meant for the plant and were arrested for trespassing after they refused to leave. In the melee the Fort Worth chief of police scuffled with Foster, the union's district president. The next day the Texas and Pacific Railroad obtained a court injunction banning picketing on its property. Over a year later, in July 1947, A. C. Bjork, general foreman of the Texas and Pacific Railroad shops, found a package outside his front door, 2927 Travis Avenue, containing four dynamite sticks wired together, a cap and, ominously, a partially burned fuse. Mr. Bjork knew of no reason to explain the incident. The Tarrant County sheriff cracked down at the plant, restricting "sideline picketing" to Grant's Lane, the street leading south from the main gate, on the grounds that picketers represented a traffic hazard and violated Texas unlawful assembly laws. The sheriff's new orders limited the main picket line to twenty-five persons, relegating all other supporters to an adjacent union property. In addition, the sheriff threatened to arrest anyone using the union loudspeaker, claiming neighbors had complained about the noise. The next day he made good on that threat, arresting a speaker and cutting the microphone wiring, doing $3,000 in damages, according to union officials. Afterward, the sheriff and union compromised, allowing the use of a smaller, quieter PA system. On May 24, 1946, the eighty-four-day strike ended with both sides accepting the War Stabilization Board recommendation of a $0.15 an hour pay hike that increased the top hourly wage for skilled worker to $1.73, the same increase the company had offered in January 1946 when the union demanded $0.30.[18]

No one was ever convicted for the bombings, but domestic problems brought some interesting allegations to the public light. During an October 1948 divorce hearing, the estranged wife of John F. Foster Jr., president of the IAM Lodge 776 (Fort Worth), alleged her husband kept dynamite at their home during the 1946 Convair strike and told her that the union had dynamited properties of nonstrikers. Foster admitted buying five sticks of dynamite but claimed it was after the strike and was used to remove tree stumps.[19]

On December 17, 1946, Fort Worth flexed its economic and political muscle, embarking on an ambitious annexation program that took in thirty-five acres in Ridglea, an area west of Arlington Heights along Camp Bowie Boulevard, and in Handley, Texas, a town east of downtown along Lancaster Avenue. The new territories increased Fort Worth's geographic area almost 54 percent, to 100 square miles, making it larger than both Dallas, under ninety-five square miles, and Houston, only seventy-four. The addition added $10 million to the property tax rolls and 14,000 residents, requiring the hiring of 46 more police officers, raising the department's authorized strength to 357 and increasing patrol beats from twelve to seventeen. The new patrolmen earned $165 monthly while detectives and sergeants garnered $226. Not all annexations were successful. In April 1948 Fort Worth tried but failed to absorb River Oaks and Keller after plebiscites in both cities rejected annexation. Those minor setbacks were more than offset by the end of the Convair strike and the Ridglea and Handley annexations. The general mood of well-being may have played a role in the 1947 municipal election that returned all nine sitting councilmen, including five who ran unopposed. The council, still elected at large, selected the mayor from their ranks, choosing F. Edgar Deen to replace Roscoe L. Carnrike, who stepped down as mayor but remained as a councilman. Deen was reappointed in 1949 for a second term, although the vote was close, five to four.[20]

One of the first items the new council faced was a motion to assume operational control of the Lake Worth Casino after the existing contractor, George T. Smith, fell $14,000 behind in rents and had difficulty paying $8,610 due from an 8 percent commission on annual revenue over $55,000 (the figures indicated that the casino grossed $162,625 in 1945). Smith fought the motion and somehow came up with $15,690 in back rent, apparently enough to reassure the city of his good faith. It helped that the city wanted to retain overall control but did not relish running the day-to-day operations. To that end they offered Smith $32,000 for his interest in the property and a new, generous contract leasing the casino back to him for an annual rent of $5,200, guaranteed for five years. The sweetheart deal allowed Smith to reopen Lake Worth Casino on September 28, 1947, after five months' closure.[21]

The council considered progressive ideas to solidify the city's financial base. They seriously studied consolidating with Tarrant County to eliminate waste and duplicate costs, but dismissed the proposal, choosing instead to increase property tax valuations from 66 to 75 percent of appraised worth, a stroke of the pen that added $1,176,000 to tax revenue. At the same time, they raised the property tax rate $0.10 cents, to $1.84 per $100 valuation, the two measures funding a $9.6 million budget for the fiscal year beginning October 1, 1947. To cap off a rather busy period, the council named W. O. Jones as city manager at an annual salary of $15,000. Jones had served in an acting capacity for a year after Sam Bothwell, city manager for seven years, resigned.[22]

The new budget granted teachers a pay raise, increasing starting teacher pay from $1,440 to $1,620 and maximum pay for holders of bachelor's degrees from $2,400 to $2,760 and from $2,700 to $3,000 for master's degrees. Even with the raises, Fort Worth teachers remained comparatively

Mayor Roscoe L. Carnrike and City Secretary E. S. Birdsong signing city bonds, January 20, 1947. Courtesy *Fort Worth Star Telegram* Collection, Special Collections, University of Texas at Arlington Libraries.

underpaid in 1948, averaging $2,007 to $3,231 with a bachelor's degree and $2,232 to $3,456 with a master's (some salaries exceeded maximums due to extra duty pay, similar to overtime). In a survey of teacher pay in sixty-one American cities, Fort Worth ranked forty-ninth, the lowest of any Texas city. The problem of low teacher pay was common in most Texas cities; Houston (forty-first) and Dallas (thirty-eighth) also placed in the bottom half, while San Antonio (twenty-ninth) and Amarillo (twenty-eighth) barely edged into the top half. In June 1948 salaries were readjusted to lower the minimums and increase the maximums, setting the range for bachelor degrees at $2,200 to $3,800 and $2,232 to $4,000 for master's degrees. Despite the lingering pay issue, Fort Worth students seemed to do well, generally testing above average, but with some deficiencies. In 1948 Fort Worth fourth graders scored 4.6 overall (4.0 was average) and sixth graders graded 6.5 (6.0 average) despite performing well below grade standard in American history (4.8) and world history (5.0), respectively. Enrollment growth may have affected student performance; administrators in September 1948 reported a 60 percent jump over 1947 in the number of first-grade students, registering 3,756 white and 649 Black students (schools remained segregated).[23]

Care for displaced and abandoned children lay primarily on Tarrant County, with a few private agencies providing some support. In 1946 the Tarrant County Orphan's Home, a three-story building on five acres, averaged housing and feeding seventy-seven children at a daily cost of $1.35 per child, a rate considered so high that serious consideration was given, but rejected, to closing the home and sending the children to Lena Pope Home, which charged considerably less. In September 1948 Tarrant County Probation oversaw 358 children (331 white and 27 Black)—155 housed at Lena Pope Home, 79 at Tarrant County Children's Home, 22 in free foster homes, and 17 in paid fosters, plus another 85 housed by various private agencies.[24]

Fort Worth's general medical care fared better than most large Texas urban areas, at least in terms of bed supply. In 1947 Tarrant County reported 3.7 hospital beds per 1,000 population, significantly below the recommended 4.5 but better than Dallas County's 3.6 (Dallas), Harris County's 3.4 (Houston), and Bexar County's 2.6 (San Antonio). The relatively favorable standing probably was aided by the recent expenditure of $29,210 to convert the second floor of the old City-County Hospital into a polio ward. The study may have fostered complacency. Ethel Ransom Memorial Hospital (for Blacks; ERMH) was the only Fort Worth hospital out of 180 statewide that applied for grants in a $75 million federal hospital construction program.[25]

The Fort Worth council also took important steps to improve the city's aviation infrastructure. By the postwar period, aviation had become an important part of the Fort Worth economy, contributing $10 million in 1947—$4.7 million from private aviation and $5.4 million from commercial airlines that employed 1,350 plus another 451 working at the regional CAA office. In March 1946 the council designated 2,400 acres two miles southeast of the Quartermaster Depot and northwest of Everman for a new $6 million airport that would become Spinks Airport. A more ambitious plan in October 1947 involved converting Midway Airport on Highway 183, twelve miles east of Fort Worth's eastern limits and six miles north of Arlington, into a "super-airport" costing $11.5 million, financed largely by grants from the CAA. The move signaled Fort Worth's decision to go it alone regarding a regional airport after failing for years to reach an agreement with Dallas. The initiative got off to a good start with $340,000 approved by the CAA, conditional on matching funds from the city, to build runways, taxiways, and hangars. A roadblock developed in 1948 when the United States House of Representatives denied federal funding, at least until negotiations restored the original $340,000 and added $800,000 to complete what would become Fort Worth International Airport, later Amon Carter International Airport. Dedication and ground breaking for the administration building was celebrated two years later, July 10, 1950.[26]

In 1947 the Fort Worth Fire Department was deemed critically understaffed, with only 303 firemen, 87 below the 390 mandated by a standard of 1.5 firefighters per 1,000 population. Firefighter salaries were comparable to the police department, ranging from $425 monthly for the chief to $266 for battalion chiefs, $231 for lieutenants, and $210 for firefighters. A Fort Worth firefighter since 1902 and chief since 1945, Claude Ligon, retired January 1, 1948, after forty-six years of service that included fighting the massive 1909 fire that devastated the south side. Chief Ligon blamed the conflagration on two boys taking hot coals from their mother's washpot into a garage. A serious fire in August 1947 that could have been much worse began when someone tossed a cigarette into hay at the Stockyards, inciting a blaze that burned two acres of the sheep pens, killing 2,900 sheep and thirty-five cattle worth $25,000 and destroying $85,000 in property. In 1949 an explosion at the Magnolia Refinery No. 1, 3420 North Sylvania Avenue, killed two workmen and injured nine others.[27]

The city made some major starts at developing an urban environment. In April 1948 work was well under way on the initial phase of what would become the West Freeway, with a completed section running from Summit Avenue to Camp Bowie Boulevard and plans on the books for an extension to Horne Street to open in March 1950. On January 1, 1947, the first twenty-two employees (of sixty-five eligible) retired under the new retirement plan, receiving monthly pensions ranging from $21 to $55 monthly. Pensions payments increased dramatically in September 1948 when an amendment changed the calculation to $3 per month for every year of employment, raising the average monthly benefit for the now forty-three retirees from $21.60 to $50.30, a 132 percent increase.[28]

Severe water supply issues that had plagued Fort Worth's early history were now gone, replaced by quality issues. Cities downstream on the Trinity River had, over the years, frequently complained (sometimes with good reason) that Fort Worth dumped sewage in the river. Those complaints subsided after a new sewage plant was built in 1924, but reappeared in August 1947 when Grand Prairie Mayor G. H. Turner complained to the Texas Health Department that Fort Worth had dumped raw sewage for twenty-five years without being penalized. Turner suggested that when the wind was right, the sewage gas would take the paint off houses. C. Milo Thelin, Fort Worth's director of Public Works, denied a chronic problem but admitted that up to 35 percent of the city's raw sewage had recently been pumped in the river due to a temporary problem that put the sewage plant offline.[29]

In 1947 the United States Corps of Engineers began the $10 million Benbrook Dam on the Clear Fork of the Trinity River. The dam, two miles south of the town of Benbrook where the river crossed Dirks Road, was needed to control the Trinity River and avoid a reoccurrence of the 1922 flood that that killed 13 persons and did $1 million in damages. Unfortunately, the timing was bad. Construction was still underway May 16–17, 1949, when twelve inches of rain fell overnight, causing the worst flooding since 1922, leaving at least 10 people dead and 13,200 homeless and causing an estimated $12 million in property damages. The deluge left most of the city without electricity for several days, and water service was off until May 20. Surprisingly, only five persons were arrested for looting.[30]

Only two months after the flood, Fort Worth held an eight-day centennial celebration of the founding of the fort that became a city. In December 1948 the *Star Telegram* began publishing a series of historical recollections from early settlers such as William "Bud" Browne, who served thirty years as a Fort Worth bartender. Between 1893 and 1910 Browne worked at the Palais Royale Saloon, which regularly kept $25,000 on hand to cash Rock Island Railroad payroll checks. Fiesta-cade, the eight-day official party, began

July 16, 1949, with nightly bands, street dances, and fireworks, culminating with a pageant at Farrington Field presenting twenty skits on the city's history. The *Star Telegram* marked the end of festivities with a 481-page Sunday edition, October 30, 1949, highlighting Fort Worth's history.[31]

In 1942 J. Frank Norris, an infamous local Baptist minister, celebrated thirty-four years as pastor of Fort Worth's First Baptist Church. Norris attained infamy on many fronts, being tried and acquitted of arson and shooting to death a critic while spreading his religious domain from a $2,000 tabernacle at Seventh and Burnet Streets to over $3 million in property holdings that included the Fort Worth church, the Temple Baptist Church in Detroit, Michigan, and Bible Baptist Seminary in Fort Worth with 3,000 students and alumni that included 300 pastors and missionaries. He was a national, even international, celebrity who raised $3.2 million and traveled through most of the United States and many parts of the world, meeting many foreign leaders, including Winston Churchill. In 1944 Norris's son, George Norris, tried to wrest control of First Baptist from his father, threatening to take 500 members and form another church if he were denied. In December 1944 the church board caved under the pressure, demoting J. Frank to associate pastor and naming George first pastor, only to relent the next month and return J. Frank as full and sole pastor, prompting eight high-ranking church officers, including Sunday School Superintendent Jerry Miller, to resign. In November 1948 J. Frank resigned from Temple Baptist Church in Detroit, saying he wanted to concentrate on the First Baptist Church and the Bible Baptist Seminary.[32]

Norris had always associated with right-wing causes, openly consorting with members of the Ku Klux Klan during the Klan's resurgence in the 1920s. Robert Welch, leader of an ultra–right wing political group, named his organization the John Birch Society after a graduate of Norris's seminary who became a missionary in China while also serving as an American intelligence agent during World War II. Birch was killed fighting Chinese Communist forces in 1945. In 1947 Norris attended the Southern Baptist Convention in Atlanta, Georgia (his First Baptist Church was not a member of the convention). At the meeting he attempted to grill Southern Baptist President Reverend Louie D. Newton about his views on Russia but was shouted down by other attendees who knew Norris was trying to publicly accuse Newton of harboring Communist leanings. J. Frank may have been shouted down in Atlanta but in Fort Worth he received official support. Tarrant County Assistant District Attorney W. E. Myres filed a complaint in a Tarrant County court charging that Ralph McGill, antisegregationist editor of the *Atlanta Constitution*, had libeled Norris in an editorial, "One Southerner's Viewpoint," in which he described Norris as a "Ku Klux Klan yelper" and a "loud-mouth shouter" of hate. Myres expressed regret at not having been at the convention so he too could have booed Norris. Sheriff Sully Montgomery forwarded the warrant to the Atlanta sheriff, who probably gave it all the attention it deserved. Leonard's Department Store displayed its support for the embattled preacher in a September 1948 full-page *Star Telegram* spread that congratulated Norris on his fortieth anniversary as pastor of First Baptist Church, calling him a fighter against "atheistic communism."[33]

A well-known local prolabor activist, C. W. Woodman, known as "Fort Worth's grand old man of labor," died at his home at 1600 Fairmount Avenue in October 1948. Woodman, 84 at his death, was a major figure in the Texas labor movement and was the last surviving charter member of the Texas Federation of Labor. He arrived in Fort Worth in 1903, and through the years his conservative approach helped establish and maintain peaceful labor relations.[34]

In the postwar period leading into the Cold War, accusations of Communist leanings were a serious charge that put any accused person on the defensive regardless of the degree of truth or evidence involved. Many careers were closed to Communists, including those of labor union officials. In 1947 O. A. Knight, president of the local branch of the Oil Field Workers International Union, a CIO affiliate, sued in federal court, challenging provisions of the Taft-Hartley Act requiring labor union officers affirm they were not Communists. The local US District Court rejected the petition, but Knight planned an appeal. In 1947 Mississippi Congressman John Rankin of the House Committee on Un-American Activities charged that an unidentified TCU professor was a Communist sympathizer. Rankin's information was thirdhand, coming from a man who heard it from his son, a TCU student. Even such a frivolous report (thirdhand and without collaboration) brought a denial from TCU Chancellor Dr. M. E. Sadler, who denied knowledge of any faculty member with Communist leanings. Sadler welcomed a fair inquiry, even writing FBI Director J. Edgar Hoover asking for an investigation, but the bureau declined, stating that no law violation was alleged.[35]

Fort Worth experienced major technological advances in 1948. On March 8, 1948, WBAP-FM began broadcasting, Fort Worth's first FM radio station. Most of the early programing duplicated that of WBAP's two AM stations, giving advertisers double coverage for which they were not charged extra. A more portentous event followed on September 27, 1948, when WBAP-TV presented the first television broadcast in Texas, coverage of President Harry Truman's appearance at Fort Worth's Texas and Pacific Railroad Depot, followed by three and a half hours of programming on September 29 that began with dedication remarks, music from The Flying X Ranchboys, and a feature movie presentation, *The Scarlet Pimpernel*, all sponsored by W. C. Stripling Company, a local department store. Reports indicated the television signal extended 160 miles, although the dedicated service area was less than half that. Fort Worth had an estimated 1,000 television sets that first day, most bought in anticipation at shops like Wolf & Klar Jewelers, where consumers could find an RCA television with a fifty-one-square-inch screen (approximately 7.2" by 7.2") for $341.19. Broadcasts expanded and viewership grew at a steady pace despite challenges like a seventeen-minute loss of signal when a truck struck a utility pole. On September 29, 1949, the station marked one year on the air, celebrating with almost nine hours of daily programming. By that anniversary Fort Worth had two networks, NBC and ABC, with signals that reached 16,000 televisions and an estimated audience of 64,000 (four per set) over a sixteen-county region, all supported by fifty regular sponsors. The *Star Telegram* published a twenty-page section celebrating the new medium on December 4, 1949.[36]

Chapter 8

Crime, Criminals, and Vice in Postwar Fort Worth

Prostitution, an enduring part of Fort Worth's history, received scant coverage postwar, suggesting it had either declined or gone further underground, likely the latter. Venereal diseases, often associated with sex for hire, certainly did not disappear. In January 1946 the Fort Worth Health Department reported a serious outbreak of twelve new syphilis cases in two weeks; the next month fifty-six new syphilis infections and twelve cases of gonorrhea were reported in just one week. Dr. Berke Brewer, city health director, launched a citywide education program on the high risks of exposure and established a STI clinic at the old City-County Hospital, Fourth and Jones Streets. In 1947 Tarrant County commissioners proposed turning the clinic into a Youth Health and Rehabilitation Center for juvenile delinquents, perhaps a signal that STI exposures had declined and juvenile crime had risen. No other statistics or reports suggested declining infections, and the available reports indicated prostitutes remained plentiful. In December 1950 police picked up forty-four women and twelve men in raids of cheap hotels catering to the sex trade. Police credited the operation's success to coordinated, simultaneous entries that thwarted the "grapevine" that normally alerted others. A few days later police charged twenty-two prostitutes picked up at eight downtown hotels, including one woman arrested at noon who bonded out and was rearrested that evening at the same hotel. The police response was an established pattern of occasional raids in which arrestees were immediately released on bonds forfeited as fines, all done neatly and quickly with little to no deterrent effect. The only changes in the postwar was an increase in bonds in 1950 from $10 to $25 and that women were no longer detained for STI examinations, thanks to new state regulations prohibiting forced exams.[1]

Doubtlessly, homosexuality existed from very early in Fort Worth's history, but no reports reached the public press until the 1940s. Even in the 1940s, homosexual references remained vague, omitting significant details that left the reader to fill in blanks. In 1946 Glen Atkins told police he killed Clyde Ross, the husband of his former wife, because Ross mistreated Atkins's two sons and "induced" them to do "immoral acts," often code words for homosexual practices. Also in 1946, police officers reported their surprise when a Black woman arrested with a white man in a stolen automobile turned out to be a man wearing makeup, a wig, "gay deceivers [bustle]," and sheer underwear.[2]

A sensational murder in 1949 put homosexuality in the news in clear, unambiguous terms. The story broke in March 1949 when Dr. John W. Lord, dean of TCU's Graduate School and chair of the Social Sciences Department, was found bludgeoned to death at his home seven miles outside Burleson, Texas (fifteen miles south of Fort Worth). Two students discovered the body while checking on Lord's welfare after he failed to appear for classes. A few days later, police in Big Spring, Texas (260 miles west of Fort Worth), recovered Lord's car and Arthur C. Hester, Lord's 18-year-old ward, was arrested at the Los Angeles home of a relative. The young man admitted the murderous attack, saying he became enraged when Lord refused to allow him use of a car to meet a girl in Waco.[3]

Former District Attorney Al Clyde and Eva Barnes, one of the first women involved in a Texas murder case, represented Hester at trial that April. Hester testified that he was 14 in July 1945 when Lord initiated a conversation at a Fort Worth movie theater. As they talked, Lord began touching Hester, placing his hand on the youth's leg and eventually offering money to go to Lord's home. Hester, flat broke without any means of support after walking away from a state school in Corsicana, agreed. At the home, 2513 Chicago Avenue,

Lord performed "unnatural acts" on Hester, beginning a relationship that continued for over two years, during which Lord, a widower, successfully had Hester released as his ward. At one point Hester tired of the arrangement and left for the Navy, but he returned after being booted out of the service and, once again, left broke and without prospects. In February 1949 Lord and Hester moved from the Chicago Avenue address to the Burleson area farm. Hester ostensibly worked as a cook, driver, and general handyman performing property maintenance in exchange for room and board and $50 monthly, although Hester claimed Lord seldom paid him. Dissatisfaction with being taken advantage of boiled over into rage when Lord refused Hester's use of a car to meet a woman. The youth vowed he did not intend to kill Lord and thought he was alive when he left. He admitted taking a ring and some money as partial recompense for what Lord owed him in back wages.[4]

At the trial Hester's defense attacked Lord as a homosexual who abused the defendant. Defense witness Dr. T. W. Grice testified that homosexuals routinely hid their "abnormal cravings," preyed on boys 12 to 14 years old, lived in seclusion, and were known to be jealous. Raymond Navehar, a former TCU student, claimed Dr. Lord made physical advances while they drove to Lord's Chicago Avenue home and again as they sat on a sofa, both times putting his hand on Navehar's lap and leg, advances which the student rebuffed. The jury deliberated three hours before finding Hester guilty and assessing fifty years, a partial defeat for the state, which had sought the death penalty. Days later Hester signed a statement repudiating claims about Lord's homosexuality, claiming he made up the story in hopes of getting a reduced sentence. The next day he denied the denial, offering to swear on a Bible that Lord was homosexual and charging a newsman concocted the plan as a ploy to reduce Hester's culpability, although exactly how that would happen remained unclear (the reporter denied the accusation). The Texas Court of Criminal Appeals rejected his appeal, leaving Hester to begin serving his sentence in 1949. Ten years later, in 1959, Hester was released on parole that would run until 1991.[5]

Another sensational incident came to light at almost the same time as the Lord murder case. The incident began to unravel in October 1950 when a father called police after his 16-year-old son came home with new boots that he could not explain. The boy had been a student at Poly High School before transferring to Technical High School and dropping out. He told detectives that he was the chief recruiter inducing local high school boys for a "sex perversion ring," luring the boys with promises of "easy money" as well as gifts such as shirts and, presumably, boots. He admitted taking two unnamed boys to a tourist cabin on East Lancaster Avenue on September 29, 1950, where they met four men, all wearing lipstick and dresses. The evening began with dancing but soon turned to "petting" and "unnatural sex acts." One gullible lad claimed his participation had been forced, that the 29-year-old man, who claimed to be a German spy, threatened him with a gun. Given the lack of corroboration, his story was most likely an improbable face-saving attempt. The police also put little stock in it, filing sodomy charges against all three youths as well as the four men: Charles S. Journey, 59 years old; Charles E. Nelson, 18 years old; Horace T. Little, 19 years old; and Fritz Karl Schneider, 29 years old. Journey, who had recently moved from Fort Worth to California, owned property in both states, including the Lancaster Avenue tourist cabins where the sex party took place. Police later arrested a 36-year-old British war bride living in Arlington Heights, charging her with performing "indecent and unnatural sex acts" on a 14-year-old Poly boy during the party, the allegations sustained by photographs. The woman, whose husband worked late nights, admitted going to the tourist cabin because she was bored but denied the indecency charge. Journey, Nelson, and Little were indicted but unadjudicated without explanation (apparently detectives also dropped charges against the woman and three boys). The fourth man, Fritz Karl Schneider, was convicted of sodomy in February 1951 and given two years for an "unnatural sex act" committed on a 15-year-old Poly boy. The court records revealed that Schneider was 38 years old, not 29 as reported in the original description, probably indicating he had lied about his age along with the fanciful story about being a German spy. An interesting side note: A month after his arrest, Journey sold the Rockwood Inn, a tavern at 1816 Jacksboro Highway, for $9,000 to Tarrant County Sheriff Sully Montgomery. The sheriff's involvement in a business deal with an alleged pedophile stirred up so much bad press that Montgomery quickly resold the property (at a profit).[6]

The tourist cabin incident seemed to signal a more open journalistic approach to homosexual indiscretions, that or incidents simply became more common. A rash of arrests for indecent exposure in 1950 prompted a police crackdown on sex offenders. Two incidents occurring that autumn have familiar links to Fritz Schneider. In November 1950 an 18-year-old boy found wandering downtown at 3:00 a.m. told officers that a 29-year-old taxi-man paid him and other boys $5 to $10 to "perform unnatural sex acts" at the man's hotel room on Burnet Street. The accused admitted the charges but claimed they happened months earlier, during the summer. The suspect was not identified but his age, hotel domicile, and timing of the incident in the autumn of 1950 suggest it was Schneider, perhaps out on bail. Likewise, in December 1950 detectives arrested a 39-year-old man after two Carswell airmen reported he had initiated "illicit relations" after buying them food and drinks. The accused, previously charged with sodomy according to the police report, was registered at a downtown hotel under a fake French name and falsely claimed to be a medical doctor. Once again, the reports did not identify the accused, but the timing of the arrest coming just after the affair with the boys and just before Schneider's conviction, that the accused in both cases lied about his occupation (spy/doctor) and claimed European heritage, that he was already charged with sodomy and was 39 years old (or 29), suggest that it could well have been Schneider.[7]

Precinct One Constable O. M. "Jimmie" Myer was charged with several sexual offenses, including sodomy of young girls. In October 1946 Myer was tried for sodomy committed against an 11-year-old girl, but the jury hung, failing to reach a verdict, and in January 1947 he was acquitted of aggravated assault of a 9-year-old girl. Before 1947 was out, a grand jury returned an indictment on three charges of aggravated assault, two of false imprisonment and one of assault with intent to rape. One of the charges stemmed from an October 10, 1947, assault on Mrs. Johnny Ward Wilmoth, while the other five involved assaults on December 5, 1947, involving Rosa Lee Hart and Celina Caldwell. At trial, Ms. Hart and Ms. Caldwell testified Myer picked them up outside their work and took them to a tourist cabin on Jacksboro Highway, where he gave them alcohol and attempted to force himself sexually on both. Myer admitted taking the two to the cabin but claimed they were robbery suspects and that he used beer to get them to talk. Once again, the jury deadlocked, but this time District Attorney Al Clyde promised to retry the case in February. That became problematic when Myer resigned as constable and checked into a Veteran's Administration Hospital in Hot Springs, Arkansas, for treatment of stomach ulcers. Clyde opted not to pursue the case as long as Myer remained out of state.[8]

In postwar Fort Worth illegal narcotics replaced alcohol as the controlled substance garnering the most attention, although drugs were never as widespread as illegal liquor. No evidence suggests that alcohol consumption diminished in the 1940s, but the intensity level for law enforcement involvement declined and became less newsworthy after Prohibition ended. Fort Worth certainly had numerous bars and taverns and lots of boozers; a 1948 study estimated 6,000 problem drinkers lived in Tarrant County. Determining the exact number was impossible, but enough serious drinkers existed in 1948 to justify the establishment of an Alcoholics Anonymous at 807 West Richmond Street, Scott B. Lackland serving as director.[9] Downtown was the center for the direst cases, alcoholics without a fixed abode who lived in the streets. In 1946 Tarrant County Judge Clarence Kraft (of sterilization infamy) called for the dismantling the old stone water trough on the Courthouse Square, complaining it had declined into disuse except as a collection point for wine and whiskey bottles. Judge Kraft's recommendation may well have also been a product of his lack of appreciation for history and nature, among other failings. Kraft also called for removal of trees lining the courthouse sidewalks, complaining they were ugly and attracted birds that fouled the area with their defecations.[10]

Many drug forms appeared, although some that are common today were rare, at least initially. In 1947 Tarrant County Sheriff Sully Montgomery ordered a complete jail shakedown after inmates reported drugs were commonly available. Investigators found nothing, but Montgomery admitted "goof balls," or stimulants, had been found earlier on two prisoners. Morphine had been around Fort Worth for decades and remained fairly common. In 1947 a 32-year-old, lifelong Fort Worth resident succumbed to a morphine overdose after a capsule burst in his stomach. On Monday the victim disembarked from a cruise ship in New Orleans after swallowing two rubber-wrapped capsules containing seven drams of morphine worth $4,000. On Wednesday in Fort Worth he was rushed to a hospital after recovering only one capsule, indicating the second had burst. He confessed his misadventure shortly before dying. A 1950 federal government report described cocaine as relatively insignificant, citing only one prosecution nationally in fifteen years, but just one year later Treasury agents reported cocaine was appearing in substantial quantities. If cocaine existed in Fort Worth, no reports were noted by the local press from the end of the war to the end of Truman's presidency.[11]

Heroin was present, but press reports related to it appeared infrequently, perhaps because the drug was relatively expensive, which limited its use, and was difficult to prosecute. In 1950 a US Bureau of Narcotics agent told a Fort Worth audience that aggressive enforcement had caused a thirteenfold increase in the price of heroin, pushing the cost of daily fixes to $40 to $50. Price inflation may have been a force prompting some users to opt for prison, where they would be forced to kick the habit. Charles L. McCarthy, an admitted narcotic's addict, and a 23-year-old woman, both convicted of forging checks, asked the court for prison sentences so they could kick their heroin habits. Regular users remained. In July 1948 Fort Worth Police seized heroin, hypodermic needles, and a cooking spoon at a downtown hotel where they arrested three men and two women.[12]

Aggressive enforcement tactics by federal agents were alleged as a factor leading to the shooting death of George Jenkins, a US narcotics agent. In February 1947 George Miller, an ex-Alcatraz inmate and reputed former kingpin of narcotics for the Southwest, was out on bond on two Fort Worth burglary charges when he, his brother, and a third man spotted Jenkins walking with a woman near a Dallas grocery. Miller jumped out of the car and chased the agent into the store, where he gunned him down, then waited to surrender at the scene, telling officers that he acted in self-defense because Jenkins had threatened him.[13]

Marijuana possession, which dominated drug arrest reports, was treated as a serious crime and punished accordingly. The noticeable increase in local news concerning marijuana seemed to mark 1948 as the year the drug arrived in a major way. That year an 18-year-old boy was sentenced to five years for selling weed. He admitted the crime but insisted he had been framed because the federal agent had not identified himself as a law enforcement agent. His conviction was followed by the charging of Louise McClune, 24, of Fort Worth, and Thomas Snell, 29, of Cleburne, for marijuana possession. The couple pled not guilty in Fort Worth US District Court and were awaiting trial. In the early morning of July 6, 1948, Fort Worth Police and federal agents launched the city's largest drug raid since 1933, capping off a month-long investigation. Officers made seven arrests at a downtown taxicab stand on the city's north side and in Handley, confiscating nine ounces of marijuana and four taxicabs used in the distribution of marijuana cigarettes for $1. The next week police arrested four men and two women, seizing marijuana at a Jacksboro Highway tourist camp. Marijuana arrests were the main reason behind a 35 percent jump in narcotics arrests reported by Untied States Treasury agents in 1949 compared to 1948. In 1949 30 percent (or 1,599 of 5,273) of narcotics arrests made nationally were for marijuana. That year federal agents also confiscated almost 4,000 pounds of marijuana. Local enforcement action remained steady in the ensuing years. In January 1950 two men from Massachusetts were arrested in a Main Street pool hall after they were seen rolling marijuana cigarettes. The arresting officers recovered enough marijuana to make twenty-five cigarettes. In July 1950 Fort Worth Police arrested six marijuana dealers, including John Robert "The Goon" Butler, known, along with his wife Bertha, as Fort Worth's biggest marijuana dealers. Officers found twenty-one cultivated marijuana plants growing in the couple's backyard.[14]

The frequency of reported burglaries of pharmacies and doctors' offices and cases of fraudulent prescriptions suggested that prescription medication abuse was common. In September 1948 a pharmacist at Scott Drug Company, 3130 East Belknap Street, recognized a man presenting an opiate prescription as having purchased the same narcotic the previous week. The pharmacist held the man for police after discovering the prescription was forged. In just two days in July 1949, four doctors' bags were stolen, presumably by addicts seeking narcotics. Of course, reported cases represented just the tip of the iceberg; many offenses went unreported and few reported cases resulted in arrests.[15]

The only local dedicated narcotics treatment facility, the USPHSH, one of only two federal drug treatment centers, was overwhelmed treating active-duty military and veterans with mental or emotional issues. On July 1, 1947, the hospital's 897 patients included 513 active-duty military and 237 patients referred by the Veteran's Administration (discharged veterans) suffering from a host of mental issues, but only 101 drug addicts committed by courts plus another 46 voluntarily committed. The patient load included 36 women patients housed separately from the men.[16]

Gambling, the most common vice, occupied a lot of police resources. In May 1946 vice and patrol officers arrested 679 gamblers, collecting $8,405 in fines, an average of just over $12 per charged person. Dice games accounted for almost 80 percent of gambling arrests.

Chart 8.1 Fort Worth Gambling Arrests, May 1946

Form	No. arrested
Dice	538
Policy Writer (numbers game)	95
Bookmaking	26
Slot Machines	9
Card Games	8
Punch Boards	3

Source: Fort Worth Press, June 14, 1946, p. 17.

Dice had been common in Fort Worth for as long as the city had existed. Jim Thompson wrote that in the 1920s dice and card games ran twenty hours a day, taking up several floors at the Hotel Texas and many other downtown hotels.[17]

The never-ending parade of raids and arrests followed by releases on forfeited bonds constituted the appearance of effort without any real commitment to deterrence. If police wanted to close a notorious gambling den, they could have walked a few blocks from headquarters to the Diana Hotel, 1207½ Main Street, a well-known casino. The hotel's link to gambling was laid bare in April 1946 when a lone robber attempted to rob three men in the hotel lobby. The men had just left the dice game on an upper floor when they were accosted. One of the three victims, Clem Roberts, was shot three times and died a few days later. Whether from embarrassment or anger over not finding a suspect, officers began raiding the Diana Hotel regularly, hitting it every day in May and sometimes twice a day, making 177 arrests, an average of almost 6 per day. After a brief lull the raids resumed in October with seven persons arrested in one raid. Many joints around town offered dice and card games, but simple gambling devices like slot machines and punch boards were ubiquitous, available in many cafés and shops. In December 1946 four vice officers destroyed forty-six slot machines (valued at $150 each), seven punch boards, and five automatic dice boards they had confiscated in November, many from taverns and cafés.[18]

Most arrests made in the almost regular raids were low-end operators and players, while high-stakes operations were generally left alone. In April 1950 Fort Worth Police arrested a known Arlington gambler (otherwise unidentified) after he shot at R. G. Rossi, owner of a Calhoun Street tavern, because Rossi (a white man) refused to serve him a beer, saying, "We don't sell to white men." The rebuffed customer turned assailant had thirty-eight $100 bills on him, two of which he used to pay his $200 bond before walking out of jail. In January 1947 Texas Ranger Captain M. T. "Lone Wolf" Gonzaullas announced an antigambling enforcement drive for the fifty-eight counties under his command (including Tarrant County) as a response to a rash of murders linked to gambling. Gonzaullas promised to target actual casinos, not just the low-hanging fruit of marble boards, slot machines, and punch boards. Someone must have read the paper, for an overnight check found all known Fort Worth gambling locations closed. The Rangers had better luck at the Top O' Hill Terrace (the Hill) on August 9, 1947, where they confiscated and destroyed $25,000 in gambling equipment and arrested nine employees and fifty patrons. The successful operation was unusual; in most cases the Hill's precautions were an effective deterrent. In this case officers bypassed them by crawling through an adjacent field from the rear, avoiding the front gate's guard post with a buzzer that alerted the main building. Once reaching the main entrance, the Rangers waited in hiding until the door opened to admit patrons, then rushed in to find operating roulette, dice, and blackjack tables, as well as slot machines, items usually stowed in adjacent wall panels before officers entered. Several players and employees tried to escape via a thirty-yard tunnel only to be met by Rangers waiting at the exit. Most of the gambling equipment was destroyed after the owner, Fred Browning, waived his right to contest. Browning paid his personal fine of $200 plus court costs ($13), as well as $100 and costs for each of eight arrested employees and $10 plus costs for fifty patrons, shelling out a total of $2,267. The news report claimed Captain Gonzaullas had opted not to file felony charges, which would have required public disclosure, to avoid embarrassing several prominent Fort Worth and Dallas citizens among the detained. Gonzaullas added that a search warrant on a private home might be legally problematic—a strange position given that the Hill was a known casino.[19]

The obvious class favoritism brought several complaints, prompting District Attorney Al Clyde to ask for a grand jury investigation. Captain Gonzuallas agreed to appear if asked, adding that there were other reasons for downgrading the charges that the press had ignored. He lambasted the press further, claiming that they had "half-quoted" him and that he did not care if suspects were "big or little." Others, identified as "Fort Worth observers," questioned why the Top O' Hill, a swank joint frequented by wealthy elites, was singled out when many other gambling joints were running full tilt since the lifting of the recent "shutdown." The bad publicity seemed to stir the Rangers into activity. By the end of the month, they charged twelve café operators, including several on Northwest (Jacksboro) Highway and Mansfield Highway, with permitting gambling on their premises. The Rangers returned the next week to six joints on Northwest Highway, this time arresting five men for "intermittent gambling." The same week Fort Worth Police raided a gambling house in the 1000 block of Main Street with an early-warning system, an outside lookout who hand signaled an inside accomplice at a switch that activated an electric lock on the front door and a buzzer that alerted the staff to secret the gambling equipment. Despite all the precautions, officers were somehow able to detain twenty-four persons found gambling and charge four—Roy Hurley, Johnnie Williams, H. D. Anelly, and Leroy "Tincy" Eggleston—with keeping a gambling place, a more serious charge that carried $1,000 bonds, while patrons charged with simple gambling were released on $200 bonds.[20]

Afterward things remained relatively quiet for several months. One of the few reported incidents, the confiscation of three marble boards in September 1948, was a low-level operation initiated after wives complained their husbands had lost all their paychecks on the devices. Marble boards, coin-operated machines similar to pinball, were so common that a class of crooks arose specializing in breaking into them. In 1947 police arrested two juveniles, 15 and 16, and a 22-year-old reform school graduate and marble board shark known for his ability to open the games using only a wire. All three were charged in several thefts and burglaries. The 22-year-old, head of a youth gang operating on the Northside and Lake Worth, was described as a "young Fagin" who picked out and cased likely spots, then sent the younger boys to do the actual burglary. Little to no activity involving more elaborate operations appeared, but absence of reporting did not mean absence of gambling. The evidence suggests that gambling continued unabated during the cycle of low enforcement. In January 1949 Mrs. Joyce D. Dillard testified in her child custody hearing that she worked for a man who ran dice tables in several Fort Worth taverns, a claim confirmed by her husband, who said her ties to gambling was one reason he was "through" with her. Mrs. Dillard described a widespread operation similar to chain stores, but she only identified the Dude Ranch Inn, 3400 Azle Avenue, owned by Buck Stuart.[21]

On May 6, 1949, Norman D. Bailey, a former Dallas Police captain who resigned from the force in 1935, was arrested at a downtown Fort Worth hotel trying to bribe Fort Worth councilman C. C. McKnight. Bailey claimed to represent a New York gambling syndicate looking to set up operations in Fort Worth and willing to pay five councilmen (a council majority) $500 each, per week, for influence and protection. He provided two pages of instructions that called for dismissing the chief of police and putting the vice squad under direct council control. Two city detectives, posing as fellow councilmen, arrested Bailey, who quickly bonded out. Fort Worth police dismissed Bailey's story about New York connections, believing he was, at most, a front man for a Dallas gambling interests interested in Fort Worth. Bribes involving Dallas gamblers were not unknown. Recorded telephone conversations played in the 1947 trial of gambler Paul Rowland Jones, accused of trying to bribe Dallas County Sheriff Steve Guthrie, identified Top O' Hill as under payoff protection. Prosecuting Bailey became unlikely after he checked into the Veteran's Administration Hospital in Waco, claiming memory loss caused by shell-shock from World War I and a Dallas County court filed a lunacy charge against him. Tarrant County District Attorney Sidney Hellman disclosed the former police captain had been hospitalized fourteen times for mental disorders since 1932. The grand jurors cited the mental issues in no-billing Bailey.[22]

The incident contributed to a widely publicized formal investigation into local gambling that reinvigorated enforcement. Councilman McKnight appealed for a grand jury investigation into gamblers involved in bribes and payoffs but found the panel had already begun an inquiry. Jurors asked anyone with relevant information to appear May 18, 1949, but the massive 1949 flood canceled the hearing. Police Chief Dysart admitted gambling existed in Fort Worth and always had but maintained that police did their best to control it. To that end the chief initiated a flurry of enforcement activity that seemed to concentrate on one segment of the population. Officers raided a back room at 309 East Ninth Street where they arrested twenty Blacks, all released on $10 bonds. Two days later they charged six more African Americans found at a dice game at 704 East Seventeenth Street and eighteen at dice and card games at 910 Jones Street. Despite the single-focus enforcement effort, African American citizens still supported the police. In October 1949 residents of East Terrell Street petitioned for police action to close a gambling house in the 800 block. The council, which earlier had jumped into the gambling controversy and then quickly out of it, punted, referring the request to Chief Dysart, who explained that officers had raided the joint a dozen times, but it kept reopening. Some balance was restored May 13, 1949, when police arrested fifteen whites (ten women and five men) found gambling at 1510 Houston Street.[23]

Religious leaders proved an effective force in rallying enforcement actions. Reverend Karl Bracker, president of General Ministers Association (GMA), supported the grand jury investigation. He pointed to a yearlong GMA study that determined prostitution, slot and pinball machines, and obscene literature were available all over the city, although he noted that much of the activity had gone underground since the public outcry. A few days later, Reverend Bracker discovered a burning railroad flare on his front porch, 4301 East Lancaster Avenue. He remained undaunted, leading a large delegation to the city council on May 25, 1949, to complain about slot machines openly displayed in many businesses. Reverend W. Fred Swank of Sagamore Hill Baptist Church also questioned police efforts, saying he regularly saw slot machines and marble boards in businesses and had witnessed two policemen sitting beside two slot machines at a café without taking any notice. Reverend Swank was one of few to raise the race question, asking why police had no difficulty arresting Black gamblers but could not find white gamblers in country clubs and hotels. The council took no action other than to call for cooperation with law enforcement, a response that Reverend Bracker termed a whitewash of the problem. Interest waned after the grand jury ended its term without indictments or a report. Even the GMA moved on to other matters, petitioning the Fort Worth Cats to end Sunday night baseball games and to provide a separate seating section where beer was banned. Judge David McGee instructed the new grand jury, empaneled July 8, 1949, to prosecute police officers who tolerated gambling, telling the jurors that the existence of slot machines was common knowledge. The order meant nothing since it left the onus outside the court.[24]

Dice, slot machines, and board games were prevalent, but bookmaking also flourished despite efforts to stifle horse racing information. In August 1949 Texas agents seized a high-speed ticker tape machine supported by multiple phones in the Turf Bar, Seventh and Commerce Streets. The machine, operated by S. S. "Ned" Mayo, provided up-to-date odds used to make scratch sheets by local bookmakers like Harry W. Smith, Rube Harris, and David Bronstein. It had been originally placed in the Ellison Building, 102½ East Weatherford Street, in 1946, then moved down the street. Bookmaking was harder for local police to find and prosecute, but they made the occasional arrest. In August 1949 two downtown police raids resulted in a bookmaking charge against Tom Daly and operating a gambling house against Clyde Neal and Robert Kemper.[25]

A *Dallas Morning News* article published on October 8, 1950, described Fort Worth as "wide open" for gamblers. Their reporter visited several clubs in Fort Worth and Tarrant County, finding open dice games, roulette wheels, horse race bookmaking, and slot machines. He carried an "admittance card," a pass handed out in many Dallas night clubs granting access to Fort Worth gambling spots, but was freely admitted everywhere without questions. The reporter expressed wonder not only at open gambling but also at the heavy police presence on Jacksboro Highway, a center of Fort Worth gambling. He reported seeing two state highway patrolmen, two police motorcycles, and a police patrol car in the area of the 2222 Club, Fort Worth's swankiest casino with stakes rivaling Las Vegas and a national reputation that reached all the way to Maine. The club drew celebrities like Dick Kleberg of the King Ranch, Speaker of the United States House of Representatives Sam Rayburn (reputed to down two bottles of whiskey a night), and big game hunter Frank Buck. Downtown gambling spots tended to attract a less affluent clientele, but most offered a full range of games. One downtown spot over a grill had a blackjack table but concentrated on bookmaking for horse races in New York, New Jersey, and Chicago (odds were posted on large boards), as well as wagering on football and baseball games. Eastside clubs tended to be on the lower socioeconomic scale, with the exception of a swanky club off Highway 183 known for its dice, roulette, and slot machines. At least half the eastside patrons came from Dallas, many arriving by chartered buses. A staple of Fort Worth gambling clubs burned in a "mysterious fire" in 1949. The Starlite Club at 1301 Jacksboro Highway, built in 1927, had operated as the Ringside Club, 400 Club, Cuckoo Club, and Vivian's before being destroyed. The first alarm came in at 5:30 a.m., ninety minutes after the cleaning crew left at 4:00 a.m.[26]

Chief Hawkins roundly denied the Dallas newspaper's allegations, although his follow-up remarks admitted that gambling existed. The confession was obvious, given that Fort Worth Police had recently filed 500 gambling cases. Hawkins specifically denied that Fort Worth was a gambling resort town or that slot machines were prevalent, insisting that his officers confiscated all they found. He explained that prosecuting gambling in private clubs was difficult because their restricted entry allowed employees to hide or dispose of evidence. Chief Hawkins also vehemently denied that he transferred the vice unit supervisor to break up an entrenched payoff system, claiming he had intended to assume direct control but found the added duty too demanding and appointed Sergeant R. E. Pinckard. All the publicity revived the GMA demands for vigorous enforcement.[27]

The uproar brought the usual reaction, a rush of police activity prominently displayed in the news, followed quickly by a return to the status quo. In October 1950 Chief Hawkins went along on a raid on the Westmoor Club, 5800 Camp Bowie Boulevard, where officers confiscated two slot machines, dice equipment, and a punch board and made twenty-one arrests, including several employees charged with operating a gambling place. The next week gambling charges were filed against ten bars and cafés clustered around downtown on Main, West Ninth, West Seventh, and East Belknap Streets, as well as spots on East Lancaster Avenue and West Berry Street. In every filed case, undercover vice officers had received cash payouts from pinball and marble board machines. By November reports surfaced that gambling had been cleaned out of Fort Worth, although gambling dens remained outside the city limits, especially on Jacksboro Highway, where the clubs were said to be "as open as the courthouse." Tarrant County Sheriff Sully Montgomery denied that gamblers operated openly, although his own officers raided the Dude Ranch, 3400 Azle Avenue, charging Giles G. Gillian with operating gaming devices, seizing three slot machines, and destroying a dice table.[28]

The World War II and postwar periods witnessed the beginnings of a rash of murders of gamblers and associated hoodlums that continued into the 1960s, taking several lives. Exactly when the carnage began, as well as the precise number of victims, remain under debate. Elston Brooks, a local reporter and columnist, counted ten starting with Nelson Harris in 1950, clearly ignoring several homicides that predated Harris. Ann Arnold comes much closer, beginning the count in 1943 with James "Red" Kavanaugh, but many consider Louis Tindall, killed in 1944, to be the first victim. The final act is also an open question, with most reports suggesting that the last victim died sometime prior to 1960, although at least one assassination after 1960 qualifies to be included. Less disagreement exists about the cast of characters, and certainly the main actors are obvious.[29]

One of the early fatalities, J. L. "Spec" Montgomery, was shot to death in 1947 by Lawrence Albert "Blackie" Wells in front of the Senate Club, 106

East Weatherford Street. "Spec" Montgomery ran a live racing wire service for bookies that Sam Ellison, a former Tarrant County deputy sheriff, had set up in the 1930s. Ellison was subsequently forced out in a "rumble" with Roy Patton and Bert Wakefield, manager of the 2222 Club in the 1940s and a friend of Benny Binion. Patton and Wakefield took over the service, running it until 1942 when Patton died and Montgomery assumed control. "Blackie" Wells operated a domino parlor in the Ellison Building owned by Montgomery, and the two had contentious history over rent that almost resulted in a shootout in 1944. In that instance Montgomery reached for a pistol in his waistband, but Wells beat him to the draw, preventing an exchange of gunfire but leaving hard feelings. Their acrimony reached a boiling point after Wells learned Montgomery had again threatened him, prompting Wells to drive to the Senate Club armed with a shotgun he had picked up from his home. On arrival Wells saw Montgomery standing outside the club and advanced toward him, firing as he went and killing him. At trial in January 1948 several witnesses confirmed Montgomery was known to carry a gun and had threatened Wells. Wells's attorney, W. P. McLean, put Dr. Jack Furman on the stand, who testified that cirrhosis of the liver from syphilis had made Wells nervous and edgy, impairing his mental state. The jury convicted Wells, sentencing him to thirty-five years.[30]

Just months later, on March 6, 1948, Lon Holley, a known criminal who operated a River Oaks café and liquor store, was killed by two gunshots to the back of his head. Holley left home that evening after receiving a phone call. Before leaving he gave his wife the names of Frank Cates and Jim Thomas, telling her that if he were not back by midnight, she should assume something had happened. Holley was found the next morning slumped in the front seat of his car in the 2400 block of Robert's Cutoff, a secluded spot just a half mile from his home. His death came just one week before Holley was to be tried for six robberies committed the previous December. His lawyer was poised to mount a vigorous defense, having subpoenaed thirty persons to testify, a circumstance that may have contributed to Holley's death. District Attorney Al Clyde believed Holley was killed because coconspirators feared he would be convicted and try to reduce his sentence by trading information about a $16,000 bank burglary in Rosebud, Texas, or the killing of Dr. Roy Hunt of Littlefield, Texas (a crime for which Jim Thomas had been convicted, although the conviction had been overturned). Detectives interviewed Thomas but dismissed him as a suspect after he provided an alibi. Joe Spurlock, lawyer for Old National Life Insurance Company, tried unsuccessfully to deny payment on Holley's life insurance policy, arguing at an inquest that Holley had voluntarily exposed himself to harm, making his death a virtual suicide. No one was ever charged with his murder.[31]

The evening of September 30, 1948, Que Robert Miller was found shot to death in his car at Oakland Lake (also known as Fosdick Lake) in what Detective A. C. Howerton described as a gangland execution, gunshots to the neck and above the left eye. Miller, a former sheriff of Foard County, Texas, had served time for misapplication of public funds and faced several counterfeiting charges, and his brother, Sydney A. Miller, was an accused murderer out on bond in the death of a farmer slain to prevent his testimony in an oil swindle case. Miller left his lodgings at Westmoor Motor Court, 5800 Camp Bowie Boulevard, around 8:00 p.m. and was last seen playing pool in Dallas at 9:15 p.m., just two hours before patrol officers found his body at 11:30 p.m. Witnesses identified a diamond stickpin recovered in the Westmoor room that Miller had worn in Dallas that evening, suggesting that he had returned to the Westmoor before leaving with his killers or to meet them. Informants claimed Miller died because he had sold "phony" drugs, but no one was ever charged in his murder.[32]

On November 22, 1950, at 9:15 a.m. Nelson Harris, a 41-year-old local hoodlum, and his pregnant wife were killed in a massive explosion while sitting in a car parked in their driveway, 3105 Wingate Avenue. Carswell Air Force Base bomb experts determined that a blasting cap set off nitroglycerine attached to the starter, destroying the car and spreading debris over a wide area, drawing a crowd of 1,000 onlookers. Harris had a history of gambling and narcotics. In 1940 he was convicted and sentenced to two years in Leavenworth Penitentiary for activities with the Green Dragon narcotics ring. After his release, he lived in Midland and Odessa before returning to Fort Worth to work as a bouncer and operate taverns and cafés, including the 2929 Club on Crockett Street and Nelson's Place, 2236 Northwest Highway, where he ran a craps game. Harris associated with Herbert Noble, a Dallas gambler whose wife had been killed in an explosion meant for him (Noble would be killed by a bomb planted near a mailbox in 1951). Despite his record and clear gangster ties, Harris had close relationships with Sheriff Sully Montgomery; at his death he carried a deputy sheriff commission card signed by the sheriff.[33]

Investigators found so few people willing to talk about either murder that they speculated a "clam up" order had gone out. They did learn Harris was a suspect in a West Texas burglary in which a safe had been blown and that he had acted as an "advance man" for two local "gypsy" groups known for phony fortune teller scams and as thieves. Detectives sought to question Ray Pool, an oil field worker and associate of Harris, but were unable to locate him. On December 6, 1950, police rounded up ten known gamblers and associates, detaining them for interrogation in hopes of sweating information out of them. The group included James C. Thomas (out on bond pending his fourth trial in two murders), Carl Tiffin Hall (owner of the Mexican Inn), Howard Stripling, John T. Reynolds, Ernest Hays, and Dick Crownover (found with Stripling); Andrew Floyd (an associate of Tiffin Hall); Elmer Sharp (a café owner); and Grady and Robert Whitehead (brothers). Floyd was arrested at 5000 Crown Road just across the street from 5005 Crown Road, where "Tincy" Eggleston was hiding out along with Jack Blackman, a hoodlum from Nevada, adding fuel to suspicions of a Nevada connection. Those rumors grew when unconfirmed reports suggested "Russian Louie" Strauss had also been seen in town. Strauss was a known gunman who operated Tahoe Village Resort in Lake Tahoe and associated with Bugsy Siegel at the Flamingo Hotel and Casino in Las Vegas. Detectives also questioned Frank Cates, a suspect in Lon Holley's death, and Jack Nesbit, whom Dallas Police had questioned in the bombing death of Herbert Noble, a Dallas gambler. No one was ever charged in Harris's death.[34]

The plot thickened two hours after the Harris bombing when Leroy "Tincy" Eggleston, a known associate, gambler, and general hoodlum, found a quart of nitroglycerin jelly under the hood of his car at his home off Highway 81, south of Fort Worth. Eggleston discovered the bomb when he checked the car after hearing of Harris's death. Carswell bomb experts removed and detonated the explosive at the farm. Underworld gossip reported that both Harris and Eggleston were targeted because of their efforts to take over Fort Worth gambling, a lucrative prize worth an estimated $3 million annually. Harris and his wife were the fourth and fifth unsolved gangland killings since the 1944 slaying of Louis Tindall, followed by Lon Holley and Robert Que Miller, the latter two killed in 1948. Eventually, between 1940 and 1960 perhaps as many as sixteen Fort Worth gangsters met violent ends. Not every gangster's death during the span fit neatly into the pattern. In 1950 Clyde "Tuffy" Neal Jr., a known bookmaker and gambler, was killed, but not as a result of gangster infighting. Neal, manager of the Maddoc Recreation Club, 1313B Main Street, got into a dispute with Tommy Potts inside the New Annex adjacent to the Skyliner, 2238 Jacksboro Highway. The two carried the confrontation outside where they fought over Potts's pistol until it discharged, mortally wounding Neal.[35]

Chapter 9

Policing in the Postwar

On May 16, 1945, R. E. "Bob" Dysart became chief of Fort Worth police, replacing T. G. Curry, who stepped down to become captain over training. Dysart, with the department since 1920, received a monthly salary of $400. The change at the top may have been prompted by a rash of reports concerning dice games that proliferated downtown. Many dice operators set up their games on the upper floors of buildings three stories or higher with elevators, allowing street level lookouts to race upstairs if police were spotted. In addition, the department had been stung by several allegations of officers mistreating prisoners. One of Dysart's first moves was to assign to each jail shift a sergeant charged with ensuing humane treatment. The success of the effort was questionable. An autopsy revealed that Israel Standifer, found unconscious at the jail on January 3, 1946, died due to hemorrhaging from blows to his head. Chief Dysart did not publicly assign blame for the death, but he demoted Sergeant J. E. "Skinny" Helm and suspended three patrolmen for ten to fifteen days. In 1949 Dysart resigned as chief to return to his old captain's rank and was replaced by Lieutenant George Hawkins. Dysart remained as captain only a few months before leaving to head Fort Worth's Civil Defense Office for one month before becoming chief for Lubbock Police at a monthly salary of $587.[1]

Traffic enforcement, which had become a significant police function in the 1920s, expanded as the number of cars on the streets multiplied in the postwar boom economy. On September 4, 1947, Texas adopted the Uniform Traffic Code, defining and standardizing traffic regulations throughout the state while maintaining local ordinances and traffic signals that conformed to state standards. The main traffic route between Fort Worth and Dallas, Highway 80 (Lancaster Avenue in Fort Worth), was Texas's busiest road; a metered checkpoint near Arlington recorded 13,943 vehicles in one twenty-four-hour period. Most Highway 80 drivers began and ended their journey in either Fort Worth or Dallas, the majority of eastbound traffic stopping in Dallas and most westbound traffic stopping in Fort Worth. West of Fort Worth the traffic load dwindled by over half, to only 6,205 vehicles per day. Another few thousand vehicles traveled between Fort Worth and Dallas using Highway 183, a secondary intercity route. Intercity roads not going to Dallas carried significantly lower daily vehicle volume: 2,050 per day on the Decatur Road, 1,940 combined on Highways 81 and 174 to Cleburne, 1,710 on Granbury Road, and 1,600 on Northwest Highway (now Jacksboro Highway) to Azle and Jacksboro.[2]

As traffic increased, so did traffic fatalities. In the first full postwar year, 1946, Fort Worth traffic deaths declined to only twenty-one (twelve were pedestrians) and Tarrant County fatalities fell from seventy-eight in 1945 to sixty-nine (thirty-two pedestrians). Sixteen of the sixty-nine reported county fatalities occurred on the county's deadliest road, Northwest Highway (Jacksboro Highway). The drop in mortality may have been partially a product of accelerated drunken driving enforcement that increased DWI arrests from 4 in 1944 to 49 in 1945 and 127 in 1946. Certainly, emphasis on traffic enforcement increased. Fort Worth Police added three officers to "white cars," special units designated for traffic accident prevention and investigation, bringing the unit to nineteen officers. They had a lot to do. In 1947 Fort Worth Police investigated 8,222 traffic accidents, over half occurring at intersections. After 1946 traffic deaths began to rise, reaching thirty-one in 1948 and fifty-one in 1949 when Fort Worth nosed out San Diego, California, for the nation's highest traffic fatality rate among cities with a population of 200,000 to 500,000. Accidents rose comparably to 9,625 in 1949, reaching a daily average of over 26. December 1946 was the city's worst traffic month on record to that point,

View of frozen Lake Worth and Lake Worth Casino, January 22, 1940. Courtesy *Fort Worth Star Telegram* Collection, Special Collections, University of Texas at Arlington Libraries.

with 10 fatalities and 2,001 collisions, an average of over 64 accidents daily. In 1950 Tarrant County recorded 91 traffic-related deaths, the highest ever to that point and 8 more than the previous record set in 1935.[3]

The end of Prohibition signaled a reduction but not an end to police involvement in alcohol-related ordinances. Intoxication arrests were common and spiked during certain holidays, especially New Year's Eve, when city police often brought in 100 drunks. The number of arrests declined substantially on New Year's Eve 1947 due to snow and ice blanketing the streets. Adverse conditions eliminated most traffic and all fatalities and reduced drunkenness arrests to only twenty-four. The cold lingered, freezing the north end of Lake Worth to a depth of eight inches, supporting skaters and a few cars. Despite the cold alcohol-related arrests experienced a steady growth curve. In 1946 Fort Worth Police made 12,638 arrests for drunkenness, followed by 12,795 in 1947 (2,650 women) and 13,476 in 1949 (almost 37 per day). There was no doubt that Fort Worth had its share of alcoholics; a 1950 study estimated it was home to 8,000 problem drinkers, about 4 percent of the population.[4]

Officials tried to develop programs to deal with hard-core alcoholics, many with multiple arrests that skewed statistics and placed burdens on the city jail. One man had been jailed over 300 times for drunkenness. At the beginning of the 1940s the standard procedure was to take intoxicated detentions to the Tarrant County Jail, where they served three days' incarceration. Postwar, the county jail began releasing drunks after only a few hours to reduce food service costs and relieve jail overcrowding. That change prompted Fort Worth in 1947 to fine habitual drunks, those with two prior convictions for intoxication, $200 plus court costs, a sum few prisoners could pay, forcing them to serve out the fine working seventy-seven days on a road gang doing general maintenance. The plan intended to break the cycle of arrests with short detentions followed by rearrests. Longer incarcerations reduced the number of intoxication arrests by incapacitation and encouraged chronic alcoholics to avoid public exposure where they could be arrested. After a two-week trial the results showed a decrease in the city's average jail population to 68, substantially fewer than the 100 averaged before the change. The only downside was an increase in escapes since road work put men in the open where they could simply walk away. In the first month of operation two prisoners did just that, walking away from a road gang on Boat Club Road.[5]

Traffic control and dealing with intoxicated persons, with occasional exceptions, were rather routine jobs, but police work could be anything but mundane. In January 1948 Officer James L. Ruddle was shot in the abdomen during an exchange of gunfire with a burglar at Uncle Dow's Package Store, 615 East Hattie Street. That afternoon detectives arrested Jesse James Halliburton at his home. Halliburton, suffering from a gunshot wound to his right hand, admitted the burglary but refused to comment on the shooting. On August 2, 1949, Officer Walter O. Whatley died from injuries he suffered the previous week in a collision with an automobile while chasing a speeder in a third vehicle. Whatley was the first Fort Worth policeman to die in a traffic incident in twenty-five years. A recently enacted state retirement code amendment entitled Whatley's widow to $75 monthly retirement benefits plus $6 for each of her two children, a grant the city shamefully denied, arguing the death was off-duty since Whatley died in a hospital days after the collision. The recently established Fort Worth POA promised to take the matter to court if the council did not relent. On November 20, 1950, Officer Alfred D. Childress was shot by Hiram Hall, owner of the Cherokee Inn, 506 West Magnolia Avenue, who mistook the patrolman for a burglar. Childress and his partner entered the bar after they discovered the front door open at 4:30 a.m. Hall, in an attached bedroom, fired three shots at what he thought were burglars, striking Childress in the torso. Ten days later the officer was still in St. Joseph's Hospital and unable to move his left arm, but hoped to return to work.[6]

An off-duty Fort Worth police officer died while heroically trying to save his children from a fire. The morning of February 11, 1950, Officer James M. Warren and his family were asleep in their upstairs bedrooms when they awoke to flames engulfing the house. Warren and his wife alerted the children, ushering them outside in the thick smoke, but once in the clear they discovered two had not made it out. The father ran back inside, somehow gathering both and making it outside despite sustaining severe injuries. Unfortunately, all three died from their burns. The local American Legion posthumously granted Officer Warren their award for heroism, a well-deserved honor.[7]

Police brutality charges against several officers led to a grand jury investigation. In December 1949 a man acquitted of assaulting a police officer charged that officers beat him with blackjacks. District Attorney Stewart Hellman presented the complaint to the grand jury with recommendations that they broaden the scope into other allegations of police brutality. Hellman appealed for citizens with relevant knowledge to come forward, but few responded. The grand jury report cited the lack of witness responses in dismissing claims of a widespread problem, arguing that only 8 persons appearing with complaints out of an estimated 47,000 people that officers had dealt with each year suggested that mistreatment was the exception, not the norm. The report concluded that Fort Worth had one of the best police departments in the state.[8]

A few officers faced serious discipline. Cornelius Leahy, a police officer since 1929, was terminated in 1950 after being charged with DWI while on duty. A couple began following his patrol car after seeing him weaving in traffic on South Main Street, trailing him until he stopped and they were able to telephone police headquarters. Responding officers found a whiskey bottle in the patrol car and learned Leahy had failed to report for several hours (officers were required to contact dispatch periodically). Leahy had a history, having been suspended sixty days a year earlier for being drunk on duty. In addition to losing his job, Leahy, who pled guilty, was fined $50 plus $35 in court costs and had his driver's license suspended for six months. Police Officer H. C. Hall Jr. was suspended for five days, then terminated for punching Principal Weldon Wells of Forest Hill Elementary School. Hall confronted Wells after the officer's son, a student at the school, reported Wells had put him out of the car, making him walk home. Hall later learned his son had lied and apologized to Wells. The Civil Service Commission reduced the punishment to six months' suspension.[9]

Fort Worth Police experienced significant expansion to accommodate the city's growing population and recent annexations. All the additional territory and population added five districts to the map, increasing the police beats to seventeen, each staffed with a two-officer car. In January 1947 forty-six new hires (all but three World War II veterans), average age 27, began a two-week academy class. For ten days the recruits attended morning classes at the old post office and worked afternoons with veteran officers. Their addition brought total police strength to 350, including 22 civilians. The detective squad also expanded to 37, plus 2 detectives assigned to downtown foot patrol to monitor bars and hotels where criminals frequented. In 1950 Chief Hawkins asked the council for 50 more officers to correct for attrition that had dropped the department to only 326 officers and to allow officers to patrol smaller beats. At the time 156 officers were assigned to patrol.[10]

Comparing crime statistics over the years is difficult due to the sporadic availability of data and shifting reporting categories and dates. The statistics for 1941 and 1946 cover fiscal years ending August 31, while the reporting periods in 1947 and 1948 ended September 30.

Chart 9.1 Police Statistics, 1941, 1946, 1947, 1948, and 1949

	1941	1946	% Change
Staff	234	348	+49
Patrol cars per shift	12	17	+42

(Continued)

Chart 9.1 Continued

Detectives	24	39	+63
Arrests (includes citations)	20,410	27,368	+34
Stolen Cars	215	558	+160

Source: Fort Worth Star Telegram, August 29, 1947, p. 4.

	1946	1947	% Change
Stolen Vehicles	577	455	–21
Robberies	60	75	+25
Burglaries	951	1,006	+6
Cases filed	1,833	2,147	+17

Source: Fort Worth Star Telegram, October 24, 1947, p. 31.

	Jan–June 1948	Jan–June 1949	% Change
Murders	13	10	–23
Aggravated Assaults	109	130	+19
Robberies	2	56	+2,700
Burglaries	536	634	+18
Thefts	1,619	1,708	+5
Auto Thefts	198	210	+6

Source: Fort Worth Star Telegram, September 19, 1949, p. 4.

Analyzing the data is difficult because of the gaps and discrepancies. Annual statistics are available for 1946 and 1947, while all we have for 1948 and 1949 are the first six months of each year. Automobile thefts seemed to have taken off postwar, although a dip appeared after 1946. Only 215 cars were reported stolen in 1941, but the number almost tripled to 577 or 588 in 1946 (reports differ), declined slightly to 455 in 1948, and held steady at just over 400 annually in 1948 and 1949. Robberies overall seemed to be steady at rather low numbers, ranging from 60 to 75, discounting 1948 when only 2 were reported. Burglaries seemed to have increased steadily, rising from 951 in 1946, to 1,006 in 1947 and, if half-year trends held, to the 1,100 to 1,200 range in 1948 and 1949. The general summation is that car thefts and burglaries increased steadily throughout the 1940s.

Robberies, which remained rather constant through the postwar period (except for 1948), often involved known perpetrators. One active hijacker,

Ivan Pool, met his end in April 1946 during a robbery in Pantego, a suburb between Fort Worth and Arlington. Pool, who lived on East Lancaster Avenue, had already served three hitches in prison. At his death he had $1,000 in his wallet and was wearing a diamond stickpin. Pool was working alone when killed, but many robbers enlisted accomplices. In December 1947 T. S. Walls, a Fort Worth Police identification clerk and later chief of police, recognized a man arrested for drunkenness at the Greyhound Bus Station as Argyle E. Guyton, a known hijacker who had served seventeen years in prison. Through interrogation and information gathered from Guyton's hotel room, detectives were able to identify and detain an associate, Howard H. Herndon. Both men talked openly (probably under rather intense questioning), spilling details about eight recent robberies and fingering partners Johnnie Bevil, Zach McWiggins, and Ralph Nobles, as well as two unidentified lesser partners in crime. Other hijackers must have taken their place, for armed robberies continued at a high rate, hitting forty-four in the first two months of 1950, only twelve fewer than in the first six months of 1949. In response, officers raided night spots downtown on Main and Houston Streets and the north side where criminals congregated, arresting ninety-four men and nine women. Prosecution also stiffened. In April 1950 Tarrant County criminal courts sentenced sixteen convicted robbers to an average of thirty years in prison (another ten cases were pending).[11]

Juvenile crime that had exploded during World War II continued to increase after the war. Juveniles arrested for criminal offenses, as well as any picked up for running away from home or other civil matters, were taken to either city or county jails. A TCU study found that in 1945 some 744 juveniles stayed overnight at the Fort Worth Jail before being released to Tarrant County Probation officers. The report strongly recommended a separate juvenile facility be made available twenty-four hours a day, but the best the city could do was fashion a juvenile ward within the existing jail. The Tarrant County Jail remained the eventual destination for most detained juveniles, whether they were charged criminally or simply held civilly, and the Tarrant County Probation Department served as the primary agency handling juveniles. In 1945 county officers dealt with 1,200 children, sending 354, to the county jail, 117 girls and 237 boys. In 1946 Fort Worth and Tarrant County authorities detained 1,332 juveniles a total of 2,526 days in county custody, an average of just under 2 days per detainee. Fort Worth accounted for 1,084 (or over 80 percent) of the 1,332 total juvenile detainees but was responsible for only 48 percent of incarceration days (1,233). That 1,084 juveniles spent just 1,233 days in Fort Worth custody indicated that most youths were either released or transferred to the county within one day.[12]

Economic issues delayed the development of better juvenile detention facilities. The city jail continued to place boys in a separate cell a few feet removed from adult prisoners, while girls were held briefly in the jail matron's office before being taken directly to the county jail. The city kept a matron on duty twenty-four hours a day, a difficult bit of scheduling considering there were only three: Mrs. Lucille Underwood, Mrs. Hallie Cook, and Mrs. Ila Rowe. The Tarrant County Jail offered slightly better accommodations, with separate cells for girls and boys on the third floor, the women's floor. White girls were separated from adult women and other juvenile girls detained for "health" charges (STI treatment), but African American girls enjoyed no such considerations and were thrown in with other Black women without concern for age or health status. In 1948 the League of Women Voters inspected the Fort Worth and Tarrant County jails. Their report disparaged the city facility as completely inadequate but also faulted the county for its sparse accommodations consisting of two communal cells (one for each sex), each with a sitting room and iron cots but no entertainment options other than magazines. The league determined the only acceptable solution lay in a completely separate juvenile facility.[13]

Adults housed at the Tarrant County Jail complained loudly about the meal service. In January 1947 prisoners protested the quantity and quality of food by burning mattresses. Sheriff Sully Montgomery met with two prisoner representatives. One prisoner claimed he had lost over twenty pounds on the set menu of one ounce of cereal in the morning and a half plate of beans at noon and dinner. The only exception, a Sunday lunch with roast beef, was praised, but not the Sunday evening dinner of three small cookies and a cup of coffee. Three years later complaints resurfaced, leading to a dietician's review that described jail meals, costing about ten cents each, as deficient in calories and essential elements. Sheriff Montgomery ordered increases in portion size and the addition of fresh vegetables.[14]

The state of Texas became the driving force in the establishment of minimums for police and fire pay and work standards. The state had begun setting recommended minimum wages for police and fire personnel after World War I, but the lack of enforcement meant that Fort Worth and other cities simply ignored them. In January 1945 the Tarrant County district attorney chided the city for paying entry level police $145 monthly, $5 below the state minimum of $150. The city relented in 1947, raising starting pay to $165 with an increase to $191 after one year, followed by $10 monthly increases every five years up to twenty-five, a maximum of $241 monthly. In 1948 the state increased minimums for both police and firefighters to $200, immediately raising the pay of thirty-eight police officers and fifteen firemen. The city compensated for the increase by cutting $10 from the thirty police officers with less than five-years tenure who earned $210 monthly. The cut caused an uproar from embittered officers who noted that Dallas officers earned $200 monthly plus a $75 annual uniform allowance. City administrators reacted defiantly, threatening to implement a state clause that allowed reclassifying officers with fewer than eighteen months service as trainees who could be paid only $165 monthly. The audacious and vindicative plan brought a harsh reaction from District Attorney Al Clyde, who warned that failure to meet the state minimums would bring noncompliance fines.[15]

Continuing frictions over retirement and pay contributed to the adoption of state civil service statues governing police and fire and the formation of a Fort Worth Police Officer Association. Most city employees, including police and fire, had been covered for years by a local city civil service system, but in 1947 Texas enacted a state system open to lower political subdivisions (cities and counties). A plebiscite on adoption set for December 2, 1947, faced hearty opposition from the city council that published a list of fifteen objections focusing on potential costs and the erosion of local control. More opposition came from *Star Telegram* columnist Tony Slaughter, who worried that the state system mandating that vacancies be filled by exam scores would open both fire and police to Black applicants. Firefighters strongly favored promotional exams to end what many in the department saw as a system in which poor firemen who were good "mixers" were promoted because of support from civic groups. The state civil service system passed easily,

3,133 to 1,179, but the city unsuccessfully fought its adoption in the courts, arguing it constituted an unconstitutional affront to local control. In March 1948 the Fort Worth Police Officers Association (POA) organized to advance police causes and raise work standards. Detective Arthur Conway (A. C.) Howerton, well-known as Fort Worth's first homicide detective and for buying suspects steak dinners to loosen their tongues, became the first POA president. That August 19 the POA held its first civic event, a Kiddies Day Picnic at Forest Park for all children (except Blacks, who were not permitted in Forest Park except for Juneteenth). The association furnished ice cream and sodas but asked parents to pack extra sandwiches for any children without lunches. One of the POA's first political efforts came in 1950 after the city council tabled a new state retirement plan with liberalized benefits, arguing that the state plan did not apply since Fort Worth already had a retirement program. The FWPOA, represented by Texas State Representative Doyle Willis, sued for compliance in the Seventeenth District Court.[16]

Tarrant County courts were an active and growing part of the local criminal justice system. The court's workload grew significantly postwar. Misdemeanor convictions rose from 206 in 1944 to 504 in 1945 and 526 in 1946, almost tripling in two years, an increase the district attorney credited to speedier prosecutions. Felony prosecutions followed a similar upward trajectory. In the two years between September 1, 1946, and August 31, 1948, the Tarrant County grand jury returned 1,559 felony indictments, almost a third, 499, for theft. In that period Tarrant County courts held 669 trials, receiving 658 convictions and 11 dismissals. Murders accounted for 36 of the 669 trials and 33 of the 658 convictions; 30 of the 33 murder convictions received a sentence other than death or life imprisonment. The courts handed down only three death sentences, two for murder and one for rape, and sentenced four persons to life, three for burglary and one for murder.[17]

In 1948 two sensational crimes shocked Fort Worth. On April 8, 1948, a 9-year-old girl was abducted from Hemphill Street and taken to Trinity Park, where she was brutally sexually assaulted, leaving physical injuries that took time to heal and emotional trauma that remained long afterward, especially afflicting her at night. The crime inflamed the police and public, sparking the biggest manhunt since a search for a cop killer in the 1920s. Over several weeks of intensive investigation, detectives interviewed numerous suspects before focusing on William R. Ray, a sergeant stationed at Carswell. Ray and his car matched descriptions given by the victim and evidence recovered from inside the vehicle was linked to the victim. The airman confessed to both military and civilian investigators, even writing the child's parents an apology. Defense lawyers obtained a change of venue to Corsicana, Texas, where trial began July 7, 1948. At trial Ray tried to disavow his confession, claiming that Air Force officials forced his signature by keeping him days and nights in a "dungeon" and that Fort Worth detectives threatened to prosecute his wife unless he confessed. Ray admitted picking up the girl on Hemphill Street, but claimed he blacked out and could not to remember what happened afterward. In what must have been a horrible experience, the victim testified, providing key details of the crime and identifying Ray as her attacker. The defense, left with little to work with, tried to produce sympathy by having Ray's 2-year-old daughter in the courtroom. All went for naught; Ray was convicted and sentenced to death. The Texas Court of Criminal Appeals upheld the sentence in March 1949. Ray's relatives approached the victim's parents, asking that they join in a plea for leniency. The family refused at first, calling the police and complaining to the district attorney when Ray's mother and father showed up at their home. Later, they relented and traveled to Austin to ask for commutation to a life sentence only to withdraw the request after learning a life sentence would have left Ray eligible for parole. Ray was executed by electric chair at Huntsville on the early morning of June 9, 1950, just over two years after the assault.[18]

A sensational triple murder rocked the news in November 1948. On October 30, 1948, Richard Duke, 31 years old, and his father-in-law, 56-year-old G. C. Bilbrey, died within minutes of each other. The initial report ruled the deaths natural causes, but an autopsy, requested by a reviewing physician, revealed lethal levels of strychnine poisoning in both men. Investigators broadened their inquiry, exhuming the body of Mrs. Dorthea Duke, the 26-year-old wife of Richard Duke and daughter of G. C. Bilbrey, who died in February, reportedly from heart failure. After the postmortem found strychnine in Mrs. Duke's system, suspicion focused on the lone surviving family member, Mrs. Ada Bilbrey, wife of G. C. Bilbrey, mother of Dorthea Duke, and mother-in-law of Richard Duke. Detectives took Mrs. Bilbrey to Austin for a polygraph, followed by questioning at Harris Hospital under sodium amytal, known as a truth serum. The investigation seemed stalled after Mrs. Bilbrey passed both tests, but two weeks later detectives charged her in the murder of her husband, G. C. Bilbrey, with charges pending on the other two cases. The prosecution rested on portions of a capsule found in G. C. Bilbrey's stomach during the autopsy, suggesting that he had taken poison disguised to look like medicine or a dietary supplement. Mrs. Bilbrey went to a local hospital claiming illness, although doctors could not find anything wrong with her, other than weakness from reduced mobility. After discharge she remained bedridden at friend's home, where detectives arranged for her to be booked and immediately released on a bond made by her attorney. Prosecutors suggested that Mrs. Bilbrey poisoned all three because of a love interest in her son-in-law, Richard Duke, but District Attorney Al Clyde believed she was motivated by jealousy over her husband's relationship with another woman and religious fanaticism that caused her to disapprove of her daughter and son-in-law's lifestyles.[19]

At an inquest held the end of November 1948, Mrs. Bilbrey's lawyers argued she lacked opportunity because she was never alone with her husband or Mr. Duke when poison would have been administered. Lt. Cato Hightower testified that the lie detector operator told him Mrs. Bilbrey defeated the polygraph exam because she was a pathological liar. Judge Frank Hurley ruled that Mr. Bilbrey and Richard Duke died by poisoning by "person or persons unknown" but refused to rule on Mrs. Duke since her death certificate still listed heart failure as the cause of death. Despite the problems Clyde won indictments on all three deaths. Mrs. Bilbrey expressed relief at the news, claiming she wanted the opportunity to prove her innocence at trial, but Clyde dismissed the response as false bravado made after learning of the charges. Six months later, in August 1949, a new district attorney, Stewart Hellman, petitioned the court to dismiss all indictments, claiming he was unconvinced of her guilt and could not ask a jury for a conviction.[20]

The 1933 mail truck robbery of $72,000 at the Texas and Pacific Station resurfaced in 1948 thanks to a deranged person searching for missing loot. R. O. Harris, owner of a twenty-acre farm near Handley where the three murdered coconspirators were last seen, found an intruder rummaging around a rock wall on two consecutive nights, getting close enough on one occasion to exchange blows and shoot at the trespasser. Detective A. C. Howerton speculated the prowler, likely of unsound mind, was looking for $35,000 never recovered from the 1933 robbery or narcotics known to have been stored onsite ($60,000 in drugs had been removed from a secret compartment within the house after the robbery). The FBI was called in after a third straight nighttime visit on September 23, 1948. Three days later, September 26, the intruder returned for the last time, never to be seen or heard from again. A perhaps final chapter was added in 1950 when a federal judge issued a nunc pro tunc order changing the robbery sentences of O. D. Stevens from consecutive to concurrent, moving his parole eligibility date from 1953 to 1950. Stevens's original murder convictions in the deaths of his three accomplices had already been overturned in state court, leaving only the robbery charge. Another associate, Bill May, was executed for the murders.[21]

Another sensational murder occurred on October 10, 1949, when Elizabeth Finch; her two children, Penelope, age 8, and Richard, age 7; and Mrs. Finch's mother, Mrs. Edith Walker, were all found shot to death at 3820 Rusty Dell. A neighbor, checking after not seeing the children leave for school, discovered the bodies. Investigators found all the doors and windows secured and a pistol next to Mrs. Finch's body, leading to the conclusion that she had killed her mother and two children before taking her own life. The children's father, an American Airlines pilot in Michigan visiting his mother, confirmed that Mrs. Finch had filed for divorce and her divorce lawyer reported she was distraught when they met the previous week.[22]

A notorious Fort Worth hoodlum met an appropriate end in 1949. Melvin Lee "Blackie" Lawson was a regular police character with eighty-six arrests by Fort Worth Police dating all the way back to 1936. He was most commonly jailed for assaults but also faced various charges ranging from murder, forgery, attempted rape, and carrying a slingshot. In 1937 Lawson killed two men in separate fights, one dying from a skull fracture when his head struck the pavement and another succumbing from assorted injuries, but he was never charged in either death, although he did receive a three-year sentence for forgery that year. While serving that sentence, Blackie became a trustee truck driver, hauling cattle from Louisiana to the Huntsville prison. During one trip he stopped off in Fort Worth (a significant detour from a direct route) long enough to get into a fight and be stabbed. Released from prison in 1939, Lawson was set for trial in 1945 on a charge of maiming Connor Wester at a Main Street café and was also charged with assaulting a juror, DWI, and selling liquor without a license. From all those charges he drew a four-year sentence, but Lawson seemed to have an in with authorities, or at least enough charm to sway them. In 1947 Governor Coke Stevenson issued a reprieve, conditional on Lawson's vow not to return to Fort Worth. He proved unable to stay away. In October 1947 Lawson was arrested at a Jacksboro Highway motel after giving a taxi driver a bad $2.15 check, a misstep he blamed on drunkenness. Sent back to prison, Lawson was released on January 22, 1949, only to be rearrested the next day for fighting. The incorrigible brawler finally met his end in April 1949 at the Ninth Street Club, 101½ West Ninth Street, where he had challenged the house, shouting that he was the toughest man in Fort Worth. Most of the patrons chose to leave but one, William L. "Buddy" Looper, a rancher and liquor store owner, apparently moved too slowly, antagonizing Lawson, who followed him up the stairs and into the street while brandishing a knife. The man with the knife lost when Buddy emptied a revolver, retrieved from his car, killing Blackie. The rancher claimed self-defense and the grand jury agreed, no-billing him on the murder charge.[23]

Chapter 10

African Americans and Others in the Postwar

Public manifestations of segregation continued to be blatant and pervasive. Schools, theaters, parks, virtually all places of accommodation serving Blacks (many did not) maintained segregated seating and toilets. Wartime necessity brought many Blacks into industries and businesses that had previously been exclusively white, but the integration effect did not extend outside plant grounds, as business social events remained segregated. The *Star Telegram* hosted two annual picnics each year, one for white employees and one for African Americans. In 1947 the "Colored" picnic with barbecue, games, and music was at Greenway Park; the next year the celebration was moved to I. M. Terrell High School. In 1950 Convair held its Christmas party for African Americans at the Masonic Mosque Building, 2213 East First Street.[1]

Shut out of virtually all white society, Blacks developed their own social outlets. The annual Juneteenth celebration, a distinctively African American affair, featured a variety of events. The 1946 party began with a breakfast at Greenway Park sponsored by the Ruth Charity Club, followed by swimming at Dixie Park (a city park pool reserved for Blacks), and a parade that departed at 2:30 p.m. from the historic Black commercial center at Ninth and Calhoun Streets going north to Belknap Street, where it turned east to Greenway Park. That evening a baseball game at LaGrave Field pitted the American Negro League

Kansas City Monarchs against the Indianapolis Clowns, followed by dances at North Side Coliseum and the Masonic Mosque. Black veterans returning to Fort Worth established several separate military social organizations. In January 1946 the McCrumby-Brooks Branch, Post No. 5617 of the Veterans of Foreign Wars, opened at 1600 Jones Street with thirty-one charter members; two years later eighty-six veterans established Fort Worth's first Black American Legion Post, the Eugene Brown Post No. 21 at Baker Chapel AME Church, with special seating provided for white visitors. Major African American entertainers appeared at Will Rogers Auditorium, usually with a "Special Section" for whites. On April 15, 1946, Duke Ellington and his orchestra played and Marian Anderson sang in concert on January 25, 1948.[2]

Segregation had a clear economic dimension with severe impacts. Blacks faced racial discrimination in gaining admission to the technical education boom of the postwar period. The Veterans Administration funded training to facilitate the transition of ex-servicemen into the civilian workforce, often with tuition-free classes and many that paid stipends. The idea was noble, but the implementation often was not, especially when allocating classes. Racial bias clearly played a role in the selection process, routinely placing more whites into training programs for highly skilled jobs while relegating Blacks to less skilled trades paying less. The situation for Black women was even worse, often limiting them to household services training, although Fort Worth and Dallas programs offered typing classes, something Houston did not.[3]

In November 1947 the Fort Worth Independent School District tried to correct the imbalance by opening a "Negro branch" vocational school, the McDonald College of Industrial Arts, at I. M. Terrell High School with classes in shoe repair and leather work, radio repair, auto body repair, auto mechanics, welding, machine work, and cooking. Reby Cary, a graduate of Terrell High School and a future FWISD board member and Texas state legislator, served as dean of personnel at the college from 1947 to 1950 when the campus moved to the Prince Hall Masonic Mosque, 2213 East First Street. The Southwestern College of Industrial Arts for Negroes (SWCIAN) on East Belknap Street that opened in 1946 became the state's largest African American vocational school. SWCIAN enrolled 850 students taught by forty faculty, all with degrees and 90 percent holding teaching certificates. In 1947 the VA suspended veteran's subsistence payments (stipends) to the school's students after receiving numerous complaints alleging inadequate or nonexistent instruction. SWCIAN was one of five schools indicted by a federal grand jury in Oklahoma City for "fraudulent representations" in tuition reimbursement claims involving payments to 482 veterans. The fraud cost the Veteran's Administration $60,000 in tuition payments and another $20,000 in subsistence payments to students, many of whom never attended classes.[4]

The inferior state of Black education was one of segregation's most egregious secondary effects, victimizing the future of Black students forced to attend poorly funded public schools where they received substandard instruction. The poor education they received left many unqualified for college or for jobs demanding high skills, fostering a legacy of stunted educational development that hindered economic advancement. Disparity in education existed at every level from academic to industrial training. The negative effects of a segregated, second-class educational system showed up in racial disparities in military rejection rates. During World War II the army rejected one-third of African American draftees for lack of educational development, four times the 7.4 percent rejection rate for whites. That racial effect was especially pronounced in the South, a region that historically underfunded all education, including that of Black students. Black men from the South were five times more likely to score below average as their counterparts from New England. The costs associated with poor education had wide-ranging implications, effectively relegating African Americans to nonprofessional careers. Negative outcomes were even more dramatic for African American women. In 1950 Texas had a population of 501,834 Black women, but only 7,307, fewer than 2 percent, worked in professional occupations, the overwhelming majority, almost 85 percent (6,186), as teachers and another 6 percent, or 440, as nurses. In 1950 Texas had only nine Black women working as medical doctors. The situation for professional Black women in 1950 was poor, but it still represented improvement from 1900 when only 1,840 Texas Black women were considered professionals and 1,097, or almost 60 percent, were teachers, and substantially better than 1940 when 5,414 Black Texas women were considered professionals and 4,928, or 91 percent, were teachers.[5]

It would be years before significant changes would come, but an early effort at desegregating schools developed in Euless, a suburb between Fort Worth and Dallas. In October 1949 the parents of thirteen Black children in Mosier Valley, a historically Black neighborhood established by former slaves and free Blacks, sued the Euless Independent School District for violating separate but equal mandates by busing its Black students to Fort Worth rather than providing separate local schools. The lawsuit argued that the Euless district, which covered Mosier Valley, had an obligation under the doctrine of separate but equal to provide equal local facilities. District administrators countered that the few Black students made separate schools uneconomical and that the children received a better education at Riverside Negro Elementary School or Carver Negro School in the FWISD. In April 1950 FWISD official Elden Busby testified in US District Court that sixteen area school districts, including Euless, contracted with FWISD for Black education, adding that the district also received white students from twenty-two school districts that did not offer all grade levels. The court sided with the parents, ordering Euless to provide separate facilities or integrate, a ruling the district appealed.[6]

While the issue lingered in the courts, Black parents tried to register their children at Euless Elementary. In September 1950 35 Black school children were turned away to face an unruly crowd of 150 angry whites. The white protestors turned part of their ire on media representatives, punching Gene Gordon of the *Fort Worth Press* and taking both his camera and the camera of a Black photographer, but only warning a WBAP-TV cameraman to stop filming. The next day Euless began work on an abandoned school south of Highway 183, a dilapidated, two-room frame building without heat, electric power, or inside toilets, to convert into a Black elementary school. In the 1950s Fort Worth would annex Mosier Valley as part of its eastward expansion to Greater Southwest International Airport.[7]

The argument advanced in Euless, that the lack of available Black facilities effectively obviated pretensions to separate but equal, was adopted to attack inequities in higher education. The obvious inconsistency between the doctrine and poor to nonexistent Black colleges and graduate schools was so glaring that in 1947 the Texas legislature appropriated $3 million to build a

Black college in Houston and a Black law school at the University of Texas at Austin (UT). Hermann Sweatt, a Black man denied admittance to the UT Law School, sued, citing the inadequacy of the hastily created Black law school. The United States Supreme Court agreed in *Sweatt v. Painter* that the thrown-together Black law school was not equal to UT Law. In the autumn of 1950 Sweatt and three other Black men began studies at UT Law. One of the new students, Dudley Redd, operated the Red and White Café in Fort Worth. Redd expected to practice locally but failed to graduate.[8]

Health care was another critical human need diminished by segregation. In some cases medical care was simply not available; in others racial disparities downgraded the quality of care. Discrimination began with the trip to a hospital. Eight ambulance companies, most affiliated with local funeral homes such as Shannon's; Lucas, Owens, and Brumley; and Ray Crowder served Fort Worth's white citizens, but only Davis Ambulance transported Blacks. Once in an ambulance, Black emergency patients went to Black wards at John Peter Smith, the county supported hospital, or to limited Black facilities at St. Joseph's Hospital, Harris Hospital, or All Saints Hospital, or to ERMH, 1200 East First Street, operated by Dr. R. A. Ransom and his son, Dr. R. A. Ransom Jr. Dr. Ransom Sr., opened his hospital in 1919 at 417 East Fifth Street, then moved to 509 Grove Street before, in 1929, converting a rooming house of twenty rooms at 1200 East First Street into a small hospital. Along the way the hospital's name changed from Negro Baptist Hospital to Fort Worth Negro Hospital and finally to Ethel Ransom Memorial in memory of Dr. Ransom's wife (she died in 1937). Black hospitals, providing care for the lowest economic group, struggled to stay afloat financially. In 1949 city inspectors ordered ERMH to close by April 1 after deeming the structure a fire hazard and unsanitary. Dr. Ransom Sr. tried to relocate to the Carver Hotel Building on East Fifteenth Street, but city officials quashed the plan, citing the building's frame structure as a fire hazard.[9]

Long-term care for Black patients with chronic conditions ran into severe funding issues. In March 1946 City Health Director Dr. Berke Brewer suggested the city council add an African American wing to the Elmwood Tuberculosis Sanitarium to correct a deficiency since no local clinic accepted Black tuberculosis patients. In 1947 Fort Worth's Tuberculosis Society hired a social worker from Dallas, Nancy Kinnebrew Goss, to oversee Black care, taking over the task from Black staff borrowed from the state tuberculous association. Ms. Goss was well qualified, having done graduate work at the University of Michigan and the University of Chicago. Dr. Ransom Sr. tried to relieve a shortage of long-term care providers for African Americans by opening a care home at the Carver Hotel to house three African Americans with chronic conditions. Once again, city inspectors intervened, citing the doctor for operating a health care facility without a permit. In a rare display of understanding, the Fort Worth Corporation Court acquitted the physician, ruling he had acted in good faith and had since transferred all three patients to a licensed facility. Inadequate health care for Blacks was not just a Fort Worth problem. In 1949 Dr. R. C. Rowell, superintendent of the State Hospital for Epileptics at Abilene, Texas, reported that no Blacks were among the hospital's 1,351 patients and that no state or private institution accepted African American epileptics. Despite the obvious need, a $400,000 appropriation to add two Black wings was left out of the 1949 state budget.[10]

Black soldiers in uniform did not escape racism. In November 1949 Wellington Valentine, an African American army corporal, was at the Zanzibar Café at 951 East Rosedale Street with three friends when two military policemen and two Fort Worth Police officers entered, reportedly in response to a report that one of the four had become intoxicated and loud. Valentine left the bar voluntarily only to be arrested outside by officers who struck him repeatedly, beating him and another Black serviceman while they were being transported to the Air Force detention facility. At the military jail Valentine was repeatedly slapped for being "a smart Nigger" and forced to fight another inmate. Corporal Valentine contacted the NAACP for their assistance in prosecuting the abuse. The organization's legal staff sent appeals to Secretary of the Air Force Stuart Symington.[11]

Whites most aggressively defended racial lines defining neighborhoods, using various tactics, including force, to block Blacks from all-white areas. In January 1947 a group led by Carter Riverside High School Principal T. E. Wentworth met at Avenue J Baptist Church, Wallace Avenue and Avenue J, to protest a Black subdivision planned for east of South Ayers Avenue and south of Rosedale Street. The city council solved the supposed problem by rejecting

E. F. Crites, Judge Marvin H. Brown, and W. A. Meacham at a Riverside Civic League Banquet, November 16, 1943. Courtesy *Fort Worth Star Telegram* Collection, Special Collections, University of Texas at Arlington Libraries.

the proposal, citing a lack of adequate city services, a fault that was totally within their power to correct. Two years later, in 1949, another Black housing project for the Rosedale Street and Evans Avenue neighborhood was met by intense white backlash that coalesced into the Home & Business Protective League (HBPL), formed that November at East Van Zandt School to resist "the incursion of the Negro into white areas." It followed the example set by the Riverside Civic League formed in 1943 in the Riverside area. Vernon Seals, 311½ Tennessee Street, chairman of the HBPL, was a committed segregationist who advocated expelling Blacks from Fort Worth. He suggested that George Armstrong, owner of Texas Steel and an ardent segregationist, build a residential subdivision outside the city limits where Blacks would have their own police, fire, bus service, and utilities. The league relocated to Harmony Baptist Church after school officials, citing the controversy, withdrew their sanction for meetings at East Van Zandt School. The HBPL asked white real estate agents to discourage Blacks from considering properties in white neighborhoods.

They also organized protests against the sale of Missouri Avenue Methodist Church (white) to St. Andrew's Methodist Church (Black). St. Andrews had outgrown its existing facility on 1063 East Rosedale Street while Missouri Avenue Methodist had been losing members.[12]

Integrated housing conflicts spread beyond the Rosedale Street and Lancaster Avenue areas of the eastside. In June 1950 Rosedale Park residents, meeting at Bible Baptist Church, 2700 Putnam Avenue on the fringes of east Fort Worth, asked developers behind a planned rental housing project to exclude Blacks, a request the builders promised to consider, assuring residents that they had no wish to lower property values, which would downgrade their rental rates. Also in June residents of Handley, slightly north and east of Rosedale Park, petitioned the Fort Worth City Council to block a proposed $2 million Black housing project planned for the area between Handley and Stop Six, the latter a historical Black neighborhood. B. T. Johnson, the group's attorney, warned that the development would become a refuge for rapists, making the area unsafe for women at night. The council pointed out that the proposed site was outside the city limits and, therefore, outside their control. The builder, Fox and Jacobs, abandoned the project anyway, stating they would find a location acceptable to all. In 1950 Fort Worth's near west side neighbors threatened lawsuits to stop African American–designated housing planned for the 1900 block of West Morphy Street. Herman Heath, president of the Forest Park Civic League leading the movement, expressed confidence, boasting that the group had defeated a similar proposal for North Mistletoe Heights.[13]

The success of white segregationists in blocking new Black-designated housing aggravated an already serious housing shortage at the same time that freeway construction created more demand. In 1949 the North-South Freeway extension from Rosedale Street to Morningside Drive displaced over 230 residential housing units, including 100 Black-owned properties. Affected homeowners were compensated for their properties and for costs to relocate their houses or to purchase suitable replacement housing, but finding suitable lots or alternative housing was a major problem for African Americans homeowners struggling in an already tight postwar housing market made worse by severe limits on where Blacks could relocate. The addition of Black citizens made homeless by freeway construction forced many families into unsuitable housing. The problem was national; in 1946 the National Urban League estimated that 80 percent of Black Americans lived in substandard housing. In 1950 the Supreme Court attacked segregated housing by invalidating property restrictions based on race, creed, or color. Following the ruling the FHA began requiring mortgage applicants affirm their property deeds did not carry racial restrictions. Ending housing segregation would take many more years, but the court ruling was an important step.[14]

As in school desegregation, opponents practiced evasion and resistance to blunt ameliorative measures, leaving Blacks to deal with racially imposed housing shortages for years. A broad *Star Telegram* survey published in July 1950 identified housing as the most pressing need facing Fort Worth's Black community. Many factors played a role in creating a severe housing crisis for African Americans, but perhaps most important was the growth of the Black population. The Black population of Fort Worth had surged 53 percent from 25,254 in 1940 to an estimated 40,000 in 1950, ten years later. Many of the new arrivals, Black and white, came seeking defense work. That population shift from rural to urban occurred at the same time that the war ended residential construction, creating a gap between demand and supply that only got worse. The FHA estimated that Fort Worth needed at least 2,000 dwellings but feared the actual need was much larger. As bad as the raw numbers were, they did not tell the whole story, especially concerning Blacks forced into unfit housing. The Fort Worth Housing Authority deemed 5,222 of 7,709 Black dwellings substandard, a condition they blamed on the dearth of new construction needed to replace the unsuitable. They were right about the lack of building; fewer than 200 of 22,786 building permits issued between 1940 and 1949 were for Black housing, statistics that jibed with estimates that only 250 to 500 new residences for Blacks had been built in all of the 1940s. The demand was certainly there; in 1950 a development of 100 new 4.5 room houses in Hollywood Hills (east of the Stop Six neighborhood) offered at $4,655, completely sold out.[15]

A remarkable study by Lady George Munchus-Forde in 1941 provided a wide range of statistics on Black economic conditions in Fort Worth that, although prewar, offered significant insights. The study began with a chamber of commerce report showing the average value of Black-owned homes was only $1,586 and that Blacks paid on average $13.39 per month for housing (rent or mortgage), but that many paid much less. The statistics confirmed that 4,056 Black families spent only $5 to $10 monthly for housing, 270 paying $5 or less. In contrast, few Black families lived in higher-end housing; only 504 Black families paid $15 to $20 monthly, only six paid $20 or more, and only one Black family lived in a home valued at $20,000 or more. In addition, Blacks tended to be renters rather than homeowners; only 1,852 Blacks were homeowners versus 4,056 renters. The lack of Black homeowners was positively correlated to presence of so few Blacks in professional occupations. In 1941 nine Black doctors, seven dentists, and four lawyers served all of Fort Worth.[16]

The scarcity of housing in designated Black neighborhoods coupled with a growing population left African Americans no other choice than to relocate into white neighborhoods, a move that often prompted robust responses. In 1946 Black encroachment into the Maddox Avenue–Rosedale Street area sparked a spate of bombings that damaged numerous homes and businesses, including the house of Edward Williams, a veteran, at 824 East Maddox Avenue, and the Apex Beauty Salon, 801 Missouri Street. In March the grand jury asked for witnesses or anyone with information concerning race-related bombings to appear and testify. No one showed up. Two years later, on May 25, 1948, a bomb did $1,000 in damage to a house at 1400 Evans Avenue, but the home's three occupants, Robert L. Macklin, a 27-year-old taxi driver, his wife Johnnie May and her sister, Ruby Lee Harris, escaped unharmed. The Macklins, the only Black family in the 1300 and 1400 blocks of Evans Avenue, had moved in only five days earlier after buying the home for $4,500. The former owner, Mrs. J. T. Lockley, reported receiving several bomb threats. Macklin and his brother-in-law, John Harris, began taking turns guarding the property all night. Five weeks later, the morning of July 1, 1948, around 3:00 a.m., Robert Macklin fired three shots at a white man he saw running from the hedges who had placed something under the house. Macklin threw the smoking bundle into the street where it exploded, damaging a curb. Days later, an arsonist struck the Stop Six Store, 1809 Amanda Avenue, off East Rosedale Street, doing $2,000 in damages to the business owned by A. O. Alexander, a white man. The blast caused no injuries, but a Black family living over the store moved out, saying they felt threatened. An African American woman, Almita Robinson, appeared before the city council to ask for more police protection. She told the group that Black families lived in constant fear of bombings.[17]

Housing was a serious problem, but African Americans were denied many urban accoutrements. Municipal libraries were closed to them except for a branch at the Black YWCA, 1916 Crump Street. Mrs. Ella Mae Shamblee served twenty years with the Fort Worth Public Library, retiring in 1946 after being the YWCA branch director for six years. Parks and recreation facilities were separate, relegating Blacks to either Lincoln Park on the north side, only 3½ acres with few amenities, or Greenway Park off East Belknap Street, the only fully developed park option covering sixty-six acres with ball fields and tennis courts, as well as a makeshift golf course built by citizens. In 1947 the city council, acting on a request from 100 citizens, spent $24,000 for forty-one acres east of Miller Street and north of Ramey Avenue to become a Black-designated park. In 1950 Jesse Mitchell of the Fort Worth Negro Golf Association petitioned the city council for access to Fort Worth's three eighteen-hole municipal golf courses or construction of a Black golf course. The park superintendent recommended building a Blacks-only golf course on city land just east of 1700 East Ninth Street.[18]

Several community organizations worked to improve the community. Some were Black versions of mainstream white organizations, such as the Black YWCA that offered classes in various skills and topics and other wholesome diversions for young African American women. A "Negro division" of the local Community Chest was created in 1951 with a $4,000 budget. The Bethlehem Center, sponsored by Methodist women, opened in 1940 at 929 Leuda Street, then moved to 970 East Humbolt Avenue in the most populous of Fort Worth's ten Black neighborhoods. The center offered family nights, classes for the blind, and training to develop the "civil, social, moral and spiritual life of Negroes." Fort Worth Blacks also organized local chapters of their own national organizations. The Fort Worth branch of the Urban League focused on improving health outcomes through lectures and instruction in family health practices and through events like Negro Health

Week held April 1948. The local NAACP chapter concentrated on developing political involvement via voter registration drives. In January 1947 its members distributed poll tax cards at Wayside Church of Christ in God. Through their efforts Mrs. Bertha Dews became the first African American deputized by Tarrant County to collect poll taxes; six others would soon follow in her footsteps. The local branch took a giant step forward, successfully subscribing a fund for a full-time secretary, the collection jump-started by a $200 annual pledge from Dr. R. A. Ransom Sr.[19]

Many other organizations were founded locally. In 1947 the Crime Prevention Society, a social welfare organization led by Reverend W. L. Brown of Macedonia Baptist Church, helped 586 adults find jobs, counseled 10,000 Black youths, cared for 30 delinquents released to their care by probation officers, and provided aid to another 70 adults, all on a $6,000 annual budget. In 1947 Our Lady of Mercy Negro Mission had 200 members and a school with 190 students. Father Brophy, a member of the Society of St. Joseph, a missionary order dedicated to work among African Americans, established the mission in 1932. The Lake Como Community Center, 5201 Wellesley Avenue, was dedicated in June 1948 thanks to $3,000 in donations that paid for the house and its remodeling. The center offered a range of recreations and space for girls and boys clubs, employment services, a health clinic, a library, a kindergarten, and a day nursery. In September 1950 a fundraiser to pay off the center's debt and expand its day nursery featured a mock election between Jackson Moore and W. H. Wilbur (both WWII veterans) for the "Bronze Mayor of Lake Como and Harlem Hills," the office going to whomever collected more money.[20]

By 1950 Fort Worth's African American community had developed a solid separate commercial and social infrastructure. A study that year listed the existing service providers:

Chart 10.1 African American Businesses in 1950

	No.
Theaters (plus 2 white theaters that allowed Blacks in their balconies)	4
Dance Halls	20

(*Continued*)

Chart 10.1 Continued

	No.
Cafes	91
BBQ Stands	15
Ice Cream Parlors	6
Taverns	30
Pool Halls	16
Hotels (rooms $2.00 to $2.50 nightly)	3
Dentists	7
Doctors (two older and semiretired)	6
Hospital (plus Black wards at city-county hospital and a few others)	1
School-Age Children	6,992
Black High School (I. M. Terrell)	1
Combined Elementary-Junior High Schools	5
Elementary Schools	4
Churches	69
Bank	1
Neighborhoods	14

Source: Fort Worth Star Telegram, July 30, 1950, p. 10.

The list omitted the YMCA where visiting Black athletic teams stayed and the Black YWCA on the north side.

One of Fort Worth's most prominent Black churches, Mount Gilead Baptist, endured a major leadership schism that spilled over into the courts. In 1947 police were called on a Sunday to break up a melee between supporters of Reverend W. M. Bowden and an opposition group headed by Deacon Robert Wilson that sought Reverend Bowden's removal. The confrontation turned violent after Bowden supporters refused to accept a plebiscite that approved his ouster, 114 to 29. Bowdenites charged the results were fraudulent, that nonmembers, including children and "crap-shooters," had been allowed to vote. Reverend W. C. Jones claimed the pulpit but Bowden, supported by the Negro Baptist Ministers Union, took the matter to the Sixty-Seventh District Court. Judge Walter Morris, telling the litigants that they were acting "as bad as white people," ordered another vote overseen by a neutral authority, a logical step that nonetheless failed when the two sides could not agree on the third party, sending the dispute back to court. Judge Morris appointed an outsider, R. V. Nichols, a deacon of Broadway Baptist Church and a lawyer, as a court master charged to find a compromise resolution. The opposition called the order the same as binding mediation and balked, filing a protest in the Ninety-Sixth District Court while the pro-Bowden faction returned to the Sixty-Seventh District Court, where Judge Morris, probably relieved at the opportunity, dismissed the suit in favor of the other court. The Ninety-Sixth District Court took bold action, restoring Bowden to the pulpit and prohibiting Reverend Jones and seven other opposition leaders from interfering with church activities. Jones and sixty followers vowed to attend services that Sunday but promised not to cause a disturbance.[21]

Segregation was so pervasive and strongly defended that few incidents of Black resistance appeared in the 1940s. In August 1948 Fort Worth Police officers responded to Hilltop Park (Black designated) after whites reported Blacks had forced them to leave the tennis courts. By the time officers arrived, all parties were gone. The same month police were called to a downtown drug store after a Black man demanded food service. The insistent customer, an East Indian, was released after the store refused to sign a complaint. City buses, strictly segregated by criminal statutes, became the scene of several racial confrontations. John Willie Horn, an African American, was arrested July 26, 1948, after a white man complained that Horn sat next him and refused to move. Horn claimed he had simply fallen into the seat when the bus stopped suddenly. Horn's employer, a white man, paid his bond and took him to the Buxton Clinic, 4139 West Rosedale Street, for treatment of body welts and facial bruises that Horn claimed came from police beating him with a rubber hose. Despite the injuries, Horn refused to lodge a complaint, saying that "it wouldn't do any good." The employer did complain, sparking an investigation in which the officers admitted a physical altercation that occurred when Horn became "arrogant" and uncooperative, requiring force to get him into a cell. In January 1950 Leonard House, a 21-year-old Black man, was stabbed when he refused to give up his bus seat to a white man standing in the aisle. The irony was that House was sitting in the Black section near the rear door where the white man had been moved due to overcrowding.

House said he agreed to move when he debussed at the next stop, North Main and Thirty-Third Streets, but was stabbed just below the heart when he rose to leave. No arrest reports followed, suggesting no charges were ever filed—no great surprise since police tended to be rather lax in investigating white on Black crimes. On July 4, 1949, Black residents chased and detained a panel truck carrying eight young white men who had driven through Como hurling "torpedo bomb fireworks" at residents. The young whites confessed, saying they were just "having fun." Six juveniles were let go with only lectures while two 17-year-olds were charged with malicious mischief and released on $10 bonds.[22]

Postwar Fort Worth African Americans began a campaign for Black police officers, something many cities, including some in the South, had already done. In 1946 the Interdenominational Ministerial Alliance joined the Urban League and Reverend Louis Martin, rector of St. Andrews Episcopal Church, in petitioning the city council for Black police officers. The council initially rejected the proposal based on negative reactions from City Manager W. O. Jones and Police Chief R. E. Dysart. Dysart claimed Black officers could only patrol Black neighborhoods, at variance with the premise that police officers should serve all citizens. He added that cities with Black officers had reported that "these people" (Black police officers) had failed to obtain cooperation and assistance "from their own people." Both Dysart and Jones also suggested that it would be difficult to find suitable applicants. Fourteen months later five African American men registered for the police entrance exam after new state civil service rules opened the door to all applicants. All five had at least two years of college, a rarity in American policing of the period. Robert B. Howard and Clarence Pollard each had two years of college, and Ollice M. Thomas, a teacher at I. M. Terrell High School, and his brother Lawrence L. Thomas were graduates of Wiley College, while Edward L. Willis graduated from Lincoln University. Only Ollice Thomas passed the written test, but he withdrew from the oral portion after learning he would have to resign as codirector of distributive education at Terrell. At the next exam, June 27, 1949, seven Black males registered and two passed, although one subsequently withdrew. The remaining Black applicant, F. L. Willis, made it to the eligibility list, where he sat and waited, repeatedly passed over by the city council and police administrators. In 1951 the Interdenominational Ministerial Alliance revived the issue, pointing out that Fort Worth was the only major Texas city without Black officers. The group protested when Chief Howerton continued to ignore Willis, who met all the requirements.[23]

The police and the law enforcement system in general had a problematic relationship with Black Americans. For years Fort Worth Police maintained separate sections dedicated to crimes committed by African Americans. In September 1945 C. D. Bush and W. E. B. Kearney were in charge of Negro Thefts and Burglaries in the detective office. A typical police response to any crime surge was to bring in in dozens of Black men for questioning. In October 1945 a sustained increase in assaults resulted in police raids on five Black nightclubs, where officers arrested seventy patrons and confiscated two firearms. Adjudicating Black suspects made an important advance in the narrow sense that lynchings declined nationally and ended locally. The last person lynched in Fort Worth, Fred Rouse, was murdered in 1921, but the threat remained viable, especially for Blacks charged with sexual assaults involving white women. In reality, the legal process reacted so quickly and harshly in Black on white crimes that little distinguished it from lynching. On August 16, 1948, a 33-year-old newly married white woman was sexually assaulted at her home near Ten Mile Bridge Road. She escaped to notify authorities, sparking a manhunt involving numerous police officers aided by a large citizens' posse and three airplanes to search the rural area around the home. An aircraft spotting a suspect, identified by his red shirt, and was able to land and detain Cleveland Stovall Jr. Stovall had recently been released from prison for stealing $3 from a telephone coin box. After he confessed to the assault, police moved Stovall to an undisclosed jail in another city to forestall a lynching. District Attorney Al Clyde, exclaiming that "swift justice is essential in this type of case," recalled the grand jury (jurors were on scheduled vacation until August 24) to issue an indictment and had the Tarrant County sheriff notify state highway patrols between Texas and Yellowstone Park to locate the district judge who was on a driving vacation. It took a lot of effort, but the trial began on August 30, 1948, two weeks after the assault; Clyde, apologizing for the delay, explained that along with all the other issues, the seriousness of the case required a large jury pool and the assignment of a defense lawyer. On August 30 the trial began with jury selection that ran until 3:00 p.m., followed by three hours of testimony and summations, then a break for dinner, after which the jury deliberated forty minutes before issuing a guilty verdict and sentencing Stovall to death, the whole affair taking a total of ten hours. Stovall appealed but was denied by the Texas Court of Criminal Appeals in June 1949. Three months later, September 11, 1949, he was executed at Huntsville State Prison, one year and twenty-six days after the crime.[24]

Assaults on two white women in one week in March 1950 launched a general roundup of Black men. In one sweep police picked up 150 African American men in the south end of downtown around the Texas Employment Commission, 921 Lamar Street, quite some distance from the crime scenes on the north side and near Magnolia and Eighth Avenues on the short southside. All were released after questioning failed to produce usable leads. Wholesale detentions without probable cause for "investigation" were not only common but also defended by Chief Hawkins as necessary to prevent the "criminal class" from causing "trouble." On March 25, 1950, Arthur Lee Sherrod, a 20-year-old Black man, was arrested following an attempted assault on a 71-year-old white woman on Samuels Avenue. Sherrod confessed to other assaults and was sentenced to life in prison, a rare defeat for the prosecution, which had sought the death penalty.[25]

Racism played a major role in the 1948 presidential election, both at the national and local level. President Harry S. Truman, running for his own term in 1948, faced Southern backlash over his challenges to segregation, splitting the Democrats and threatening the party's Southern dominance. Truman's supporters, led by Texas Governor Beauford Jester, held a barbecue dinner in Fort Worth in April 1948. George W. Armstrong, former owner of a local steel company and ardent reactionary and segregationist, was one of Truman's most vocal critics. Armstrong carried extreme political positions, calling Franklin Roosevelt a socialist, railing about Northern Communists and socialists who he was convinced ruled the United States, and advocating the disenfranchisement of African Americans through repeal of the Constitution's Fourteenth and Fifteenth Amendments. Armstrong ran a paid political statement in the *Star Telegram* addressed to "My Fellow Citizens," urging voters to turn from the mainstream Democratic Party and to the Southern candidate running as a Dixiecrat. After Truman's election Armstrong tried to seize control of the Jefferson Military Academy of Natchez, Mississippi, offering a $50 million endowment, conditional on his right to appoint three of the five trustees, giving him majority control that he planned to use to exclude Blacks and Asians and ensure the teaching of white racial superiority. Jefferson Military Academy was no liberal bastion—the school had already banned Blacks—but balked at ceding control. The trustees rejected the offer.[26]

The 1949 city council elections were notable for having thirty-two candidates, the most ever for the nine council seats, and for including two African American candidates, Robert L. Thornton, running for Place 4, and H. J. Blackwell for Place 8. Their candidacies worried racists, although neither had much of a realistic chance with, at most, only 7,000 Blacks registered out of 32,000 eligible voters. Robert Lee Thornton, born in Paris, Texas, where he graduated from the Negro High School in 1926, claimed an impressive background as the first Black recruiter in World War II, a graduate of the University of California at Los Angeles (UCLA), holder of a master's degree from New York University (NYU) and a teacher of distributive education classes at Prairie View University from 1944 to 1948. It was all too good to be true, and it was not. The Navy confirmed Thornton had served as a recruiter in 1943 and 1944, but was not the first Black to do so, and both UCLA and NYU denied Thornton had earned degrees or had ever registered as a student. The entire Tarrant County delegation to the Texas legislature presented a resolution condemning Prairie View University for hiring Thornton without verifying his credentials. The college dismissed him, although they cited expense account issues and not false credentials as the cause. Just days before the election Thornton canceled his campaign, claiming the physical and mental strain was too much, but his withdrawal came too late to remove him from the ballot. He received 526 votes, coming in last in a multiperson contest won by J. R. Edwards, with 8,300 votes. The second Black candidate, H. J. Blackwell, carried three boxes and received 882 votes but lost to Ed Baker.[27]

A Fort Worth African American who had risen to wealth and political prominence died and a new leader emerged. One of the state's primary forces promoting African American economic and political clout, William M. "Gooseneck Bill" McDonald, succumbed in 1950 at his home, 1201 East Terrell Street, where illness had confined him for two years. McDonald, Texas's first Black millionaire, became a dominant figure in Texas Republican Party politics from 1896 to 1912 before the "Lily-Whites" took over the party. He was laid to rest in the Trinity Colored Cemetery on Grand Avenue. McDonald's fortunes had sunk over the years, but he left an estimated $100,000 estate to his fifth wife. In 1948 Dr. George D. Fleming of Fort Worth was appointed to the executive board of the national NAACP, catapulting him to national recognition. General John J. Pershing, commander of the American Expeditionary Force in World War I, died in 1948, leaving funeral instruction for Sergeant Charley Wycoff, an African American stationed at Carswell, to blow taps at his funeral. Colonel Alan D. Clark, Carswell field officer, was sure the wishes would be respected.[28]

African Americans were the most visibly oppressed group, but others also faced discrimination. The Asian population of the United States in the 1940s remained small, amounting to only 321,000 in the 1950 Census, miniscule compared to 15 million African Americans. The Asian presence in Texas was even more limited, but despite their small population, Asians still faced discrimination. In January 1947 actor Dean Jagger flew to Albuquerque, New Mexico, to marry Gloria Jean Ling after the couple were refused a California marriage license due to state laws prohibiting marriage between Caucasians and "Orientals." That June a bill removing restrictions from American GIs marrying Japanese women went to the United States Senate after passing the House. The bill faced surprisingly little opposition, perhaps due to the conviction that not many veterans would take advantage.[29]

Hispanics, largely from Mexico, represented a significant slice of the national population, numbering 3.2 million in the 1950 Census. They were a large historical presence in Texas and Fort Worth. In the 1950 Census 2.9 percent of Fort Worth's population, or 8,139, had a Spanish surname, but due to undercounting and language issues, the actual number of residents of Hispanic descent would certainly have been much higher. Like African Americans, Hispanics faced overt racism and discrimination. Journalists regularly used derogatory terms. A 1947 newspaper article, "13 HOT 'WETBACKS' FOUND," reported thirteen undocumented aliens discovered inside a truck, and a 1950 article described the journey of five "Wetbacks" from Guanajuato, Mexico, who took a $120 taxi ride from Del Rio, Texas, to Fort Worth ("wetback" was a derogatory term for Hispanics derived from the idea that unregistered immigrants entered the United States by swimming the Rio Grande River). Mexican immigrants and their descendants in Fort Worth's "Mexican colony" celebrated Columbus Day in 1947 at San Jose Catholic Church, where they named Lupe Rivera queen. On January 9, 1948, a four-page monthly publication, *El Eco Latino*, became Fort Worth's first true Spanish-language newspaper, replacing a mimeographed newsletter, *El Boletin.* The record concerning development of a local culture is largely undone, at least in anything other than a few anecdotal accounts. Certainly, we know it was there, but the history remains largely unwritten, with a few exceptions. By the early 1940s Marine Theater on North Main Street ran Mexican and other Spanish-language films seven days a week, and a local baseball team, the Aztecs, played teams from other cities. While "Mexicans" attended Fort Worth's white schools, their status in other institutions, such as medical care, was limited. In 1948 Dr. R. A. Ransom, operator of a clinic for Blacks at 1200 East First Street, was charged with performing an abortion on a "Mexican" girl. Dr. Ransom denied the allegation, asking that everyone withhold judgment until the trial. The incident suggests that while Hispanics had some access to the white health system, at times they turned to African American clinics.[30]

Many Anglos valued the contributions Mexican workers made to the economy. Judge Joe Montague represented the Texas and Southwest Cattle Raisers Association before a United States congressional hearing reviewing the Justice Department's accelerated program of capturing and returning undocumented Mexican laborers. Montague and the association opposed the program as inimical to the need for general agricultural labor, then in short supply. Anglo support rested more on hard economics than altruism. The existing treaty covering Mexicans working in the United States set a minimum rate of $2.05 per hundredweight for cotton pickers, a price many farmers and ranchers bypassed by hiring unregistered pickers they could pay less.[31]

Chapter 11

The Postwar Economy

Preparation for the postwar began while fighting still raged. Planners recognized that transitioning to a peacetime economy presented many challenges for returning veterans and businesses. A 1945 federal aid package gave veterans hiring preferences in civil service positions and increased rationed food allocations for new business ventures to help jump-start nondefense commercial startups that had been largely nonexistent since March 1, 1942. Fort Worth launched a program to make significant infrastructure upgrades to the sewer and water systems in anticipation of increased demands when veterans returned home, swelling the population. The challenges posed by the postwar economic transformation looked so daunting that many feared an economic downturn that would throw the United States into another depression cycle.[1]

Postwar planning accelerated with Germany's surrender in May 1945 but was constrained by prevailing projections that the Pacific war would run into 1946 or even beyond. The $85 billion federal budget for the fiscal year beginning October 1, 1945, assumed the war would last through the summer of 1946. Still, the end of the European front brought significant changes, decreasing defense appropriations $20 billion to $70 billion for the 1945–1946 fiscal year and beginning a massive rerouting of railroad rolling stock to redeploy men and equipment from the East to the West Coast, an enormous task that would require 65,000 additional workers, 4,500 in the Southwest alone, in an already stretched labor market.[2]

Japan's surrender brought wild celebrations, but also abrupt and massive cutbacks in defense outlays, creating uncertainty for American workers. On August 13, 1945, a Monday, Fort Worth celebrated VJ Day with more intensity than it greeted VE Day. Banks and shops closed, people shot off fireworks, and hundreds drove through downtown, honking and cheering while late-night partyers filled clubs to the wee hours, thanks to the end of curfews that May (a national midnight curfew for places of entertainment had been issued in February 1945). Even before the party started, production cutbacks were well under way with shifts canceled that Saturday, August 11, for most defense industries. On August 15 the *Star Telegram* reported rampant wholesale contract cancelations and warned more were expected within twenty-four hours. The cancelations created massive layoffs. By August 17, 1945, an estimated 42,000 workers across the nation were idled; by the end of September the number rose to 960,913, including 600,000 dismissed the last week of August who filed for $20 weekly unemployment benefits. In August the federal government lifted manpower controls for nineteen North Texas counties, although retaining them in Tarrant County. The sea of suddenly unemployed workers seemed certain to be swelled by large numbers of returning military personnel, posing a dire situation that Texas newspaper editors chose as the top story of 1945. In May 1945 some 8.3 million Americans were in the military; by Christmas 3 million were discharged and 4 million more were released that summer, adding 7 million to the ranks of the jobless. The local economy reeled from canceled increases in B-32 production that eliminated 10,000 jobs in just one year, approximately 50 percent of Convair's workforce.[3]

Cancelations and cutbacks were a serious blow to the local economy, but even in the chaos hopeful signs emerged. On August 17, Convair, already beset by cancellation of the B-32 contract, cut back to one forty-hour shift a week and glum company officials refused to deny more layoffs were planned. On the Monday after VJ Day, the local USES received 1,641 applicants but referred only 641. Despite the poor showing, the office remained optimistic, pointing out that 462 new jobs had recently opened and another 2,525 were expected within a month. The actual figures came in significantly better, with 2,948 new jobs added by August 28 at the same time that 2,500 women and students left the labor market to return to homemaking or to attend school. Harold Foster, assistant manager of the chamber of commerce, painted a rosy picture, predicting that jobs would be plentiful, although he conceded that wages might fall 10 percent. Foster proved to be overly optimistic for the short-term. In mid-October 1945 the number of registered unemployed reached 7,984, approximately 8 percent of the local workforce—high but not close to Depression-era percentages. Overall, the Fort Worth economy seemed stressed but capably began the postwar transition.[4]

Things were difficult during the initial transition period, but Fort Worth survived the outbreak of peace without severe long-term economic problems thanks to its success at maintaining most existing industries while also developing new business ventures. In 1946 the four local aircraft manufacturers, Convair, Globe, Johnson Aircraft, and American Eagle, were either producing aircraft or scheduled to begin soon. Convair, the largest, was best positioned, with sufficient orders to last three years, and Globe Aircraft had a stable outlook, with an $18 million backlog of military and civilian orders for its Swift GC-1A. Unfortunately, the backlog and stability evaporated, leaving Globe near bankruptcy and forced into reorganization with $1.5 million in debts and no cash. Fort Worth's other major industry, meat packing, actually came out of the war and into the postwar stronger and richer than ever. In 1944 and 1945 approximately 406,000 head of livestock worth $145 million passed through the Fort Worth Stockyards, a huge figure that dwarfed the $2.43 million value of livestock traded in 1916 just prior to American entry into World War I. Fort Worth's major munition plants, Texas Steel and American Manufacturing, kept some of their war production while successfully diversifying into other products. Conversion and adaption of defense industries helped, but civilian construction, mothballed in the war, proved to be the critical force driving postwar economic success. In the first three months of 1946, city building permits reached $8 million, much of the work dedicated to opening 2,522 new businesses during the fiscal year ending October 31, 1946. The expanding old and new businesses created 24,600 new jobs, raising total employment to 116,000 in December 1946, an impressive 15,000 more than the wartime peak of 101,000. Jobs drew in workers, adding 85,000 residents, increasing Fort Worth's population to an estimated 293,000 in 1945.[5]

Another major force smoothing the economic transition lay in pent-up demand for consumer goods, items that were largely unavailable during the war. The full impact of that demand may have been delayed by rationing and price controls that lingered well past September 1945, although some were eased. The first new 1946 car for the civilian market rolled off the assembly line on August 13, 1945, and the first new car delivered in Fort Worth in four years arrived in October, a Ford donated for the use of the chief of police. It would take time for automobile production to catch up to demand, leaving many buyers to enter waiting lists that reserved 25 percent of new cars for veterans and gave priorities to traveling salesmen. While the OPA no longer rationed cars, it continued setting their prices at the average cost in January 1942, with adjustments for engineering changes. Perhaps no area held more pent-up demand as construction of infrastructure and new homes, both virtually eliminated during the war. In the first year after peace in September 1945, federal, state, and local governments awarded $2.5 billion in public works contracts. Texas broke ground on a $175 million highway construction program and began building cabins, tourist facilities, lodges, and roads at Big Bend and other state parks. Fort Worth eased construction restrictions in May 1945, permitting projects up to $1,000, then removed all restrictions in September, resulting in a flood of more than $2 million in city building permits in just two months, the most since 1942. In October 1945 Fort Worthians overwhelmingly approved the $20 million bond package funding several construction projects, and in November TCU kicked off a $4 million construction campaign. In 1946 most remaining restrictions ended when the WPB removed twelve commodities from rationing.[6]

Fort Worth's economic transition benefited from an aggressive campaign to capture available federal money. Fort Worth was the first city in its four-state region to apply for Federal Works Agency funding, winning $5,600 for survey work for a $200,000 waterworks project, followed by successful applications funding survey work on two huge reservoirs that were part of a $17 million Trinity River flood control project. In June 1945 Fort Worth added grant applications for six new fire stations, improvements to Marine Creek, and an extension of the North Main Bridge, costing $69,000. Credit for the early aggressive appeals owed a lot to the chamber of commerce's 1943 Postwar Planning Committee's master plan to speed postwar economic conversion through expanding facilities in the aviation industry, transitioning defense plants into civilian production, and restoring free enterprise (removing price controls and rationing). In August 1945 the city council acknowledged a debt to the committee's construction plan in its launch of a $20 million bond package for $6 million in waterworks projects and $19 million for rights of way for interstate highways (other funds making up the difference). The centrality of the chamber's economic focus can be seen in its 1945 slogan, "Winning the War Comes First! Winning the Peace Comes Next."[7]

The flush of funding eased but did not completely eliminate transition trauma. Those at the bottom of the labor pool fared the worst as demand for unskilled labor dropped while the market for skilled and semiskilled workers remained strong. On February 1, 1946, J. R. Ellis, area director of the USES, lamented that the registry held only 1,392 job openings but 11,000 unemployed workers, more than twice the 5,000 on file in August 1945, just before the war ended. Ellis attributed the rise in unemployment to layoffs in aircraft and ordnance industries and a construction slowdown from material shortages that many blamed on labor strikes.[8]

By 1947 the local economic picture began to show improvement as employment increased 11,900 for the year, rising to 111,400, while unemployment dropped to 7,300. Ninety percent, or 10,800, of the new hires in 1946 were returning servicemen referred by USES, a success that left only 2,000 ex-GIs receiving servicemen's readjustment allowance—a sharp decline from 4,070 in April 1946. Many new employees went to work at one of the 2,374 (also reported as 2,522) new businesses opening in 1946, the most since 1943. Most of the new concerns were small, but together they added $50 million to the area's annual payroll. The Fort Worth Stockyards also had a good year in 1946, although overall receipts were down slightly from the previous year. Cattle and calves received fell to 1.35 million and sheep, which had set all-time records in 1945, also declined, but Fort Worth remained the world's largest sheep market. In contrast, swine (567,000) and horses and mules (70,000) arrived in greater numbers than in 1945. The strong economy enabled Fort Worth to register a 20 percent increase in employment, better than Dallas's 6.9 percent, San Antonio's 10.4 percent, or Houston's 3.6 percent. The 1946 employment surge was part of a six-year span in which Fort Worth's workforce increased 56 percent, from 76,000 in 1940 to 120,000 in 1946. Most of the new jobs lay in manufacturing. Between 1940 and 1946 Fort Worth experienced a 259 percent increase in production workers, the most of the fifty largest United States cities. Much of that jump was due to Convair, which still employed 10,500 in 1947, ranking as the largest employer in the Southwest with a monthly payroll of $1.5 million (an average of $142.85 per worker, per month). The Stockyards, the largest south of Kansas City, Missouri, and its associated businesses employed another 7,000. Convair and the packinghouses provided the economic base that spawned 2,522 new businesses, creating 14,000 new jobs in 1947. The new concerns joined the existing commercial sector of 2,603 retails shops, 436 wholesalers with $285 million in annual sales, and 575 manufacturers. All the businesses, large and small, produced over $1 billion in annual bank clearing and a per capita income of $1,439.[9]

Improving economic conditions forced some dislocations. Evictions from Ripley Arnold Housing Project, suspended during the war, resumed as rising wages pushed families beyond the $1,600 annual limit. Between 1942 and 1946 some 490 families had voluntarily moved out, but forced evictions were suspended until 1947. In 1949 the Fort Worth Housing Authority began upgrades to the Victory Apartments in White Settlement, the former Liberator Village, which was still home to 300 families despite many units having fallen into substandard conditions. The remodeling converted the barracks-like structures into one, two, and three-room apartments renting for $30 to $40 per month. Vacancies at the bottom rung of the economic scale signaled that the housing crisis had begun to subside, although it would take more time for the effect to be complete.[10]

Between 1939 and 1947 the Fort Worth economy outperformed all Texas cities over 100,000 population in percentage growth in wages and number of workers. The economic effects arrived dramatically in 1940 when the number of manufacturing employees almost doubled compared to 1939, to

13,955. The upward movement continued at a significant pace. Between 1939 and 1947 total wages rocketed from $7.2 million to $58.4 million, an incredible 708 percent rise that eclipsed Dallas's 343 percent, Houston's 325 percent and San Antonio's 306 percent. Much of the increase stemmed from growth in industrial workers from 7,000 in 1939 to 25,000 in 1947, a 257 percent climb compared to only 94 percent for Dallas. Another study covering 1940 to 1947 confirmed the remarkable growth. In that period the number of manufacturing workers increased 144 percent in Fort Worth, the nation's largest percentage gain, while Dallas tied with Milwaukee for second with a 54 percent rise, San Antonio was fourth with 53 percent, and Houston was fifth with 52 percent. In 1947 Fort Worth's total wages, $58.2 million, were larger than Dallas's $57.2 million and almost equal to New Orleans's $59 million.[11]

Between 1940 and 1947 Fort Worth recorded the nation's fifth highest percentage increase (224 percent) in dollar amount of checks, all the more spectacular since no other Texas city ranked in the top eighteen. A similar result was seen in bank debits, which rose 257 percent, the largest increase in the state, exceeding Houston's 231 percent (third) or Dallas's 225 percent (fifth) and sufficient to rank Fort Worth twenty-ninth nationally. The increase continued in 1948 when bank clearings reached $1.3 billion. The robust banking activity supported increases in commercial activity that expanded Fort Worth's retail sales from $92 million in 1939 to $369 million in 1948, a 297 percent increase that ranked seventh in the state, behind sixth place Houston (256 percent), fifth place Dallas (262 percent), and fourth place San Antonio (263 percent). The rest of Texas also did well, with seven cities placing in the top fourteen nationally. Corpus Christi led the nation with a 320.1 percent increase in retail sales, followed by El Paso at 299.1 percent, while Fort Worth with 297.1 percent ranked fifth, San Antonio tenth, Dallas eleventh, Houston twelfth, and Austin fourteenth (no percentages were provided for the last four). In addition, Tarrant County's wholesale volume surged 338 percent, rising from $148 million in 1939 to $649 million in 1948, making Tarrant County the fourth largest retail and wholesale center in the Southwest after Harris and Dallas Counties and Orleans Parish, Louisiana.[12]

In the 1940s Fort Worth's population also had the second largest percentage increase of any Texas large city (San Antonio was first with 60.9 percent growth), adding almost 57 percent to its population to reach 277,047 in 1950, up from 177,662 in 1940, although a substantial portion of the growth came from annexation. Tarrant County provided a broader study unaffected by annexations. In the 1940s the county added 60 percent to its population, rising from 225,521 in 1940 to 361,253 in 1950, significantly outperforming the overall state increase of 20 percent to reach 7.7 million. The second largest Tarrant County city, White Settlement, had a population of 10,836, followed by Arlington with 7,691. Population growth aggravated an already strained housing situation, stimulating home construction that began to close the gap between demand and supply. In 1947 a $3.5 million development of 500 houses, each costing between $5,000 and $6,000, began in the Diamond Hill neighborhood north of Twenty-Eighth Street and west of Denton Road. Downtown development included a five-story Leonard's Brothers building at First and Throckmorton Streets, adjacent and just south of their three-story center and the $2.9 million Continental Life Building, a five-story structure planned for Seventh and Main Streets, former home of the Burton Building that was demolished in 1949. All the work pushed building permits steadily upward, to $22.9 million in 1946, $27.8 million in 1947, and $29.5 million in 1948.[13]

All the economic good news was reflected in selected statistics comparing 1940 and 1950. The results for the first three categories—bank clearings, bank debits and building permits—are striking in their scale as increases ranged from 257 to over 500 percent.

Chart 11.1 Statistical Comparison Between 1940 and 1950

	1940	1950	% Increase
Bank Clearings	$345 million	$1.2 billion	257
Bank debits	$1 billion	$3.8 billion	278
Building Permits	$4.8 million	$29.9 million	523
Water meters	46,169	71,000	54
Manufacturers with 10 or more employees	1,049	1,785	70

(Continued)

Chart 11.1 Continued

	1940	1950	% Increase
Labor force	98,900	146,500	48
City employees	1,496	2,386	59
Square miles	58.1	102.5	76
Property valuation	$167 million	$367 million	119

Source: Fort Worth Star Telegram, June 27, 1950, p. 14.

Many cities benefited from the huge defense industry wrought by World War II, but Fort Worth's experience seemed unique in degree. Mayor T. J. Harrell boasted that few cities had made more of an industrial contribution to the war effort than Fort Worth. Convair was the major factor behind that boast, but many businesses contributed to Fort Worth's industrial and commercial development during World War II. Between 1939 and 1947 Fort Worth added ninety-eight manufacturing plants, a 34 percent increase from 284 to 382 that multiplied the number of production workforce 257 percent and payrolls a whopping 708 percent. Commercial development did not stop at the city limits; in 1945 some 1,116 Tarrant County companies employed eight or more workers. Growth at such an accelerated level would not have been possible absent the major stimulus that accompanied huge defense budgets. Texas did not receive a particularly large share of wartime defense contracts, but Fort Worth companies won more military contracts than any other Texas city, outshining Dallas, Houston, and San Antonio. Between June 1, 1940, and October 1, 1944, just over four years, the United States appropriated $205 billion for defense, of which Texas received only $7,560,140,000 in defense contracts, or less than 4 percent. However, Tarrant County and Fort Worth garnered the lion's share, 22 percent, or $1,679,160,000 in defense contract, compared to just $930,951,000, or 12 percent, for Dallas County. Defense contracts amounted to a mere $2,100 per capita for Dallas, hardly a pittance compared to $6,000 per capita in Fort Worth. Part of the credit for that result may have been owed to the Fort Worth Chamber of Commerce's prescient move to begin planning for the coming war and its aftermath.[14]

Industrial growth led to corresponding population increases, putting serious demands on the area's infrastructure. Mayor Harrell cited industrial expansion as the catalyst behind a 25 percent population surge, from 207,667 in 1940 to 259,102 in 1945, and a 33 percent rise in the labor force, from 76,054 in 1940 to 102,000 in 1944, the last full year of the war. The explosion in civilian population at the same time that thousands of airmen arrived at Tarrant Field and surrounding bases prolonged the crises in housing and city services, creating problems that lingered long after the war.[15]

All the economic upswings helped relieve indigent care, but funding for charities faced mounting problems in the postwar period. In 1942 the local Red Cross collected $214,509, oversubscribing its fund by $60,000, perhaps a reflection of war patriotism driving support for an agency devoted to emergency incident relief. After 1945 local charities again faced increasing demands that stretched resources. The Union Gospel Mission, 1514 Houston Street, directed by the Reverend Joesph Green, was a critical provider of basic human needs to the dispossessed. In February 1947 the mission provided 889 nights of free lodging and 826 free meals, averaging thirty people fed and housed each day. In addition to food and shelter, the mission held religious services each day at 5:00 p.m. (faculty and students from Southwestern Baptist Theological Seminary conducted the services on Fridays and Saturdays), receiving seventy-four professions of faith in February 1947. In March 1947 the Milk and Ice Fund, another private charity, reported daily demand had increased to 2,000 quarts costing $0.185 each, ballooning expenditures 300 percent, a demand that so outstripped donations that the fund accumulated an $8,100 overdraft, the largest in its history. The dire financial situation forced a pay-as-you-go policy, but the debt continued to grow, hitting $11,000 despite pleas for donations. The Goodfellow Fund, a private Christmas charity run by the *Star Telegram*, ended the 1941 season with a $1,100 deficit on expenditures of $11,630, with the majority, $7,262, spent not on toys and candy but on basic clothing so poor children could attend school. The funding struggle resumed postwar, leaving a $2,048 deficit on expenditures of $36,336 in 1946. The Community Chest, providing lunches for underprivileged children, had to scrape to cover a two-cent increase boosting lunches to fourteen cents. In February 1947 the county juvenile office reported dependency cases had put the County Children's Home at capacity and were straining capacity at Lena Pope Home.[16]

The war and Cold War were the major economic forces of the 1940s, but Fort Worth also experienced the effects of an incipient migration pattern that favored the Sunbelt, the warmer regions of the South and Southwest. In the five years between 1944 and 1949, commercial development in the Southeast, Southwest, and West outstripped the national average, while the Northwest lagged slightly and New England, the Mideast, and the Midwest performed significantly below average. The positive effect was most pronounced in Florida, Arizona, and California, the three states accounting for 48 percent of all business growth, but Texas shared in the disproportionate growth.[17]

The war complemented and accelerated that national economic transformation benefiting states in the South and West, helping to improve their economic position relative to the North and East and creating a widespread industrial base that survived and expanded in the postwar. A War Production Board study found that American manufacturing increased 51 percent during World War II, a tremendous national achievement in only four years. That increase was led by twenty-one states that outperformed the national average, particularly ten states, nine in the South and West, that more than doubled their industrial equipment holdings. Texas ranked fifth in percentage increase, rising from the fourteenth largest in industrial output in 1939 to tenth largest in 1944.[18]

Chart 11.2 Top Ten States in Percentage Increase of Industrial Equipment During World War II

State	% Increase
Nevada	714.2
Utah	369
Arkansas	218
Kansas	173.4
Texas	**172.8**
Oklahoma	122.8
Louisiana	137
Arizona	131.7
Wyoming	124.5
New Mexico	118

Source: Fort Worth Press, August 11, 1945, p. 7.

By all standards Fort Worth changed between 1940 and 1945, most notably by becoming more commercial and industrial while also adding substantial population. Growth is a two-edged sword, and what happened in World War II carried both positive and negative effects. Fort Worth's experience, although perhaps different in degree and intensity, was similar to that of many cities. Perhaps the most compelling domestic effect of the World War II experience was the durability and the longevity of its impacts. Fort Worth and the nation as a whole became something quite different during the 1940s, becoming more populous, more industrial, and more urbanized.

Part 2

Fort Worth in the 1950s, 1951–1960

Chapter 12

Fort Worth in the 1950s

In the 1950s the local economy continued to do well, thanks in part to defense spending stimulated by the Korean War and the Cold War. Fort Worth made some important initial infrastructure investments in opening a regional airport and building the first freeways, including the Turnpike. The Turnpike connecting Dallas and Fort Worth had a serendipitous consequence as the catalyst for an Arlington entertainment complex that now includes stadiums for the Texas Rangers and the Dallas Cowboys and Six Flags Over Texas.

Gambling and prostitution, the major vices confronting police after the end of Prohibition, flourished with little permanent enforcement response or effect, despite a sustained public airing of corrupt ties between many in law enforcement and gamblers and pimps. That exposure may have played a major role in developing awareness that would eventually undo those relationships. The most sensational event of the postwar criminal world involved the ongoing serial murders of Fort Worth's most infamous hoodlums, creating a list of dead rogues that approached totality. Two high-profile robberies also vied for the top crime story of the decade, one involving Cuban revolutionaries and the second a brazen plan to rob Carswell Air Force Base.

Police work in the decade was noteworthy for a sustained increase in juvenile delinquency, especially in organized youth gangs, as well as a growing police involvement with traffic and a modernization trend that established the first crime lab, polygraph section, and undercover operations.

Fort Worth's African American community largely remained isolated from the developing national Civil Rights Movement of the 1950s, although local Blacks made some aggressive moves to open municipal parks and other recreation facilities to all people. The most spirited point of contention developed over efforts to integrate traditionally all-white neighborhoods, a movement largely dictated by necessity as an expanding Black population spilled over the existing racial boundaries and into white areas. School integration received only limited attention as most local leaders waited for compliance with the 1954 *Brown* decision. An exception was Mansfield High School, where violent opponents coalesced into mobs thwarting court-ordered integration. Fort Worth schools remained noncompliant with the *Brown* decision, as did most of Texas and the American South.

Chapter 13

Fort Worth Enters the 1950s

The 1950 Census described the average Texan as a white, 28.8-year-old urban dweller (urban defined as 2,500 or more population) living in a household of 3.3 people and earning $2,831 annually ($54.44 weekly). Fort Worth, with a population of 278,778, was the thirty-eighth largest city in the United States behind twenty-fifth San Antonio (408,442), twenty-second Dallas (434,462), and fourteenth Houston (596,163). Fort Worth politics was remarkably stable and remained so through most of the 1950s thanks to domination by the Citizens' Committee for a Greater Fort Worth (CCGFW), a conservative business-centered group. With the exception of 1937, CCGFW candidates exercised majority council control every year, beginning in 1925 when Fort Worth adopted the city manager system. In 1950 T. J. Harrell served as CCGFW chair and Roscoe Carnrike, a former mayor, and Marvin Evans were cochairs. In the 1951 municipal election all nine incumbents endorsed by the CCGFW won reelection (only two had opposition). The nine councilmen named J. R. Edwards, a retired businessman, mayor.[1]

In the aftermath of the 1951 vote a grassroots political movement arose to challenge the business-centered CCGFW. The opposition initially coalesced around firefighters seeking to replace five city councilmen who had blocked a

Fort Worth City Hall and Public Library, 1952. Courtesy W. D. Smith Commercial Photography, Inc., Collection, Special Collections, University of Texas at Arlington Libraries.

plebiscite that would have reduced firefighters' workweek from seventy-two to sixty hours. The movement focused on defeating those five, taking no position regarding the other four incumbents: M. M. McKnight, Edgar Deen (a former mayor), Ray Crowder, and Ed Baker. As other city employees and progressives joined in, the scope broadened and organized in December 1952 as the People's Protective League (PPL), running a full slate of nine council candidates for the 1953 election. In January 1953 a third group, the Fort Worth Voters League (FWVL), chaired by Toy Cocker, formed around discontent with the council's seeming indifference to rampant vice. The FWVL eventually aligned with the PPL, supporting seven of their nine candidates, although relations between the two were not without rancor. In March 1953 George Seaman, chairman of the Riverside Civic League and a segregationist, came close to brawling with Buddie Thompson, a sitting councilman, during an FWVL dinner at the Hilton Hotel. Other internal problems developed in the contest for Place 8 covering the Riverside area (council seats were elected at large but candidates were designated for specific neighborhoods). A local businessman, upset that the CCGFW candidate, Melvin Miller, lived in TCU, entered as a third candidate for Place 8. The PPL/FWVL alliance proved formidable, winning four contests outright (admittedly three of the four were also endorsed by CCGFW) and forcing the other five races into runoffs. Mrs. Joe Spurlock, one of the coalition candidates, was the first woman to make it to a Fort Worth council runoff. PPL/FWVL candidates won all five runoffs, defeating five incumbent councilmen and making Mrs. Spurlock the first woman on the Fort Worth City Council. M. M. McKnight, a labor leader and incumbent councilman who had received the most votes of any council candidate in the 1953 and 1951 elections, was favored for mayor, but the eight councilmen and one councilwoman chose Edgar Deen instead.[2]

Just months after the election, City Councilman T. L. Carleton was arrested for arson involving a $150,000 fire at the Bender Hotel, 1201 Commerce Street. The blaze began August 24, 1953, with an explosion in Fort Worth Radio Supply, a ground-floor business owned by Carleton. Suspicions arose when investigators discovered Carleton had recently increased the shop's insurance coverage. Enough evidence was secured to indict Carleton, but a weeklong trial resulted in a not-guilty verdict.[3]

The 1955 council election featured candidate slates from four political organizations: the FWVL, the CCGFW, and two new groups, the Better Government League and the Fort Worth City Council Committee. An African American, Dr. R. A. Ransom Sr., running for Place 1 as a "Native Son," came in second with 5,031 votes, putting him in a runoff with Joe Owen, who received 9,513 votes (other candidates shared 6,976 votes). Unfortunately, Ransom, the first African American to make it to a runoff, lost, leaving Fort Worth to wait several more years for its first Black councilperson.[4]

Over two-thirds of the $10.7 million municipal budget went to funding the FWISD that, in the 1952–1953 school year, taught 39,828 white and 5,120 Black students. The budget kept lunches at $0.25 for elementary and $0.30 for junior and senior high grades while also providing 54,446 free lunches for impoverished students, an average of 724 free meals daily. FWISD avoided the teacher shortage affecting most of Texas in 1952, perhaps because salaries exceeded the state minimums. The state-mandated minimum starting salaries of $2,403 for holders of a BA, with $3,012 guaranteed after twelve years, were considerably lower than FWISD's rates of $2,750 and $4,550, respectively. In contrast, FWISD was slow to develop sufficient programs to accommodate the developmentally challenged. In 1954 some 2,500 FWISD students were classified as challenged (then termed "retarded"), but only 250, 10 percent, were enrolled in special education classes. The Fort Worth Council on Retarded Children called for expanded special education classes for 1,900 students estimated to have IQs between fifty and seventy, the established range for special education classes. The council argued that insufficient special education classes carried high social and economic costs, leaving challenged students without the rudimentary skills that could have qualified them for low- and semiskilled jobs, condemning thousands to dependency who might have supported themselves.[5]

In the early 1950s Fort Worth still struggled with the housing crisis that had begun during the Depression and deepened during the dearth of residential construction during World War II. In 1952 Fort Worth's 89,380 housing units, 59.4 percent owner-occupied, had an average value of $7,200, rather substantial for the period, but the real housing problems lay in the lower end of the market, where more than 21,000 units, almost 24 percent of all housing, were deemed structurally dilapidated or were without a bath, and another 8,854 lacked indoor plumbing of any kind. Substandard housing tended to be concentrated in poorer neighborhoods that were nonwhite, creating a clumping effect of large swaths of blighted housing, or slums. The Fort Worth City Council established a Housing and Sanitation Board charged with slum eradication, an ambitious undertaking. In September 1953 board member R. B. Billings issued a report identifying 25,190 substandard dwellings: 14,355 without toilets, 7,720 structurally dilapidated, and 3,115 without water service of any kind. The board developed an eight-point plan to strengthen codes, increase enforcement, and develop a privately financed loan program to help fund improvements for the noncreditworthy.[6]

The legacy of postwar strikes carried over into the 1950s along with a tendency for management to take a general hardline. The $14.9 million city budget for 1951–1952 received praise for reducing the standard workweek for 1,100 staff from forty-four to forty hours without a cut in pay and for granting a $10 monthly increase for police and firefighters, raising their base pay to $267, but union garbage workers balked at the elimination of fixed monthly salaries of $228 for drivers and $205 for helpers based on a forty-hour week. Under the new scheme, garbagemen became hourly workers, earning $1.18 to $1.32 an hour for forty-four hours a week, all at straight time with no overtime pay. Union workers walked out on October 8, 1951, demanding a return to the guaranteed monthly wage and one-and-a-half pay for overtime. The first day, a Monday, only eight trucks staffed by nonstrikers went out, leaving sixty-five trucks idle, but the number of rolling trucks grew each day as more strikers returned and the city hired other workers. After four days the two sides agreed to the forty-hour workweek with double pay on holidays, returning all 260 workers effective Saturday, October 13.[7]

Workers at Pangburn's Candy Company struck at the end of 1951, but the company continued operations using nonunion staff. A marked rise in intensity was noted in January 1952 as the walkout entered its sixth week with no signs of progress. Crude firebombs were found outside the homes of two nonstriking workers, neither doing significant damage. In one case a worker's husband found a paper sack with a burnt fuse on the front porch and in the second a neighbor saw smoke coming from a package on the porch at 2613 Northwest Twenty-Sixth Street, the home of Mrs. W. L. Swink. Mrs. Swink reported she had received threatening phone calls in the days before the firebombing.[8]

Workers also walked out at American Manufacturing Company on September 10, 1952, beginning a strike that turned violent five days later. A picketing striker, Edward Griner, was hit in the mouth with a rock, and the next morning at 1:00 a.m. a bomb blast damaged a car at 904 Hawkins Street, the home of I. F. Williamson, a nonstriking worker. Mrs. Williamson blamed the Steel Workers Union for the bombing. The next day, September 17, the strike ended with a two-year contract granting a dime an hour pay raise, the same increase the company had offered before the work stoppage. Police involvement in strikes put officers in a difficult situation in which they could be accused of favoritism. In 1959 police administrators were criticized as strikebreakers after they charged eighteen Blacks picketing

Trinity Valley Iron and Steel, 3400 Bryce Avenue, with vagrancy. All were released on $10 bonds.[9]

In the 1950s the Cold War between the Soviet Union and the United States carried the very real potential of becoming an actual war, a lurking threat that was major and persistent. The potential for nuclear war spawned serious discussions about ways to protect the populace in such an exchange. In 1951 R. E. Dysart, an ex-chief of police before becoming Fort Worth's civil defense director, told Black civil defense workers (even civil defense meetings were segregated) that preparation was the key to surviving a nuclear attack. Lieutenant Colonel Burton K. Lyons of the 49th Armored Division, speaking at a 1951 Fort Worth business luncheon, said a nuclear bomb detonated at Seventh and Main Streets would destroy everything in a one-quarter mile radius, kill 90 percent of the population within a half mile, reap extensive damage over two miles from the center, and cause 30,000 deaths and 60,000 casualties, but that Fort Worth would survive and rebuild. Lyons's optimism was no more outlandish than a 1951 *Star Telegram* article, "The A-BOMB and YOU," that recommended protecting yourself during a nuclear attack by sheltering in a covered area while covering your nose with a folded handkerchief. Fort Worth joined most of the rest of the country and Canada on June 14, 1954, in a mock nuclear attack, code named Lemon Juice, that began at 11:46 a.m. with a B-36 dropping a "bomb" at ground zero, Seventh and Grove Streets. Fort Worth did not participate in a follow-up drill, Operation Alert, in June 1955 that exposed problems in communications and revealed that warning sirens had inadequate range.[10]

All the publicity created an atmosphere where the unthinkable seemed possible. An unintended example occurred on June 19, 1953, when many Fort Worthians mistook a massive explosion at Wilfong Fireworks Company as a nuclear attack. The blast, northwest of downtown near Carswell Air Force Base, created a mushroom cloud that resembled an atomic bomb explosion and damaged nearby houses but caused no deaths. The local civil defense coordinator complained that many persons drove to the scene, ignoring training directives to avoid impact sites. Hysteria over nuclear war was closely linked to fears that Communism was creeping into America through innocuous channels. In 1954 Fort Worth District Dental Society President

Dr. W. O. White canceled plans to add fluoride to the water supply after the city council succumbed to scare tactics linking fluoridation with Communism and race mixing. In 1953 a more realistic anti-Communist effort, headed by A. M. Herman of the Fort Worth Jewish Federation, raised funds to support Jews behind the Iron Curtain.[11]

The 1950s saw major technological innovations that would reorder life. Television had appeared earlier but came of age after 1950, making the '50s the first television decade. In 1951 Fort Worth viewers could tune in to three local channels—WBAP (channel 5), WFAA (channel 8), and KRLD (channel 4), the latter two Dallas based—with weekday programming beginning at either noon or 1:00 p.m. and running until around 11:00 p.m. WBAP aired Texas's first color broadcast on May 15, 1954, a three-hour local variety show. Electronic computers had also appeared earlier but took an important step in September 1951 when the Massachusetts Institute of Technology developed an artificial brain with 32,768 memory cells capable of high-speed electronic computing. In 1954 local department stores—Cox's, The Fair, Stripling's, Meacham's, Monnig's and Washer Bros.—began accepting tokens issued by the Charga-Plate Stores of Greater Fort Worth, allowing customers to charge purchases automatically, the first credit cards accepted by multiple local shops.[12]

Not all in the 1950s was new and advanced. In 1949 the city of Fort Worth still had a four-man rat control crew that killed between 1,000 and 2,000 rats each month. Pestilence associated with rodents and other carriers may have played a role in periodic sharp rises in communicable diseases. In 1933 tuberculosis afflicted 59.6 persons per 100,000 population nationally, but by 1953 its incidence had declined to only 20.1 (almost two-thirds fewer), although Fort Worth and Dallas were significantly above the national average with 27.7 and 30.6, respectively, while San Antonio led all medium-size US cities (those with a population between 200,000 to 500,000) with a horrible rate of 83.0. Cancer had a similar local presence, accounting for 562 deaths in 1956 for all of Tarrant County, a mortality rate of 110.8 per 100,000 population, significantly less than the national rate of 145 but slightly more than 106.6 for the state. Polio remained a chronic major health issue with periodic outbreaks that spread quickly. In the first seven months of 1952,

82 cases were confirmed in Fort Worth and another 42 in the rest of Tarrant County; three days later 23 more cases were confirmed, bringing the total exposed countywide to 147. The rapid onslaught filled the polio ward at City-County Hospital with 63 patients, taking over 30 percent of the 200 available beds. Overcrowding became so severe that City-County and Fort Worth Children's Hospital put new patients on a waiting list. In 1951 a $1.25 million gift from the Tom B. Owens Trust allowed Fort Worth Children's Hospital, 2400 Winton Terrace (valued at $750,000), to merge with Cook Memorial Hospital, 1212 West Lancaster Avenue (valued at $2 million), creating W. I. Cook Memorial Hospital for Children.[13]

Plagues were a major factor in creating funding crises for indigent health care. In 1951 City-County Hospital spent $751,569, considerably more than its $651,567 budget, sparking sharp debates over steps to correct the imbalance. Many blamed the polio outbreak that ravaged poor neighborhoods, infecting patients most likely to be charity cases. That argument certainly had merit but was insufficient to explain all the problem. In 1955 County Auditor Star Williams criticized John Peter Smith Hospital (the former City-County Hospital, renamed in 1954) Administrator Lowell Hudson and his staff, citing shoddy accounting of hospital supplies. Administrator Hudson drew more flack for his mother's stay as a charity patient at the hospital that left a $408.65 unpaid bill. In addition, Hudson suffered from divided loyalties, concurrently serving as a director of National Underwriter's Life Insurance Company, a conflict of interest aggravated by whispers that he had hospital staff do insurance company work. Hudson denied wrongdoing but paid his mother's hospital bill before resigning his $11,000 per year hospital position on August 5, 1955. Tarrant County Commissioners also looked for cost reductions in pauper burials that were contracted to Harveson and Cole Funeral Home at $99.50 for services and $34.00 for burial plots at Mount Olivet Cemetery.[14]

On June 16, 1951, Fort Worth welcomed General Douglas MacArthur just two months after he had been relieved of command in April 1951. General MacArthur, arriving by car from Dallas as part of a whirlwind tour of Texas, was greeted by a crowd estimated at 150,000 standing along the route of his motorcade escorted by twenty-five police motorcycles to the

Pike Drive-In Theater, where he was greeted by Amon Carter and a crowd of 1,000. Afterward, he rested and dined at the Fort Worth Club before a 1:00 p.m. speech at Farrington Field.[15]

Several prominent and noteworthy Fort Worthians died in the 1950s. Pastor J. Frank Norris succumbed while at youth camp in Florida. Norris, 74 years old, led a notorious life—charged but acquitted with arson, killing a critic and engaging in long-running feuds with religious leaders like Dr. Louie D. Newton, president of the Southern Baptist Convention, whom Norris accused of supporting Communism. A Fort Worth character, J. W. "Daddy" Flynn, died February 27, 1955, at 89 years of age. "Daddy" Flynn came to Fort Worth during World War I to be near his son stationed at Camp Bowie and quickly made a name for himself as a snappy dresser, a Damon Runyon character who wore many hats, serving as a plant manager and Deputy United States Marshal but becoming best known as a boxing trainer and manager who brought many top-name fighters to town. Flynn was also an associate of shady characters. In 1952 informants accused him of acting as a bagman paying off police to protect gamblers. One of the most important figures in Fort Worth history and a critical force behind the city's development, Amon G. Carter, died June 23, 1955, at his home, 1220 Broad Avenue. Carter worked tirelessly to promote Fort Worth through his newspaper, the *Star Telegram*, and in multiple other projects, most famously the 1936 Centennial Celebration. The *New York Times* called Amon Carter a "one-man chamber of commerce for Fort Worth and West Texas."[16]

In 1950 the Korean War accelerated national defense spending, once again stimulating the Fort Worth economy, although the effect took some time to reach Texas. In the war's first six months (July 1950 to January 1951), California garnered 18 percent of all defense contracts, the most of any state, followed by New York with 16 percent, while Texas lagged far behind with only 1.6 percent. California continued to do well throughout the conflict, but Texas businesses gradually won larger slices of the pie. The resulting commercialization effect was part of a clear trend the Bureau of Labor Statistics identified in 1953 of factories leaving the East and Northeast for the West and South, especially California and Texas.[17]

Convair, built to gigantic proportions during World War II, was well positioned to reap substantial defense contracts. In April 1951 the Fort Worth plant celebrated its ten-year anniversary, marking a decade in which it produced over 3,000 planes, many rolling out during the production heights of 1943 and 1944 when 200 B-24s left the mile-long assembly line each month. Employment topped out at 30,609 in 1943, producing a $55 million annual payroll that rose to $60 million in 1944, a major factor supporting the Fort Worth economy. Postwar, employment declined to fewer than 20,000, but by 1951 production of the B-36 bomber and other military equipment once again took employment to the 30,000 level, making Convair the largest employer of all American aircraft manufacturers and its $100 million payroll the largest of any single plant in the Southwest. Convair's annual wages varied slightly as the workforce rose and fell but exhibited a clear upward trend that accelerated as the years advanced. In the ten years after ground was broken in 1941, Convair paid out $371.8 million in wages; just three years later total wages almost doubled, reaching $688.8 million, a massive infusion of capital that was reflected in before-and-after commercial statistics. In 1940, just before Convair construction began, Fort Worth, with a population of 177,662, had annual bank clearings of $355.8 million; ten years later the population had risen 56 percent to 277,047, but bank clearings had increased 308 percent to $1.4 billion; the next year they hit $1.6 billion. Bank deposits showed a similar trajectory, rising from $112.5 million in 1940 to $518 million in 1952, a 360 percent increase. By 1955 Fort Worth's twenty banks held $732 million in deposits, up from the previous high of $687 million in 1954. Direct wages were Convair's largest contribution to the Fort Worth economy, but the company also bought enormous amounts of goods from local suppliers. From its start to 1954 the company spent an estimated $55 million for supplies, services, and parts.[18]

Other economic statistics reflected a strong and growing economy. City building permits dipped slightly from $47.7 million in 1950 to $42.7 million in 1951 but rebounded in 1952 to $44.4 million. In the first four months of 1952 Fort Worth built 2,551 new homes, and was the fifth largest nationally in residential home construction behind Los Angeles, Chicago, San Diego, and Dallas (Dallas barely edged out Fort Worth for fourth with 2,630 new homes.) From 1951 to 1952 Fort Worth retail sales grew from $508 million to $574.4 million, per capita income increased from $1,606 to $1,754, and average family income inched up from $5,229 to $5,829. Fort Worth's per capita income in 1951, $1,606, was significantly higher than the state average of $1,412 and above the national average of $1,584. For context, in 1951 medical doctors averaged $12,518 a year and lawyers $9,375.[19]

Convair's success was mirrored and complemented in 1951 by two major additions to Fort Worth's aviation industry. On March 27, 1951, Bell Helicopter announced construction of a plant near Hurst, Texas (but in Fort Worth city limits), costing $27 million and employing 2,000. Six months later, in October, Carswell Air Force Base began work on a $19 million program to extend the runway and build the world's largest hangar and a huge military hospital. Lengthening the runway required closing part of White Settlement Road and extending Grant's Lane south to connect with Highway 183.[20]

One of the more important achievements of the first half of the decade was the development of a major commercial airport. Greater Fort Worth International Airport's grand opening on April 25–26, 1953, drew 30,000 visitors who listened to a dedicatory speech from the secretary of the Air Force. The first official flight, an airliner from New York City, arrived just after midnight on April 26, en route to Los Angeles. In November 1954 Fort Worth, at the urging of Civilian Aeronautics Board, offered to sell Dallas one-half of the field for $2.7 million and rename it Dallas–Fort Worth International Airport, but the Dallas City Council unanimously rejected the offer, arguing the area needed two airports and that traveling to the airport just east of Arlington would burden Dallasites. The airport opened as air service transitioned to jet service, significantly reducing travel time. When transcontinental air service had begun in the early 1930s, flights from New York City to Los Angeles took forty hours, beginning with a rail journey to Cleveland, Ohio, where passengers boarded a flight to Fort Worth, where they took sleeper airplanes with fourteen beds for the final leg to Los Angeles. In 1936 American replaced the rail portion with air service, reducing travel time to eighteen hours; in 1953 jet service lowered total time to under seven hours, ending sleeper flights. In 1958 American Airlines began offering nonstop DC-7 jet service to New York City leaving Carter Field at 10:30 a.m. and arriving at 4:55 p.m.[21]

The economic successes of the early 1950s were not just about aviation; many other major businesses arrived and existing concerns thrived. The biggest nonaviation economic news for the area came on August 5, 1951, when GM announced the acquisition of 255 acres in east Arlington for a Buick-Oldsmobile-Pontiac assembly plant. The announcement culminated the tireless efforts of Amon Carter and Tom Vandergriff of Arlington, assisted by many others, who had worked since 1934 to attract a GM plant. Less than three years later, on January 23, 1954, Amon Carter bought the first Buick to roll off the assembly line. In 1952 Chicago Pneumatic broke ground on their new $4.5 million plant on Highway 81 (near the Quartermaster Depot), which would employ 500. The previous year Fort Worth had celebrated the seventy-fifth anniversary of its first large commercial concerns, railroads. The first train to roll in to Fort Worth, arriving at 11:23 a.m. on July 19, 1876, consisted of a mere four flatcars and a caboose pulled by a wood-burning Engine No. 20 of the Texas and Pacific Railroad, Engineer James Kelly at the controls (in 1951 Kelly's daughter still lived in Fort Worth). During the next three-quarters of a century, Texas and Pacific remained a major commercial force, employing 2,120 workers in 1948 to handle 1,568,287 freight cars. In 1953 Tandy Leather, soon to form part of Tandy Corporation, a multinational retailer, purchased its thirtieth store, Burgess Handicrafts of Chicago.[22]

Two major freeways that began in 1954 helped change vehicle travel patterns. A real estate developer's donation of twenty-six acres jump-started construction of a four-lane, $8 million highway running from the intersection of Highways 183 and 377 east to Highway 81 (now I-35), and work began on the Dallas–Fort Worth Turnpike, a thirty-mile, stoplight-free link between the two major cities. In 1955 W. O. Jones, who had served nine years as Fort Worth city manager, resigned to head the Turnpike's construction.[23]

For all that happened, the biggest story of 1954 may have been a missing reptile. On September 18, 1954, Pete the Python, an eighteen-foot snake, escaped from its enclosure at the Fort Worth Zoo, apparently climbing an eight-foot fence to freedom. Zookeepers discovered the absence only after a live chicken left in Pete's pit was found alive the next day. The news prompted the zoo's closure and sent all twenty-five staff searching the surrounding environs, joined by firefighters and police officers and a sound truck broadcasting warnings throughout the park. As a precaution, the zoo's four poisonous snakes were destroyed. Amon Carter offered $500 for Pete's safe return. News of the escape spread across the nation, with the *Chicago Tribune* reporting Fort Worth streets were deserted and homeowners kept their windows tightly closed (the author, a young boy at the time, feared Pete would find him). Some local businesses tried to cash in, offering Pete burgers and fashions for Pete watching. After two weeks Pete turned up the evening of October 3 in the zoo's primate area, his presence given away by chimpanzees raising such a ruckus that Ed Baker, a zoo night watchman, alerted zoo staff, who discovered the errant Pete was the source of all the commotion. Pete became Patricia in December 1957 after caretakers found several eggs in her cage. She died of malnutrition just weeks later, in February 1958, after refusing to eat for six months. Patricia's remains went to TCU.[24]

surrounding environs, joined by firefighters and police officers and a sound truck broadcasting warnings [illegible] the [illegible]. As a precaution, the zoo's [illegible] poisonous snakes were destroyed. Amon Carter offered $500 for Pete's safe return. News of the escape spread across the nation, with the Chicago *Tribune* reporting Fort Worth streets were deserted and homeowners kept their windows tightly closed (the author, a young boy at the time, feared Pete would find him). Some local businesses tried to cash in, offering [illegible] and [illegible] for Pete-watching. After two weeks, Pete turned up the evening of October 3 in the zoo's primate area, his presence given away by chimpanzees [illegible] such a [illegible] [illegible] zoo [illegible] zoo staff who discovered the errant [illegible] was the source of all the commotion. Pete became [illegible] in December 1957 after caretakers found several eggs in her cage. She died of malnutrition just weeks later, in February 1958, after refusing to eat for six months. [illegible]

Chapter 14

Crime, Criminals, and Vice, 1951–1955

Judging from reported police activity, gambling continued to be widely available in the first half of the 1950s. Many forms were mentioned, but dice and poker seemed most common. Wagering on horse races may have waned; only one incident was publicized, a January 1951 raid on a second-floor office in the Ellison Building initiated by a tip from a prominent but unidentified businessman (perhaps a sore loser). The sincerity of the police in that effort seemed questionable given that the two operators somehow managed to escape, supposedly leaving via a side office. They left behind extensive bookmaking equipment, racing forms, sporting sheets, five telephones and records detailing a $2,000 profit made in just two days. If wagering on horse racing had indeed waned, it may have been the victim of neglect due to a myriad of other choices. El Paso Sheriff Joe Campbell, visiting Fort Worth in February 1951, reported gambling was wide open throughout the city and county. Other observations supported the sheriff's statement, but rampant illegal gambling was not unique to Fort Worth. In 1951 Galveston Mayor Herbert Cartwright admitted gambling and prostitution were widely available in his city, and Corpus Christi Mayor Leslie Wasserman was indicted in 1952 for accepting bribes from gamblers.[1]

The mayor's indictment was a public expression of an obvious but quiet reality that the Texas Crime Commission in Austin recognized—that open gambling could not have existed without the incompetence or cooperation of local officials. The evidence supports the latter, that an unsavory, closed-door relationship existed between some in law enforcement and gamblers. In January 1951 police arrested thirty-six men and women at several known gambling joints operating after hours: the Skyliner Club, 2238 Jacksboro Highway; Westmoor Club, 5800 Camp Bowie Boulevard, managed by Ray Culbertson; and the Convair-Carswell Club, 812 North Henderson Street. At the Skyliner Club the raiders found two on-duty patrolmen, Howard Stephenson and A. B. Prine, in the office of W. D. Satterwhite, the club's manager. Two on-duty police officers hobnobbing with a casino manager was suspicious, but no one seemed to notice or feel the need to explain their presence; police administrators only faulted the two for not notifying dispatch they were out of the car and, therefore, away from radio communications.[2]

Suspicions surrounding links between police and gamblers strengthened after lawyers Ross and Doss Hardin turned over a memorandum discovered in the business papers of Nelson Harris, a local gambler killed in a bombing on November 22, 1950. The document, written in Harris's handwriting on the back of a café business card, appeared to list police payoffs:

Chart 14.1 Memorandum Found in Nelson Harris's Papers

Capt. Dur	$30.00
Howard	$50.00
Burk	$30.00
Lt. E. Lee	$25.00
Bevill	$25.00
Scout C.31 (Cox)	$50.00
7.-3-3 to 11-11 to 7	$75.00
Vice	$125.00
C.H.	$100.00
Sarge Field	$20.00

Source: Fort Worth Star Telegram, February 7, 1951, pp.1 and 4.

The names matched or were similar to several high-ranking police personnel, all of whom denied knowledge of the list or payoffs. Chief George Hawkins dismissed claims that "C.H." referred to him; Captains Karl Howard, R. H. "Rip" Burks, and J. B. Dearden, as well as Lieutenant D. W. Bevill, made blanket disavowals of payoffs or of gambling's existence beyond small-time operations. Mayor Edgar Deen chided their statements, saying he knew of eighteen big gambling houses operating in Fort Worth. Deen, along with the rest of the council and City Manager W. O. Jones, offered a $1,000 reward for information confirming police officers took bribes. At their request a recently empaneled grand jury launched an investigation into gambling and narcotics. The jurors subpoenaed all of Harris's s papers and called several witnesses, including City Manager Jones, ex-chief of police R. E. "Bob" Dysart, two police supervisors and a detective, and the entire vice squad: Sergeant R. E. Pinckard, Carl Brewer, T. R. Sanders, Orville Baker, H. F. Hopkins, Felix Crowe, and A. E. Jordan.[3]

Nelson Harris was an exception to most hoodlums in that he apparently kept extensive financial records, many of which were turned in to the grand jury. Ray Harris, Nelson's brother, arrived from Midland, Texas, with a fifty-page statement documenting twenty years of alleged police payoffs made to a captain, sergeant, and two detectives, along with the names of several other police officers tied to gamblers. Ray explained his eagerness to cooperate as a product of disappointment with the lackluster investigation of his brother's murder. He added that Tiffin Hall, a local gambler since 1920 and owner of the Mexican Inn, knew all about payoffs. Austin Harris, another brother, testified that Nelson regularly paid off police officers and that the 2222 Club hired Nelson to draw customers away from the Camp Bowie dice game, another large gambling operation. Austin furnished thirteen financial ledgers showing Nelson and three partners made $2,320 in one month off the Camp Bowie dice game. Mrs. Jessie Harris, Nelson's ex-wife, testified that a local gambler threatened her if she talked to the grand jury about Nelson's payoffs or admitted having been a hostess at the 2222 Jacksboro Club rather than a parking attendant.[4]

Records kept showing up documenting bribes and lucrative gambling operations. The *Star Telegram* provided a journal of Nelson Harris's income and expenditures listing several police payouts, including a $10 entry on November 5, 1949, marked "11 to 7 Sarg" and information on a nonstop, weeklong dice game run by Harris and others at the Camp Bowie night spot. Jay Harris, a Midland barber, also appeared with a trunk full of Nelson's papers. An anonymous source submitted bank records showing an unidentified former vice officer made several cash deposits between August 1949 and October 1949 totaling $3,880, considerably more than his annual salary. The accused officer claimed the money came from cattle sales and that he could provide receipts. Louis Welch, a city councilman, thought the case for collusion was clear and confirmed by the open presence of slot machines and other gambling devices all over town. In March 1951 the grand jury appointed John B. Honts, a former district attorney in Dalhart, Texas, as special prosecutor, replacing District Attorney Stewart Hellman, who left office in 1952 after serving since 1949.[5]

The list of witnesses included the famous and infamous, as well as regular citizens. Reverend J. Frank Norris, a historical gadfly who often railed against vice, testified. Benny Binion, a well-known local gambler before moving to Las Vegas and opening a casino, refused to return to Texas but was interviewed in Las Vegas, where he denied any gambling interests in Fort Worth, Tarrant County, Dallas, or any other place in Texas. N. C. Coke, a Texas and Pacific Railroad fireman, told jurors he had seen thousands of dollars wagered on dice games at four downtown hotels. Several police officers were questioned about their ability to buy expensive homes and cars on small city salaries.[6]

The investigation, like others in the past, stirred authorities into an accelerated rush of raids distinguished by the inclusion of a few previously ignored venues like country clubs. Perhaps they were motivated by new federal regulations in 1951 that removed slot machines from the Non-Commissioned Officers and Officers clubs at Carswell and the Quartermaster Depot (the clubs increased dues to offset the lost revenue). On February 21, 1951, a wide-ranging operation confiscated ninety-three slot machines, including twenty-one removed from River Crest Country Club, twenty-two from Colonial Country Club, and sixteen from Glen Garden Country Club, as well as others from the local VFW, American Legion, Elks Club, Knights of

Columbus, and assorted clubs inside and outside the city. The haul represented almost one-third of the 320 slot machines estimated to be in use in Tarrant County. Word of the crackdown spread quickly, allowing some operators to secret their slots and other gambling devices. The next day District Attorney Hellman accompanied officers on raids that found nothing at the Top O' Hill, the East Side Club, or the 2222 Club where owner William C. Kirkwood escorted the officers on a guided tour. Marble boards, regular features in businesses and shops, also disappeared. One operator removing his machines told the businessowner he would return them once the heat was off. In the case of the country clubs, making arrests was one thing, but getting convictions proved more difficult. In March the grand jury no-billed seven private club managers, including those at River Crest and Colonial Country Clubs. In April seventeen persons charged with keeping slot machines or marble boards pled guilty and received $100 fines plus court costs and forfeiture of the machines. In May 1951 police arrested twenty-five persons for gambling, but they were the more traditional perpetrators; almost all were Black men found shooting dice or playing poker in private homes or small clubs. The return to focusing on small-time operations run by African Americans signaled that the heat was coming off and normality had returned.[7]

Sixteen persons indicted in April 1951 from the February raids constituted a list of some of Fort Worth's most prominent gambling community: Fred Browning of the Top o' the Hill; Bert Wakefield, Phil Long, and Les Hutt, all of the 3939 Club on Jacksboro Highway; W. C. Kirkwood of the 2222 Club; George Wilderspin of the East Side Club; W. D. Satterwhite of the Skyliner; Tiffin Hall of the Mexican Inn; and H. D. "Red" Oden, Frank Cates, Les Hutt, Phil Long, A. R. Floyd, Dewey Ingram, Mack Taylor, Pete Ford, Oscar Donley, Jerry Rosenberg, Ivie Miller and L. J. McWille. Most quickly made $1,000 bonds. One of the indicted, Tiffin Hall, was subsequently arrested on suspicion of gambling by Houston vice officers. Hall, freed the next day, told reporters he was in Houston regarding an oil deal and denied he was a gambler, although he admitted meeting with the owner of a swank Corpus Christi gambling club. Bert Wakefield, operator of the 3939 Club, tried to avoid prosecution on two gambling counts by fleeing to Las Vegas. The ploy worked for a time, thanks to the Nevada's governor's refusal

Tincy Eggleston playing cards while awaiting trial, October 22, 1951.
Courtesy *Fort Worth Star Telegram* Collection, Special Collections, University of Texas at Arlington Libraries.

to extradite, at least until Sheriff Sully Montgomery seized Wakefield at the Clark County Courthouse and spirited him to the airport.[8]

Indictments continued in July 1951 when the grand jury indicted Leroy "Tincy" Eggleston, Weeks Baxter, and Ernest Harris on charges that included keeping a gambling table, bank, or gambling house and/or keeping slot machines. Tincy Eggleston's trial began and ended on December 10, 1951, after the state's main witness, Mrs. Essie Graham, testified she could not remember any connection between Tincy and the dice game at the Skyliner Annex, 2238 Jacksboro Highway, or between him and Harris or W. D. Satterwhite, operator of the Annex. Mrs. Graham's memory failure contrasted to her testimony before the grand jury that she worked as a shill for Nelson Harris's dice game at the Annex and had direct information linking Tincy to the club's gambling, the salient evidence supporting his indictment.

W. H. Hames, owner of the Skyliner, the grounds where the Annex was located, also suffered a memory loss that left him unable to recall details of the lease agreement. The general amnesia forced a directed not-guilty verdict, also ending the case against Satterwhite.[9]

Prosecution continued to grind away slowly before coming to a virtual halt. In October 1951 the General Ministers Alliance expressed regret in the delayed prosecution, but their displeasure had little effect. In February 1952 District Attorney Hellman dismissed all unadjudicated felony charges stemming from raids conducted on March 20, 1951, stating that prosecution was impossible because all the witnesses were gamblers. In a plea deal, twenty-six defendants pled guilty to misdemeanor charges, twenty paid $100 to $500 fines, and six (Tiffin Hall of the Commercial Hotel, Bert Wakefield of the 3939 Club, Howard Lee of the Court Hotel, W. C. Kirkwood of the 2222 Club, George Wilderspin of the East Side Club, and Fred Browning of the Top O' Hill Terrace) paid $1,000 fines; six others, including the only African American, Albert Huey-You, had all charges dropped. In August 1952 Hellman requested the dismissal of the twenty-six remaining charges against eighteen persons, claiming insufficient evidence. No police officers were indicted, a strange outcome in an investigation with so much incriminating evidence. Rumors, probably true, held that that the failure to prosecute stemmed from a behind-the-scenes deal in which Chief Hawkins agreed to resign and be replaced by a new administrator who would clean up the police department.[10]

The local investigation was followed by a federal grand jury, impaneled on March 17, 1952, that probed vice and corruption in the ninety-nine counties of the Northern District of Texas. The panel heard from thirty-two witnesses, including many law enforcement officers and known gamblers such as Ernest Cavitt, a Black taxi driver and operator of the Midtown Bar who kept a ledger of police payoffs. The investigation focused on Sheriff James Ralph "Sully" Montgomery, the son of former Fort Worth Chief of Police O. R. Montgomery. The jurors focused on Montgomery's purchase in November 1950 of the Rockwood Inn from Charles Journey, at the time under indictment for sodomy, and the property's sale only two weeks later for a $4,000 profit. The sheriff's financial involvement with a charged felon had occasioned numerous "adverse comments," but the federal panel only indicted Sheriff Montgomery for tax evasion, alleging that he reported incomes of $10,112 in 1948, $9,903 in 1949 and $7,826 in 1950 (he was paid $7,500 as sheriff), but had earned $16,422, $19,290 and $14,300, respectively. Assistant District Attorney A. L. Wardlaw, indicted along with Montgomery, resigned, but Montgomery continued in office.[11]

At trial Wardlaw's two ex-superiors, ex-District Attorney Al Clyde and then current District Attorney Hellman, denied any knowledge of payoffs, but W. H. Getzendaner, a bookie with a café on Henderson Street, and Clarence Cleere, a marble board operator, testified they made $50 payments each month to Wardlaw. Getzendaner, who had paid a $500 fine on a gambling charge stemming from the Tarrant County grand jury investigation, told the court he made payments through J. W. "Daddy" Flynn, a former US deputy marshal whom Getzendaner employed as a bagman to deliver and collect from bookmakers. Flynn denied knowing Wardlaw or having ever passed money to him. Several other witnesses, including Lawrence Blythe and Julia Hensley, testified they routinely paid Wardlaw "counsel fees" to get their hot check cases prosecuted. Wardlaw was convicted on two counts of tax evasion and sentenced to three years in prison.[12]

Montgomery denied all culpability at his trial, a claim refuted by Getzendaner, who swore Montgomery summoned him to the sheriff's office in 1948 to demand $50 monthly for protection, later raising the amount to $75 when Getzendaner added a dice game. He added that Montgomery was a silent partner in a marble board game run out of a cigar stand in the Flatiron Building. Car dealer Ed Etier testified he had seen Paul Suggs, Montgomery's high school friend, pass hundreds of dollars to the sheriff. Montgomery claimed his excess income between 1948 and 1950 came from side bets with acquaintances and from repayments of a 1925 loan of $3,000 so Suggs could buy a successful California business. He admitted Suggs had given him $800 in cash on a few occasions to thank him for the loan and for taking him home after he became intoxicated at a north side bar. Unfortunately, Mr. Suggs could not testify, having committed suicide earlier in 1952. Montgomery admitted his error in not reporting the gifts and winnings but blamed it on the sheriff's office bookkeeper, Robert Deen, who was also recently deceased. The sheriff emphatically denied receiving money from Ernest Cavitt or Clarence Cleere. Montgomery was convicted on all three counts and sentenced to seven years' prison time.[13]

A few months later (April 1953), the US Fifth Circuit Court of Appeals in New Orleans granted new trials to Wardlaw and Montgomery. During the retrial in January 1954, Wardlaw's defense claimed a violation of his Fifth Amendment rights against self-incrimination, that Wardlaw had believed the matter was civil and not criminal when he turned over his financial records. The court agreed, acquitting him on January 29 and Montgomery one week later.[14]

In the 1950s the Tarrant County Sheriff's Office had other issues with the district attorney's office. In 1951 Tarrant County Chief Deputy Sheriff A. B. Carter was indicted for double billing $11.70 for transporting mental patients to Wichita Falls State Hospital. Even in 1951 a criminal complaint over such a small amount was unusual. Rumors suggested the charges were part of a series of improper payments Carter received. Unfortunately, new District Attorney Howard Fender dismissed all the charges in December 1953, citing missing evidence. Relations between Fender, elected in 1952, and the new sheriff, Harlon Wright, got off to a rocky start. In July 1953 Fender and two investigators detained ninety African Americans shooting dice at 5400 Ramey Avenue, then outside Fort Worth city limits. They telephoned the sheriff's office for assistance, forcing Sheriff Wright to scramble to find transports, a process that took so long that many detainees simply walked away, leaving only twenty-seven, whom Fender released, telling them to report to court on their own. He blamed Wright for what he considered an intentional tardiness meant to chastise, but Fender may have taken the matter too personally; transporting ninety prisoners represented a serious demand on resources. Perhaps, with time, the new district attorney realized it was better to leave street-level enforcement to the police and sheriff; no other reports surfaced of Fender leading raids. In September 1954 he did go on a raid at 107 Northwest Twenty-Eighth Street, a gasoline station with nightly gambling, but as the guest of Fort Worth Police Chief Cato Hightower.[15]

All the uproar over gambling may have driven some operators out of the business, but it did not end gambling in Fort Worth. Certainly, there is little evidence supporting the optimism of Fred Meredith, chair of the Texas legislature's Crime Commission, who in 1952 credited citizen groups and local grand juries for ending gambling in Texas cities. In fact, in November 1954 the Tarrant County Crime Commission reported enforcement had waned to the extent that many gamblers reopened their operations, especially on Mansfield Highway, an area also known for alcohol sales to minors.[16]

A couple of well-known gambling sites did close, but their departure had more to do with circumstances than gambling enforcement. In March 1953 a $35,533 federal tax lien for back taxes was filed on the 3939 Club on Jacksboro Highway co-owned by Les Hutt, one of the indictees of March 1951 who paid a $500 misdemeanor gambling fine. That December a $4.5 million real estate development was announced that would raze Top o' Hill, but the Hill was saved in May 1956 when the Bible Baptist Seminary bought the property's forty-six acres, incorporating the land with a fifty-acre E. L. White tract they had purchased in 1955. The sale marked a rather ironic ending for the highest-profile casino in North Texas with an infamous history reaching across the nation and all the way to top of state politics. It had all begun with Fred Browning, an inveterate gambler estimated to have won and lost $8 million during his lifetime. Browning had various interests that included horse racing; he stabled forty-one thoroughbreds in Cresson, Texas (twenty miles southwest of Fort Worth) and promoted boxing matches, but he was most well-known for turning a tearoom into a thriving casino that attracted the wealthy and famous. Local and state agencies raided the Hill several times over the years but never were able to close the games permanently, perhaps a testament to influential silent supporters. In 1935 Texas Ranger Captain Tom Hickman was dismissed after loudly accusing a Texas assistant attorney general of tipping off the club about a forthcoming raid. Browning sold Top o' Hill in 1952 only to repurchase it the next year, using $70,000 borrowed from Benny Binion. Browning died later that year from heart failure, leaving the club's future in doubt. Binion might have taken over if he had not faced his own problems; he was sentenced in December 1953 to five years in Leavenworth Penitentiary for income tax evasion, along with a concurrent four-year Texas sentence for running a Dallas numbers game that netted $1 million in 1949.[17]

New spots opened to fill the void left by the Hill's demise. A June 1955 Tarrant County grand jury report mentioned a posh gambling resort operating out of at a ranch house in Parker County just across the Tarrant County line, one-half mile north of Highway 80. The club, run by A. M. "Boston" Smith, with financing by investors in Midland and Las Vegas, catered to the wealthy. Entry was only by invitation, and once inside guests received complimentary drinks and steaks. "Boston" Smith denied running house games but admitted guests often played cards. Parker County Sheriff John Young also scoffed at the claims, chiding the Tarrant County grand jury for interfering in Parker County.[18]

Fort Worth Police continued raiding local gambling joints, often aided by insider information. Acting on a tip in April 1954, Fort Worth officers entered Harry Hooser's Champagne Room, 2427 Forest Park Boulevard, but were stymied by a locked door that barred entry into the basement game room. By the time the door was opened, all activity had stopped, but officers still charged three persons with vagrancy and confiscated a poker table and other gaming paraphernalia, as well as $1,620. Also in 1954, a father upset after his son lost his savings, reported Redmen's Club (formerly the East Side Club), 5126 East Belknap Street, where police arrested eighteen persons and hauled away a truckload of gambling equipment.[19]

Widespread gambling on a grand scale involving a lot of money begat violence, contributing to a rash of gangland murders that began in the 1940s and continued into the 1950s and beyond. One of the first to die in the 1950s, Herbert Noble, was a known Dallas hoodlum and gambler who escaped so many attempts on his life that he became known as "The Cat" with nine lives. Noble's wife was not as elusive, succumbing in 1949 to a car bombing meant for her husband. In 1951 Noble escaped the tenth recorded attempt on his life when a bomb destroyed his Beechcraft airplane parked outside his Grapevine area home. Noble told investigators he suspected two Fort Worth men he had spotted just before the blast, but refused to identify them, telling police he preferred dealing with them personally. Noble's luck finally ran out on August 7, 1951, the twelfth assassination attempt in five years. He fell victim to nitroglycerin planted under the roadway in front of his mailbox that was detonated as he collected the mail. Investigators found wires at the scene leading to a car battery on a small knoll where assassins had lain in wait. Suspicion turned to four Fort Worth ex-convicts, two of whom Noble had spotted, but no one was ever charged.[20]

In August 1951 Fort Worth detectives traveled to Durant, Oklahoma, to question Herbert Deere, a local rancher jailed for killing Jim Thomas, a known Fort Worth gambler and all-around hoodlum suspected in several gangland murders (Thomas lived at 2317 Hillcrest in Fort Worth). Thomas had a long record. He received twenty-five years in 1931 for a bank robbery in Nebraska, was involved in a shootout in Texas, and was implicated in several Fort Worth murders, as well as the murders of a West Texas couple. Thomas was out on bond charged in the West Texas homicides when Deere killed him in a dispute over a truck. Deere cooperated with authorities, identifying several questionable characters he had seen with Thomas, including Frank Gates, a Thomas associate involved in gambling and various criminal activities, and Jack Nesbit, a forger, thief, and murderer known as a nitroglycerine expert.[21]

Tincy Eggleston, one of Fort Worth's most notorious gamblers and gangsters, was a suspect in several high-profile incidents. In June 1952 he and Paul Tomlin, another known gangster, were charged in a Stephens County burglary in which a safe containing $4,000 cash and $130,000 in bonds was taken from Henry Compton's ranch. The safe, weighing 650 pounds, was found behind the Benbrook Dam spillway. Tincy, Sid Foley, and Cecil Green were also prime suspects in a December 7, 1953, robbery of a private poker game in Austin in which three armed men took cash and jewelry worth over $11,000. Austin Police arrested all three, charging Foley but releasing Tincy and Green without charges. Foley suspected one or both had informed on him, creating rancor that grew after Foley's wife left him for Tincy. On Sunday, December 27, 1953, Foley spotted his ex, Green, and Tincy at Jacksboro Highway and Northwest Twenty-Eighth Street and began shooting as Tincy and company sped away while returning fire (the only injury was facial cuts to Tincy from broken glass). Two days later Foley saw his wife and Rita Davis, Green's girlfriend (or wife, depending on whom you asked), in Foley's car at 400 West Central Avenue where they had stopped to scour newspaper apartment ads. Foley jerked Mrs. Foley out of the car but was sent running when Ms. Davis pulled a shotgun. Foley's ex took the opportunity to drive away in Sid's car, stranding Rita Davis, who telephoned Green to collect her. Police officers responding to reports from neighbors, arrested Green and Rita at the scene, and nabbed Foley and Tincy when they showed up later at police headquarters. The four were paraded before roll calls to familiarize patrol officers, a common practice at the time, but they were released the next day (it was likely that both women refused to file charges) with orders to stay out of Fort Worth under threat of being arrested on sight for vagrancy.[22]

Tincy may have turned to home invasions. He was arrested, along with Cecil Green and Harry Huggins, for the May 19, 1953, murder of oilman William P. Clark at his mansion home, 2232 Winton Terrace West. Clark's death initially had been ruled a suicide, despite evidence that jewelry and other items were missing from the house, but was reclassified a homicide after further investigation and an autopsy. The case lingered for two years without progress until Huggins, under questioning about an unrelated burglary, confessed that Clark's estranged wife, Mary, had offered the three $10,000 and any jewelry they found to kill Clark and make it look like a robbery. Mrs. Clark was motivated by her husband's petition to annul their marriage after two years, which would have left her with nothing from his $750,000 estate. Huggins admitted that he, dressed as a Western Union messenger, attacked Clark as soon as he opened the door, but denied participating in the murder, claiming Tincy did the shooting. News of the death and arrests made national news, especially after Mary Clark was arrested as an accomplice. Whatever else she may have been, she must have been a tough customer to survive eighteen straight hours of interrogation without breaking. Tincy was arrested at 1519 West Pulaski, the apartment of a 21-year-old blond woman, Evelyn Robertson, a fact his wife, Walterine Watson Eggleston, found unpleasant (police reported Tincy had kept the woman in the apartment for a year). Huggins, as the lone cooperating witness, was in considerable danger. The Tarrant County Jail placed him in a secure, single cell reserved for prisoners under death sentences, but Huggins bonded out, only to be rearrested March 9 inside John Hancock Paints, 900 West Magnolia Avenue, prompting an added charge as a habitual criminal that carried no bond. In April 1956 Huggins was sentenced to five years for the Clark murder and two years for the burglary, leniency granted at the request of Captain O. R. Brown, who testified to his cooperation.[23]

Huggins told the court at Mary Clark's trial that he thought they were going on a routine robbery but began to have doubts after William Clark asked if his wife had sent them to kill him. Tincy remained with William in an upstairs bedroom while Huggins and Green searched the house for cash and jewels. During the search they heard a shot, followed by Tincy hurriedly coming downstairs shouting they should leave. Later, Mrs. Clark gave them $6,000 in cash, which the three split along with whatever they had found in the house. An employee of Cox's Department Store testified he saw Mrs. Clark and Tincy together several times at the store acting like they were a couple, that Mary ordered a gown after Tincy indicated his approval. The defense attacked the supposed relationship, presenting a bank employee resembling Tincy who claimed to have often accompanied Mary on shopping sprees. Mary admitted dalliances with other men, describing amorous letters she sent to a New York broker and a relationship with a man named Slaughter who got into an altercation with her sister at a north side bar. Despite the testimony of a co-conspirator, the jury returned a not-guilty verdict for the widow Clark. Both Tincy and Green were killed before they could be tried, leaving only Huggins to serve any time for the murder. Detective Captain O. R. Brown planned to pay bills with the $6,000 reward he received from the slain man's estate and brother.[24]

Tincy was suspected, but was never charged, in a home invasion of a fellow gambler and hoodlum, Gene May. On May 21, 1953, three men entered the May home, 3719 Encanto Drive, holding the family hostage while searching for cash and valuables, then leaving with $6,620. Police believed that Tincy and Cecil Green were two of the trio but failed to develop sufficient evidence to file charges on either. May was no angel. Two years after the home invasion, he was a prime suspect in an October 27, 1955, robbery in San Antonio in which $13,600 was taken. May admitted to being in town at the time gambling but indignantly denied the crime, arguing he already had two Cadillacs and a $120,000 home in Westcliff and did not need to rob.[25]

Tincy remained in the area, often showing up at Edell Evans's home, 7267 Hardesty Street in Richland Hills (a suburb east of Fort Worth), a known dice game center. Harry Rogers of Dallas filed a complaint with the Tarrant County sheriff charging that Tincy slugged him the evening of February 14, 1955, after Rogers questioned the dice game. Sheriff's deputies raiding the home the next day confiscated 4,000 pairs of dice, poker chips, and playing cards and arrested Evans, who confessed and paid a $42.50 gambling fine. Eggleston, accompanied by two lawyers, turned himself in at the sheriff's office on the assault charge. Talking to reporters, he admitted being a gambler but refused comment on the specifics of the assault, saying only that he had been in Fort Worth on and off and had not been bothered.[26]

In 1955 two of Fort Worth's most notorious gamblers/gangsters met their ends. The first to depart, Edell Evans, known as Mr. Five by Five because of his stocky build, was well known to Fort Worth Police, who had orders to arrest him on sight. Evans dabbled in many vices but concentrated on gambling and pimping prostitutes through the Evans Stock Company, where a telephone call would bring a woman in a taxi to your door. In March 1955 police arrested Evans for vagrancy and investigation, generic charges, after getting a tip that he was at the Parrish Inn, 3920 East Belknap Street, a known gambling den. Evans ran a crooked dice game at his Richland Hills home, using magnets controlled by a person in the attic to move the dice. On April 3, 1955, Evans left home, telling the maid that he was going to meet a man named Cecil at a Jacksboro Highway tavern. He never returned, but his bloody car was found several days later near Irving, Texas, and sent to the state crime laboratory in Austin, where the blood was determined to be human. An anonymous woman caller reported a man at a party bragged that Evans had been "planted," meaning killed and buried, most likely near Lake Worth, the location surmised from the boaster's remark that Cecil Green, driving Evans's car, lost control at a dip in the road near Casino Beach. From that sketchy information investigators searched fields around Jacksboro Highway and FM 1886, finding Evans's body in a shallow grave about 300 yards west of the northern end of Lake Worth. He had been shot in the head and suffered other wounds. Street information suggested that four experienced gamblers, perhaps including Tincy Eggleston and Cecil Green, who lost $80,000 at his dice table, ordered his death after learning the game was rigged.[27]

Fort Worth Police Chief Cato Hightower and Tarrant County Sheriff Harlon Wright with gun at site where Edell Evans' body was recovered, November 1, 1955. Courtesy *Fort Worth Star Telegram* Collection, Special Collections, University of Texas at Arlington Libraries.

Evans's wife, Dorothy Jean Evans, a widow at 23, moved to Cleburne, where she became a local celebrity known for flashy clothes and a pink Cadillac. In 1956 she entered into a relationship with Hobart Upham, an oilman many years her senior, who lavished her with gifts. An IRS audit assessed her $84,134 in unpaid taxes on the gifts, suggesting the items had a total value in the neighborhood of $500,000. Mrs. Evans quickly paid the tax bill. A few months later she took out a marriage license with Don Walker, a Santa Fe Railway electrician in Cleburne.[28]

The second local gangster to die in 1955, Cecil Green, was killed during an ambush outside the By-Way Drive-In, 5605 Jacksboro Highway, the evening of May 2, 1955. Green and Tincy Eggleston were in Green's Cadillac in the parking lot when car lights from the Double-Bar Club, next door at 5563 Jacksboro Highway, illuminated them and gunfire erupted from at least two shooters. Green, hit seven times, fell to the floor, but Tincy, with only minor injuries from broken glass, escaped, running from the car while emptying his own pistol. Tincy told the police he thought the assassins were out-of-towners, that he got a good look and did not recognize them. Tincy went into deep hiding, leading his wife, Walterine Eggleston, to file desertion charges in May 1955, reporting her husband had not been to their home at 1216 West Beddell Street in two months (the assault occurred less than a month prior but Tincy could have abandoned the home earlier). In his absence she and their daughter were left destitute, devoid of financial assistance since April when Tincy had given her $200. To heap insult on insult, Tincy used cash he received from selling his wife's jewelry to buy his young blond girlfriend a $750 ring. Mrs. Eggleston was only 34 in 1955, but she had been with Tincy for nineteen years, the two having married when she was only 15.[29]

After Green's death the *Star Telegram* ran photographs of eight "of at least nine underworld characters" slain since 1943; the list included Ray Sellers, Nelson Harris, Lon Holley, Que R. Miller, Herbert Noble, Lois Green, Jim Thomas, Edell Evans, and Cecil Green. The front-page spread included a blank space asking who would be next. Some historians such as Richard Selcer accepted the list as final, the last entry in a string of gangland assassinations going back to 1943, but that claim ignored several more killings, including Tincy Eggleston and Sid Foley, to name only two.[30]

Just two months later, in August 1955, an anonymous tipster reported Tincy's car abandoned in the Buddies Super Market, 3220 North Main Street. Investigating officers found a blood-stained interior and a spent shotgun shell as well as Tincy's hat and coat. Tincy's wife reported that he left home August 25, 1955, telling her he was going to meet someone on the north side. After leaving, he stopped off at his blond girlfriend's home before leaving about 5:00 p.m. and disappearing. Police focused their search on a rural area four and one-half miles west of Saginaw, Texas (a suburb just north of Fort Worth), based on a report from a couple parking in the area who heard a gunshot. Tincy's body was eventually found in in an abandoned well and removed using grappling hooks. Tincy died from shotgun buckshot wounds in his head, armpit and right side.[31]

Informants provided various explanations that were all over the map. One held Tincy had been killed by a man who owed him $5,000, while another suggested an Oklahoma-Dallas syndicate issued the hit after Tincy and Edell Evans had refused to share several thousand dollars fleeced from gamblers at Evans's crooked dice game, contradicting earlier reports that Tincy killed Evans after being victimized by the crooked game. One outlandish account from a Panamanian private investigator, Colonel Gaspar Mendez, claimed the Lucky Luciano crime syndicate contracted with Tincy in Los Angeles, along with two other men, to assassinate President José Antonio Remón Cantera of Panama, who was killed on January 2, 1955, in Panama City. According to the fanciful report, Tincy was paid $20,000 for the hit and given $15,000 for the two accomplices, but he gambled away the $15,000 and was killed for that indiscretion. Mendez claimed that a German Schmeisser machine gun confiscated from a stolen vehicle recovered in Hurst, Texas (a suburb northeast of Fort Worth), on August 16, 1955, had been used in the Cantera assassination. No hard evidence ever developed to support the Mendez account. A more likely tie to Tincy's demise turned up in December 1956 when a road crew discovered a rusted twelve-gauge shotgun, a pistol and two bank sacks with a few coins in a culvert off Saginaw-Watauga Road, less than a mile from where Tincy's body had been recovered. Investigators suspected it was the murder weapon but could not prove it, and no one was ever charged.[32]

Tincy's widow attempted suicide in March 1956, shooting herself in the stomach with a .38-caliber pistol. Just before the shooting, Walterine telephoned Fort Worth Police Captain O. R. Brown, telling him she wanted everything she left to go to Carole Ann, the couple's 14-year-old daughter, then married and living in Odessa, Texas, followed by a gunshot. Brown dispatched officers who found her in the hallway, wounded but still alive. Recovering at St. Joseph's Hospital, Mrs. Eggleston told the staff she was broke, unemployed, desperate, and tired.[33]

In May 1955 former Fort Worth Motorcycle Officer James Clyde "Chuck" Parrish shot and killed Willkie "Blackie" Matthews, former owner of Blackie's Buggy Wheel on Jacksboro Highway. The shooting occurred in Parrish's room at the Valley View Tourist Court, 2306 East Belknap Street, following an argument over a dice game. An appeals court overturned Parrish's conviction in the murder, and in 1960 Criminal District Judge Willis McGregor dismissed the charge at the request of the district attorney after the key witness, J. W. "Happy Jack" Jones, was slain in New Mexico. In August 1956 Marvin Woodie Dunham, a hoodlum with a record that included four convictions for robbery and multiple theft offenses, was critically wounded by a gunshot to the stomach as he sat with Parrish in a car at a 3401 East Lancaster Avenue parking lot. Dunham and Parrish refused to provide police with any information.[34]

Few pedophilia cases appeared in the local press, but the evidence suggested that it was more common than the few press reports indicated. In April 1951 Edwin Louis Johnson, a 38-year-old chemical plant employee, was arrested for indecent exposure and enticing a child for immoral purposes. At the time Johnson was out on bond for soliciting a child under 14 to commit sodomy, and a July 1950 incident in which he took a 5-year-old girl off the street, claiming he only wanted to ask directions (of a 5-year old). Fortunately, the family began an immediate search that found Johnson and the girl in a nearby wooded area. The girl's father, Jesse Roy Shaw, was arrested for shooting Johnson before police arrived. Johnson's second arrest, coming while he was awaiting trial on the 1950 offense, precipitated a review of pending sex crime cases that found only one sex crime case had been adjudicated while seven indictments, including that of Johnson, were waiting trials, suggesting that there had been either a sudden rash of cases or a tendency to drag out prosecutions. The police had no control over court schedules, but they did what police do, launching an accelerated enforcement drive. Two of the first casualties, Francis Dudley Randles and Rogene Edmund Colgrove, both adults, were arrested for sodomy committed at 2:30 a.m. at the Texas and Pacific Railway Station. In May 1951 Donald Hughes, a Carswell airman, was quickly arrested after he forced a 7-year-old girl to commit sodomy, his capture made easier because the victim recognized Hughes as a resident of the same apartment house. Ironically, Hughes was a newlywed, having married only three days earlier, on May 28, 1951. In another case Harold

Arnold, a machinist, received a suspended sentence after he was found guilty of fondling a 9-year-old girl.[35]

Pornography, outside of printed forms, was rare but available. On the evening of November 13, 1953, two undercover police officers were part of a crowd of 200 men at the Annex of the Skyliner Club watching stag films and live sex performances by nude couples, at least until police officers arrived in force to end the show. The newspaper report did not go into specifics describing the performances but did note that the cast included both whites and Blacks, including one interracial couple, a Black man with a white woman. W. D. Satterwhite, the Annex operator, claimed ignorance, saying he rented the club for a private party that, according to the renters, would feature business films and a striptease act. Police arrested the eight "performers" and a 19-year-old in the audience.[36]

In the 1950s Texas became a major transit point for marijuana just as the drug expanded from its original base among Mexican Americans in border states to a national clientele. United States Commissioner of Narcotics H. J. Anslinger explained marijuana's rapid spread by its relative cheapness, easy availability, and ease of use, requiring no devices to ingest. He cautioned against assuming the drug's popularity meant it was harmless, warning that "murderous and maniacal tendencies result from 'reefer' smoking" and that its addiction drove boys and men to commit robberies, thefts, and burglaries and turned girls into prostitutes and thieves. P. A. Williams, supervising federal narcotics agent over Texas, Louisiana, and Mississippi, warned that Texas's border with Mexico made it the center of a national drug traffic chain supplying marijuana to the nation. Williams conceded his twelve agents assigned to all of Texas were inadequate to the challenge and had to rely on local agencies to shoulder most enforcement. He praised Tarrant County for assigning an assistant district attorney and investigator to narcotics enforcement, noting they had filed seven drug cases in the first six months of 1951 after only ten cases had been filed between 1948 and 1951. He also praised Fort Worth Police vice officers for breaking up a barbiturate racket and curtailing marijuana distribution, driving up the price to $12 a pound and a "stick" (cigarette) from $0.50 to $1.25. He added it was time for Fort Worth to establish a dedicated narcotic squad. At this early stage, arrest figures were relatively low, suggesting either the problem was not widespread or enforcement was ineffective. In 1954 Houston led Texas cities with 284 drug arrests and 146 convictions, followed by Dallas with 146 and 42, and Fort Worth with only 44 and 33, respectively.[37]

Arrest statistics reflect marijuana's increased availability and its growing popularity among white youths, although whites seemed less likely to be prosecuted. Prior to the 1950s drug use, especially of marijuana, tended to be concentrated among Hispanics. Author Jim Thompson, who worked as a Fort Worth hotel bellboy in the 1920s, regularly supplied hotel guests with marijuana, cocaine, and heroin he bought in the "Mexican Quarter" along North Main Street. By 1954 Fort Worth Vice Officers D. A. Mahan and H. O. Middleton would describe local marijuana use as rampant among white teenagers, and W. E. Naylor, chief of the Texas Department of Public Safety's Narcotic's Section, called teen drug use the state's biggest dope problem, blaming its spread on young people trying marijuana to avoid being called "chicken." Incredibly, Naylor also claimed marijuana was addictive, capable of hooking users to a habit costing $36 daily, forcing them into other crimes, especially theft. Mrs. Maxine Burlingham, superintendent of the Texas State School for Girls at Gainesville, affirmed the prevalence of drugs, especially marijuana, among young white delinquents. According to her statistics, 33 of 180 committed girls admitted they had been exposed to dope, largely marijuana or "goof balls (barbiturates)." Most of the 33 ended up at the state school because of sexual promiscuity. For example, Katharine Calloway, age 14, and Shirley Butts, 15, were adjudicated delinquent in 1952 based on testimony that they had attended a sex and marijuana party with six boys, frequented Black night clubs and shoe shine parlors, and kept late hours. Ms. Calloway was placed under the supervision of Tarrant County Probation Officer Lynn Ross, but Ms. Butts was remanded to the State School for Girls, presumably because she was older.[38]

A few minors entered the federal treatment program. The USPHSH reported patients as young as 16 in their five-month addiction treatment program, but they remained a small part of their caseload; only eleven patients were under 20 in January 1955. Critics dismissed the lack of youth addiction treatment as a nonissue since neither treatment nor punishment had shown impressive results. It was true that treatments had not shown much success. The two federal narcotics hospitals at Fort Worth and Lexington, Kentucky, reported high recidivism and only a 5 percent success rate. In one noteworthy case, a patient just released from treatment used heroin on the train ride home. Despite the lack of success, confinement rates for narcotics use rose dramatically. Secretary of Health, Education, and Welfare Oveta Culp Hobby reported that between 1945 and 1947 the Fort Worth USPHSH averaged only 25 narcotic patients, but during 1950 to 1952 the average soared to over 350. Hobby credited the meteoric rise to increased drug use coupled with the federal government's doubling down on penalties for violations of the Harrison Narcotics Act of 1914, increasing maximum sentences to forty years and, in certain cases, sanctioning the death penalty.[39]

Local drug enforcement tended to focus on marijuana, more specifically on African Americans with marijuana, which seemed to involve a lot of musicians. Vice Officers D. P. Mahan and H. O. Middleton worked a case for weeks on an East Lancaster Avenue nightspot where marijuana cigarettes were sold, most often to white teenagers. Sellers tried to hide their involvement by putting the marijuana cigarettes in a handkerchief or a regular cigarette package and dropping them so the buyer would pick them up from the floor rather than directly from the supplier. In July 1951 the two officers using an unknown buyer were able to arrest five Blacks at the club, including a club musician. Patrol officers responding to a fight on Luella Street arrested a couple for possession after they found marijuana in the woman's purse. In December 1953 two musicians, one from New York City and one from Detroit, were returning from Juarez, Mexico, when they were stopped and their vehicle searched, turning up 2,047 grains of marijuana (133 grams or 4.75 ounces). In December 1953 four Black men were found with marijuana inside an Evans Avenue hotel. Three of the charged pled guilty, two receiving three years and the third two years, but the fourth went to trial and walked free after the judge dismissed the case, calling the evidence too circumstantial.[40]

In 1951 an undercover narcotics officer posing as a student at Wichita Falls High School, identified Amelia Palmarez of Fort Worth as a major marijuana supplier for the North Texas area, reporting he bought $30 worth of marijuana from her. Ms. Palmarez, 65-years old, was described as a "witch doctor type" dealing in curative herbs from her home, a shack at Ninth and Kerrigan Streets. A subsequent raid by Texas Rangers and Fort Worth Narcotics Officer H. F. Hopkins confiscated several sacks of marijuana and a marijuana "tree" growing on the property.[41]

The incidence of reported drug use exploded in the 1950s compared to earlier decades, bringing an intense public scrutiny that demanded action. In 1953 the United States Congress began a series of investigative hearings on drug use. In 1955 Texas Senator Price Daniel convened a committee hearing in Fort Worth on the tripling of narcotics convictions in Dallas, San Antonio, and Fort Worth since 1945. The committee heard from 346 witnesses, a long list that included police officials and narcotics traffickers. Charles Beland (see p. 227) was called but was unable to attend due a mortal illness (he died shortly afterward), but his wife testified, although she could offer little new information after being off drugs for years. Chief Hightower reported most Fort Worth dope came from Dallas and Temple or from Mexican border towns and that a lot of marijuana arrived from San Antonio and white heroin came in from both coasts. Harry Huggins, partner in crime with most of Fort Worth's gangsters, testified that he had used cocaine and morphine and had seen Tincy and Cecil Green use those drugs as well as marijuana.[42]

In 1953 Fort Worth Police launched a large roundup netting ninety-eight narcotics arrests, almost equally divided between whites and Blacks. Most of the arrests were made in cheap rooming houses and bars populating the south end of downtown, places like Grover's Hotel, 1502½ Main Street, where lodgers could get a room for seventy-five cents or sleep on a dormitory cot for less, or the Roxy Hotel, 1409½ Main Street, a walkup hotel for the indigent offering a cot in a room shared with as many others as could be squeezed in for fifty cents. The Roxy posted two house rules: no bay rum allowed and lights out after 10:00 p.m.[43]

Patrol officers also made the occasional narcotic arrests. In June 1953 a man on probation for marijuana possession took off when he saw two patrol officers at Eighth and Calhoun Streets. Officers retrieved a packet they saw him throw that contained forty-three marijuana cigarettes. The Parrish Inn, long known as a gambling den, was also a center for drugs. In March 1955 officers approaching Bobby Teel sitting with a woman in the club's parking lot saw the woman toss a matchbox containing eight marijuana cigarettes. That same month patrol officers arrested a Black man at 900 Calhoun Street carrying twenty-six marijuana cigarettes.[44]

Paregoric, a mixture containing opium used to control coughing and as an antidiarrheal medicine, was widely abused. A 57-year-old man told reporters that he had used cocaine, heroin, codeine, and morphine for thirty years to alleviate hangovers before turning to paregoric, known as Big G, because it could be bought at four Fort Worth drug stores for $0.50 without prescription or restriction, much less than the $15 to $20 for other drugs. City Narcotics Investigator Kenneth Glass agreed that paregoric had become a big problem with easy availability at unethical drug stores. Some medical professionals abused opiates. In 1954 Barbara Shockley, a surgical nurse at St. Joseph's hospital, was arrested and charged with fraudulently procuring narcotics. Ms. Shockley admitted her guilt, saying she turned to drugs to relieve tensions from her divorce and the death of a parent.[45]

The "great white father" of Fort Worth's illegal drug in the 1950s was John Thomas Lott, a white man living at 1702 South Jennings Street. In 1953 police arrested Lott and several accomplices based on evidence supplied by Floyd Luke Watkins, a Black special agent of the United States Narcotics Bureau. Most of the incriminating evidence came from a wire recording worn by Watkins, one of the early uses of wired informants. The state described Lott as a major drug promoter. In one infamous incident, he spread a drug cache on a bed and gave everyone an injection of their choice. Lott was sentenced to ten years for conspiring to distribute drugs, and his four accomplices, Johnny "Yank" Reed, Larry Pierce, Joe Shaw, and Doris Shaw (also known as Doris Miller), all African Americans, received five to ten years.[46]

Doris Shaw began serving her sentence but joined Lott, Reed, and Pierce in an appeal on the grounds the search was illegal and that having only one defense lawyer for all four Black defendants constituted improper representation. The US Court of Appeals in New Orleans reversed all four convictions, agreeing that the warrantless search of a rear shed where officers recovered 128 grains of narcotics was illegal and that one attorney defending four defendants constituted improper representation, also adding that the court erred in admitting Lott's criminal history. The retrial of all four (Lott, Reed, Pierce, and Shaw) began March 22, 1955, with separate counsel for each defendant. Lott was reconvicted, receiving a reduced sentence of five years at Leavenworth. He reappealed, charging the government knowingly used perjured testimony, that Agent Watkins had admitted lying in an affidavit. Watkins had been held in protective custody at the Tarrant County Jail during the trial but had left after the trial and had to be located and returned for the second appeal.[47]

The Beland family, long associated with Fort Worth narcotics, remained active in the drug trade before falling to the ravages of time. The family matriarch, Lucy "Ma" Beland, moved from Grandview, just twenty miles south, to Fort Worth in 1908. In the city she and her family became heavily involved in narcotics, thefts, and prostitution, racking up thirty convictions between 1921 and 1947 and earning the FBI's designation as the nation's leading dope runners. They remained involved into the 1950s, although age and the consequences of their lifestyle had begun to wear on them. One son, Charles Louis Beland, born in 1900, developed a lengthy drug history after first being arrested and sent to Leavenworth Penitentiary for narcotics in 1920. On his release Charles immediately returned to the drug trade, earning several more convictions, including a seven-year sentence in November 1941 for a host of offenses committed with accomplices Charles Shiffen, Abe Chapman, and Jack Leftak. All four initially went to Leavenworth, but Beland was transferred to Alcatraz after he developed such an efficient drug supply line that his arms and legs became covered with needle marks. In March 1945 Charles was again paroled and returned to Fort Worth. On April 30, 1951, he and another son, Joe "Pusher" Beland, were arrested along with Estha Hamilton Beland, Charlie's wife, and Ruby Allen, Joe's companion, at Joe's home, 1401 North Riverside Drive. The two men were convicted and sentenced to five years in prison for sale of narcotics while Mrs. Joe Beland (Ruby Allen) received five years for possession of narcotics. Joe "Pusher" also had a lengthy history, having been first arrested in 1926 and sentenced five times to Leavenworth where he served a total of seventeen years before dying in prison of natural causes in 1951. Two years later in 1953 "Ma" Beland died at 5536 Calmont Avenue, the home of her daughter, Alice Beland Hamilton, who was married to Francis "Dago" Hamilton, holder of an extensive history of narcotics and theft convictions. Charlie Beland died November 26, 1955, of throat cancer, but his wife, Estha, survived until 1982. A daughter, Willie Beland, also known as Lucy, worked as a prostitute while amassing a series of narcotics arrests. She married Leslie James, who had at least five narcotics convictions between 1931 and 1953. Willie died of lung cancer as a charity patient in 1956. Another daughter, Cora, followed the family tradition, working as a prostitute while still a teenager and dying in prison of a drug overdose.[48]

Homosexuality, then a criminal offense in Texas, remained largely hidden, its presence only hinted at in news reports. One such incident came to light the evening of January 28, 1952, when Albert Reagen, a 51-year-old lawyer, was found in a gully off Bluff Street clad only in underwear, shorts, and shoes. Reagen said he met two 17-year-old boys at a downtown hotel coffee shop and was walking with them to watch television at their place when the two attacked, cutting his arm and leg and taking his suit and $3. Police found the two young men nearby, still carrying Reagan's suit. The two, both members of the Tenth Street Gang, a notorious downtown youth gang known to carry knives and commit thefts, admitted meeting Mr. Reagen but denied attacking him. In March 1954 Carl Gee Jr. was indicted for sodomy after forcing two 11-year-old boys to commit "unnatural sex acts." It was not Gee's first brush with the law; in November 1953 he was arrested in Buck Sansom Park in the back seat of car with two boys. The youths told officer that Gee lured them into the car with promises of farm work.[49]

Prostitution remained, but the police seemed to have lost their focus, perhaps because corruption and the abbreviated life spans for local gangsters had shifted the public's attention to gambling and gamblers. In March 1951 raids at four small downtown hotels, centers for prostitutes, netted a mere seven women, a paltry figure. Police Sergeant Pinkhard credited the low tally to daily police checks at twenty-five hotels and motels known to cater to the sex trade, suggesting the extra scrutiny had forced many working women to leave for easier locales. Reports supported enforcement's impact, but the effect seemed more to displace than eliminate. The 1951 grand jury report recommended a local crime commission that would promote vice enforcement, but nothing happened until January 1952 when grand jury Foreman Sam Braswell announced an organizing committee had formed to create the Tarrant County Crime Commission, Inc. The group's charter called for reducing crime by directing public attention to problem areas, assuming awareness would bring enforcement. In November 1954 the commission reported prostitutes had largely abandoned downtown Fort Worth but were common in surrounding motels and would travel to downtown hotels if called.[50]

On such suburban operation was busted in March 1955. Police arrested Mary Isbell, 20 years old; Jackie Wilson, 21 years old; and Betty Barns, 25 years old, in an Arlington Heights apartment where they operated a call girl service. Mary Isbell reported earning $150 nightly on calls to local hotels and tourist courts, where she received $50 a visit or "date." Also arrested were Teddy Wilcher, the 24-year-old leader of the group, and husband of Mary Isbell, and J. C. Mize, 27 years old. All five had recently returned to Fort Worth after relocating to Dallas for several weeks to escape the extensive police attention on prostitution directed at bringing down Edell Evans, a known pimp and gambler. The group's downfall may have been due to its parsimony. Hotel and tourist camp porters tipped off police to the group's operation after Wilcher and Mize refused to pay for referrals.[51]

An April 1953 valedictory report by the outgoing Tarrant County grand jury complained about rampant prostitution at tourist camps and of children as young as 14 working and being served alcohol in bars on Jacksboro Highway, Mansfield Highway, and downtown Fort Worth. The two issues were often related in that many prostitutes were quite young. In 1954 a 14-year-old girl testified in court that Tommy Brewster, a known trafficker of young prostitutes, seduced her in a downtown hotel before forcing her into prostitution at the Rio Lodge Motel, 1850 Jacksboro Highway. Brewster was convicted and received a forty-year sentence, an unusually severe sentence that was likely impacted by his reputation as a corrupter of youth. An appeals court voided the conviction, bringing Brewster's release on a $15,000 bond, pending a new trial. Brewster did not let his legal troubles change his tendency to exist on the fringes of legality. In August 1954 he and Eugene Webb, a known Fort Worth burglar, were with George Mann in Tulsa, Oklahoma, when Mann was arrested for passing counterfeit $20 bills forged in Fort Worth by Thomas C. Davis, 1527 Northeast Thirty-Sixth Street. Davis admitted he printed $8,000 in $20 bills that Mann and Joe Fernandez passed in various cities.[52]

Chapter 15

Policing, 1951–1955

After sixteen difficult months fraught with corruption scandals, Police Chief George Hawkins resigned and was replaced by Roland R. Howerton on April 25, 1951. Howerton, who joined the force in 1930 and rose through the ranks to become the department's first assistant chief, earned a monthly salary of $640. He quickly made major changes to the upper command structure, naming R. E. "Dick" Tarvin assistant chief and H. Clay Bishop night chief. Also in 1951 Barney Finn, founder of the Fort Worth Police fingerprint section and a nationally known fingerprint expert, died of heart disease. Finn studied fingerprinting at Fort Leavenworth, Kansas, before taking over the Fort Worth Police Identification Section, serving from 1913 to 1934 when he resigned under accusations involving misappropriated Police Benevolent Association funds.[1]

In his first year Howerton faced a series of issues involving financial payoffs. He had been chief just over two months in July 1951 when the grand jury indicted twenty-eight Fort Worth police officers for bribery involving kickbacks from wrecker operators. At the time police tows were unregulated, leaving field officers free to call any wrecker, an open system in which tow truck drivers paid for referrals. The indictments were quashed by District

Attorney Heilman, who ruled the payments did constitute a crime as the bribery statue was written and interpreted. Chief Howerton ended the problem by establishing a wrecker rotation system, eliminating officer involvement. A similar arrangement involved under-the-table payments from lawyers and bondspersons paying officers for referrals. The system became public knowledge in March 1954 when the grand jury criticized the practice. Chief Cato Hightower, who replaced Howerton in 1953, banned the practice, promising to fire any officers taking payoffs.[2]

In June 1952 Officers A. V. Hickman and C. D. Ferris, patrol car partners, were indicted and terminated for demanding and receiving $35 from Lewis McCline, a porter at the La Verde Tourist Camp, 2221 Jacksboro Highway, a known haunt for prostitutes. Ferris appealed, but the Civil Service Commission upheld his termination after a couple testified that they heard the officers threaten to arrest McCline if he did not pay. The district attorney dropped criminal charges against Ferris, but Hickman was tried, convicted, and given a two-year suspended sentence.[3]

Financial malfeasance among police may have been related to poor pay and negative work issues. A 1952 federal grand jury report described the Fort Worth Police Department as understaffed and underpaid. The POA suggested staffing would improve if new recruits were not required to spend $200, over a month's salary, for uniforms before they even started work. Just four days later, on April 14, 1952, twenty-nine new police officers began a four-week academy covering first aid, law, firearms, care and use of equipment, and one week of traffic control. A subsequent grand jury report in 1955 recommended a joint city-county crime laboratory staffed by trained professionals and the hiring of African American investigators in the district attorney's office.[4]

Officers also struggled with alcohol abuse and domestic violence, two issues that drew less censure than they do today. In August 1951 Chief Howerton suspended Detectives Tom Hoote and J. W. Montgomery for fifteen days after they were caught drinking on duty. Two months later he accepted the resignation of Officer Jackson Roland and terminated Officer Eugene Robertson, a trainee without civil service protection, after the two were found in a squad car drinking beer with two women. An egregious example of shifting standards was seen in the case of Officer Ralph Sandlin, arrested and charged with aggravated assault after allegedly striking his wife hard enough to bruise her cheek. When the criminal charges were dismissed at the wife's request, Chief Howerton canceled the disciplinary action, saying it was a "domestic matter."[5]

Misconduct in professional discharge of duties seemed to be a rarer issue. In August 1952 Chief Howerton suspended Officer E. M. Bilger for fifteen days and F. J. Boyle for three days after Bilger admitted using a baton to strike a traffic violator complaining about a citation. Both officers admitted their mistake and apologized. In 1952 Mrs. Eula Nicolay, owner of the Nicolay Hotel, 1401½ Calhoun Street, sued Vice Officers H. O. Middleton and Don P. Mahan for $4,000 after they arrested her as a vagrant inside the hotel she owned (the charge was dismissed). The officers countered that the hotel was a known haven for prostitutes and they had just arrested two women and three men in the hotel's rooms for vagrancy, the common charge for prostitution arrests. They added that Mrs. Nicolay had been arrested for vagrancy several times since 1939, as recently as nine months earlier. Officer Billy W. Thomas was dismissed after a captain found him playing dominoes with three African American men in a domino parlor on Bonnell Avenue. His partner, left in the patrol car, a rookie on his first tour of night patrol, was retained without punishment.[6]

The new Civil Service Commission became a real force mediating disciplinary actions. In September 1951 the commission reinstated Officer Clifton Harris, fired for unbecoming conduct regarding an affair with Juanita Fort while both were married to others. The reversal may have come from a lack of certainty; both Mrs. Fort, since divorced from C. B. Fort, owner of the Old Mill Inn, and Officer Harris denied the relationship. In October 1951 the commission returned Officers Newton Stone and Charlie Williams to work after the grand jury no-billed them on theft charges stemming from allegations they took $300 from William Kessler after finding him asleep in a car. Both men received back wages for income lost while suspended.[7]

Most police officers served honorably and competently in an occupation that could become dangerous at any time. In August 1951 Officers H. L. Stephenson and T. J. Stevenson were wounded in the 200 block of

Cooper Street by two shotgun blasts fired by Thurman Wilson, a 17-year-old Black youth upset because police had stopped him three times in one month. The officers were driving away after questioning and releasing Wilson when he fired, causing non–life-threatening wounds. The evening of July 2, 1952, Fort Worth Patrol officers were involved in two unrelated shootings within blocks of each other. In the first incident, Officer C. K. Hawley shot Max Serrano outside a bar at 1316 South Main Street after Serrano shot another patron and fired on arriving officers. Four hours later Officer R. B. Dean shot a burglar lunging at him with a tire tool inside the Motor Lunch #3, 308 West Magnolia Avenue.[8]

On February 7, 1952, Detective Henry Cleveland was killed, Detective A. L. Armstrong was shot in the chest, and Dallas Police Detective H. C. Holloway was shot in the leg at 1933 Queen Street in the Meadowbrook neighborhood. The three officers, along with Dallas Detective T. O. Pope, were at the residence to talk to Robert Barber about a January 2, 1952, robbery at the Birch Café in Dallas in which bandits got away with $15,000. Upon their arrival Pope and Armstrong waited at the rear while Cleveland and Holloway went to the front door, where they were admitted by Robert's wife, Mrs. Doris Barber. Cleveland was checking the bedroom for the suspect when Barber fired from an adjoining bathroom, killing Cleveland and wounding Holloway and Armstrong. Detective Pope ended the carnage by shooting Barber in the chest, arm, and leg when he ran out the front door.[9]

While recovering from his wounds at St. Joesph's Hospital, Barber overpowered a sheriff's deputy, took the deputy's pistol, and fled on foot before forcing a woman from her car and driving away as officers fired. He subsequently abducted a Texas Wesleyan College student, having him to drive to Mansfield, Texas (fifteen miles southwest), where Chief Howerton and Cato Hightower, together in a car, spotted the vehicle. They recaptured Barber and released the student unharmed. Barber was convicted in Cleveland's death and given a fifty-year sentence but planned an appeal, alleging the officers illegally entered his home without a warrant. Barber eventually dropped the appeal as part of a plea bargain on the Dallas robbery in which he pled guilty in exchange for a seventy-five-year sentence, leaving him eligible for parole after twenty-five years.[10]

Two other police officers died in 1952, both in traffic collisions. On June 17, 1952, at 4:35 a.m., Officer Charles W. Hoffman died from injuries received when his motorcycle collided with a car at Northwest Twenty-First Street and Ephraim Avenue while he was chasing a speeder. Ironically, Hoffman had recently asked Motors Sergeant Lawrence Wood for a transfer, stating he thought his luck had run out on motorcycles. The POA donated $200 to his widow and started a fund. Just days later, June 20, Motorcycle Officer Namon L. Cox was killed in a collision with a car at Hemphill Street and Woodland Avenue.[11]

On Christmas day 1955, around 11:00 p.m., Police Officer Marvin Wills was found in a field south of the Western Hills Hotel, clubbed and shot four times. Wills, assigned to the warrant division, was off duty at the time working as a hotel house detective. His body bore bite marks to the hands and legs, indicating a close, violent struggle, and his duty pistol was missing, suggesting he may have been shot with his own weapon. His killer was never caught and his widow, Mrs. Mable Willis, was left destitute without a pension since his death occurred off duty. She received only a $4,500 settlement from the hotel's insurance provider, less one-third that went to her lawyers.[12]

Chief R. R. Howerton's tenure was marked by criticism from within and without the police department over what some saw as harsh and strict discipline. The grumbling drew a vote of confidence for the chief from the General Ministers Alliance in April 1953, issued because the ministers had heard that underworld figures were out to "get his job." Their support was not sufficient. A week later Howerton stepped down to assistant chief, saying he wanted to bring harmony to the department wracked by adversity. Cato Hightower, on the force since 1936, became chief the same day, with a monthly salary of $650. Hightower's appointment did not immediately squash dissension within the ranks. Rumors flew that five higher-ranking department personnel planned to discredit the new chief by slacking off prostitution enforcement, letting the number of prostitutes swell, then publicly making arrests to make it appear Chief Hightower had let vice run unabated. A 24-year-old north side hooker identified an officer from a photo spread who approached her about resuming work.[13]

One of Hightower's first initiatives was to institute night patrols targeting a new street gang, the Tenth Streeters. The gang formed in 1953 around members of the Southsiders Gang that police had run out of downtown (the Southsiders remained active, just out of downtown) and the Tenth Street Gang broken up by police pressure fifteen months earlier. A reporter interviewed a 16-year-old Tenth Streeter who joined the gang after being arrested for writing bad checks. The miscreant lad carried a switchblade knife but claimed some packed guns. Rank-and-file members were identified by drake haircuts (ducktail), upturned back collars, and low-slung trousers with the belt buckle on the side. More seasoned members who had been to Gatesville, the state reformatory for boys, sported a Gatesville Cross tattoo on their hand. The gang supported themselves by thefts and burglaries, but when not doing either, they spent considerable time cruising, looking for girls.[14]

In 1953 the Southsiders Gang became involved in a series of confrontations with Handley youths. The problem came to police attention after Southsiders curbed a car of three young men from Handley, beating them with clubs and chains. Officers arrested Clarence "Red" Fisher (17 years old and the reputed leader of the Southsiders) and Charlies Crow (16 years old) at the gang's hangout, a pool hall at Hemphill and Terrell Streets. Fisher and Crow both sported drake haircuts, and Crow had a "Gatesville Cross" tattoo while Fisher had a tattooed blue dot on his chin, supposedly marking him as a "hep cat." The two admitted the confrontation with the Handley youths but denied using anything but fists. Fisher—along with Leon Benton and Glen Furstenberg, both 17 years old—spent five days in jail before being released. They were immediately rearrested on the way home after officers stopped them for a traffic violation and found clubs and chains in the car.[15]

A rash of incidents followed in which youths thought to be gang members curbed and attacked motorists or pedestrians. In October 1953 three young men, ages 20 to 21, were arrested after they beat two men standing outside the Hotel Texas, saying they did so because the victims were dressed "fancy." The seemingly random, unprovoked beatings prompted the district attorney's office to promise stern prosecution for "hoodlums terrorizing Fort Worth with their thrill beatings." Many residents started carrying weapons in their cars. One motorist fired a shotgun at two young men who curbed his vehicle on Ederville Road near the Meadowbrook Golf Course.[16]

Juveniles were responsible for a high percentage of crimes in the early 1950s. In five months between September 1, 1954, and January 31, 1955, some 25.85 percent of all persons criminally charged in Fort Worth were between the ages of 10 and 17. Arrested youths tended to be most often charged with burglary, theft, automobile theft, and aggravated assault.

Chart 15.1 Charges Filed by Fort Worth Police, September 1, 1954–January 31, 1955

Crime	Total Cases	Persons Charged	Charged Juveniles
Auto Theft	491	66	26
Burglary	1,103	124	67
Rape	11	10	4
Robbery	80	28	4
Aggravated Assault	156	103	21
Theft	1,870	110	27

Source: Fort Worth Star Telegram, March 2, 1955, pp. 1–2.

Considerable debate surrounded the rise in juvenile delinquency. One of the more outlandish explanations came in 1954 from a Southwestern Baptist Theological Seminary student, Reverend Albert Johnson, who blamed salacious comic books for leading youths astray, an assertion seconded by youth authorities who called comics a destabilizing force. Mayor Deen recommended the council consider setting up a censorship board to review and restrict comic books.[17]

Post–World War II traffic surged as cars once more became readily available, requiring more police resources for traffic enforcement and control. In the fifteen years between 1940 and 1955, the number of vehicles registered in Tarrant County rose 176 percent, putting an additional 131,433 cars on the roads at the same time that the city's geographic area expanded 106 percent. Police staffing failed to keep up as the department added only 88 percent more officers in the same period, creating an inequity that strained field officers.

Chart 15.2 Growth in Population, Police Officers, Geography, and Registered Vehicles, 1940–1960

Year	Population	FWPD Officers	Area (sq. miles)	Vehicles Registered (Tarrant County)
1940	177,662	224	61.57	74,534
1950	278,788	352	n/a	~150,000
1955	343,685	423	127.34	205,967

Source: Fort Worth Star Telegram, June 15, 1955, p. 8.

Officers certainly stayed busy, issuing 28,353 citations in the first three months of 1954, almost 10,000 a month, with an average fine of $5.92. Parking violations, 16,075, accounted for over half (56 percent) of the total but were of rather low value, averaging only $1.30, while speeding, the second most frequent violation, carried a hefty average fine of $15.15. Speeding drew a lot of attention because police blamed it for a countywide spike in traffic fatalities in 1951 to ninety-five, a record high for Tarrant County. To counteract the trend, Fort Worth Police spent $1,200 in April 1954 for a radar unit that measured speed more accurately and less dangerously than pacing, the common practice to that point. After two weeks issuing only warnings, officers began writing citations using radar on January 28, 1955, handing out 142 in the first six days, considerably higher than the 30 a week averaged by motorcycle officers. Despite the new technology, Fort Worth traffic deaths increased to thirty-two in 1955, a 56 percent rise over 1954. By 1956 Fort Worth Police owned three radar units.[18]

In the 1950s police broadened their driving while intoxicated (DWI) enforcement at the same time that DWI prosecution went through a defining process. In the nine months prior to June 26, 1951, the Tarrant County district attorney filed 390 DWI charges, an average of over 43 per month, winning convictions or guilty pleas in 355 cases. Sentencing became somewhat standardized in 1954 after a court of appeals ruling mandated a jail sentence of three days, fines, and license suspension for first convictions. County Court Judge W. H. Tolbert expressed anger at the ruling, complaining that jail time and license suspension reduced court fine income, then a substantial $102,474 annually, that more than funded the court's annual operating cost, around $37,000, the excess going to county coffers. Judges also had misgivings about accepting intoxylizer results. An Alcometer purchased in 1952 for $845 sat unused for two years after courts mandated that a trained chemist operate the machine. District Attorney Howard Fender advised police to bypass the requirement by collecting a suspect's breath in a balloon, permissible for any peace officer, and sending the balloon for analysis by a chemist. One DWI incident was noteworthy. In July 1952 two patrol officers detained City Councilman Ray Crowder on suspicion of DWI but released him after Sergeant K. R. Bailey, called to the scene, decided an arrest was not necessary. Sergeant Bailey ordered the officers to take Crowder home, a strange decision if he was not impaired. Chief Howerton, questioned about the incident, said he supported the field supervisor's decision.[19]

Criminal statistics appeared only sporadically, but a partial report covering the first six months of 1952 showed a surge in murders. In the six months from January 1 to June 30, 1952, Fort Worth recorded thirty murders, thirteen more than in the same period in 1951 and one more than Dallas, but far behind fifty-one in first-place Houston. Increases were also shown in robberies (74), burglaries (974), and auto thefts (433), while declines were registered in aggravated assaults (67) and thefts (2,080). The upswing seemed to have ended in 1955 when 7,000 fewer offenses were reported than in 1954, a significant 7.6 percent decline.[20]

Electronic burglar alarms developed as a law enforcement tool in the 1950s, perhaps contributing to some crime reductions. One of the first central alarm systems was installed in 1952 at A. J. Lee's Grocery, 1302 Evans Avenue. The store had been burglarized several times, costing at least $15,000 in losses and damages before A. J. Lee, the owner, installed an alarm from American District Telegraph. The evening of July 2, 1952, a burglar raising a window tripped the alarm, summoning officers who fired two shots at a fleeing suspect but missed. Albert Smith and his two brothers owned Diamond Hill Market, 1912 Northeast Twenty-Eighth Street, the scene of many burglaries. The brothers developed and installed their own alarm system using dry cell batteries to power several "traps" or trips, all connected by wires running from the store to the homes of Albert and a brother, both living within a block. Albert telephoned police when the alarm sounded the evening of February 20, 1955. Officers arriving within minutes caught two burglars who had broken in through the roof.[21]

A lot of police work involved handling repeat, low-level offenders and youthful indiscretions. Fort Worth officers named James Franklin Moore their number one headache. Moore, arrested nine times in the first six months of 1951, had a lengthy arrest record with numerous convictions for thefts, assaults, burglaries, and indecent exposures. In his 40s in the early 1950s, Moore had spent half his life incarcerated. He blamed his troubles on kleptomania and other mental issues that stemmed from the loss of a leg in the Navy, for which he drew a $144 monthly disability pension.

In April 1953 Officer E. D. Moyers demonstrated professionalism, single-handedly ending a TCU panty raid by promising to arrest the first person to enter the women's dormitory, bringing jeers from men and the pajama-clad women hanging half out of dorm windows, but no challenges. His restraint contrasted with the overreaction of a TCU nightwatchman who fired a shot into the air during a similar event the previous night.[22]

In the 1950s rank-and-file officers and firefighters sought better working conditions, achieving limited success. By the postwar most city employees were on an eight-hours, five-days a week schedule, but police officers continued to work six days, forty-eight hours a week, and firefighters were on duty seventy-two hours weekly, neither receiving overtime pay. In 1951 voters defeated a charter amendment that would have reduced police to a forty-hour work week and firefighters to sixty hours with overtime pay over forty hours (voters also rejected five initiatives funding museums). In February 1952 many of Fort Worth's 360 police officers met at the Hotel Texas to discuss various issues, including deficiencies in the pension system that left Detective Cleveland's family without benefits after his on-duty death. The department's 410 sworn officers and 28 civilian staff in 1954 renewed requests for a forty-hour week as well as pay for court appearances, then uncompensated if the officer was off duty.[23]

A principal—perhaps the principal—figure in the fight for better benefits was veteran homicide Detective A. C. Howerton, brother of Chief R. R. Howerton. A. C. was the first president of the POA and Fort Worth's first dedicated homicide investigator. On October 1, 1952, he and his partner, Detective

D. S. Dean, marked twenty-one years together, during which they investigated an estimated 600 homicides, 500 suicides, and numerous robberies. The two were opposite personalities; Howerton was extroverted while Dean was taciturn. A. C. Howerton played an important role in securing a city retirement plan with higher retirement benefits, including provisions for disabled officers and surviving family members, changes that benefited most city employees other than firefighters, who remained on a state retirement plan.[24]

In the mid-1950s the council authorized significant improvements to the police department while struggling to bring pay to regional standards. In September 1953 Fort Worth approved a $100 annual uniform allowance for police, a move Chief Hightower hoped would result in plainclothesmen dressing better. On June 21, 1954, the department opened its first firearms range, a $9,000 open-air facility on two fenced acres off Lake Shore Drive, three miles north of the Lake Worth Casino. Sergeant Oliver Ball, the first rangemaster, instituted standards developed during his attendance at the FBI's National Academy that required officers fire fifty rounds each month with a minimum score of sixty. During the first qualification round the range discovered 21 of the 415 pistols (.38 caliber) that officers carried would not fire. In 1955 a proposal reached council to raise police salaries $25 a month to help close the pay gap with other major Texas cities. At the time Fort Worth officers earned $300 monthly working a forty-eight-hour week, short of the $325 Dallas officers received for a forty-four hours, $350 for forty hours in Houston, and $300 for forty-four hours in San Antonio.[25]

Fort Worth had its share of notorious crimes in the first half of the 1950s. The most newsworthy involved the robbery of $248,000 from Manuel Madgreaga and Caandido Torres, (spelled Manuel Madriaga and Candido de la Torres in later sources), revolutionaries committed to overthrowing Cuban President Fulgencio Batista. Madgreaga and Torre initially told police they arrived at the Western Hills Hotel on September 23 to visit friends, but they eventually admitted they had traveled from Mexico City at the urging of Sam Brown Cresap, a Fort Worth car dealer, who assured them they could easily buy guns in Fort Worth. On October 5, 1952, Cresap and Duarte, a Cuban munitions expert, left the hotel to examine weapons in Dallas, leaving a man Cresap introduced only as Johnny playing cards with Madgreaga and Torre in the room. Around 3:30 a.m. Johnny, claiming he heard a noise, opened the door, admitting two masked men, one carrying a submachine gun, while Johnny pulled a revolver. The three bandits tied the two Cubans before leaving with the money. Madgreaga and Torre escaped their bounds to call police, who were on the scene when Cresap returned, making a great show of surprise about the robbery. Investigators were unconvinced and arrested him. From mug shots provided by Fort Worth detectives the Cubans identified Orvil L. Chambless (sometimes Chambliss) as one of the three robbers. Chambless was an ex-convict from Oklahoma known as the "flying bootlegger" from his use of a private plane to move alcohol. Detectives issued a warrant for Chambless, who was believed to be hiding in Oklahoma along with the mysterious Johnny. At the Dallas FBI office the two victims combed through 3,000 photographs to identify Gene Paul Norris, a well-known hoodlum with twenty-five arrests and six convictions in Texas. Chambless was arrested in Oklahoma City and FBI agents nabbed Norris in Duncan, Oklahoma, where he operated a machine shop. On October 24, 1952, Chambless, out on bond, was shot through a picture window while sitting inside his home near Oklahoma City. Hit in the leg and chest, he was taken to a local hospital where he was kept under guard in good condition.[26]

On November 3, 1952, an anonymous tip led police to a pasture five miles north of Azle (twenty-five miles northwest of Fort Worth), where they found a buried thermos containing $128,000 of the Cubans' stolen cash, as well as a fruit jar holding $4,250 taken two months earlier in the robbery of Mr. and Mrs. Sam Andrews of Kilgore, Texas. The Andrews were bound and gagged, similar to the Western Hills Hotel robbery. Officers, secreted nearby, lay in wait for several hours until Floyd Hill arrived and began digging up the cache. Hill, of 2712 Skyline Drive, Fort Worth, was a known criminal from Oklahoma with four prison sentences who had been released from Alcatraz just three months earlier. Over five years later, in 1958, a Bryan County, Oklahoma, woman hoeing in a field near Norris's shop, found a metal box containing weathered bills. She sent the money to her daughter, who turned it in to police. Detectives suspected it was Norris's share of the Western Hills robbery. Norris had boasted of burying the loot to wait until it was safe to spend.[27]

Hill and Norris were tried for the robbery, but Chambless and Cresap escaped prosecution. In 1953 state and federal grand juries no-billed Chambless and a jury acquitted Norris, accepting his argument that at the time of the robbery a machine shop injury had left him unable to walk without the use of a cane. In January 1954 Floyd Hill pled guilty to a reduced charge in exchange for a twenty-year sentence, avoiding a possible death sentence for robbery committed with firearms. As part of the plea bargain, Hill also pled guilty to robbing the Kilgore couple. In January 1956 the Tarrant County district attorney dismissed the lone remaining indictment against Sam Cresap, effectively ending his legal jeopardy for the Western Hills robbery.[28]

One of the sadder criminal incidents occurred in 1952 when Mrs. Rubye Ray was charged with murder in the death of her 5-year-old foster son, Charles. Ruby's husband, Johnny Ray, called authorities after finding the child dead when he came home from work. An autopsy revealed Charles had suffered 256 cuts as well as internal injuries with hemorrhaging. Mrs. Ray only admitted she had backhanded the boy in frustration.[29]

A twisted insurance fraud conspiracy captured local headlines in 1953 and 1954. David F. Hagler, a vice president of United States Asphalt in Fort Worth, plotted with Frank A. St. Claire to fake his own death and collect a $200,000 life insurance policy. The original plan involved buying a body from a funeral home for $500, but the conspirators opted to produce a corpse themselves, reportedly murdering William Reed Matthews, a former soldier who went missing in October 1953. The scheme opened on October 10, 1953, when police near Davis, Oklahoma, found Hagler's burned car with a badly charred body inside. The sloppy plan quickly began to fall apart, starting with dental records that confirmed the deceased was not Hagler and an autopsy that determined the victim had been alive when the fire started (no positive identification was ever made on the remains). Hagler appeared in public a few days later, claiming that he had blacked out after an extended drinking spree and could not remember anything in the interim. That story came under serious doubt when St. Claire gave a written confession detailing their plan, although he denied direct involvement in the victim's death. What seemed like an open and shut case became more difficult when St. Claire committed suicide in his Irving, Texas, home, apparently upset over falling finances he blamed on adverse publicity from the case. The loss of the key witness doomed the prosecution's case, leading to Hagler's acquittal by an Oklahoma jury.[30]

The Tarrant County Jail experienced violent escapes in consecutive months of 1953. Floyd Hill, charged in the Western Hills / Cuban case, was one of ten prisoners who overpowered three guards on February 18, 1953 (sixty-five other prisoners refused to leave their cells). One of the ten was captured almost immediately and six others were taken within a few hours, but Hill and two men held for the same sexual assault remained free for several days. Eventually only Hill remained outstanding, an outcome police credited to underworld assistance. A witness reported seeing a car, later identified as that of a former Alcatraz inmate, near the jail at the time of the break. The getaway car would have given Hill the means to leave quickly, avoiding responding officers who saturated the area. Of course, coordination with the outside meant the break was planned and scheduled rather than a crime of opportunity. Hill was captured soon after the FBI added him to its Ten Most Wanted List.[31]

The February escape may have increased anxieties, contributing to a violent reaction the next month that cost the lives of three escaping prisoners. On March 22, 1953, several prisoners armed with knives fashioned from bed slats and with bars of soap wrapped in cloth overpowered a guard on an upper floor, then took the elevator to the basement where they rushed jail staff. In the melee Jailer W. P. Foster shot and killed Bobby D. Baker (a leader in the February 18 break), Lloyd D. Lesher (also in on the earlier break), and William H. Ford and wounded C. L. Eubanks. Three other prisoners making it to the basement—Manuel Hernandez (also part of the February 18 break), David Smith, and Stewart Freeman—retreated from the gunfire and were detained by Louis Riley, a Black trusty. The survivors, ranging in age from 17 to 20, were charged with attempted escape. Sheriff Wright blamed the rash of escapes and on poor staffing that left some shifts with only four jailers on duty.[32]

Both the city and county jails continued to face chronic issues of overcrowding, poor staffing, and rising costs. In 1952 a downtown café won the contract for prisoner food service for the Fort Worth Jail with a bid of

$0.41 per prisoner, per day, to provide sandwiches and coffee for the morning and evening meals (there was no lunch). The Tarrant County jail, much larger with an average population of 165, spent only $0.15 per day. The cost difference may have been behind a new city contract in 1955 that lowered the per diem to $0.275 for a bacon and egg sandwich in the morning and a ham and a bologna sandwich in the evening, both served with coffee. Councilman Thompson, who had earlier proposed building a $60,000 penal farm at Lake Worth, renewed his call, arguing it would offer potential savings from prisoners producing and preparing much of their food.[33]

The fire department fought a large fire that ranked as the second largest in the city's history. On August 4, 1953, seventy-five firemen fought for hours to contain a fire at a Cold Springs Road Cotton Compress, placing such a large demand on personnel that off-duty firemen were called out. The blaze caused $1 million in damages, second only to the great 1909 fire that destroyed much of the south side.[34]

Chapter 16

Race Relations, 1951–1955

The 1950 Census revealed a clear demographic shift of nonwhites (census categories included "Negroes," American Indians, and Asians) away from the South. Between 1940 and 1950 the thirteen Southern states of the Confederacy added only 55,637 nonwhites, less than 1 percent, but the nonwhite population of the eight industrial states in the North, Midwest, and West increased 1.5 million, a 55 percent increase. Both regions had similar increases in their white population, the South adding 4.4 million whites, a 16 percent upswing, while the white population in the North, Midwest, and West increased 14 percent. The opposite regional racial population trajectories revealed a clear movement of Blacks from the rigidly segregated and more rural South for the more open and urban North and Midwest and the rapidly industrializing West. Fort Worth avoided a significant disparity between white and Black population growth rates, an outcome that may have been the product of its sizable defense industry, most notably, Convair. Between 1940 and 1950 Fort Worth added 101,116 residents, a 57 percent increase, growing its population from 177,662 to 278,778, without significant racial disparities. Fort Worth's white population increased 68 percent, from 143,505 to 241,651, while the African American population ("Negroes" in the census) grew almost 56 percent, from 23,754 to 36,933. Fort Worth's percentage increase reflected the best trends in both regions; its Black population growth equaled that of the industrial states of the North, Midwest, and West while its white population increased at four times the rate of the South and the North, Midwest, and West.[1]

All the new residents aggravated the existing housing shortage, especially for African Americans shut out of most neighborhoods by rigid segregation. As the Black population grew, Blacks had little option but to spread outside traditionally Black neighborhoods, a forced movement that occasioned considerable conflict. The city attempted to provide relief via rent-subsidized multiunit housing projects. In January 1951 the Fort Worth Housing Authority announced, "Negro Housing Project to Be Built on North Side," some 300 units reserved for low-income Black families on a six-block site bounded by Thirty-Third and Thirty-First Streets and McKinley and Loving Avenues. Monthly rents, adjusted according to income, ranged from $12 for a $700 annual income to $30 for $1,800, the maximum allowable annual salary. No white backlash developed, probably because the area already had a substantial African American enclave of ninety-seven Black families, four businesses, and one church. However, Black residents meeting at Worth Hills Baptist Church complained that builders underbid their seized properties. In January 1952 city zoning okayed construction of a $2.3 million rent-subsidized Black housing project at 5000 East Rosedale Street that would become J. A. Caville Place. Caville Place opened on December 21, 1953, with rents averaging $23.69 monthly for an average annual income of $1,496, well below the maximum allowable of $2,000 for a family of two or $2,200 for a family of three or four. The two developments, along with H. H. Butler Place, were reserved for low-income Blacks, while Ripley Arnold Place housed low-income whites. Commercial developments targeting African Americans faced tougher sledding. The city council killed a zoning committee recommendation to rezone Cravens and Hedgeman roads to commercial use after white citizens complained the proposed shops would bring more Blacks to the area. The council promised to reconsider the matter later.[2]

The housing projects helped but were insufficient to substantially alleviate the shortage or the deep and systemic sanitary issues plaguing much of Fort Worth's low-income housing. In 1951 Councilman Ed Baker called for action to correct appalling sanitary conditions common in Fort Worth's fourteen Black neighborhoods, most seriously the lack of sewer connections and flush toilets that left many residents relying on "pit toilets," or outhouses that were sources of pestilence and disease. The *Star Telegram* blamed lax code enforcement and the city's failure to extend sewer lines into Black neighborhoods for creating a situation in which 3,500 nonwhites lived in 1,000 housing units without flush toilets or sewer service. The article named a poor area off Summit Avenue with more than twenty habitations that was without sewer connections, including a house at 2216 Winneca that was home to eight persons from two families paying $32 monthly rent for a dilapidated house with only a pit toilet. The Como neighborhood on the west side was one of the worst blighted areas, especially Libbey Avenue, where blocks of homes were without sewers, forcing residents to use pit toilets. One family of three paid $20 monthly for a house at 5206 Blackmore without lights, gas, or water that was thirty yards from the nearest pit toilet. Another unidentified area was home to 250 families living in 152 housing units, all without sewer connections.[3]

The city council appointed a special committee to find funding for extending sewer connections and flush toilets to all of the city. Dr. George Flemmings, local head of the NAACP, criticized the committee's membership, which included several councilmen, for its lack of Black representation. At an off-the-record conference at a local hotel, the committee reviewed city ordinances governing housing and sanitation in slum areas, searching for ways to eliminate inequality in public works. The quick and obvious fix would have been to enforce existing ordinances requiring sewer connections and flush toilets for all homes, but that proposal faced pushback from landlords concerned about costs. One white slum lord rented thirty-two one- and two-room housing units to Blacks for $2.00 to $2.75 a week that he had bought fourteen years earlier for $500 each. He admitted that the units had become so rickety that they were then worth no more than $200 each and that all thirty-two lacked indoor plumbing, providing only shared outside taps for water and shared outhouses. The landlord stated that installing flush toilets, at a cost between $150 and $300 each, would be so financially unfeasible that he would demolish the properties rather than comply. He did not mention that in fourteen years, he would have collected $46,592 in rents even at the $2.00 minimum rate. In a statement of the obvious, City Councilman Tom McCann, chair of the citizens' committee in 1953, accused a few large property owners of exploiting the poor and illiterate to make huge profits.[4]

Lester Granger, head of the National Urban League, lambasted sanitation in Fort Worth's Black neighborhoods. During a 1951 visit he reported conditions were no better than he had seen in 1946, especially concerning the widespread use of outdoor toilets. Granger argued that Fort Worth had fallen behind other Southern cities like Little Rock, Arkansas; Atlanta, Georgia; and Memphis, Tennessee, in slum eradication. He cited Memphis's Dixie Housing Project as a progressive Black housing reform that had demonstrated slum removal was economically sound, that the cost of renovation was returned in reduced costs for city services. Granger cited studies showing slums cost up to six times more for fire, police, and health protection and five times as much in disease and juvenile delinquency as sanitary, well-maintained neighborhoods. Fort Worth may have lagged behind other cities, but the problem was widespread. A 1956 National Urban League report that surveyed ten cities (Fort Worth included) named substandard housing as the biggest problem facing Blacks.[5]

The separate Black culture that developed under segregation reached a high level of achievement in the 1950s, fostering several organizations dedicated to improving conditions. The Crime Prevention Society, led by Executive Director Reverend M. W. Knox, took a holistic approach to crime reduction using a variety of community activities. In one year the society attacked the deleterious effects of unemployment, finding jobs for 896 adults and 286 juveniles, and converted 286 persons during religious services at the county jail and the Ritz Theater. They also took 550 children to the Shrine circus and 255 to the Texas State Fair in Dallas, all on a $7,500 budget. African American girls could take advantage of many services provided by the Black YWCA, 1916 Crump Street, as well as a summer camp at Lake Murray in Oklahoma. The white YMCA broke color lines for one two-week term each summer when Black youths could attend Camp Carter, located on Fort Worth's west side. In 1951 the "Negro section" of the Community Chest, headed by Reverend O. P. Felder, launched a $5,000 funding drive with a parade that began at Burnett Park, followed by a dinner at the McDonald Branch (Black) of the YMCA. Black residents also organized to support the general March of Dimes fund in appreciation for care provided for five Black children stricken with polio. The organizers designated Sunday, January 28, 1951, for collections at local churches.[6]

In 1952 the only home for impoverished aged or sick African Americans was threatened with closure after the fire department deemed it a fire hazard (the Tarrant County Home for the Aged did not admit Blacks). The home was made possible by Lutie McFarland, who willed her house at 1510 West Peter Smith Street to the Fort Worth Welfare Association on the stipulation that it be used for the benefit of Black residents. In 1940 Mrs. I. V. Amie began serving as home manager, providing care for up to ten aged and infirm men and women using funding from welfare payments and old age grants that barely covered daily expenses and left little for repairs. Sid Richardson and Amon Carter saved the home by jointly funding the $6,000 needed to bring the structure up to code, freeing Mrs. Amie to use private donations for new furniture and equipment.[7]

Childcare also survived financial crises. The North Fort Worth Community Center and Day Nursery, caring for twenty children of working Black mothers, had opened in 1948 using $4,424 in donations to buy a house and move it to 2923 Lincoln Street, a donated lot. Children at the center received care and instruction, two meals, and a snack, all for only $0.75 for under 2 years of age and $0.50 for older, an artificially low rate insufficient to meet expenses that was made possible through fundraising efforts spearheaded by Mrs. Henrietta Starr. Natal care in the Black community suffered a loss on October 6, 1954, when Mrs. Mattie E. Willis, 72 years old, died at her post, at the bedside of an expectant mother (the mother was taken to the City-County Hospital, where she delivered a girl). In fifty years as a midwife, Mrs. Willis, 5329 Libbey Avenue, delivered an estimated 2,000 babies (for a $25 fee), including most children born to Como parents.[8]

A sign of mature development can be seen in the beginnings of African American groups devoted to the high arts and society. The Ambassador's Club began holding an annual debutante ball in 1948. In 1952 the group presented six African American debutantes, all college students, at North Side Coliseum. In December 1957 they presented four young women at the Tenth Annual Ball. In 1952 the Texas Academy of Fine Arts for Negroes, formed to promote music and dance, accepted its first class of seventy-five students. Two years later, in May 1954, the academy presented its first recital at I. M. Terrell High School with reserved seating provided for whites. Black leaders with national standing visited Fort Worth. On April 27, 1951, Thurgood Marshall, chief counsel for the NAACP, spoke at St. James Baptist Church on the role of Black troops in the Korean War. Fort Worth's Negro Business and Professional Women's Club scheduled a talk by Langston Hughes, but Mrs. Lucille Smith announced they canceled the appearance after learning of his connections to "subversive organizations."[9]

All the emphasis on developing separate organizations reflected a lack of progress in integration. Fort Worth was slow to integrate its major sports team, the Fort Worth Cats baseball club. The color line for the Texas League, the Cats' regional baseball league, had been broken in 1952 by Dallas pitcher Dave Hoskins, but the Cats did not field their first Black players until 1955, when the parent organization, the Brooklyn Dodgers, sent outfielder Edward Moore and shortstop Maurice Wills. Plans were underway for an Alcoholics Anonymous dedicated for Blacks after the local Information Center on Alcoholism received numerous calls from African Americans seeking help with alcoholism.[10]

While Fort Worth did not play a major leading role in the Civil Rights Movement of the 1950s, local Blacks did actively campaign to desegregate municipal parks. The parks movement developed in conjunction with efforts to improve Black housing, then split to become a separate entity. Fort Worth's main park facilities—the zoo, Botanic Gardens, and Forest Park Swimming Pool—were closed to African Americans except on Juneteenth, when they opened that one day to large numbers. In 1951 some 5,000 African Americans celebrated Juneteenth at Greenway Park, designated for Blacks only, but 8,000 went to Forest Park, enjoying the zoo, rides, and swimming pool (the pool would be closed afterward so the city could drain and refill the water). In his criticism of Fort Worth's Black housing, Lester Granger of the Urban League, added the injustice of excluding Blacks from parks and golf courses built using their tax dollars. His comments may have prompted the 1951 committee on sanitary housing to recommend allowing supervised groups of African Americans to the zoo (including access to the rides), Botanic Gardens, and the Lake Worth picnic grounds. The city did make one minor adjustment, opening Worth Hills Golf Course on Juneteenth, drawing eighty-five Black golfers to the course on June 19, 1951, the first African Americans to play at any of Fort Worth's four municipal courses.[11]

The Worth Hills concession only served to highlight the inequality of Fort Worth Black golfers having to travel to Dallas to play when Fort Worth had four municipal golf courses. In January 1952 the Fort Worth Negro Golf Association appealed to City Manager Jones, citing a recent United States Civil Court order requiring Houton to either desegregate its golf courses or provide comparable separate facilities. The Park Board realized the situation was unsupportable under separate but equal and began planning a Black golf course on land the city purchased that joined sixty-five acres donated by the Tarrant County Water district lying between the railroad tracks, Lancaster Avenue, I. M. Terrell High School, and the Trinity River. Construction, funded by the city and a Harmon Foundation grant, began in 1953 on the $160,000 William E. Harmon Recreation Center and a nine-hole golf course, with plans to expand to eighteen holes and add baseball diamonds and a playground.[12]

The opening did not end demands to open city golf courses to Blacks. In June 1954, Dr. R. A. Ransom, acting as a member of the Citizens' Committee, led a delegation to petition the city council for unrestricted access to all municipal golf courses, including cafés, locker rooms, and showers. The petitioners, including several golfers who had recently been turned away at Z. Boaz Golf Course, pointed out that Dallas, Houston, San Antonio, and many other Texas cities had desegregated their municipal courses. Their petition stipulated that Harmon Golf Course would be opened to whites. Court appeals proved more effective than appeals to council. In November 1955 the courts ordered Fort Worth golf courses to end exclusions by race. Eight Black golfers teed off at Rockwood Golf Course, marking the opening of all four municipal courses—Rockwood, Z. Boaz, Meadowbrook, and Worth Hills.[13]

The drive to open golf courses spawned a broader movement seeking to desegregate all park facilities and city services. In May 1952 Reverend Prince F. Jackson of the Negro Allen Chapel AME Church led a delegation to the city council to complain about the inequality African Americans endured in many municipal services, including deficient swimming pools, inadequate parks and playgrounds, unpaved and ungraded streets, poor garbage collection, and limited sewer service. Reverend Jackson blamed many of the deficiencies on the 1951 all-white committee on inequality that, he charged, had failed to significantly improve substandard housing and sanitation in Black neighborhoods or address basic inequalities. A councilman who was also a committee member tried to defend the committee, arguing that the process was ongoing, that they were still gathering information to determine the appropriate steps. However, when questioned he could not recall the date of their last meeting. Dr. G. D. Flemmings, president of the local NAACP chapter, warned that Dallas attorney U. Simpson Tate was prepared to take the matter to the courts if the council failed to act. The issue lingered into 1955 with the council stalling, delaying, and setting unreasonable conditions, at one point demanding that Blacks pledge not to attempt integrating white pools before they would agree to build separate pools in Black neighborhoods. One councilman, A. P. Owens, urged a harder stance, suggesting that the city needed to get "these Negroes on the line and let them know what is what." Dr. Flemmings and the NAACP remained steadfast in their commitment to sue if Blacks were not granted pool access by the coming summer. Eventually, four Black swimming pools were bult, a temporary victory that also delayed integrating city pools. Progress was slow but inevitable; in 1961 Dr. Marion J. Brooks, a Black man, was named to the Park Board.[14]

Federal courts and agencies proved to be the most effective resources in the battle to open public facilities to African Americans. In December 1951 the Civilian Aeronautics Agency threatened to cancel $1.5 million in federal funds designated for the Houston Airport after a police officer forcibly removed an African American woman from a "white" taxicab outside the airport terminal (Houston, Fort Worth, and many Southern towns had segregated taxicabs). The woman, a national NAACP officer, reported the incident to federal authorities. Faced with the loss of federal funding, the airport desegregated all facilities, including toilets and taxicabs. On September 1, 1955, a federal order ended school segregation on military bases, creating legal conflicts in many Southern states where statues mandated segregated schools. The US Office of Education solved the dilemma by taking over military base schools, running them independently of state and local systems.[15]

Carswell Air Force Base was a melting pot of diversity existing alongside a rigidly segregated community, a confluence that occasioned some confrontations. In 1953 the Filipino wife of Air Force Sergeant Robert Reed, an African American stationed at Carswell, became a naturalized United States citizen, which presented a problem since Texas defined Filipinos as whites and state laws prohibited marriages between whites and Blacks. Other issues arose simply because many Black servicemen were from more progressive areas and were less willing to accept strict Southern racism. In 1952 a Carswell airman questioned the right of Fort Worth Vice Officers O. H. Middleton and Dan Mahan to enter Porters' and Waiters' Night Club, 811 East Terrell Street. The dispute became a standoff with 200 supporters blocking access to the club, sparking calls for assistance that brought thirty-five officers. The airman, who had a police radio in his car, was turned over to Carswell Base officials.[16]

The Supreme Court's 1954 ruling on desegregating schools was met by widespread delaying tactics and little compliance. Resistance took many forms, some more ridiculous than others. Dallas alderman C. K. Bullard suggested Dallas emulate Highland Park (an upscale Dallas suburb) that barred Black residents, allowing only servants employed by whites to live in the city and only onsite at their employment. Bullard recommended whites fire Black servants and employees, which would, he reasoned, force them to leave Dallas, thereby removing Black students from the school district and ending school integration. The Texas State Board of Education presented a more mainstream response common in the South, unanimously voting to continue segregation until directed otherwise by a state authority. In July 1955 the Fort Worth Board of Education adopted the board's recommendation, ordering schools to remain segregated. Local NAACP President Dr. George Flemmings tried to remain reasonable while facing the unreasonable. He granted that delay might be necessary in a large school district like Fort Worth, but only on the condition that the forbearance would lead to sincere integration efforts. To that end Dr. Flemming suggested the school board and Blacks join together to develop integration plans. The same pattern of resistance practiced by Fort Worth was repeated across the state, receiving widespread support from Texas political leaders and politicians across the South. In fact, many Southern governors, including Texas Governor Allan Shivers, ran and won on promises to maintain segregation. In 1955 twelve Southern states formed the Federation for Constitutional Government dedicated to resisting integration through interposition, economic boycotts, and intimidation, as well as encouraging Blacks to relocate north. Texas sent ten delegates to the founding convention, including Fort Worth resident and former Governor Coke Stevenson, who served on the advisory committee.[17]

A few voices spoke out against resistance but were too few to be more than marginally effective. TCU Chancellor Dr. M. E. Sadler led a committee of seventeen leaders from the Council of Churches that condemned evasion of the *Brown* decision. Still, throughout the 1950s integration in Texas hardly advanced beyond a few school districts with small numbers of Black students. An Associated Press survey in 1956 determined Texas had approximately 2 million students of all races and that 500,000 attended integrated schools, a seemingly impressive 25 percent, but the raw figures were misleading, tending to suggest integration was more advanced than was true. The numbers provided no information on how many Black students attended integrated schools; the truth was that very few did. In 1956 all the desegregated Texas school districts lay west of Fort Worth in West Texas, a region with a small Black population, guaranteeing that the few integrated schools had very few Black students, so the 500,000 students at integrated schools were almost all white. East Texas, where most Black Texans lived and where school districts had large Black student populations, remained completely and rigidly segregated, ensuring that the majority of Black students attended segregated schools. Resistance to school integration did not significantly begin to subside until 1962, when Leo Brewster ruled Texas's dual system of segregated schools unconstitutional in *Arlene Flax et al. v. W. S. Potts et al.*[18]

The main racial battles in Fort Worth occurred not over schools but over segregated neighborhoods. A major confrontation developed in 1953 when Lawrence Peters, a 35-year-old Black man employed nearby at Allied Mills, 401 North Beach Street, paid $4,278 for a house at 109 Judkins Street in an all-white section of Riverside. On August 21 Peters and his family moved into their two-bedroom home. Upset white neighbors met at Riverside Elementary School to form the Riverside Civic League, dedicated to preventing Black home ownership in the area bounded by Belknap and East First Streets, Sylvania Avenue, and Riverside Drive. Mack Dumas, Rayford M. Shelton, and George Brown took major roles in the league along with Chairman George Seaman, a former city councilman. Seaman blamed realtors, particularly McDonald and Company, for encouraging African Americans to move into Riverside, alleging that they told Blacks the city council had designated it a Black neighborhood. Under pressure, McDonald Realtors canceled all future listings in the area. The league sought to buy out Peters, offering all his equity plus moving expenses (he rejected the offers). They also placed 500 yard signs, donated by a local printer, stating "This house not for sale to Negroes" on the Peters' block and many surrounding streets. Some whites opposed the league, not necessarily from an enlightened sense of racial justice but from a conviction that the battle was already lost, that the area was fated to become majority Black and the best option for white owners was to sell to the highest bidder, regardless of race, and relocate to a white neighborhood. A few African Americans also opposed integrating neighborhoods. One such group, led by R. L. Thornton, proposed aligning with the Riverside Civic League in the common cause of segregation. They were the exception; most Blacks supported integration. Dr. George Flemmings opposed segregation vehemently, actively pressuring Black separatists not to meet with the league.[19]

The crazies took over much of the Riverside debate. George Seaman claimed that the racial upheavals had lowered property values $5 million and were the work of do-gooders following tenets set forth by Communists and their fellow travelers in the NAACP and Urban League. Seaman also accused Black agitators of driving through neighborhoods, loudly voicing their intention to buy houses, as a ploy to stir up emotions and run off whites. In September 1953 a Black family moved into 113 Judkins, next door to Peters, but left after enduring constant heckling from whites shouting that they were not wanted. Hecklers included George Seaman, now chair of the Riverside Merchants and Home-Owners Association (RMHOA), a more radicalized group that required members sign an affidavit affirming they were white, perhaps to ward off Black separatists. Seaman admitted the RMHOA had heckled the family but denied threatening to bomb them. Another Black Riverside resident, Mrs. Mary Thornton, 2764 Nies Street, sought emergency leave through Red Cross for her husband stationed in Korea with the US Air Force, claiming she needed him to protect her from white mobs who congregated nightly in front of her home, shouting threats, throwing debris in her yard, and, on one occasion, firing a shot through the living room window.[20]

Threats and heckling became bombings and spread to other neighborhoods. In October 1953 an explosion rocked the area around Peters's home, doing no damage but bringing out crowds of whites and Blacks. On November 2, 1953, a dynamite blast at 1:00 a.m. demolished Peters's car parked in his driveway at the same time that the house next door, 113 Judkins Street, was set afire with gasoline. Police were unable to identify the culprits, even with a $250 reward offered by the Fort Worth branch of the NAACP. Peters still refused to move. He telephoned FBI Director J. Edgar Hoover about the lack of response from Fort Worth Police; Hoover agreed to have FBI agents investigate. George Seaman of the RMHOA blamed Blacks for the violence, especially the Urban League, claiming they staged the incidents to build sympathy for Black victims. Seaman had no proof for his claims but asked the grand jury to investigate. Two weeks later another blast struck the home of L. V. Johnson, 1514 Kennedy Street, in an "all-Negro neighborhood" off East Lancaster Avenue, blowing in windows and the front door, ripping off siding, and uprooting a bush. Johnson was an African American real estate agent who handled the sale of several Riverside homes to Blacks. He denied instigating the moves, claiming white property owners approached him to open the listings to Blacks.[21]

Several months of relative quiet were broken at 1:11 a.m., September 11, 1954, when a bomb destroyed a car and damaged the home of Kerven Carter Jr.

at 5736 Diaz Avenue. Carter, an English teacher at Dunbar Junior High School, lived across town from Riverside in the Como neighborhood, but his parents had recently moved into 158 North Judkins Street between two white families. Carter reported that whites yelled at him when he visited them and that he had received several hang-up calls. George Seaman downplayed the Diaz bombing as an isolated incident in a period so calm his group had not met in months. He suggested it would take Blacks moving into TCU, Ridglea, Westcliff, or Westover Hills (upscale white communities) to rekindle interest. Police Chief Hightower assured Dr. Flemmings and a delegation of Black leaders that the police were doing their best to investigate the bombings.

The next month a small explosion damaged another Como neighborhood home at 5318 Wellesley Avenue belonging to Mrs. C. M. Johnson. Mrs. Johnson believed the incident was in response to her husband inquiring about a Riverside home for a woman without transportation. While he was viewing the property, he saw a white man writing down his license plate number and assumed he used the registration to identify the residence. Two weeks later two African American men, James Hardin of 5420 Fernander Drive and David Holman of 5525 Libbey Street, began patrolling Como by night as security officers for Hardeman Detective Agency. Their presence may have pushed the crazies back east. The next incident occurred in the 1600 block of East Cannon Street, a predominantly white area, where whites stoned and threw bottles at a house recently sold to N. Ford, an African American. The white owner reported he sold to the Fords after whites refused to buy the house.[22]

Racial turmoil provided the fuel for a minor Klan resurgence. In 1955 a Texas assistant attorney general reported several churches were providing financial support to an Alabama Klansman organizing Klan chapters in twenty-two Texas counties. Historical ties between churches and the Klan were nothing new; J. Frank Norris, longtime pastor of Fort Worth's First Baptist Church, was openly pro-Klan, and his successor, the Reverend Homer G. Ritchie, preached that if God wanted all races to be one, he would have made them one, sermonizing that segregation was God's divine plan on earth. Other groups arose to fight integration. The Citizens' Council of Tarrant County, chaired by Howard Beard, formed in August 1955 to oppose integrating schools, parks, swimming pools, and golf courses. Chairman Beard believed that integration would bring violence and a Klan resurgence. Several council members publicly vowed to remove their children if Fort Worth schools integrated. In September 1955 fifty Citizens' Council members attending a Texas State Board of Education meeting applauded the board's order to ignore court ordered school integration until a deadline was stipulated. Some groups and individuals fought integration but refused to join segregationist groups. Dr. B. E. Masters, President Emeritus of Kilgore Junior College, warned a crowd of 700 at the Texas Hotel that integration would lead to "mongrelization" of the white race. Dr. Masters urged listeners to remain wary of educational and religious leaders errantly teaching that segregation was not Christian. Again, the occasional voice of reason tried to break through. Masters was followed by Mrs. H. V. Shank, 2705 University Drive, a former missionary, who endured boos and catcalls when she called for an end to segregation and support for integration.[23]

By the 1950s lynching had ended in Fort Worth but African American males accused of assaulting white women could be assured of speedy trials and harsh sentences. In November 1952 two Black men abducted a 21-year-old housewife after she got off a city bus at East Rosedale and Arch streets. The two took her to Greenway Park where they raped her several times over the course of two hours. Less than one month later, on December 10, 1952, Willie Lee Gage, a 40-year-old Black man with a criminal record, was sentenced to death for the attack despite professing his innocence. Gage's defense lawyer, Al Clyde, a former Tarrant County district attorney, conceded the question of guilt to focus on attacking the death penalty, telling the jury that a death sentence would never have been considered if Gage were white. One week later, the second suspect, 19-year-old James Oliver confessed and was given a life sentence. Gage, still professing his innocence, died in the electric chair on April 23, 1954, five months after the crime. In fairness, the judicial system had made some progress in treating accused African Americans fairly. In 1953 a sexual assault charge by a white woman against Woodrow W. Wynne, an African American male, was dismissed after a court bailiff reported the victim asked him if the defendant was in the court, revealing she could not recognize him. That did not imply discrepancies in treatment based on race had disappeared. In 1954 James Earl Rhodes, a 16-year-old African American charged with sexually assaulting a 15-year-old African American girl, was given a choice between the Gatesville State School for Boys or marrying the victim. Originally, Rhodes chose the former but on reconsideration opted for the latter, followed by a justice of the peace wedding.[24]

A serious drive to hire Black police officers gathered steam in the 1950s. In August 1952 James Andrew Green scored 95.8 on the police civil service exam, higher than all fifteen white applicants and five points higher than his closest competitor. Green, a graduate of Springfield College in Missouri, was a Marine Corp veteran of World War II and journalist in charge of the Bethlehem Center, 970 East Humboldt Street, a nondenominational church community outreach program. Chief Howerton acknowledged that both Dallas and Houston had Black officers and promised to give Green a fair opportunity. Howerton made good on his pledge, getting city council approval in October to hire four Black officers to patrol Black neighborhoods from 6:00 p.m. to 2:00 a.m. A second entrance exam was held October 17, 1952, to expand the list of Black candidates needed to fill all four slots. Unfortunately, Green was dropped from the applicant list after an investigation determined he did not meet the requirements, although the reason was not disclosed.[25]

Fort Worth Police hired four of the nine Black applicants who passed the October exam: Travis G. Bell, Jack D. Gray, Bennie Griffin, and Charles S. Wright. The recruits began six weeks of training on January 1, 1953, followed by foot patrol—Bennie Griffin and Jack Gray on East Ninth Street and Travis Bell and Charles Wright on East Rosedale Street. The four worked from 6:00 p.m. to 2:00 a.m. without a patrol car, leaving them without radio communications (they telephoned in every hour) or the means to transport prisoners. They attended roll call, then were driven to their assigned areas by white officers, creating problems when some white officers objected to riding in the same car with Blacks. Officer D. W. Stevenson drew a fifteen-day suspension for refusing to do so. Chief Howerton praised the officers, saying they had caught burglars and hijackers, but his comment that "those **boys** [emphasis added] haven't made a bad arrest" displayed clear racism. Jack Gray and another unidentified Black officer were dismissed without public explanation while still on their six-month probation period. Still, the bar had been lifted. Black and white applicants were encouraged to take the next entrance exam scheduled for June 5, 1953, to fill twenty-six vacancies. In 1953 several Blacks were hired, including Lonnell E. Cooper, who would serve with honors for twenty-seven years and later become a constable.[26]

Texas's exploitation of Mexican immigrants received national coverage. A 1951 *Look Magazine* article called "Mexicans" in Texas the "most downtrodden and defenseless group" in the nation (a questionable statement), forced to endure discrimination in education and the military draft as well as economic exploitation, especially by ranchers and farmers in the Rio Grande Valley (unquestionably). Mexican immigrants, drawn by farm wages paying twenty to forty cents an hour, congregated along the Rio Grande Valley, where they lived in unsanitary slums with little access to education. Neville Penrose of Fort Worth, chair of Texas's Good Neighbor Commission, admitted the state had some problems but countered that Texas was the only state with an agency dedicated to correcting injustices. The truth was that many Texas ranchers in and outside the Valley exploited cheap immigrant labor, often using underhanded tactics. Texas Governor Allan Shivers hotly denied a charge from a New York congressman that Texas opposed stricter immigration laws from a desire to exploit "wetbacks" (a derogatory term derived from crossing the Rio Grande River to enter Texas). Governor Shivers would have had a hard time denying that exploitation existed in many forms, from routinely paying workers less than the minimum wage to ranchers retaining wages from arrested and deported workers, including cases in which employers turned in undocumented workers simply to avoid paying back wages. There is no question that Texas agriculture depended on immigrant labor. In 1954 Judge Joe Montague, acting as a lawyer for cattle raisers, criticized the Justice Department's accelerated program to capture and return undocumented workers at a time when Texas faced critical shortages of cotton pickers. Shortage or not, many cotton farmers preferred undocumented workers, whom they could pay less than the $2.05 per hundredweight set by treaty between the United States and Mexico.[27]

Hispanics, whether natural born citizens or immigrants, undocumented or documented, often lived in squalid shacks without running water or sanitary

Lieutenant Joe Galloway pinning badge on Charles S. Wright, one of the first Black Fort Worth police officers, December 31, 1952. Courtesy *Fort Worth Star Telegram* Collection, Special Collections, University of Texas at Arlington Libraries.

facilities, conditions that spawned and spread diseases. Tuberculosis disproportionately afflicted Hispanics, accounting for 205 deaths out of every 100,000 Latinos compared to only 31 of 100,000 Anglos. San Antonio, with a majority Hispanic population, was particularly hard hit, having the highest tuberculosis rate in the nation. Health care was often unavailable for Mexican immigrants or available in limited circumstances and, when available, was often too expensive. The benevolence of a rancher providing an employee medical care was noteworthy enough to warrant a 1952 *Star Telegram* article, "Young Wetback Full of Kind Words for Texans." Luzino Biyeda of Hidalgo, Mexico, slipped across the border to work at a ranch, where he suffered a wound that became infected, leading to pneumonia, which would have killed him if his employer had not taken him to a hospital and paid for his care. In 1952 the Fort Worth Council on Social Agencies conference praised educational opportunities available to local "Latin Americans," claiming that discrimination did not exist in Fort Worth schools, a true statement as far as access in that Hispanics attended neighborhood schools with Anglos. In contrast, the report complained that Hispanic communities remained woefully underserved in health care and that the quality of care, when available, was low or too remote, that few clinics or medical professionals officed in predominantly Hispanic neighborhoods. The council especially criticized the lack of resources for Hispanic orphans, noting that only one orphanage, St. Teresa's, accepted Hispanic orphans.[28]

Mexican Americans of Fort Worth benefited from support agencies that tried to fill the gaps left by municipal and medical providers and provide community events celebrating their unique culture. The Wesley House, a 1914 white structure at 2131 North Commerce Street operated by the Women's Division of Christian Services of the Methodist Church, served for years as an important institution aiding Mexican immigrants and local Chicanos. The Wesley House provided social and sports activities for youths, kindergarten classes, English classes, a library, sewing machines mothers could use to make clothes, and a television at a time when many households could not afford one. The community joined together to celebrate Mexican Independence Day on September 16. In 1953 the festivities included a parade and a ball at San Jose Catholic Church, where Maria Bell Carmen Trujillo was crowned queen. The ball was a big part of the celebration. In 1954 Fort Worth's Junior GI Forum chose Margaret Morales of 2729 Weisenberger to represent the chapter in the annual queen contest. Unfortunately, sectional differences between Hispanics of the north side and south side sometimes exploded into violence. A dance in September 1955 at Immaculate Heart of Mary Catholic Church, 100 East Pafford Street, turned into a brawl between the two groups, leaving one north side youth shot in the hip and one stabbed and a south sider stabbed. That fight may have been related to an incident in June in which a south side resident, Pete Castillo, 33 years of age, was killed. One of the participants in the June slaying, Thomas Martinez, 17 years of age, said every time the Hispanics from the north and south sides came together, a fight ensued.[29]

Chapter 17

Fort Worth in the Last Half of the 1950s, 1956–1960

Some harbingers of the future appeared in the second half of the 1950s. Foreign automobiles became a noticeable, albeit still small, part of the American market. In 1956 Americans registered 107,675 new imported vehicles, exceeding six figures for the first time, an impressive achievement but still miniscule compared to the 5.9 million American cars built that year. Volkswagen, accounting for almost half the imports, 50,011, harbored hopes of selling 100,000 vehicles in the American market for 1957, a lofty goal considering production already so lagged demand that customers went on a waiting list. Space exploration became more than a theory on October 4, 1957, with the launching of Sputnik I by the Soviet Union, followed quickly in November by Sputnik II, which weighed six times as much and carried a dog. The Soviet space successes shocked Americans, who had assumed technical superiority but now feared the Russians would be first to the moon. Another glimpse into the future received little notice. Dr. Edward Teller, speaking in December 1957 in Tulsa, Oklahoma, warned that excess carbon dioxide would heat the earth by the end of the century. Teller proposed a rapid conversion to nuclear energy to forestall the looming threat. The North Texas area received an early ecological awakening of sorts in 1960 when a study found the Trinity River between Fort Worth's Texas Electric service plant and the town of Rosser in Kaufman County (about sixty miles southeast) was too polluted to support fish life. Several cities lay on the affected watershed, but the report blamed Fort Worth and Dallas for 83 percent of the effluent and 67 percent of the organic loading. Dallas was by far the bigger polluter, creating almost four times as much river pollution as Fort Worth.[1]

The 1950s saw major advances in the highway infrastructure that reduced commutes between North Texas's two large cities. Proximity, being only thirty miles apart, dictated that Fort Worth and Dallas would have close economic ties. In the sixth decade of the twentieth century a large part of that commerce traveled over two-lane roads clogged by traffic and delayed by numerous intersections. That changed on August 20, 1957, at 6:00 a.m. when the Fort Worth–Dallas Turnpike opened, providing uninterrupted transit. In the first twenty-four hours 16,330 vehicles traveled the Turnpike, 6,998 going westbound from Dallas and 5,912 eastbound from Fort Worth (the other 3,420 presumably entered at various other points). The success of the Turnpike clearly demonstrated the benefits associated with freeways, paving the way in 1957 for an overhead route across the southern end of downtown Fort Worth. The overhead's completion in 1960 did not bring joy to all concerned. Attorney Elton Hyder, owner of several downtown buildings along Lancaster Avenue between Throckmorton and Jones Streets (adjacent to the overhead), complained the freeway increased property valuations while pushing the area, now bypassed by overhead traffic, into seediness, frequented by pigeons and "winos" (street persons frequently suffering from alcoholism) so numerous that it was difficult to walk without being assaulted by pigeon droppings or obscene language. Hyder recalled losing a prospective renter because a passed-out man blocked the building's entryway. Statistics supported the gist of Hyder's claims. Of over 100 buildings in the southwest quadrant, thirty-five were vacant, thirty-six were bars or liquor stores, and forty had declined and decayed to the point of being uninhabitable.[2]

The Turnpike also made possible a major sports and recreation venue in Arlington, centrally located midway between Fort Worth and Dallas. The Turnpike's quick access from both Fort Worth and Dallas made the concept of an Arlington stadium not only feasible but also enticing. In 1958

Architect's Drawing of a domed stadium proposed for Arlington, August 20, 1960. Courtesy *Fort Worth Star Telegram* Collection, Special Collections, University of Texas at Arlington Libraries.

Tarrant County Commissioners determined that leases, preferably to a major league baseball or football team, would more than fund construction of a $5 million stadium. In October 1959 Dallas County joined Tarrant County in approving a $9.5 million bond package to build a 45,000-seat stadium that would, it was hoped, attract a Major League Baseball team. The adopted plan was scaled down from a proposal for a 70,000-seat domed facility that would have predated the Astrodome. In August 1961 an $8–10 million amusement park was announced to be built in far east Arlington. The park, centered around a theme of "Texas Under Six Flags" (changed to Six Flags Over Texas), would be "bigger and better" than Disneyland. Even with the Turnpike, the two large entertainment centers may not have happened without the GM plant, the stimulus that transformed Arlington from a sleepy town to a growing city. On July 1, 1956, the *Star Telegram* celebrated Arlington's growth with an article, "Arlington: After 80 Years of Progress, 1876–1956," that credited GM for almost tripling Arlington's population in four years, from 7,691 in 1950 to 21,972 in 1954. Arlington's growth showed no sign of letting up; 1,542 new homes were built in 1955. In 1960 Arlington recorded a population of 44,775, a whooping 482 percent increase since 1950.[3]

Fort Worth also took some major economic strides in the late 1950s. In 1955 it annexed 21.5 square miles, second nationally only to El Paso, which added 34.5. Only the failure to absorb Haltom City kept Fort Worth from outgrowing El Paso. In 1954 John Willis, upset over a perceived lack of city services, started a movement to dissolve Haltom City's incorporation as the first step to eventual annexation by Fort Worth. A Fort Worth alderman, Buddie Thompson, polling the city council, found all members favored the annexation, but Haltom City voters rejected the proposal in a plebiscite, killing the idea.[4]

On November 13, 1957, at 2:00 p.m., a massive clock with twenty-five-foot-tall numbers visible for three miles began revolving atop the thirty-three-story Continental National Bank. In 1960 Sears announced plans for Seminary South, Fort Worth's first regional shopping center, on eighty-five acres at West Seminary Drive and the South Freeway, then occupied by Katy Lake. The center, including a Stripling's Department Store, was scheduled to open in the autumn of 1961. In 1958 the $6 million South Holly Water Treatment Plant became operational, raising the city's water output to 129 million gallons daily. A four-foot main line connected the new plant and the old North Holly Pump Station.[5]

Highway and other construction required large amounts of material, including gravel, which figured into a major financial scandal in 1958. On February 5 the Tarrant County purchasing agent disclosed serious questions had arisen regarding large purchases from a Mosier Valley gravel pit. In March 1958 the grand jury subpoenaed Jess Gray, road supervisor for Tarrant County Precinct Three, to testify, but Gray checked into a Dallas mental health hospital, then disappeared from sight. Precinct Three Commissioner W. Earl Johnson terminated Gray after the grand jury returned indictments against him, Commissioner Johnson, and Dwight Plemons, a jeweler, charging all three as owners of the Mosier Valley gravel pit listed as belonging to Plemons. The indictments alleged the three conspired to issue fake purchases orders for gravel never received, swindling the county out of $20,000.[6]

At Johnson's September 1958 trial the county auditor testified that Tarrant County paid the gravel pit $34,200 between December 1955 and September 1957, supposedly for 136,803 cubic yards of gravel, but two engineers estimated the total gravel removed could not have exceeded 44,940 yards, one suggesting that the total taken was probably no more than 25,024 yards. The defense countered with their own engineer who claimed the pit was capable of having supplied all the gravel billed, although he admitted on cross-examination that he had not inspected the property recently and could not identify the specific pit involved. The previous owner told the court he sold the pit to Plemons for $6,262 in March 1956 and that in the year before the sale, the county bought just $125 worth of gravel. The county auditor reported county gravel purchases spiked just ten days after Plemons took over, and truck drivers testified that records showed them hauling gravel on rain days when they had hauled rock instead. Bank officers corroborated that Plemons was only a straw owner, presenting records indicating that most of the pit's revenue went to Commissioner Johnson. The ledger included checks signed by Plemons that were deposited to Johnson's personal account for $2,400 in November 1955 and $6,262 in March 1956, the totals equaling 90 percent of all the money drawn on county warrants to the pit while Plemons retained just 10 percent. Johnson swore the deposits were payments on a loan he made so Plemons could buy the gravel pit, although the deposits greatly exceeded the pit's purchase price. The jury found the county had been cheated out of thousands but ruled the evidence linking Johnson to the swindle was insufficient. A year later the district attorney's office recommended dismissing all twenty remaining indictments against Johnson, Gray, and Plemons, saying the evidence would not sustain convictions.[7]

The cultural scene benefited from two major initiatives. Since the end of the war, support had grown for a new Casa Mañana to be built at the site of the original structure erected for the 1936 Texas Centennial Celebration. In 1945 voters approved a $500,000 bond package funding the center, but construction stalled for lack of a sustainable plan that would generate sufficient income to repay the bonded indebtedness. In 1954 the issue was revisited with little progress until a citizen's group in 1957 proposed the city relinquish operational control and lease the theater to a private production company for $25,000 annually, an amount sufficient to cover bond payments. The original plan called for two aluminum domes with 1,400 seats for plays and 800 for movies, but was scaled back to a single dome just north of the original 1936 site. The first season presented six musicals, starting with Cole Porter's *Can-Can*, which opened July 5, 1958, to a full house paying $25 per couple. In 1959 the council approved a contract with the Amon G. Carter Foundation for a museum of Western art built and operated by the foundation on city land lying between Camp Bowie Boulevard and West Lancaster Avenue. The Amon Carter Museum of Western Art, featuring works by Frederic Remington and Charles Russell, opened on January 24, 1961. Amon Carter wanted the museum adjacent to Will Rogers Auditorium to complement his tribute to Rogers and, perhaps, to improve the auditorium's profit and loss statement. The Will Rogers complex closed the 1959 fiscal year in the red, which was blamed on lost conventions due the lack of air conditioning and adequate hotel rooms.[8]

Ambitious construction outlays combined with a $42.3 million bond program stretched finances, forcing a close look at finances. A 1958 public forum had a serious discussion on implementing a municipal income tax, most of the debate focusing not on the tax itself but on whether or not residents should be taxed on all income or only that portion earned within the city limits. The idea did not sit well with voters; in November they overwhelmingly rejected both the income tax, by a margin of three to one, and a second amendment to increase the maximum property tax from $1.90 per $100 valuation to $2.20.[9]

The two defeated taxing measures may not have been timely or welcome, but a good argument existed for increasing the city's revenues. In a 1959 survey of taxes, fines, fees, and rental incomes of forty-one of the nation's largest cities, Fort Worth was the thirty-ninth lowest, taxed with $56.16 per capita in municipal income, higher only than last-place San Antonio ($36.23) and Birmingham, Alabama ($51.41). Texas's two other large cities, Dallas and Houston, collected significantly more per capita, $67.55 and $64.52, respectively, but both were below the national average of $87.33. Fort Worth ranked considerably higher in per capita annual property taxes, coming in at twenty-seventh with $30.37, a reflection of the city's reliance on property taxes in the absence of sales and/or income taxes. Once again, San Antonio came in last, number forty-six, receiving only $24.95 per capita in property taxes, but Dallas, $44.06, and Houston, $47.44, scored above the national average of $36.73 per capita. San Antonio was an outlier, existing in a special state apart from the rest of the state and nation, while the other three Texas metropolitan areas hovered near the national mainstream, albeit with a marked overdependence on property taxes. Statistics from a 1960 Census survey of per capita expenditures in twenty-seven Midwestern cities between 250,000 and 1 million population paralleled the earlier findings. Fort Worth's per capita expenditure of $62.41 ranked twentieth of the twenty-seven cities, less than thirteenth-ranked El Paso, $104,78; seventeenth Dallas, $70.50; and nineteenth Houston, $64.74. San Antonio at $40.04 came in at twenty-sixth, surrendering last place to Phoenix, Arizona, $38.70. In contrast, Cincinnati, Ohio, spent the most per capita on municipal government, $155.05.[10]

Financial stresses may have contributed to instability in the city hall power structure that ousted a city manager. The CCGFW, a group of leading businessmen that included Marvin Leonard, had dominated Fort Worth local politics for years. In the April 1959 city council election, the CCGFW endorsed three of five incumbents and six newcomers, including one woman, Mrs. Reecy McKnight. One of the excluded incumbents, Councilman T. D. Thompson, accused the CCGFW of supporting higher property taxes, benefiting downtown business property holders at the expense of everyone else. Despite the mild split, the new council retained a CCGFW majority and a probusiness slant, returning Tom McCann as mayor and John Justin as mayor pro tem. The new council focused their dissatisfaction on City Manager F. Frank Davis, who resigned after receiving endorsements from only two councilmembers. Davis, 50 years old, had thirty-three years with the city that began in 1926 when he was 17. His departure should not have been much of a surprise in view of Fort Worth's track record with city managers. In the thirty-four years since going to the city-manager form in 1925, eight city managers had come and gone. W. O. Jones, the longest serving, lasted nine years, from 1946 to 1955, and left voluntarily, as did O. E. Carr and Sam Bothwell, but the other five resigned under pressure or were fired. Davis's replacement, L. P. Cookingham, had been city manager of Kansas City, Missouri, for nineteen years before resigning when the Pendergraft political machine returned to power. Cookingham received an annual salary of $30,000, making him the highest paid city manager in the state.[11]

The financial situation came to a head in 1959, forcing major reductions and some realignments. The crisis focused on funding John Peter Smith Hospital (JPS), the county's largest supplier of indigent care. Since its founding in 1939 as the City-County Hospital, relocated from downtown, Fort Worth and Tarrant County had jointly covered gaps between the hospital's income and outgo, but rising costs had driven that cost to an unsustainable level. The financial problems were directly related to the doubling of demand; the daily patient load averaged 145 and traffic in the emergency room saw 90 persons a day, stretching hospital facilities that had scarcely changed in twenty years. The imbalance between demand and supply created room shortages so severe that patients often spent a day or more in a hallway waiting for a room to open. In April 1959 voters approved a separate hospital district with taxing authority, funding JPS and the tuberculous hospital, removing both from the city budget. In January 1959 the city council dropped insurance coverage costing $30,000 annually, making Fort Worth self-insured and eliminating the city's welfare system, a $233,000 budget item, effective January 1, 1961, referring all relief enquiries to the county system or private agencies.[12]

The Union Gospel Mission (UGM), 1514 Houston Street, was one of Fort Worth's major private relief organizations. The UGM, founded in 1888, served Fort Worth's indigent through their worst days, including the Depression years, providing lodging and two meals a day, each preceded by religious services. Breakfast at 8:00 a.m. consisted of coffee, doughnuts, toast, and, sometimes, milk gravy, while dinner at 8:00 p.m. had a rotating menu of pinto beans, black-eyed peas, stew, or vegetable soup, all served with bread. Donations from local businesses helped keep each meal under $0.03, but overall costs hovered around $1,000 monthly. In March 1960 Reverend Rodger Q. Florence became superintendent, taking over the mission that in the first two months of 1960 served 11,214 meals, an average of 190 a day, and provided 3,432 nights of lodging, an average of fifty-eight persons per day.[13]

Fort Worth schools remained underfunded, with teachers' salaries below those in comparable cities. In a 1960 survey of Texas's ten largest cities, Port Arthur paid the highest starting annual wage, $4,200, and Fort Worth was dead last at only $3,850. A national study the same year looking at forty-three comparably sized school systems ranked Fort Worth twenty-ninth in teachers' salaries. Funding issues were widespread, affecting more than just teachers. The $20.9 million budget for the 1960–1961 school year represented an expenditure of only $297 per student, stressing a system stretched thin by substantial growth in the student body. Between the 1951–1952 school year and 1960–1961, Fort Worth schools added 26,548 students, an increase of 60 percent.[14]

The 1950s have been associated with the formation of a youth culture separate and distinct from mainstream culture. Music was a major expression of that new identity, and there was no bigger force moving music than Elvis Presley, described by Elston Brooks, a *Star Telegram* reporter, as a "21-year-old Memphis blues singer with long sideburns and black denim trousers." Brooks added that Elvis's appeal was boosted by the hip movements incorporated into his performance. On April 20, 1956, Elvis performed two shows at North Side Coliseum ($1.50 general admission, $2,00 reserved), entertaining 7,000 screaming fans while protected by twenty police officers.[15]

The new youth culture of the 1950s had an unpleasant side personified in the image of a juvenile delinquent prone to violence. The tendency for violence was displayed in clashes between rival high schools, often in conjunction with athletic contests. A 1956 basketball game between Poly and Paschal High Schools turned into a brawl involving up to 500 that spilled outside the field house, sending several students to hospitals, and taking twenty patrol cars, likely the entire shift, to end the melee. Later that night high school students barricaded 4700 East Lancaster Avenue and police arrested seven youths at a south side drive-in where several hundred congregated. Principals O. D. Wyatt of Paschal High School and C. A. Thompson of Polytechnic High School called for reestablishing the All-Schools Better Relations Organization they had formed in 1946 after a spate of near-riots disrupted athletic events. In 1958 another Paschal-Poly brawl caused the district's high school principals to seriously consider canceling the rest of the high school football season.[16]

Paschal and Poly received most of the attention, but other schools got involved. In September 1959 ten Birdville High School students were attacked during the Birdville-Poly football game at Farrington Field. Afterward, Birdville Principal Julius Bussey advised students to travel in groups at any Farrington Field event. Two days later Haltom City Police arrested six youths, including two Birdville students, they found with clubs, brass knuckles, knives, and other weapons in their car. The youths admitted going to Poly High School looking for fights but left when the principal confronted them. Statistics seemed to suggest that juvenile delinquency had risen in the post–World War II era. In 1933 Tarrant County's lone juvenile probation officer handled 209 cases, sending 23 offenders to courts for adjudication; twenty-five years later, in 1958, the chief juvenile probation officer and his ten assistants handled 2,151 delinquency cases, referred 138 to courts, and administered 2,933 dependency cases, 196 going to court.[17]

Another facet of the 1950s youth culture, beatniks, faced hostility from police and the courts. Beatniks to some degree rejected mainstream society's values in favor of an alternative lifestyle, manifesting their uniqueness by their distinctive dress and by hanging out at counterculture coffee houses. Fort Worth's best-known center for the alternative lifestyle, the Cellar, was a bohemian spot that opened in 1958 at Tenth and Main Streets. The owner, Pat Kirkwood, was the son of the owner of the 2222 Club on Jacksboro Highway, a legendary gambling den catering to an upper-class clientele. An insight into beatnik attire came from an October 1959 forgery warrant arrest report for Diane Keller, a waitress at the Cellar. The arresting detectives reported Ms. Keller was wearing black toreador pants and a black turtleneck sweater over a man's white shirt. Some judges took questionable steps in adjudicating cases involving beatniks. In 1960 a Tarrant County juvenile court offered probation to three teenage burglars on the condition that they got rid of their "beatnik-style haircuts and sideburns." Tarrant County Criminal Court Judge J. C. Duvall took a similar approach in dealing with two adults associated with coffeehouses. He ordered William Scott, convicted of stealing a jacket from the Red Dragon, another "beatnik coffee house," to return to high school and John Anicher, day manager at the Cellar found guilty of carrying a pistol, to move to his parents' home in San Antonio.

Two counterculturists attempted to enter local politics, registering as candidates for Democratic Party precinct chairmen, but both failed to make the ballot. Peter "The Hero" Gill was rejected for not having paid his poll tax, disqualifying him from voting and, therefore, political office, and Joe "Big Mike" Callaway was scratched for not having a verifiable home address after he listed an out-of-business coffeehouse.[18]

One disaffected local youth chose to abandon the United States. In 1959 Lee Harvey Oswald, an ex-Marine who attended Fort Worth schools, including Arlington Heights High, turned in his American passport at the American Embassy in Moscow, announcing he would seek Russian citizenship. He told reporters that leaving the United States was like getting out of prison, adding he could not be happy living under capitalism. Oswald's brother, Robert Oswald, who lived with their mother, Marguerite Oswald, at 7313 Davenport Avenue, said Lee was young and looking for excitement. In September 1960, almost one year later, a crowd of 15,000 heard Democratic presidential hopeful John Kennedy speak at Burnett Park. Kennedy was met at Meacham Airport by Mrs. Edna Willy of Fort Worth, the widow of an Army aviator killed in the same World War II bombing mission that took the life of the candidate's brother, Joseph P. Kennedy Jr.[19]

By the end of the decade Fort Worth would lose one relic of its past and see another decline into insignificance. In 1959 the Milner Hotel, 911 Main Street, was razed. The building, erected in 1898 by Winfield Scott in what was known as the Scott block, opened as the Metropolitan Hotel amid boasts of offering the finest in accommodations, complete with water from its own courtyard artesian well, rooms heated by artificial gas derived from coal, and a posh bar and a restaurant with a French chef. During the Depression the hotel and its general neighborhood declined into seediness, frequented mostly by imbibers of cheap wine. The Lake Worth Casino remained, but by 1959 it was only a shell of its former self. What had been a destination, a local version of Coney Island, had never fully recovered from a mishap in the summer of 1940 when the boardwalk collapsed, sending 200 persons onto supporting pilings, injuring 56. Afterward, the boardwalk was demolished, along with the roller coaster, dooming the carnival concession that had lined it, leaving only the pavilion that continued to host dances well into the 1960s.[20]

John F. Kennedy and Senator Lyndon B. Johnson shaking hands on Seventh Street during 1960 presidential campaign, September 13, 1960. Courtesy *Fort Worth Star Telegram* Collection, Special Collections, University of Texas at Arlington Libraries.

Structures were not the only relics that passed away in the 1950s. Amon Carter, perhaps Fort Worth's biggest booster since Boardman Buckley Paddock and John Peter Smith, died in June 1955. Former presidents and celebrities of all types sent accolades and condolences. Harry H. Halsell died in Fort Worth in 1957 at the age of 96 after a full life as a cowboy-rancher who had driven cattle on Commerce Street, all recounted in nine books he wrote detailing his adventures. In 1957 death also came to Wyatt C. Hedrick, the son of a Virginia tobacco planter who became a civil engineer and established W. C. Hedrick Construction Company, responsible for building Texas

Technological University in Lubbock, Dallas's Love Field, Houston's International Airport, and several Fort Worth buildings. Hedrick owned eight ranches, several aircraft, and businesses in many cities, including Fort Worth, Dallas, and Houston. Sid W. Richardson, called the wealthiest man in American by the *Ladies Home Journal Magazine*, died in 1959 on an island he owned in the Gulf of Mexico. Billy Graham spoke at his funeral at Broadway Baptist Church. Richardson left an estimated fortune of $700 million, much of it in his vast personal oil holdings that exceeded the assets of some oil companies. A bachelor, he lived for twenty years at the Fort Worth Club, where he kept three packed suitcases, one each for cold, moderate, and temperate climates, allowing him to simply add shirts and be off at a moment's notice in one of his two aircraft. Richardson was survived by two sisters and his nephew and business partner, Perry R. Bass, who took over the business operations. Perry Bass did well, building the family fortune into the billions, much of which he and his sons used to spur and direct Fort Worth's development.[21]

In contrast, not everyone prospered in the 1950s; a few unfortunates existed in a state of poverty that forced ill-advised risks. Oppressive poverty and the lack of affordable childcare combined to create a tragedy in 1959. Firefighters arriving at an apartment fire, 1023 Northeast Twenty-Third Street, found the only exterior access door nailed shut by the parents to keep their three children, ages 1, 2, and 3, inside while they worked. All three children died from the flames.[22]

An interesting study by the TCU sociology department ranked Fort Worth neighborhoods according to socioeconomic criteria. Ridglea had the highest average annual income, $5,685, as well the highest monthly rents, $98.66, but was second in home value, $12,593, to TCU/Westcliff, where the average home was worth $16,037. TCU/Westcliff also led in average education (27.2 percent of residents over 25 years old had four years of college) and in the highest concentration of professional/executive classes (56.1 percent). Diamond Hill boasted the city's highest percentage of foremen and craftsmen, 54.2 percent, and Fairmont was the most densely populated at 15,518 per square mile.[23]

The 1960 Census showed the Fort Worth had a population of 353,388, up 74,610, or 26.8 percent, from 1950 (278,778). The Fort Worth Metropolitan

Area grew faster, adding 175,841, or 44.8 percent, thanks to a remarkable 88.9 percent increase in the population of suburban cities that added 101,231 to reach 215,096, likely an effect of the rise of Arlington after GM and the Mid-Cities after Bell Helicopter.[24] Fort Worth's Standard Metropolitan Area population was the forty-first largest in the United States, up from forty-sixth in 1950. Houston's Metropolitan Area, Texas's largest, ranked fifteenth nationally with Dallas following at eighteenth and San Antonio at thirty-third. The census estimated Fort Worth's metropolitan population in 2000 would reach 1,986,000 to 2,643,000, coming very close to the actual count in 2021 of 2,542,235.[25] A statistical comparison between 1936 and 1957 Fort Worth reveals significant actual and percentage increases:

Chart 17.1 Percentage Increases in Fort Worth Statistics, 1936–1957

	1936	1957	% Increase
Population	189,662	~370,000	95
City budget	$4.3 million	$22.4 million	421
Property valuation	$162 million	$618 million	282
Square miles	58	140	141
City employees	906	2,836	213
Firefighters	264	382	45
Police officers	207	458	121
Roads (unpaved / paved)	852 / 384	1,464 / 818	72

Source: Fort Worth Star Telegram, January 20, 1957, Section 1, p. 1.

Chapter 18

Crime, Criminals, and Vice, 1956–1960

In February 1956 William Prescott Allen, publisher of the *Laredo Times,* was jailed overnight after he refused to disclose the source behind the paper's charge that police payoffs were behind widespread gambling in Fort Worth and other Texas cities. After conferring with his lawyers, Allen claimed not to know the person's identity, but he did name six law enforcement authorities on the take (unfortunately their names were not published). In April the Tarrant County Crime Commission reported that no substantial evidence tied organized crime to large-scale payoffs in Fort Worth or Tarrant County. The sitting grand jury chimed in, stating it had found nothing to indicate or substantiate police payoffs.[1]

No denials could seriously undermine Allen's basic premise, that widespread gambling was common in many Texas cities and could not have existed without the cooperation of law enforcement. Gambling was as clear as the slot machines and other gaming devices found in taverns, cafés, and many shops and in the frequent arrests of low-end, street-level operators. A Fort Worth city ordinance adopted in 1956 authorized confiscation of pinball and marble board machines commonly used for gambling. The ordinance did not last long before Ben McDonald of Star Coin Machine

Company won an injunction prohibiting seizures pending a hearing on the law's legality. That review ruled Fort Worth's ordinance unconstitutional. Fort Worth Police took the setback in stride, simply resuming their traditional enforcement strategy, arresting gamblers and releasing them on cash bonds that were forfeited as fines. In one such operation in May 1956, three officers raiding an upstairs pool hall at 1200½ Evans Avenue released thirty-two gamblers on $25 bonds. In January 1958 Clifford Piper of Cliff's Place, a bar at 2936 East Lancaster Avenue, and William Prince of the Oui Lounge, 3509 Bluebonnet Circle, were charged with allowing gaming devices after undercover officers received payoffs from coin-operated machines. Vice Squad Sergeant Oliver Ball led a raid on an Arlington Heights home where officers arrested a woman and five men playing poker. The woman was released, but the five men put up $200 bonds on vagrancy charges, a strange charge to be applied to anyone inside a private home. Perhaps it was justified by the presence of a serious gambler like George Washington "Jettie" Bass, described as Dallas's "No. 1 hoodlum" and a top lieutenant in the Lois Green crime gang known for robberies, prostitution, and drugs. Bass was the only one of the five identified.[2]

Gambling was not just a minor vice played on coin-operated machines or a friendly game at the kitchen table, but a business often associated with serious, even deadly outcomes. In August 1956 gambler Frank Cates, suspected in the 1950 bombing deaths of Nelson Harris and his wife, was severely injured in a dynamite explosion at his home, 2806 Roberts Cut-off Road. First responders found Cates dazed and injured but more concerned about finding $1,800 he claimed to have had in his hand when the blast hit ($755 was recovered). Frank Cates had a police record of thefts and larcenies stretching back to 1915 and was linked to or suspected in many violent crimes, including several high-profile murders in addition to the Harrises. The bomb exploded just as Cates arrived home and answered the telephone. Investigators found electric wires running 250 feet from underneath Cates's house to Jacksboro Highway where they had been connected to an electrical source powering the blast. Staff at nearby Chenault's Restaurant reported two suspicious persons, one who entered the restaurant at 8:00 a.m. and remained, drinking five beers while occasionally going outside to a payphone, and a second who stayed beside a blue Buick parked in an adjacent alley. Both disappeared immediately after the blast. Police theorized the beer-swilling patron telephoned until Cates answered, then signaled the man by the vehicle to set off the dynamite by connecting the wires to the car battery. Texas Rangers investigating found a dice table and poker equipment that could be quickly set up and broken down, the type commonly used for "sneak gambling," dice games. Cates, 61 years old, remained uncooperative, telling investigators he would take care of the matter his own way.[3]

Just two months later, on October 8, 1956, Cates was found in his car on Watauga-Saginaw Road, dead from shotgun wounds. He had left home around 7:15 p.m., telling his wife he was meeting a man and would return in a few minutes. Approximately two hours later two men saw Cate's stopped car on Watauga-Saginaw Road. An hour later they checked after noticing the car had not moved and discovered the body inside. No one was ever charged in Cates's murder, but police sources pointed to Gene Paul Norris as the likely assassin. Norris was a prolific killer tied to nine deaths and suspected in as many as forty, including Cecil Green, Tincy Eggleston, and Cates. Cates was the latest in a string of gangland slayings since 1944. The list included Louis Tindall, May 1944; Lon Holley, May 1948; Cue Miller, May 1948; Mildred Noble, 1949; Hollis Green, December 1949 (ambushed at Dallas); Mr. and Mrs. Nelson Harris, November 1950; Herbert Noble, August 1951; Jim Thomas, August 1951 (in Durant, Oklahoma); Edell Evans, April 1955; Cecil Green, May 1955; Tincy Eggleston, August 1955; and Frank Cates, October 1956.[4]

Four months later, on February 2, 1957, Sid Foley was found in a garbage pit northwest of Lake Worth, a short distance from the well where Tincy's body had been dumped. Foley had been beaten beyond recognition and shot to the back of the head with a .38-caliber round. An associate of Tincy Eggleston and Cecil Green, he had fallen on slim times, subsisting on "find the pea" games played with bottle caps and selling dyed rabbit stoles as "stolen" expensive furs. Detectives learned that he had been in a barroom brawl the previous day at Danny's Place, a known hoodlum hangout on Jacksboro Highway owned by Danny Horowitz. Sheriff's investigators searching the bar found four handguns (three hidden in a sofa)—a .32-caliber, a .38-caliber and two .45-calibers—and gambling equipment. They arrested the manager, Lowell Danny McCombs, for allowing gambling devices on premises and charged George Kean, the club bouncer and known associate of Foley, with three counts of aggravated assault after he attacked Investigators E. N. Buie and Ed Max and Texas Ranger Jay Banks. The four guns were sent to the DPS laboratory in Austin along with a .32-caliber bullet recovered at the garbage pit. A few days later, a child walking in a field near where Foley's body was dumped found furs taken during a January 16, 1957, home invasion at 4551 Vermont, the residence of David Zips. The furs raised speculation that Foley met his fate in a dispute over division of the Zips' goods, but, again, no one was ever charged, although police suspected George Kean.[5]

Just a few months later, in December 1957, George Kean vanished. At the time of his death, Kean was involved in a struggle for control of local rackets, but he dismissed concerns about his welfare, telling police he was too small-time to warrant assassination. In September 1958 an anonymous caller reported Kean's body had been dumped at Lake Worth near where Edell Evans and Sid Foley had been found. Officers searching the area found a body, but dental records confirmed it was not Kean (the identity was never determined). Another tip sent Fort Worth Police Captain O. R. Brown and Tarrant County Sheriff Harlon Wright to Lake Huron in Michigan, where they found Kean's buried body. Once again, suspects were everywhere, but witnesses and solid leads could not be found. Suspicions focused on Midwestern mobsters reportedly upset over increased police pressure they blamed on Kean's robberies. A history of peevishness existed between Kean and local hoodlums. Earlier, a disgruntled mobster had tipped off police to Kean's hideout, leading to a shootout in which Tommy Brewster, a Fort Worth procurer, was killed but Kean escaped unharmed. Jimmie "The Greek" Tsermengas told Detroit Police that he had accidentally killed Kean when a gun went off as they fought over it. The rift that led to the struggle began when Tsermengas and Kean, along with Thomas Smith and Danny McComb (Smith and McComb were also known Fort Worth hoodlums), were driving to the Michigan area where they planned to commit several robberies. Two Illinois police officers stopped their car, but the four men, all armed, disarmed the officers. Kean wanted to kill both policemen, but Tsermengas refused (the two officers later thanked Tsermengas for saving them). That dispute created hard feelings that later erupted in a drunken argument over who was tougher and the physical struggle in which Kean was killed. One of the three survivors called in the erroneous Lake Worth tip to divert the investigation away from them and the area. Some have suggested Kean was the last victim in the chain of notorious Fort Worth gangster murders, but that honor may well belong to James "Chuck" Parrish, a former police officer turned gambler and gangster. Parrish died in a classic gangland execution, killed when his car exploded as he drove on Forest Park Boulevard on March 20, 1965. Depending on where the line is drawn, either fifteen or sixteen senior Fort Worth gangsters met ignoble ends between 1944 and 1958 or 1965.[6]

The deaths of so many well-known and active gangsters left detectives without their routine response of rounding up the usual suspects whenever a major crime occurred. In June 1958 bandits invaded Melvin Evans's home, 4117 Clayton Road West, tying up the family while they searched for a nonexistent safe. Investigating detectives complained that their normal response, questioning known police characters, had been closed by all the deaths. In time, B-listers and young acolytes would emerge to fill the void, although they never seemed as clearly defined and none became as infamous as Tincy Eggleston and a few others.[7]

Some of the new faces in Fort Worth crime started out with a bang in 1958. On the afternoon of August 20, 1958, three men ambushed Bobby Rae Foote in the 1800 block of Arch Street, killing him. Johnnie Green, riding in the car with Foote, told police the shooters were part of a syndicate trying to take over the call-girl trade in Fort Worth. Green picked Garrett Ramsey and Donald Gauntt out of a line up and identified a third accomplice, Larry W. Gunsolus (also spelled as Gonsolus), who turned himself in a few days later. All three were known underworld characters involved in Fort Worth vice. Many police sources considered Ramsey a worthy successor to Tincy Eggleston and Cecil Green, citing his involvement in various criminal enterprises, including burglaries, safe cracking, robberies, and prostitution. Ramsey was acquitted at trial but Gauntt, the apparent triggerman, was convicted and sentenced to ninety-nine years.[8]

Most, but not all, of those involved in the Foote killing ended up paying for their life of crime. Johnnie Green, the chief prosecution witness, was arrested in September 1958 in Texas on a California warrant for the murder of a woman whose car had been recovered in Corsicana, Texas (about eighty miles southeast of Fort Worth). Green confessed, claiming he did not set out to kill the victim but became enraged and choked her when she fought off his advances. On New Year's Day 1959 two citizens found Larry W. Gunsolus under an East Belknap Street overpass, shot three times and his throat cut, but still alive. Doctors offered little hope for recovery, but somehow Gunsolus survived to be released after several weeks in hospital, although he remained nonambulatory. He claimed he could not remember being shot but recalled his throat being slit, but he could not, or would not, say by whom.

Garrett M. Ramsey continued as a major player in prostitution circles, called by some Fort Worth's "head hoodlum," due in part to a surge in his reputation following the Foote murder. Ramsey had twenty-three arrests dating back to a 1953 assault on a Fort Worth police officer and was suspected in many murders. In June 1960 he was a prime suspect in the slaying of Royce C. Herd. An anonymous caller to the Tarrant County Sheriff's Office claimed Ramsey had just killed a man and buried him at Lake Worth. Detectives checking Ramsey's home, 3700 Sandgate, found him asleep and his Cadillac with bullet holes and a bloody interior. The awakened gangster told a fanciful tale about Herd holding him at gunpoint at a house owned by Paul English (later a drummer for Willie Nelson) when armed men kicked in the door and shot Herd, seriously wounding him. When Herd refused to go to a hospital, Ramsey put him in the Cadillac's trunk (presumably the intruders had left) and drove to a road bridge over Village Creek southwest of Kennedale where he dumped the body, then called for an ambulance, saying that an accident victim was in the road. Ramsey and Bobby Lott were jailed in the slaying and released on $15,000 bonds each, but Ramsey passed a lie detector test and was never charged.[9]

Clarence Wesley "Sonny" Evans, the son of Edell Evans, followed in his father's footsteps. Sonny started with a whirlwind of activity in July 1956 when he, 19 years old, and Robert Lee Campbell, 17 years old, assaulted four fellow prisoners while in the city jail for investigation of burglary.

Sonny was released only to be rearrested in August in a stolen car along with his brother, Dennis Gale Evans, and two other young men. He avoided prosecution after one of the two unnamed accomplices confessed to taking the vehicle and vowing Sonny was unaware the car was stolen. Afterward Sonny announced he had "squared up," that he had committed to leaving the thug life after becoming overcome with remorse at a dance where a gang fight was about to start. He promised he would no longer emulate his father but would go straight and be a "square John," crediting his transformation to God and love for a girl. The reversal either came too late or did not last long; the very next month, September 1956, Sonny was indicted for raping Elthia Williams, a 15-year-old girl, probably his intended fiancée. Elthia admitted having an intimate relationship with Sonny as well as joining him in luring Dee Stone, a 23-year-old waitress, into prostitution. At the time Sonny was waiting trial for burglarizing Jack Blair Floor Company, had another pending burglary charge in Cleburne, and was suspected in several other burglaries. He remained criminally active for years with a seemingly unnatural knack of avoiding serious prison time, including in 1966 when he was sentenced to death for rape but won a reversal on appeal. His luck ran out in 1969 when he received two life sentences for burglary and escape. Sonny died from heart failure on July 14, 1983, at the age of 46.[10]

Gene Paul Norris was a main participant in a notorious robbery attempt that went very wrong. Norris operated a machine shop in Oklahoma but regularly visited Fort Worth, where he was no stranger to the police. In March 1956 he was arrested at the 711 Lounge, 711 Pennsylvania Avenue, after the bartender reported he caused a disturbance. In June 1956 he and his new wife, the former Rita Davis and former girlfriend of Cecil Green, reopened the By-Way Drive-In, 5605 Jacksboro Highway, where Cecil Green had been shot to death in May 1955. Fort Worth Police still considered him a suspect in the Western Hills Hotel robbery but never had the proof to charge. He steadfastly denied knowledge of the crime or of the missing loot.[11]

In April 1957 law enforcement officers from several agencies began trailing Gene Paul, William G. Humphrey, and James Edward Papworth after an unidentified tipster reported they planned to rob the Carswell Air Force Base payroll, a haul estimated to be worth $500,000. The intricate plan involved holding Elizabeth Barles, a Fort Worth National Bank teller at the Carswell Base branch, and her child hostage while Norris, dressed as Ms. Barles, drove her car with a base pass to the base payroll office to await the armored bank car bringing currency used to cash payroll checks. Police officers secured the woman's home off Meandering Road while unmarked cars patrolled the area. The day before the robbery Chief Hightower, Sheriff Harlon Wright, a Texas Ranger, and other officers spotted Norris and Humphrey driving nearby, apparently conducting a dry run. The two sped off after spotting the officers, firing repeatedly as they fled. The officers, joined by two other cars, returned fire as the pursuit reached speeds of 120 mph before ending at Walnut Creek near Springtown, Texas. The bandits scampered away, shooting as they ran, and were killed in the gun battle, Norris suffering sixteen wounds and Humphrey twenty-three.[12]

Officers turned their attention to Papworth, arresting him and searching his office, 2625 Race Street, that he shared with David F. Hagler. Hagler and Papworth had met while both served time at the Federal Correctional Institute at Seagoville, Texas, Hagler for fraud in obtaining loans and Papworth for mail fraud. Papworth confessed readily but told a self-serving tale in which Norris lured him to a Jacksboro Highway tavern where he threatened Papworth's wife and son to force his cooperation in the Carswell robbery. In this version Norris somehow knew that Papworth had met not only Hagler at Seagoville but also John Wesley Taylor, a former Fort Worth National Bank manager who served nine months for embezzling $7,300 to cover gambling debts. Norris ordered Papworth to get from Taylor both the floor plan for the Carswell bank branch and the identity of the branch's teller. Papworth claimed he went with Norris during the dry run to point out the home of Ms. Barles but became concerned for her welfare and told Norris he had forgotten the address. Norris then left and got into the car with Humphrey just before the chase began. Chief Hightower dismissed Papworth as a liar, avowing that he had masterminded the robbery and initiated the contact with Norris. The chief added that Papworth also had plans to steal valuable oil paintings belonging to Kay Kimbell, a wealthy local miller and art collector responsible for the Kimbell Art Museum. At his arrest Papworth carried a pencil drawing of Kimbell's office at Kimbell Milling Company headquarters, 2200 South Main Street, where paintings were stored.[13]

Papworth's trial began in September 1957 with testimony from James W. McFarland, an admitted gambler, who said he, at Papworth's request, set up a meeting in March 1957 with Gene Paul Norris at the Beachcomber Café on Jacksboro Highway but left and did not hear their conversation. Several witnesses testified they heard Papworth discussing the robbery without mentioning that his participation was forced. Taylor confirmed Papworth developed the original idea while they were in prison and that he (Taylor) provided details based on his inside knowledge of the operations but got cold feet and tipped off the FBI after Norris vowed to kill anyone who interfered. Taylor added that he so feared for the safety of Ms. Barles and her child that he told Norris the two were dating in hopes the relationship would ensure her safety. Ms. Barles confirmed that she had keys to the Carswell branch safe and a pass to enter the gate but denied any romantic links with Taylor despite testimony placing her in Taylor's room at the Fortune Arms Hotel. The jury convicted Papworth, sentencing him to five years in federal prison.[14]

Chief Hightower blamed Norris for several murders, including that of Tincy Eggleston, Cecil Green, Frank Cates, Olen Ray Tyler, and Edward Townley and his wife, the latter two missing drug dealers who were presumed dead. Norris was also a serious suspect with a motive and the opportunity in the beating deaths of Johnnie Brannan and his wife in Houston. Johnnie Brannan had testified in a 1937 murder case in which Gene Paul's brother, Pete Norris, received a ninety-nine-year sentence. Witnesses reported seeing Gene Paul's car near the Brannan's home at the time of their deaths, but the most compelling evidence surfaced after Gene Paul's death: a receipt for a handgun that his widow discovered and turned in. The serial number on the receipt matched a pistol found near the Brannan murders. Police believed the killer tossed the weapon as he drove away.[15]

One of the era's last well-known gangsters to be killed met his end not at the hands of unknown assailants in an underworld power struggle but as a one part of a lovers' quarrel. George Rennie "Jack" Nesbit was a hoodlum suspected in many crimes, including the bombing deaths of Mr. and Mrs. Herbert Noble and Mr. and Mrs. Nelson Harris. Nesbit had fallen on tough times, working as a bouncer at Boston Smith's gaming joint on the Tarrant/Parker County line. On May 21, 1957, Nesbit arrived at 812 Scenic

Drive, the home of Lois Stripling, widow of gambler Howard Stripling, with whom he had a romantic relationship. The interlude turned sour quickly after Lois announced she was breaking off the affair, news Nesbit did not take well. When he threatened to bomb her parents' home in retaliation, Lois put four slugs in his body, killing him. Nesbit's violent past coupled with the threats convinced Detective A. C. Howerton the murder was a case of self-defense; on his recommendation the grand jury no-billed Lois.[16]

A couple on the lower hierarchy of local crime died by violent means in January 1959. A building manager, alerted by incessant barking, discovered Willard and Darlene Hauer dead in their apartment, 301 St. Louis Avenue, each shot once in the head and a gas outlet left opened in case they survived the shooting. The couple was well-known to police. Darlene had several arrests and Willard's record dated back to the 1930s; both were known associates of Tincy Eggleston, Edell Evans, Harry Huggins, and Cecil Green (Green had lived at the same address). By 1959 the Hauers had fallen on hard economic times, Willard dealing in used cars while Darlene, who had worked as a prostitute, turned to shoplifting after the years and drugs destroyed her looks. Police suspected, but could never prove, that they died in a struggle to control the local drug trade.[17]

In 1959 the Tarrant County Sheriff's Office faced serious corruption charges alleging ties to gamblers. In September 1959 Texas Rangers, along with deputies from the Tarrant County Sheriff's Office, raided Pat Kirkwood's gambling house on Copeland Road north of the Turnpike in Arlington, the last known gambling house in Tarrant County according to Sheriff Harlon Wright. The raiders arrested ten customers and four employees, including W. C. Kirkwood, father of Pat and a veteran gambler who owned the infamous 2222 Club on Jacksboro Highway. A Tarrant County grand jury investigating gambling and corruption in law enforcement looked into reports that Tarrant County Sheriff's Deputies A. P. Hurley and his partner, Bobby Morton, had tipped off Kirkwood. Both deputes denied the charge, saying they could not have told anyone because they had no prior knowledge. Hurley claimed that he first learned of the operation when a Texas Ranger telephoned after it was over, while Morton maintained he was not told until the next day. Hurley testified before the grand jury but refused to take a polygraph, saying he did not trust them, but Morton resigned, saying he did so to save Sheriff Wright from political damage. The grand jury refused to indict either deputy, ending the criminal cases. Emerging details indicated that Morton had not personally called Kirkwood but that whoever called cited Morton as their source.[18]

The Copeland Road raid generated more fallout. In March 1960 Department of Public Safety Commissioner Homer Garrison allowed Ranger Captain E. J. "Jay" Burks to resign in lieu of termination for laxity in attacking Tarrant County gambling. Garrison reported Burks had stalled and delayed multiple enforcement opportunities, that Garrison had to order him to hit Kirkwood's gambling operation, and that Burks delayed raiding A. O. Wooden's Benbrook Highway gambling den for so long that state intelligence officers took over the investigation. State agents on the Benbrook operation drew criticism from Chief Hightower for not notifying Fort Worth Police beforehand, a mistake Commissioner Garrison blamed on a misconception that the location was outside Fort Worth city limits.[19]

The grand jury also investigated allegations that the Tarrant County Jail staff assisted J. A. Avery Jr. in a September 28, 1960, escape. According to jailhouse sources, Avery bribed Jail Engineer Wayne Whittenberg with a ring to be made a trusty. Whittenberg denied the allegation, but Avery's mother confirmed Whittenberg brought her a note from Avery instructing her to give the ring to the jailer. Fellow prisoners added Whittenberg had furnished Avery with liquor on several occasions. The grand jury report lambasted Sheriff Wright, accusing him of "highly reprehensible, irregular and perhaps illegal conduct," suggesting that the next jury panel continue the investigation if corrective measures were not taken. Wright drew most of the heat, although the summary described the actions of unnamed deputies as "unsavory" but not indictable.[20]

Wright dug in his heels, insisting he had done nothing wrong and was being "crucified" by political foes. The sheriff suggested that his problems stemmed from District Attorney Doug Crouch's support for Lon Evans, one of Wright's opponents in the upcoming election. Wright also attacked allegations against Deputy Morton, arguing that the grand jury's failure to indict proved that his deputy had nothing wrong, a shallow argument that equated failure to prosecute with a finding of innocence. Wright's uphill reelection fight suffered another setback on April 7, 1960, when twenty-four prisoners rioted from afternoon to midnight, burning blankets and mattresses and breaking water lines and plumbing fixtures, causing $500 in damages. Overcrowding was a major issue behind the riot, a complaint with some justification since the county jail held 311 prisoners in a facility designed for 167. Ancillary issues included demands to increase outgoing mail limitations from two per week to three per day, access to a telephone, a service then denied prisoners, greater access to attorneys, and speedier trials, the last not in the purview of the jail or sheriff's office. All the controversies proved too much to overcome; Wright placed third in the 1960 three-person race for the Democratic nomination for sheriff. In the runoff Wright threw his support to Buster Lary, but Lon Evans, a former TCU football player, won easily.[21]

Despite raids, corruption investigations, and new legislation, gambling persisted. The Federal Wagering Law of 1951 added a new enforcement tool, requiring gamblers buy a $50 tax stamp and pay a 10 percent tax on bets. In 1960 twenty-three Tarrant County residents, including ten in Fort Worth, bought the $50 federal gaming tax stamps, leaving many who did not. In April 1960 IRS agents, empowered by the tax provisions, hit gambling operations in Pittsburgh, Boston, Chicago, Newport, Fort Worth, and a few spots in Kentucky all linked to a "lay-off" center in New Kensington, Pennsylvania, that protected bookmakers by balancing wagers. Locally, IRS agents arrested eighteen persons, including J. H. "Red" Winn and J. B. King at Winn's home, 1222 Virginia Place. Winn and King admitted they were professional gamblers but denied being bookies. The following week authorities conducted a massive operation covering fifty cities spread across twenty states that netted 100 arrests for tax stamp violations, including a bookmaking operation in two adjoining rooms of the Jackson Hotel, 1014½ Main Street, run by Jefferson "Spec" Randolph and James C. Williams. At the Jackson agents and police found three telephones, betting slips, odds charts, and racing forms. A third nationwide operation in November 1960, led by the IRS agents, arrested 109 gamblers in 105 raids in fifty-four cities, including Fort Worth and Dallas. Local officers got into the act in September 1960 when city vice officers and Texas Rangers arrested eighteen persons and confiscated $1,730 and gambling equipment at a north side upstairs pool hall.[22]

A struggle over gambling in Fort Worth between 1956 and 1959 may have led to four bombings and one attempted bombing at three barrooms known as gambling dens. On September 2, 1956, Paul's Club on Belknap Street, formerly the Parrish Inn, was destroyed by an explosion while the club was closed. The blast, fueled by gasoline attached to a crude fuse, moved two nearby cars and blew two neighbors out of their beds. The prime suspects were Jack Nesbit and C. S. Stewart (sometimes listed as S. C. Stewart), both charged with arson in Paducah, Texas. In the next fifteen months the Penguin Club, 5925 East Rosedale Street, was hit three times: on August 2, 1957, a bomb thrown through a broken window exploded in the main bar area; on December 12, 1957, an explosive tossed on the roof caused minor damage; and on the morning of December 31, 1957, a porter found five sticks of dynamite with a sputtered-out fuse in an outside planter box. Fifteen months later, in March 1959, six sticks of dynamite placed near a beer box destroyed the Jungle Lounge, 101 West Berry Street. The owners denied knowledge of what or who was behind the attacks, at least to police.[23]

In 1958 a Barber Shop War erupted into violence in several Texas cities, including Fort Worth. The conflict, pitting barber against barber, started after more established shops raised rates for regular haircuts to $1.50, an increase some newer operations resisted. The dispute over uniform prices became a power struggle pitting small independent barbers against the Texas Barber Association (TBA), a statewide organization supported by dues from hundreds of established shops. The TBA regulated pricing and hours statewide, usually to the benefit of larger operations. Many independents, largely small shops run by new barbers, refused to follow guidelines requiring shops to close on Sundays and charge the set rate. When some lowered their fee to $0.75 a price war broke out that turned violent. In February 1958 an employee of Charles F. "Pete" Hawkins, owner of Pete's Barber Shop, 5158 East Lancaster Avenue, was attacked in a café by another barber after Pete dropped the price of a haircut to a $1.00. Violent reactions spread and intensified when some barbers began opening on Sundays. On August 12, 1960, the owner of Brown's Barber Shop, 1211 South Ayers Avenue, was beaten and threatened with further violence if he did not close on Sundays. When he still refused, someone ran a stolen truck into his business. No one was charged, but Brown blamed the TBA, claiming that their agents had forced eighteen of the twenty-two shops normally open on Sundays to close. Those allegations were probably well-founded. An undercover agent of the Texas Rangers infiltrated the TBA, developing enough evidence to arrest Rex Avery, owner of a shop at 1632 East Berry Street and president of the Poly branch of the TBA, Frank Allred, and Elvin Walker, as well as two unnamed accomplices.[24]

More arrests followed as the investigation broadened. Tarrant County District Attorney Doug Crouch asked the grand jury to investigate the use of TBA funds to promote violence and the involvement of board members in that violence. Rex Avery confessed that in mid-August a collection had been taken during a Jacksboro Highway meeting to pay ruffians who would physically intimidate Brown and other opponents. Avery later recanted, claiming police had beaten the confession out of him. Charges were also filed against Robert DeArmand, Texas TBA president, for the damage to Brown's Barber Shop. The violence spilled over into the district attorney's office when Crouch refused to show David Whitlow, a TBA lawyer, the grand jury report related to DeArmand's arrest, leading a confrontation in which Crouch slugged Whitlow, busting his lip and bringing assault charges. Perhaps everyone had had enough, for things settled quickly, or at least disappeared from public view, ending the great Barber Shop War.[25]

The autumn of 1960 witnessed another exchange of blows between a county officer and a disgruntled citizen. In October Tarrant County Purchasing Agent B. O. Lange fought with Royal Hogan, owner of Hogan Office Supply, and Hogan's assistant, R. G. Little. Hogan and Little claimed Lange had given them until October 16 to submit bids, but when they arrived with bids in hand on October 13, they were told that the contract had already been awarded. The dispute turned physical when Hogan called Lange a liar.[26]

Alcohol, which had been such a major issue during Prohibition, received scant notice from police. The only enforcement action appearing in the press was a March 1958 police and state liquor agents raid on three private clubs, Town and Country Club, 4016 White Settlement Road; Seven Eleven Club, 711 Pennsylvania Avenue; and Chez ce Soir, 5428 Calmont Avenue, after undercover officers had bought mixed drinks in each without becoming members (before 1971 only members of private clubs could order liquor by the drink). No arrests were made, but the officers confiscated 200 bottles of liquor, and the state suspended each club's license.[27]

The drug trade took up most of the attention that once went to booze, especially heroin, which seem to explode in newspaper reports during the second half of the decade. The nature of the drug trade in which transfers were conducted privately made enforcement by uniformed officers difficult. Most arrests came from searches of homes or cars. In May 1956 the grand jury indicted brothers Dean and Billy Portwood, admitted heroin users, after heroin was found in Billy's home, Seventh Street and Summit Avenue. Enforcement difficulties led to the use of undercover operatives. In 1956 neither the Fort Worth Police nor the Tarrant County Sheriff's Office had undercover officers, a flaw the outgoing grand jury that year noted in its report recommending their use and the allocation of buy money to fund dope purchases. To jumpstart enforcement, Chief Hightower and Sheriff Wright borrowed undercover agents from federal agencies and the Texas Department of Public Safety Narcotics Section. DPS narcs, sporting long ducktail haircuts and loud sport shirts, "shucked jive" to ingratiate themselves with dealers. They successfully developed evidence for a mass warrant service conducted the evening of July 20, 1956, that netted thirty-one persons charged with selling or possessing narcotics and another fifty-two persons who happened to be on the premises and were charged with vagrancy. The raw figures suggested marijuana remained the bigger problem. Two-thirds of the drug arrests were for marijuana, and only six heroin capsules were recovered.[28]

Undercover investigations continued and expanded in 1957. A two-month investigation by state narcotics officers into Mexican heroin in Fort Worth concluded in early February with the arrests of Johnnie R. Dupree and Billy Ray Killingsworth and the seizure of fifty-one grams of heroin (almost two ounces) hidden inside a car's heater. Each gram of heroin produced sixteen capsules, or caps, selling for $7 each, making the cache worth $5,712 at the street level. In a contemporaneous four-month investigation, four state undercover operatives blended in at taverns and nightclubs, buying joints (marijuana cigarettes) for a $1 each. The operation ended on February 23 with fifty-two city, county, and state officers serving twenty-nine arrest warrants, all synchronized to start at exactly 8:00 p.m. to thwart alerts.

The officers arrested seventeen persons—twelve Blacks, one Hispanic, and four Anglos, including a pharmacist, George Murchinson—charged with selling narcotics.[29]

Despite the combined efforts, heroin seemed to take off in 1957 with several high-profile arrests reported. In April 1957 Robert Kennedy and his wife, Jeanine Kennedy, reputed to be Fort Worth's biggest heroin dealers, were arrested for possession of heroin at a downtown hotel. In June the court sentenced Robert to seven years and Jeanine to five. George Mann, who reportedly had taken over from the Kennedys, was arrested in July 1957 along with Bobby Jack Masters in the 1400 block of East Richmond Avenue after the two sold an undercover agent heroin worth $500. The same month a known associate of Mann, Fred Eric Burton, was arrested at a south side grocery for selling eight grams of heroin for $800 to an undercover officer. Agents were amazed at the drug's purity, testing at 45 percent heroin, much stronger than the going street level of 27 percent and worth, after being cut, as much as $12,000. Mann was not a user and not normally involved at the street distribution level, but he regularly carried heroin across the Mexican border to Fort Worth. Much of Fort Worth's drug supply came from Mexico, most often crossing the border at Piedras Negras. A Bureau of Narcotics supervisor called heroin and marijuana brought in from Mexico the two main drug problems for Texas. He added that the Mexican heroin supply struggled to satisfy even the demand in Texas, creating limited availability and high prices, but that marijuana from Mexico arrived in sufficient quantities to supply all of the eastern United States. Once across the border, major confiscations were rare. A large bust in January 1960 occurred after agents followed Willie Allen for three days before arresting him and a Mexican national at a Camp Bowie service station. The agents seized a suitcase loaded with marijuana worth $6,000.[30]

Other drugs were available from a variety of supply sources. Fort Worth Narcotics Officers K. O. Glass and Bill Hardin arrested Susie Hanlon, an All Saints Hospital nurse, for obtaining narcotics by fraud or deceit after she replaced morphine tablets with atropine, a nonnarcotic used to reduce bronchial secretions. Other hospital staff alerted police after noticing that the tablets did not dissolve properly and that patients continued to complain of pain. Ms. Hanlon confessed, admitting she backslid into addiction after kicking the habit years prior. Billy Doyle Prince and wife Imogene were arrested after police found marijuana and hypodermic needles at their home, 3509 Vinetta Drive. Prince, partners with hoodlum George Kean in a janitorial supply business, had a record for burglary and was linked to several criminal enterprises. The couple got off with only three years of probation due to concerns that the lack of a search would kill the case.[31]

The leniency shown the Princes was an exception; most courts treated marijuana as a dangerous drug meriting harsh sentences, especially for subsequent convictions. In July 1958 Robert Porter, an African American man with a newsstand/shoeshine parlor at 216 East Rosedale Street, received twenty years for selling a federal narcotic officers thirty-seven cigarettes containing sixty-seven grains of marijuana, about one-sixth of an ounce. It was Porter's second narcotics conviction, making him ineligible for parole (twenty years for one-sixth of an ounce). James Locke, convicted in 1955 for possessing marijuana, received a fifteen-year-sentence in 1959 as a repeat offender and his wife got five years for possessing marijuana at their home, 620 East Bluff Street. Harsh sentencing for marijuana violations was not unique to Fort Worth. In 1959 the Texas Court of Criminal Appeals upheld a fifteen-year-sentence given Candy Barr, a celebrity striptease artist, real name Juanita Dale Phillips, for possessing four-fifths of an ounce of marijuana. In contrast, drugs considered today as more dangerous sometimes brought lighter sentencing. In August 1958 Bobby Hemmeline, an admitted addict, was given five years of prison time for possessing cocaine and morphine.[32]

Drugs were sold in many places. Some bars had a sideline in drug sales. In 1958 Lieutenant L. E. Wood and two other officers sparked a melee at Ray's Place, 4010 Hemphill Street, owned by Ray Wilborn, that began with the detention of several men gambling on a pinball machine, then escalated to a wild fight after officers found narcotics in the socks of two suspects. The fracas required additional officers to control. After the dust cleared, Gerald Carter and Eugene McDade were charged with possession of barbiturates and, along with two unidentified men, assaulting police officers. Clubs were common outlets, but other shops/services were also involved in the drug trade.

Robert Porter, discussed above, used his shoeshine parlor to sell marijuana, and Jackson Celli did a drug business at his store, the Tote-It Grocery, 5301 White Settlement Road. Narcotics Officers H. L. Hardin and Gary Cox raided the grocery, arresting Celli after finding seventeen tablets of a controlled substance and six grains of marijuana.[33]

Street narcotics occasionally turned up on prisoners at local jails. In 1959 Assistant District Attorney Downer complained that officers transferring a DWI suspect from the city to the county jail found the prisoner so stoned on "red birds," secobarbital tablets, that he was only semiconscious and unable to stand. The cause of the intoxication was confirmed when officers found one capsule on him and two more under his cot. Another prisoner, Claude Mayfield, admitted bringing the drugs inside hidden in his socks. The stoned inmate, Michael J. Paprskar, 1607 Circle Park Boulevard, was only 17 years old in 1959 but already had nine arrests dating back to 1956 when he was 14. At the time he was in jail on a DWI charge and also out on bond on an assault to murder charge resulting from slashing the throat of a sailor who objected to Paprika's vulgar language in front of a woman. He would live a violent life, in one spree killing two men and a 4-year-old child, the son of one of the two murdered men.[34]

By the end of the 1950s clear links were established between prostitution and illegal narcotics. In February 1959 Cecilia Burks, a 23-year-old admitted prostitute on trial for bad checks and narcotics, told the court she regularly "entertained" two to twelve men a night, charging a minimum of $10 each, while working out of a north side motel that cost $1.50 to $4 nightly plus 40 percent of her earnings going to the motel's porter. The judge was so concerned about her health, saying she looked ten years older, that he ordered a physical examination. In May that year police arrested Ulric Brannon, convicted in 1947 for marijuana possession, and Celestia Free, a known prostitute, at their apartment, 809 West Leuda Street, where they confiscated morphine, opium, and capsules believed to contain unidentified narcotics. In October Sharon Shreck, a 19-year-old prostitute, was convicted of barbiturate possession and sentenced to a year and a day. The upswing in press reports may have been the product of a drive to crack down on prostitution launched by the Tarrant County Sheriff's Office in March 1959. In support of the enforcement effort, a justice of the peace agreed to increase bonds on vagrancy charges related to prostitution from $100 to $250.[35]

Cheap motels like the one Ms. Burks used seemed to be everywhere and to always be prostitution centers. In the late 1950s the Chambers Hotel at Chambers and East Lancaster Avenues was particularly notorious. In 1958 Anita Melton, 17 years old, testified that her husband, John "Cowboy" Melton, 31 years old, forced her into prostitution at the Chambers and other hotels. During John Melton's trial, Mrs. Lily Pitts, manager of the Chambers Hotel, admitted that bellhops from other hotels arranged "dates" for Anita and other prostitutes and that she received 10 percent if the assignation was elsewhere and 40 percent if at the Chambers. Robert Barker, bellhop at Fort Worth's Hilton Hotel, confirmed her story, telling the court he had provided prostitutes, including Anita, for hotel guests. "Cowboy" Melton was sentenced to four years in prison for transporting Anita across state lines for immoral purposes.[36]

Many prostitutes were young girls with no other means of support or care who worked under the protection of a male. In May 1959 several incidents involving pimps came to light. Judy Melton (possibly related to "Cowboy" Melton, above) and Sheila Weir, both 17 years old, were committed to the State Reformatory for Girls at Gainesville after they confessed to being part of a prostitution ring run by Weir's husband, Gary Weir, and Jerry Linden. Also in 1959 the Tarrant County District Attorney charged Jimmie Poteet, bartender of the 1412 Club, 1412 Main Street, with corrupting the morals of a child by arranging prostitution dates at a Jacksboro Highway tourist camp and a lower Main Street hotel for a 14-year-old girl with a subnormal IQ (the girl, a ward at the State Reformatory, confirmed the allegations). Those directing the women or girls occasionally fought over the span of their authority. In May 1959 Lawrence Britton was killed, Jack Sanders wounded, and David "Bucky" Smith jailed after a shootout at a Riverside home in a dispute over control of prostitution. Not all business expansion ventures in the sex trade worked out. In January 1958 inside Steve's Bar, Tenth and Main Streets, Mrs. Dorothy Shannon, a 33-year-old woman of dubious occupations and a lengthy police record, shot Odis Hammond, a known procurer with sixty arrests on his rap sheet, hitting him in the stomach and leg after he took $0.75 from her and suggested she work for him.[37]

The Mann Act of 1910, also known as the White Slavery Traffic Act, used in the prosecution of Cowboy Melton, made it a federal crime to transport a woman or girl across state lines for the purposes of prostitution. In June 1959 FBI agents charged Fort Worth Police characters Walter Flanagan and Robert "Red" Huddleston for Mann violations, just two of thirteen sealed indictments returned by a Dallas County grand jury that included warrants for Richard Garcia, a 24-year-old known as the "kingpin" of Fort Worth prostitution. Garcia was charged with transporting prostitutes from Fort Worth to Chicago, but he was multifaceted, facing state charges for robbing the Safeway Grocery at 1600 Northwest Twenty-Fifth Street, for automobile theft, and as a career criminal. In November 1960 Harry Kirk, a well-known local criminal, pled guilty to Mann Act violations and received a five-year sentence after he took a young woman, Toni Jackson, to Oklahoma and Las Vegas to work as a prostitute. She did quite well in Las Vegas, earning $8,000 between March and August. Before the trial Ms. Jackson, the main witness against Kirk, committed suicide in an Arlington motel, but the case continued on the strength of testimony from hotel clerks who saw the two together.[38]

Few incidents involving or even suggesting homosexuality were reported in the last half of the 1950s. Billie Don Jackson, only 17 years old, sparked a one-person crime wave in the summer of 1957 before being arrested and charged with robbery, kidnapping, sexual assault of a young woman, and forcing a cab driver to "commit an unnatural sex act." In 1959 Fred T. Leath, a 38-year-old admitted homosexual, shot and killed a 15-year-old boy, Charles Henry, at the Uptowne Motel, 612 West Third Street. Leath defended the shooting as self-defense, claiming Henry, mistaking Leath for a "pushover," tried to strongarm him and take his car. Far from being an easy mark, Leath had a violent history that included serving five years in prison for an assault-to-murder of a Dallas County youth. He refused a plea bargain offer of fifty years, which turned out to be unwise; the jury returned a death sentence. Leath, a World War II veteran, was executed at Huntsville State Prison, November 9, 1961. The only publicly reported incident suggesting lesbianism appeared in June 1960 involving three women police caught breaking into vending machines inside the closed Davis Café, 507 East Broadway Street. The three, Annie Townsend, 20 years old; Verneil Sweet, 22-years old; and Constance Cain, 26 years old, all had close-cropped men's haircuts and were distinctively attired in jeans or slacks and men's sport shirts with short sleeves (Sweet's shirt was plaid with the sleeves rolled up). Police could not recall ever arresting three women burglars, although two of the arrestees admitted to other burglaries.[39]

Guardians of public decency were fairly busy. In 1958 Fort Worth censors determined that *And God Created Woman*, a French movie starring Brigitte Bardot, was obscene and banned it. Fort Worth was not unique; several cities prohibited the film and the Catholic Church declared the only cinema in Lake Placid, New York, off-limits after it screened it. Distributors sued to remove Fort Worth's censure, but in February 1959 Federal Judge T. Whitfield Davidson upheld the city's action, and in 1961 the United States Supreme Court in a case out of Chicago affirmed the constitutionality of local censorship. In December 1959 complaints from the Reverend G. W. French of the General Ministers Alliance convinced Ellison's Furniture, 211 West Seventh Street, to remove a painting of a nude woman on display in the store. Reverend French warned that failure to maintain standards could result in the "spreading of unmentionable sex crimes."[40]

Chapter 19

Policing, 1956–1960

Chief Hightower put forward plans for decentralization and an ambitious facilities program. In March 1957 the chief moved the patrol division and motor garage to Thirteenth and Cherry Streets and relocated traffic and juvenile sections to the old Air Police headquarters, two blocks from city hall, leaving detectives, administrative offices, communications, and the jail at city hall. In December the patrol division set up shop at 1030 Burnett Street, formerly Fort Worth Cab and Baggage and Bert and Steve Cab Company, which the city bought for $142,500. An ambitious November 1958 bond package included funding for a grand new police headquarters, location to be determined, with 134,674 square feet, almost eight times the space the police occupied at city hall. The proposed building would have interrogation rooms, a crime lab, a firing range, and a jail holding 400 prisoners to replace the existing facility designed for 85. Jail expansion was sorely needed; the jail population averaged 150 daily and often reached 200 on weekends. Unfortunately, parsimonious voters rejected the police bond package as well as eight other proposals for new fire stations and street improvements.[1]

State-mandated limitations on work hours had an unintended consequence of ending two-officer patrols. In May 1959 Texas revamped civil service rules, limiting firefighters to 60 hours a week, a reduction from 67.2 hours, and police officers to 40 hours, down from 44. Fort Worth Police had already transitioned to one-officer cars on day shift, except for a few beats deemed hazardous, but the reduced work week helped convince Chief Hightower to implement one-officer staffing for all patrol cars, switching half on November 22, 1959, followed by total implementation in April 1960, the delay allowing officers to attend 24 hours of training on solo patrol. The switch was aided by the expansion from twenty-five to thirty-seven patrol beats that downsized patrol districts, putting more officers on the streets. Under the new beat plan each shift fielded forty-two officers—thirty-five in one-officer cars plus two officers assigned to patrol wagons and five sergeants. In addition, a downtown foot patrol was created to counteract a spike in business burglaries. The changes increased dispatcher workloads, requiring they assign backups and keep track of officers out of the car and away from the car radio. The latter had often been unnecessary with two-officer cars since one would monitor the radio while the second was out.[2]

Fort Worth Police also enhanced their professional support capabilities. Wendell Sowell took over as the director of Fort Worth's first crime laboratory at an annual salary of $10,025. Sowell, holder of a master's degree in science and a law degree, was hired away from the Alabama Department of Toxicity and Criminal Investigation, where he was an assistant toxicologist. The lab that opened on October 1, 1959, with a $50,000 budget was staffed by Sowell, a technician, a secretary, and a police sergeant. In January 1961 Sowell announced the appointment of Fort Worth Police's first polygraph examiner, Dee Wheeler. Wheeler had a good pedigree. In 1949 he organized and trained personnel for the original Texas Department of Public Safety Polygraph Section. Prior to his recruitment, Fort Worth Police took polygraph subjects to the Texas Department of Public Safety in Austin or to the Dallas Police examiner.[3]

The department struggled to keep its ranks filled in the face of a high turnover rate. Between January 1953 and January 1, 1960, 8 Fort Worth officers were fired and 144 resigned, an average loss of 17 officers per year. In the first two months of 1960, 25 resigned, leaving the department 25 officers short of its 543 authorized strength. Chief Hightower blamed the economy for the high turnover, but job stress may have played a role. In April 1960 City Health Director Dr. W. V. Bradshaw suggested that scheduling fewer shift transfers would mitigate negative impacts to the body's rhythm and reduce burnout. Dr. Bradshaw also revealed that 75 of the 520 policemen suffered impaired job performance from one or more physical defects, most commonly being significantly overweight. In fact, weight problems plagued half the department. Dr. Bradshaw recommended giving the most egregiously obese time to lose the excess poundage and forcefully retiring those who failed.[4]

Crime statistics continued to appear only erratically, but available figures indicated a precipitous upward trend in burglaries and thefts; substantial increases in murders, robberies, and assaults; and declines in auto theft and sexual assaults, although the 1957 statistics on sexual assaults was missing, limiting the comparison to only 1959 and 1960. The 13,130 total crimes reported in 1960 represented a of 27.8 percent increase from 10,274 in 1959, more than doubling of the statewide rise of 13.1. Unfortunately, total crimes were not found for 1957.

Chart 19.1 Selected Crime Statistics from 1957, 1959, and 1960

	1957	**1959**	**1960**	**% Change, 1957–1960**
Murders (46 in 1956)	36	64	54	+50
Sexual Assaults	?	30	22	-27 ('59–'60)
Robberies	228	247	301	+32
Aggravated Assaults	163	171	196	+20
Auto theft	1,207	963	1,019	-16
Burglaries	2,343	3,112	3,902	+67
Thefts	4,350	6,225	7,638	+76
Total Crimes	?	10,274	13,130	+27.8 ('59–'60)

Source: For 1957 statistics, see *Fort Worth Star Telegram*, April 23, 1958, p. 1. For 1959 and 1960 statistics, see *Fort Worth Star Telegram*, February 26, 1961, p. 8.

Hardcore criminal groups were a big influence on the crime picture. In 1957 the Horn family, one of the most active of the period, was suspected in at least ten supermarket robberies in the North Texas area. Billy Horn and his brothers, Robert and Dempsey, along with brother-in-law Carl Wiggins, were arrested in September and October 1957 and charged in several grocery robberies. Robert bonded out, only to be quickly rearrested robbing a market in Waco. He was eventually convicted and sentenced to thirty-five years, while brother Billy got off with only a twelve-year sentence, making parole in October 1960 after only thirty-two months.[5]

In October 1960 the Fort Worth police published a list of the ten most undesirable hoodlums, all white males with extensive criminal records. Some, but not all, were fugitives from justice at the time of publication. The list was not in alphabetical order, implying hierarchy:

Chart 19.2 Ten Most Undesirable Hoodlums in Fort Worth, 1960

Billy Joe Ellis	wanted on burglary charges
Garrett Ramsey	kingpin of Fort Worth prostitution and wanted for the murder of Royce Herd
L. E. "Danny" McComb	former tavern owner on Jacksboro Highway, a suspect in the murder of George Kean, out on bond for a kidnapping in Illinois
Jessie C. Kimbrough	out on bond for the murder of Charles Hurley and the robbery of a supermarket
Billy W. Miracle	awaiting trial on robbery of a supermarket (arrested in Las Vegas for robbery and attempted murder February 1961)
Edward J. Hall	awaiting trial on burglary and drug possession
Don A. Stacks	awaiting trial on theft charges
Zachariah D. Milligan	served prison time for assault and robbery
Virgil F. Tidwell, Jr.	forger and burglar
Raymond C. Cameron	record of burglary and narcotics charges

Source: Fort Worth Star Telegram, October 16, 1960, pp. 1 and 6.

J. Edgar Hoover, director of the FBI, sent a letter of commendation to the *Star Telegram* for publishing the list.[6]

Traffic continued to occupy increasing amounts of police attention, particularly related to significantly increased DWI enforcement. Stepped up emphasis on DWIs was credited, along with media support and traffic engineering, with reducing 1957 traffic fatalities 37 percent compared to 1956, part of a national three-year downward trend during which traffic deaths fell 3 percent. After 1957 the trend reversed, going upward while DWI arrests continued to increase. In 1958 Don Hill, regional director of the National Safety Council, praised Fort Worth Police for their enforcement efforts but criticized the paltry 32 percent conviction rate, one-third the national standard of 95 percent. Hill charged that the poor conviction rate made the city a haven for drunk drivers, citing statistics that in one six-month period, fewer than half of 213 drunk drivers arrested in Tarrant County were prosecuted and only 22 percent of the prosecuted cases resulted in convictions. The criticisms elicited a get-tough approach from District Attorney Doug Crouch, who vowed to end the practice of dismissing lesser charges if a higher charge was made, a policy that had eliminated many DWI charges. Crouch perhaps went a bit overboard with the tougher stance, going so far as to propose the death penalty for armed robberies. He may have been motivated by political concerns, fearing that his office would appear weak on crime if word got out about lax DWI enforcement and that Tarrant County had only sentenced two persons to death since 1952, Willie Lee Gage in December 1952 for a rape (executed in 1954) and Eugene Webb, convicted in May 1959. The renewed prosecutorial vigor produced results. In the first two months of 1959, 90 percent of 101 filed DWI cases resulted in convictions. In addition, the district attorney's office established standard punishments for DWI convictions that stipulated three days in jail, a six-month suspension of driving privileges, and a monetary fine for the first offense with an upgrade to a felony charge for a second offense.[7]

The last half of the 1950s was particularly hazardous for police officers. Between 1956 and 1959 three Fort Worth Police motorcycle officers succumbed to crash injuries. The first to die, James Lee Dowdy, was killed June 17, 1956, after colliding with a truck trailer while trying to catch two drag racers on North Main Street (the racers got away). Dowdy, who had been on the force for only ten months (on motors for five months), was not vested in the retirement plan, but the fund granted his widow $50 monthly for ten years and the city council chipped in $2,000. In addition, Dowdy's widow and child each received $52.50 monthly from Social Security until she remarried and the child reached 18. On October 4, 1957, Motorcycle Officer C. H. Harmon Jr. suffered fatal injuries when a vehicle struck his motorcycle at 2700 East Lancaster Avenue. Harmon, married with two children, had only been on the force four months. Motorcycle Officer L. H. Walton died May 20, 1959, from injuries sustained when a vehicle struck him as he tried to catch up to a speeder. Walton was riding without a helmet because his was at the factory having a new liner installed.[8]

A fourth motorcycle officer was shot in the line of duty and left paralyzed. On November 9, 1956, Motorcycle Officer Eddie J. Kelliher stopped Hollis G. Thom at 2528 Northeast Twenty-Eighth Street. Kelliher, likely concerned that Thom was flight risk, removed the car keys, but Thom shot the officer, retrieved the keys, and drove over the seriously injured officer while escaping. After a short chase in which more shots were fired, patrol officers stopped and arrested Thom. He received fifteen years for the shooting, but Kelliher was left paralyzed for life and unable to continue as a police officer. Kelliher sued Thom for $265,000, with little hope of collecting from a state prisoner. The police department kept the officer on the payroll for a year, continuing his $348 monthly salary, then put him on a $50 monthly pension, sweetened somewhat by $3,000 collected from donors. Kelliher overcame his injuries to live a long and full life, marrying Jo Russell and becoming an electronics technician.[9]

Several other police officers were seriously injured, including one who was killed off duty in a compromising situation. On February 4, 1957, Detective Cody Rogers, Officers J. D. Roberts and Ray Lantrip, and Reserve Officer R. B. Torrance were wounded by shotgun birdshot fired by Edward Haynes. Haynes shot when officers first arrived at his home, 1100 South Jones Street, turning a disturbance call into a running gun battle before police fire killed Haynes. In December 1957 Police Officer Joe Greene, married, was shot to death by the husband of a woman Greene was dating. The jilted husband forced the couple into a car after finding them at a Jacksboro Highway tourist camp cabin, making Greene drive to Lake Worth, where he shot him. Police Sergeant Joe Johnnie was wounded in the chest in a shootout with Herbert Lafond at Lafond's home, 908 Louisiana Avenue. Lafond, who died from return fire, had held a former employer and his family for hours before forcing the man into a sewer where he fired several shots at him. Somehow the victim not only survived but also escaped to call police. Officer A. D. Marshall and other officers arriving at Lafond's home came under gunfire that wounded Sergeant Johnnie. Detective A. A. Lewis shot and killed Clifford Davis, who ran when Lewis caught him with tools taken in a burglary. The investigation team ruled the death a justifiable homicide of a fleeing felon.[10]

One of the responding officers to the Lafond incident, A. D. Marshall, became well-known among colleagues as "Knockfire" for his ability to throw an effective punch. Marshall, no stranger to fisticuffs, decided to become a police officer when he noticed police often showed up during his many fights. His early assignments included the Rosedale and Evans Avenues area where a large, violent hoodlum had dominated and intimidated locals, controlling most criminal activity in the neighborhood. Marshall was with other officers raiding a known gambling house when the bully advanced in an obviously threatening manner. Marshall was not a small man, standing close to six feet tall and, although not heavy, possessing a solid frame built from hard work, but was noticeably smaller than the charging brute. Marshall squared himself and waited, timing a sharp blow that dropped the assailant and kept him down. Afterward, he became known to locals as "Mr. Marshall, sir."[11]

Ethics complaints continued to be a problem. In 1957 former Tarrant County Assistant District Attorney Eugene Biddle expressed concerns over complaints from several suspects charging police had beaten them into confessing. Biddle told reporters that prisoner abuse was common in many cities and jurisdictions but that he had no confirmed incidents involving local officers. Bribery allegations continued to appear. In 1958 restaurant and tourist camp complaints about police officers demanding payoffs led to a departmental directive requiring officers turn in any money or valuables received. Police officers also had many supporters. One of their most ardent fans, Mae Carlton, owned the Carlton Hotel, 1312 South Main Street. Affectionately known as Ma since 1915 by generations of police officers, Ms. Carlton regularly visited police headquarters, bringing cakes and desserts, and was a fixture at the annual policeman's ball, where she was known for energetic dancing. In June 1958 Mae was found dead on her kitchen floor, succumbing to natural causes at 80 years of age. She left funeral instructions for six officers to serve as her pallbearers, an officers' quartet to sing "The Old Rugged Cross," and Officer V. C. Ballard, an ordained minister, to conduct the service.[12]

Drinking on duty seemed to be a recurring problem, and at least one officer lost his job over drug use. In 1957 Chief Hightower terminated Patrol Officers Harold Hickman and M. M. Langley after a sergeant found them asleep surrounded by beer cans behind a Trail Lake Drive gasoline station. The two admitted falling asleep after drinking beers. The Civil Service Commission reduced the penalty to thirty days' suspension followed by ninety days' probation. In 1959 Officer W. M. Nelson was terminated after he admitted he had been drinking on duty when he drove his patrol car into another vehicle. Nelson claimed he drank to deal with an earache. In April 1958 Chief Hightower fired Officer K. O. Glass, one of the department's two narcotics officers, for conduct unbecoming related to irregularities in prescription opiate use. Acting on an informant's tip, investigators discovered that between 1956 and 1958, Glass and his wife had filled fifty-six opiate prescriptions at a south side pharmacy where the pharmacist, at Glass's request, had not registered the prescriptions as required. The list of prescribed medications included 683 tablets of Pantopon and sixteen large and eighty small vials of Demerol (both opiates) prescribed for pain by Glass's physician after a 1956 automobile crash and by his dentist. Glass filed an appeal but in June dropped the suit, effectively ending any hope for reinstatement.[13]

One of the worst ethical lapses came to light in March 1959 after Fort Worth and Tarrant County officers trapped David Sampson and Ollie Wilson inside the closed Chicotsky's Market, 3433 West Seventh Street. The two bandits surrendered only after exchanging shots with officers. Inside the store officers found cash missing, a large safe that had been forced open, and a walkie talkie. The single communications device and missing money suggested that a third person or more had managed to escape. That assumption was reinforced when officers found a vehicle nearby containing Chicotsky's boxes filled with cash. As a more complete picture evolved, detectives determined that four men entered the grocery—the two captured,

Sampson and Wilson, plus Charles Long and Harry Kirk, who left with loose cash while Sampson and Wilson remained, breaking into the safe. Officers found and arrested Kirk and Long at 1800 Sunset Terrace along with Jaquelia Anderson and Ruth Bradshaw, who were also at the house and believed to be part of an organized burglary ring. Kirk and Long gave statements implicating Detective H. L. Stephenson and Sergeant Phil Coker, claiming they provided confidential information on police informants and potential burglary sites in exchange for 10 to 30 percent of the take. Chief Hightower reported that Coker had been involved with the gang for only a few weeks, but Stephenson's involvement went back much farther.[14]

Subsequent revelations disclosed that Coker acted as a "pull-off man," diverting patrol officers away from the area while the burglars struck. In the Chicotsky's burglary Coker had the area patrol officers for a fish dinner while, unknown to Coker, other officers staked out the area thanks to a sheriff's office tip that burglars would hit either the Chicotsky's or an A&P Grocery nearby at 4828 Byers Avenue. Officers rotating between two stores were at the A&P at 3:00 a.m. when they learned the burglars had entered Chicotsky's, the information coming from a telephone tap at the Sunset Terrace address that recorded Sampson and Wilson calling from inside Chicotsky's. Coker insisted his innocence but withdrew his termination appeal, saying he had a good job in private industry and did not want to return. Stephenson appealed but resigned the night before his hearing, also claiming to have a good job. The Civil Service Board ruled anyway, upholding the termination. Chief Hightower also fired Patrolman Otus Williams after he collected $77 from fellow officers for Sergeant Coker, arguing the fund constituted a defense of Coker, a violation of departmental policy. Williams's appeal reduced his penalty to a ninety-day suspension, later lowered to thirty days by the Civil Service Commission. The grand jury declined indictments for Stephenson and Coker, closing the criminal investigation.[15]

The insular clan known as gypsies continued to be a problem, especially those operating as fortune tellers. In 1958 a rash of complaints about the old scam of placing charms in wallets led to police raids on clan homes doubling as fortune-telling centers at 1110 and 1205 Main Street, 1107 Houston Street, and 113 West Eleventh Street. Police also arrested Joe Evans, king of the local clan, under a state law identifying gypsies as vagrants, but King Joe was released on an injunction suspending enforcement. The arrest and raids did convince Evans to order an end to palm reading and fortune telling, although he allowed reading bumps on the head, claiming it was a form of phrenology and not prohibited. King Joe, driver of a new Oldsmobile, had spent the previous fifteen winters in Fort Worth as head of twenty-five families surnamed Evans, Mitchell, Stevens, and Nichols. The families traveled with carnivals during warm months and spent winters in Southern towns where the men worked as coppersmiths or did odd jobs and the women told fortunes and ran scams.[16]

In 1959 street peddlers staged an organized protest after police arrested two members of their trade for vagrancy. Chief Hightower admitted police had cracked down on peddlers, beggars, and street preachers after receiving complaints. He added that enforcement was nothing new, that the city had historically regulated street peddlers, issuing identification cards in 1953 to known, reputable operators and arresting peddlers without cards. One of the arrestees in 1959, Herman Douglas, a blind man, earned a living selling pencils, which he argued made him no more a vagrant than shopkeepers or newsboys selling newspapers on the streets. The city council passed the matter to City Manager Cookingham. Douglas sought to demonstrate the unreasonableness and harshness of the ordinance by demanding police arrest Dudley Price, a 60-year-old blind African American man who had worked the same area of downtown for seventeen years, becoming so accepted that store owners rushed to his defense. Price was not arrested but was taken to city hall and warned. Douglas's gambit worked; the absurdity of arresting the old and infirm trying to earn an honest living became obvious. The city dismissed all charges filed under the street peddlers code, including those against Douglas, and reinstated identification cards to legitimize honest street peddlers.[17]

The brouhaha over peddlers dovetailed with and added weight to an ongoing proposal for a rehabilitation program that would serve as an alternative to jail for low-level offenders. The idea became a reality in August 1958 when Chief Hightower offered nine "winos," jailed persons with a history of alcohol arrests, the option of serving thirty-day sentences at the city jail or at the Lake Worth Rehabilitation Farm operated by Reverend Henry Cooper.

Five of the nine opted for the center, where they spent their days clearing brush and tending goats, the animals spawning the nickname of the Goat Farm for the facility. The farm's funding came from the police budget allocation of $0.50 per day per inmate, up to a maximum of thirty-five persons, or $17.50 per day, a $300 monthly grant from the Parks Department in return for grounds upkeep and from private donations. After a few months the financial situation became untenable as donations failed to cover the gap between the $50,000 annual operating cost and the city's total payments averaging only $1,350 monthly, or just over $16,000 a year. In addition, a serious escape problem developed; about one-half of prisoners simply walked away by climbing over wire fencing designed only to keep the goats in. In April 1959 Reverend Cooper told the city council that the farm was officially bankrupt and needed increased funding and assigned police officers to curtail escapes. Chief Hightower was positively disposed, praising the farm for significantly reducing jail overcrowding. Fort Worth officials approached Tarrant County about sharing the almost $34,000 shortfall, but the commissioners declined, saying the precedent would require funding similar arrangements for the county's thirty other municipalities.[18]

Reverend Cooper sought alternative funding to house and feed the eighty-seven detainees the farm averaged and to cover his salary ($7,800 annually) and $5,000 indebtedness. Pleas for increased donations had little substantial success, but the Parks Department may have saved the site by agreeing to hire ten to fifteen inmates each day, paying the farm $3 per day, per man. To stretch food outlays, Cooper scoured restaurants for once-used coffee grounds and markets for soup bones and overripe fruits and vegetables, as well as grabbing surplus foods from the federal government.[19]

The Goat Farm continued to face perennial funding issues but somehow survived into the 1980s and even developed some infrastructure improvements. In the beginning most prisoners lived in tents, but in 1960 the Cosmopolitan Club began work on a 200-person barrack. Unfortunately, the club ran out of funding before the project was finished. Councilman Tommy Thompson proposed that the city appropriate $10,000 to finish the job, but the motion ran into opposition and was delayed for future consideration until Chief Hightower intervened. The chief insisted the farm was necessary, that health regulations limited prisoners to fifteen days in the city jail and the farm, serving as a "branch jail," offered an acceptable alternative for longer incarcerations. Hightower also committed to providing security, assigning five officers at an annual cost of $20,000. Things got appreciably better in 1966 when the John Fogarty Foundation completed the sorely needed new dormitory. (In the early 1980s the author, as a new Fort Worth Police officer, made several runs delivering and returning prisoners between the city jail and the farm). Meanwhile, the downtown city jail continued a Christmas Day tradition of releasing persons held on drunkenness and other minor charges, freeing 100 prisoners on December 25, 1959. Those who remained dined on bologna and pressed ham with three slices of bread and coffee. County jail inmates had it much better, feasting on turkey and dressing.[20]

Chapter 20

Race Relations, 1956–1960

The second half of the decade witnessed a broadening and intensification of the movement to desegregate schools and neighborhoods. At the same time that African Americans struggled to gain equal access to education and housing they also faced economic challenges that threatened their separate support and cultural organizations. Civil rights victories in the 1950s were few and hard-earned but proved critical for opening doors through which more fundamental changes would come in the 1960s and later.

Fort Worth's African American community opened a critically needed youth care center but had serious issues maintaining two elder care facilities. In March 1956 the Fannie C. Brown Home, named for a woman chartered as a childcare provider in 1915, opened at St. John's Baptist Church, 1109 East Fourth Street. The Brown Home provided day care for working African American mothers at a reduced cost thanks to the church donating space and utilities as well as subsidies from the Tarrant County Day Care Association. In the same year two eldercare homes for Blacks faced closure over long-standing code violations. The Fort Worth Health Department sought district court orders to close the Texas Home for the Elderly, 304 East Fourth

Street, operated by Dr. R. A. Ransom, and Eventide Care Home, 1004 Evans Avenue, operated by Dr. H. B. Dorsey.[1]

One of the most important facets of the local African American financial infrastructure also faced a financial crisis. In March 1957 Dorsey Adams, a Black real estate agent, and other depositors sued the Fraternal Bank and Trust, 401 East Ninth Street, founded by William "Gooseneck Bill" McDonald in the heart of the downtown Black business district. The plaintiffs were seeking to recover their deposits after Fraternal failed to cover several large withdrawals. The liquidity problems, caused by overdrafts and past-due loan repayments, forced the bank into receivership under A. B. Culbertson, who took aggressive steps, selling assets and suing several borrowers with large, overdue overdrafts or loans. The most egregious debtors included John and Bernice Mebane, operators of Lake Como Grocery, with $45,000 in overdrafts; Dumas Boyd, the largest scofflaw with $60,900 in past due notes and $87,705 in overdrawn checks; and three unidentified clients in arrears for a total of $19,747.[2]

The actual depth of the financial morass was worse than even the figures suggested. A newly sworn grand jury in July 1957 studying the bank's financial history found $800,000 missing and unaccounted. The investigative panel was notable for the inclusion of one of the first African Americans, O. C. Crook, and Mrs. E. L. Boswell, the first woman to sit on a Tarrant County grand jury since Texas opened juries to women in September 1955. Their findings, released in October 1957, concluded that the bank's "startling and appalling" condition stemmed from staff and others misappropriating $500,000. The grand jury issued 115 indictments for theft and embezzlement against thirty bank employees and customers, all African Americans, including I. P. Anderson, the bank's executive vice president.[3]

Blacks serving as jurors had an unintended consequence when M. F. Hawkings, owner of the Hawkins Café, Main and Weatherford Streets, discontinued juror food service effective July 1, 1956, following customer complaints over serving Black jurors. The café's reaction was part of the rigid, brazen segregation that conditioned every facet of life in 1950s Fort Worth. Newspapers regularly used base racial epithets and cartoonish depiction of African Americans. Even appearances by Black entertainers carried racial restrictions. An advertisement for an October 9, 1956, Casino Ballroom performance (tickets $2) by Little Richard, an African American rock and roll performer, stipulated "whites only." Despite the Montgomery bus boycott and related court rulings, Fort Worth city buses remained segregated in 1959, although the rules were changed to allow Blacks to sit anywhere if no rear seating was available. Confrontations over seating still happened with some frequency. Mrs. W. M. Preslar reported two Black women attacked her after she refused to let one sit next to her in the only available seat (Mrs. Preslar and a Hispanic man were sitting in a three-seat section). Segregated public accommodations were so common in the South that Black travelers relied on the *Negro Motorist Green Book*, a listing of restaurant, hotels and other businesses that accepted Blacks. Several Fort Worth spots were listed, including the Clover Hotel in the Rock Island Bottom neighborhood between the Trinity River and downtown, the Monterey Hotel and Rose Cliff restaurant near Rosedale Avenue and East Terrell Street, and the Mohawk Hotel in the southeast section of downtown in a commercial center with several Black enterprises. Segregation was prominent, hurtful, and ridiculous. The Fort Worth Public Library reported brisk demand for its few copies of *The Rabbits' Wedding* by Garth Williams, a book banned by libraries in Alabama because a white rabbit married a black rabbit.[4]

A few doors cracked open, allowing African Americans to make limited inroads into law enforcement at the county and municipal levels. In May 1956 Tarrant County Sheriff Harlon Wright hired a Black deputy, Wesley Hardeman, and promised to add a second as soon as county commissioners approved funding. Blacks were sorely needed in local law enforcement for many reasons, including a tendency for law enforcement to respond tepidly when Blacks were the victims. In 1956 ten Black businessmen appealed to the Tarrant County district attorney, asking for more aggressive prosecution in cases with a Black complainant. A 1957 grand jury report criticizing the Fort Worth Police Department's investigation of Black-on-Black crimes suggested the department hire Black investigators, arguing they were needed because of the "common knowledge" that African Americans were reluctant to talk to white officers. Chief Hightower reassigned two of the department's four Black police officers to assist white detectives, although he did not promote them to the detective rank. An important milestone was passed in 1959 when Ollice Malloy became the first African American sworn in as an assistant district attorney for Tarrant County. Even that advance was mitigated. Malloy, an ex-teacher and graduate of the University of Texas Law School, was assigned only to cases involving Black complainants.[5]

Local politics in the 1950s had not yet caught up to the changing attitudes accompanying the postwar Civil Rights Movement. In 1956 Congressman Jim Wright, later to become Speaker of the United States House of Representatives, affirmed his belief in a separate but equal system, stating that segregation did not inherently discriminate, a blatant contradiction of logic and the Supreme Court's *Brown* decision. Wright tacitly admitted his statement's inherent legal flaw by conceding a constitutional amendment would be needed to legalize segregation, an unlikely event. Without offering an alternative, Wright suggested the nation needed a "cooling off period" to calm emotions. To be fair, Jim Wright was not alone in holding on to outdated views. Joe Pyle, in a runoff against Doyle Willis for the Democratic nomination for state senator, accused Willis of courting voters in predominantly Black precincts, implying that he kowtowed to African Americans. Pyle advertised that a vote for him was "a vote against mixing the races."[6]

The Ku Klux Klan was around in the 1950s, but with a dramatically reduced public footprint and less official acceptance than it enjoyed as recently as the 1920s. The head of the Texas Klan, Horace S. Miller, moved from Walnut Springs, a small town sixty miles south of Fort Worth, to Waco in 1949. Miller and the Fort Worth Klan chapter became involved in a 1957 movement to oust White Settlement Public Works Director Clifford Johnson (White Settlement is a suburb west of Fort Worth) after rumors spread that he welcomed Black residents. Miller described the Fort Worth Klan as one of the strongest local units in the state, although he refused to provide membership figures. That statement was dubious, at best. Both the Fort Worth Klan chapter and the national organization had undergone a resurgence around 1916 that led to heightened activity and influence throughout the 1920s before weakening in the 1930s. The local chapter was also beset by an internal split in which two factions competed for dominance. Still, enough organization remained in the 1950s for the local Klan to support Odela N. Whalin, a Harris Hospital nurse fired her for refusing to care for a Black man. The local Klan presented Ms. Whalin with a Klansman hood ornament for her car. The Texas Klan suffered a serious setback in June 1957 when the Texas secretary of state rejected their charter application, claiming that their statement of purpose (education) did not meet state requirements.[7]

The weakened position of the Klan did not imply that resistance to court ordered desegregation had waned. In 1956 the Fort Worth Recreation Board expressed its fears of an "impending crisis" developing from the courts recent moves expanding desegregation orders to include municipal golf courses and swimming pools. The prospect so alarmed board member J. J. Lyles that he moved the city sell or close all its pools. Instead, the board opted to open on schedule on, June 2, 1956, under the status quo of segregation, reserving five pools for whites and the Dixie Swimming Pool, 1200 East Rosedale Street, for African Americans. The city council went along with the decision to retain segregation, adding only a suggestion that the Park Board accelerate construction of a second Blacks-only pool in Lake Como Park. Despite the victory, segregationists remained truculent. In June 1958 a four-foot alligator was found in the Dixie Swimming Pool, almost assuredly the work of racists, although no one was ever charged.[8]

Little wonder that the city did not embrace integrated swimming when its Board of Education continued to ignore the *Brown* decision. In August 1956 the FWISD Board voted to maintain strict segregation for the upcoming school year, a decision the *Star Telegram* supported, adding praise for making Fort Worth's "system of Negro schools" the most outstanding in the state. The editorial was particularly proud that that 17.5 percent of recent bond funds had been allocated for facilities serving Black students, only 15.1 percent of the district's student body. Dr. Flemmings, president of the local NAACP, was less complimentary, blasting the school board for violating court orders. He suggested Black parents ignore segregation and send their children to the nearest school. Fort Worth's nascent civil rights movement benefited from the efforts of a few dedicated supporters like Dr. Flemmings and Lenora Rolla, an African American woman instrumental in establishing local chapters of the NAACP and Southern Christian Leadership Conference. A few parents taking Flemmings's advice were turned away from Peter Smith Elementary, 715 West

Seventh Street (two children rejected) and Carroll Peak Elementary, 1212 Elmwood Avenue (three children rejected). Over the next few years several schools would refuse to register Black students. In September 1959 Sergeant Weirleis Flax, an African American stationed at Carswell Air Force Base, was referred to Como Elementary when he tried to enroll his daughter, Arlene, at the nearest elementary, Burton Hill Elementary, and the six children of Mr. and Mrs. Herbert Teal were turned away from Peter Smith Elementary and directed to George Washington Carver Elementary. The six Teal children and one Flax child became plaintiffs in a suit filed by NAACP lawyers Clifford L. Davis of Fort Worth, W. J. Durham of Dallas, and Thurgood Marshall of New York seeking desegregation of all Fort Worth schools.[9]

The battle for school integration became a contentious issue in Mansfield, a town of 1,500 twenty miles southeast of Fort Worth. Mansfield Schools provided separate facilities for Black students through the eighth grade but bussed high school students to Fort Worth's I. M. Terrell High School. In 1955 NAACP Attorney L. Clifford Davis, representing three Mansfield high school students, sued, arguing the three, along with nine other Black students, suffered hardships from being bussed forty miles to Fort Worth. The commute was long and arduous. The students boarded a 7:30 a.m. bus to Lancaster Avenue, where they debussed to walk the last twenty blocks to Terrell, retracing the same route starting at 5:30 p.m. for the return. Mansfield was only one of seventeen surrounding towns from as far away as Decatur, Texas (forty-five miles northeast), bussing Black students to Fort Worth schools. In August 1956 United States District Judge Joe Estes ordered Mansfield to admit Black high school students, the first Texas school district to face direct court-ordered integration. Angry whites surrounded the high school, preventing Blacks from entering and registering. As the protestors grew in number they spread to downtown Mansfield, where an effigy of a Black person was hung with a sign reading, "This Negro tried to enter a white school." Texas Governor Allen Shivers sent in the Texas Rangers, which also brought a large media contingent. The mob vented part of its anger on Gordon Yoder, a television cameraman, roughing him up and smashing his camera to the ground, then they turned on three staff members of the Tarrant County district attorney's office, surrounding

Police Officers R. W. Cole and Delbert Giles remove an effigy of an African American found hanging from West Lancaster Avenue Bridge over Trinity Park during Mansfield School integration riots, August 30, 1956. Courtesy *Fort Worth Star Telegram* Collection, Special Collections, University of Texas at Arlington Libraries.

them and manhandling Gary Hight before sheriff's deputies arrived. Police also had to intervene to protect the Reverend D. W. Clark of St. Timothy's Episcopal Church, who called on protestors to act like Christians.[10]

The mob ran largely unchecked for several days, becoming so threatening that administrators feared serious violence was imminent. Emboldened by the lack of control, demonstrators hung Black effigies from the school entrance and its flagpole, both with signs proclaiming, "Black Negroes Keep Out." Attorney Clifford Davis telegrammed Mansfield School Superintendent R. L. Huffman, demanding the high school admit the three students named in the suit, but Huffman insisted the students had to register at the school in person, a condition the crowd made impossible. Huffman's response was not surprising; he had publicly assured segregationists that he stood with them. Nearby Alvarado, Texas, experienced a brief uproar after rumors circulated that Blacks planned to enroll, but the disturbance quickly dissipated when no Blacks appeared at the white school.[11]

As time passed without a challenge or change to the standoff, the anti-integration mob waned, apparently confident of victory. Their confidence was well grounded. Huffman ordered buses to resume transporting Black students to Fort Worth's I. M. Terrell High School. Eight students, including two of the three desegregation suit plaintiffs, registered for classes at Terrell. Fewer than fifty listeners were present when W. Lee "Pappy" O'Daniel, a flamboyant former Texas governor running again in 1956, arrived with a sound truck. O'Daniel would have been a crowd favorite; he loudly maintained that the *Brown* ruling was part of a Communist plot. Thwarted by a mob and an effete administration, integrationists shifted to the federal courts, obtaining another injunction ordering integration. Clifford Davis sought enforcement assistance from the federal government, but Mansfield's lawyer, J. A. Gooch, won a stay to prepare a formal appeal. Texas Attorney General John Ben Shepperd, a segregationist, sought a temporary restraining order banning the NAACP from Texas, claiming the group incited racial prejudice, picketing, and riots. The suit specifically blamed Dr. George D. Flemmings. Supreme Court Justice Hugo Black of the Fifth Circuit Court rejected Gooch's appeal, but the Mansfield school board, now represented by Gooch, R. K. Hanger, and E. A. Cantey, appealed to the United States Supreme Court. In December 1956 the Supreme Court rejected the Mansfield School Board's petition for delay, but NAACP counsel L. Clifford Davis chose to wait before proceeding with a request for enforcement. In the meantime, no Black students registered at Mansfield High School. One year later the situation remained unchanged, leaving Black students bussed to I. M. Terrell.[12]

Car with racist statements and epithets parked near Mansfield High School during school integration riots, August 30, 1956. Courtesy *Fort Worth Star Telegram* Collection, Special Collections, University of Texas at Arlington Libraries.

Mansfield's stark resistance was repeated in many Southern towns, but the process went much smoother in a few places. Clinton, Tennessee, was one of the exceptions, a town facing court-ordered integration in 1956 that opted for compliance rather than resistance. In September 1957 the Clinton schools began their second year of integrated schools with eight Black students registered, all without upheavals, a vivid contrast to the Mansfield, Texas experience. Analysts credited the peaceful and successful outcome to the Clinton School Board's informed decision to accept integration, something lacking in Mansfield.[13]

Segregation continued to dominate Texas education through the end of the 1950s. Since the *Brown* decision of 1954, the percentage of Black students attending integrated schools had barely changed. In the 1959–1960 school year, five years after *Brown*, Texas public schools held 1,777,000 white and

278,000 Black students, but fewer than 2 percent of Black students, 3,600, attended integrated classes, only 350 more than in the previous year. As bad as the 1959 figures were, the actual state of school integration in Texas was actually worse than they indicated. Only 125 school districts had integrated classes, almost all in West Texas, where few African Americans lived. The 3,600 integrated African American students would have averaged only 28 per district, ensuring they were a small minority in any school. Meanwhile, six hundred Texas school districts remained completely segregated, including all the districts in East Texas, where 90 percent of Texas's school age Blacks lived. Clearly, the pace of integration was stalled where it was most needed with little hope of correction. In 1958 Dallas and Houston schools remained segregated, relying on the tired excuse that the court's failure to set compliance deadlines left the timing open. In 1959 Fort Worth schools were sued by two Black students, one the son of a Carswell sergeant, after they were denied entry to their local school. By 1960 Fort Worth and Galveston came under specific court-ordered desegregation, but they, along with Dallas and Houston, continued resistance and delay, backed by a state law prohibiting integration without approval by district voters.[14]

The situation in Texas was not unique. In 1960, six years after the *Brown* decision, five Southern states remained wholly segregated: Alabama, Georgia, Louisiana, Mississippi, and South Carolina. An Associated Press study confirmed that desegregation forces controlling most school districts in the five states were so committed to segregation that they would close the schools rather than integrate. The study suggested the situation was not much better in the rest of the South, that most schools were likely to continue segregation until forced to comply.[15]

Inferior educational opportunities forced on African Americans had ramifications beyond the schoolhouse. Gross educational inequalities negatively affected Black attitudes to education, effectively dissuading African American students from recognizing schools as a pathway to a better future. Because of the disaffection, only 65 percent of Blacks 14 to 17 attended high school compared to 80 percent of whites, intensifying an education gap that shut Blacks out of higher status jobs. A national study completed in 1958 found that only 12 percent of Black male workers held white-collar jobs compared to 40 percent of white males and that the white-collar gap between the races for women was even larger. In 1959 a presidential commission worked to spur Black representation in higher class employment positions by encouraging companies to move Black workers from unskilled, menial jobs into professional careers. The commission praised Convair for hiring and training Black electrical workers and for its addition of significant numbers of Black clerical and professional staff.[16]

Many Blacks, tired of oppressive racism and attracted by the lure of greener pastures, opted to leave the South. That trend accelerated during World War II when worker shortages made relocations easier, then continued after the war. Between 1950 and 1956 an average of 300,000 African Americans left the South each year, the outflow most pronounced in rural areas of Mississippi and Alabama, but also evident in East Texas, a largely rural section. Those who left overwhelmingly migrated to the North and West. Phillip Hauser of the University of Chicago documented Black migration in a demographic study that showed that the percentage of African Americans living in the South declined from 89 percent in 1910 to only 53 percent in 1958. The study also confirmed the movement's rural to urban effect, revealing that 90 percent of Blacks in the North and West resided in cities, but only 48 percent of Southern Blacks were urbanites.[17]

African Americans who remained in the South were often forced by the sheer increase in population to make shorter moves, from one neighborhood to another. The saturation of existing residential locations left many Blacks no choice but move into traditionally white neighborhoods. Fort Worth had experienced racial upheavals in the Riverside/Sylvania neighborhoods northeast of downtown, but in the second half of the 1950s contention shifted to the near southeast section running north and south along Rosedale Street. On September 3, 1956, a cross burning, a common Klan tactic, was held at Sycamore Park near Rosedale Avenue and Mitchell Boulevard, although the crowd dispersed before police arrived. Segregationists committed themselves to keeping the area all-white organized in September 1956 at South Fort Worth Baptist Church as the Southeast Side Civic League (SESCL) for the expressed purpose of preventing Black inroads into all-white neighborhoods around 1200 East Powell and 1200 East Ramsey.

Southeast Side Civic League Headquarters, 2302 Evans Avenue, with sign stating, "United We Stand to Keep Morningside White," 1956–1959. Courtesy Margaret B. Carter Papers, Special Collections, University of Texas at Arlington Libraries.

Once established, they quickly expanded their boundaries. League Vice President G. W. Snell announced the SESCL's 500 members were dedicated to securing the Morningside area (south of Rosedale Street and east of Evans Avenue) and all of southeast Fort Worth for whites only. The group telegrammed appeals for support to several state officials who had publicly criticized the NAACP and integration. They also handed out 100 placards proclaiming, "This Property Not for Sale to Coloreds" to property owners and picketed Highland Park Baptist Church, Evans and Harvey Avenues (an all-white area), to protest the church's pending sale to a Black congregation. The pickets and protests apparently worked; Reverend Henry Cox, Highland Park's pastor, agreed to sell to the league. The SESCL sold shares in the church property to fund the purchase and continued buying properties to block African Americans, spending $68,000 in the process. The city of

Fort Worth colluded with whites to advance the effort. After E. L. Byers, 808 Colvin Street, complained in 1958 that the city had sold several properties to Blacks on all-white Harvey Street without giving the league notice, Mayor Tom McCann promised the city would negotiate with the group on future sales. Byers proposed the city establish city parks as buffer zones between white and Black neighborhoods.[18]

African Americans slowly achieved a critical, sustainable mass in the affected neighborhoods, softening but not ending resistance. In May 1959 a few hundred people protested outside 1201 Colvin Avenue after the owner showed the property to Blacks. Don Hillin, 5012 Westcreek Drive, the Covin property owner, explained that he had no choice but to consider Black buyers after whites refused to consider the house because they believed the area was destined to become all Black or, at least, have a sizable Black presence. That assumption seemed well-founded; Black families already occupied homes just north of East Harvey Street, the historical unofficial dividing line between white and Black neighborhoods. The SESCL still fought back, circulating a petition asking Hillin to reconsider the sale. They also protested when white owners offered four houses in the 1000 block of Jessamine Street to African Americans. Segregationists were fighting a rising tide propelled not only by growing racial sensitivities but also by economics as more white property owners accepted the demographic tide that shifted dividing lines. Erich Montgomery, a Black realtor, stated the obvious, that a growing population left Blacks with no choice but to move into previously white neighborhoods. The other reality was that Black homeowners tended to react like homeowners everywhere, being primarily concerned with protecting their property values. In 1960 Black residents blocked plans for a luxury hotel with a café and swimming pool for 5700 East Rosedale Street, citing fears that the business would depress property values. White homeowners who remained adapted and learned to coexist, at least to a certain extent. E. R. Hawkins, a white Morningside resident, organized Neighbors Realty & Investment Company in 1956 to encourage whites to remain. Hawkins, speaking in March 1960 to white residents at Morningside Elementary School, argued the area had a good future "despite the fact that Negroes are moving in."[19]

Riverside, an early center of white resistance, experienced renewed racial strife in 1956 after Lloyd Austin bought a home at 209 North Judkins Avenue, an all-white block of homes valued at $8,000 to $10,000. Two years earlier a Black family moving into the adjacent block sparked loud protests followed by a white exodus that left only one white family. Austin and his family, moving into their home on September 2, 1956, were greeted by a lone neighbor yelling insults and threats to burn the house, but as word spread, a crowd of 200 protestors regularly gathered around the Austin home, even hanging an effigy with a knife in its chest. Fort Worth Police increased their presence as angry whites discussed their next steps, and the city council appointed a committee to study the problem. Austin remained defiant, bravely guarding his home alone but refusing to talk to anyone, other than to tell reporters he was fine. At one point the mob became so threatening that Austin fired wildly out a window, hitting a car belonging to Stephen Shoemaker, 19 years old, and bringing a dozen police officers led by Captain J. D. Dunwoody. After the shooting, the police took a more aggressive stance, moving the crowd away from the Austin house and setting up barricades manned by officers twenty-four hours a day to restrict entry. Segregationists and concerned citizens who just wanted a peaceful solution offered to buy the house at a profit, but Austin remained steadfast, refusing to leave until 1960 when the street was taken for freeway expansion. In a rare show of individual progress, Stephen Shoemaker eventually apologized to Austin for his conduct during the protest.[20]

Fort Worth's north side neighborhood, home to a large Mexican-American community, experienced a case of misplaced racial violence. In July 1960 someone threw a rock through the glass front door at 3514 North Nichols Street, the home of Mr. and Mrs. W. D. Martin, with a note reading "Warning Get Out While You can. N———s Are Not Wanted In This Neighborhood." The Martins were not African American. Mrs. Martin was the daughter of a German mother and an American Indian father with a "moderately dark" complexion and her 7-year-old son had a medical condition that darkened his skin.[21]

The simultaneous explosions of World War II, urbanization, industrialization, and migration meshed with an increasingly more sympathetic court system to begin the unraveling of segregation. That process did not always go smoothly or peacefully, and years fighting resistance radicalized some African Americans. The Nation of Islam, or Black Muslims, a national organization of African Americans led by Elijah Muhammad, preached Black supremacy and separatism (the *Star Telegram* report on the group in 1959 was the first time the paper used the word "Black" to indicate African Americans). A local chapter of about fifteen members met at the Muhammad Temple, 1300 East Lancaster Avenue. In 1959 Police Chief Hightower, calling the Nation of Islam an "anti-white Negro supremacy cult," ordered a close watch on the local branch.[22]

Reverend L. C. Henegan, pastor of St. John Baptist Church and leader of an African American group dedicated to preventing racial conflicts, countered that the real threat to local harmony came not from Black Muslims but from the failure to correct long-standing inequities. Reverend Henegan blamed lingering injustices on a small group of whites, gullible Blacks, and the Tarrant County district attorney's tendency to ignore racial incidents. Not surprisingly, Chief Hightower disagreed, arguing that Black movement into white neighborhoods constituted the real threat to public peace. Henegan suggested that if integration were the problem, the best approach would be to make Black neighborhoods safer and cleaner, reducing the tendency to relocate. He specifically cited the area around I. M. Terrell High School, a blighted region with rampant crime that he said more resembled a jungle than a neighborhood. Reverend Henegan warned that failure to correct that and other inequities would result in African American students registering at white high schools. The city council agreed about the Terrell High School area, calling it an "eyesore ghetto" of tumbledown-down, dilapidated shacks. In February 1960 they ordered the Fort Worth Housing Authority to begin construction of 272 housing units for Black residents. Reverend Henegan remained in the public political eye for many years. In 1956 he lost a bid for City Council Place 8 and in 1960 ran for Place 2, an open seat, but lost again. Henegan was not the first African American to file for a city council seat; R. L. Thornton registered in 1949 but withdrew from the election, Dr. R. A. Ransom ran but lost in 1956, and Almita S. Robinson, a social worker, filed for Place 3 in 1957.[23]

Restrictions and roadblocks to voter registration made direct political participation almost impossible for African Americans, forcing many to turn to other tactics. One such option was lunch counter sit-ins that had been used in Greensboro, North Carolina, and other spots in the South. Fort Worth Police instituted training in mob psychology and control after rumors circulated that similar protests were planned for Fort Worth. Store managers at the national chain stores affected by the sit-ins—F. W. Woolworth, S. H. Kress, W. T. Grant and McCory's—successfully petitioned corporate boards for permission to desegregate lunch counters to forestall more violence. Their local branches integrated in December 1960, but some independent eateries refused to follow. That December Skyline Cafeteria, 300 West Vickery Boulevard, denied service to Welton Martin, a 26-year-old African American warehouse worker employed in the same building complex. The café offered to serve him in the kitchen, but Martin demanded to eat in the dining area. Police charged Martin with trespassing, carrying a $10 fine, which he planned to appeal.[24]

Mexican Americans experienced many of the same indignities as African Americans, but their stories seldom made into local records. They faced similar implied boundary lines, limiting where they could live. Fort Worth's north side had a long-standing racial/ethnic dividing line restricting Hispanics to east of Main Street, although in the 1950s natural demographic population pressures had begun to force challenges to that boundary. The Fostepco Heights Civic League and the Diamond Hill Civic League functioned for the same purpose as the SESCL, only their motivation was to keep Hispanics out of traditionally Anglo neighborhoods. Faced with exclusion from the mainstream, Mexican Americans developed their own cultural outlets and support infrastructure. Often, that involved programs conducted in Spanish, such as a film on cancer shown in 1958 at Marine Theater and Our Lady of Guadalupe Church, both presentations followed by addresses from two Spanish-speaking doctors. Mexican Americans also held fast to their cultural heritage, with annual celebrations on Mexican holidays like September 16, Mexican Independence Day. In 1960 a crowd of 3,000 "Mexican" residents of Fort Worth celebrated at Marine Park with a carnival and a speech from the Mexican Consul, Samuel Morales Pereyra, followed by naming Lisinia Cagigal queen of the celebration.[25]

Hispanics rarely appeared in the local news, except in reports of violence, both intra- and interracial. In one such incidence in 1956, Larry Martinez was arrested for firing a shot during a fight. Martinez told police he carried a pistol because "Mexicans" could not go anywhere without other "Mexicans" starting trouble. In 1958 two carloads of "Latin American youths" engaged in a name-calling and heckling match with seven Anglos at Lake Worth's Mosque point. The confrontation turned violent, sending one Anglo to a hospital with puncture wounds from broken beer bottles and seven Hispanics to jail. That the Hispanics were arrested and not the Anglos was no surprise; Fort Worth Police tended to treat Mexican Americans with disdain. In 1957 Fort Worth officers took four members of rival "Latin American" gangs, the Rebels and the Pachecos, to a barber college and had their long hair cut. In a more serious incident, juvenile authorities committed five youths to Gatesville State School for Boys after several Hispanic youths were shot September 1, 1959, during a fight between two rival Mexican gangs. The police justified the detentions as necessary to prevent retaliation and more gang warfare that they feared would follow if the five remained in town.[26]

Chapter 21

The Economy Entering the 1960s

The economic history of Fort Worth after 1940 centers on Convair, the city's largest employer. Since its beginnings in 1942, Convair has remained a remarkably consistent economic force, with only temporary downward fluctuations in employment and payroll. Chart 21.1 shows that Convair's annual wages paid soared from $10 million in 1942 to $55 million in 1943 and $61.9 million in 1944, then declined as the war waned and ended, bottoming out at less than $20 million in 1946 when only 6,400 workers remained on the job. In 1947 wages began a sharp upward trend that continued to 1951, when the total reached $111 million, a probable effect of the Cold War and Korean War. Slight declines followed, dropping wages to around $90 million in 1954 before turning sharply upward to over $120 million in 1956, the end of the study. A milestone was passed on December 22, 1956, when, after fourteen years and a few months, Convair's total payroll in Fort Worth exceeded $1 billion.[1] (See Chart 21.1)

Chart 21.1 Convair Fort Worth's Annual Payroll, 1942–1956

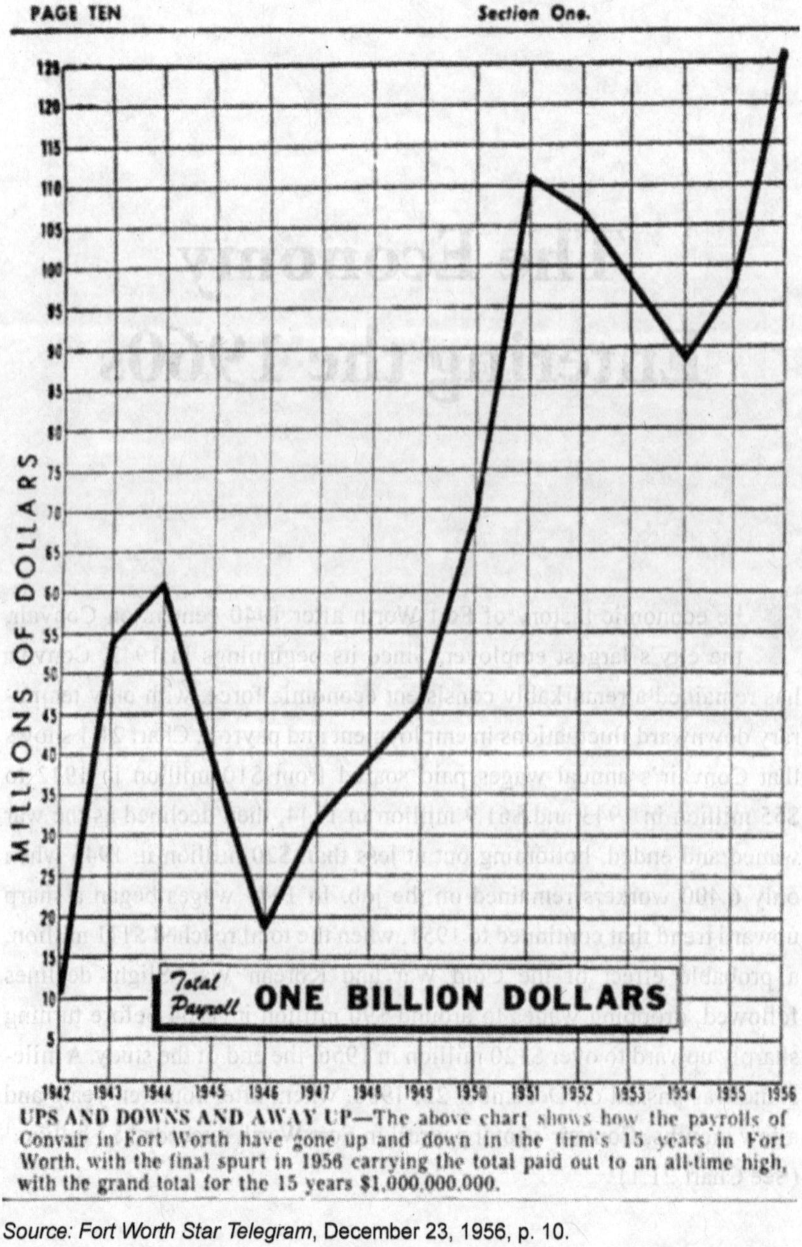

UPS AND DOWNS AND AWAY UP—The above chart shows how the payrolls of Convair in Fort Worth have gone up and down in the firm's 15 years in Fort Worth, with the final spurt in 1956 carrying the total paid out to an all-time high, with the grand total for the 15 years $1,000,000,000.

Source: Fort Worth Star Telegram, December 23, 1956, p. 10.

Convair was, and is, Fort Worth's largest employer, responsible for 30 percent of the total workforce in the 1950s, but two of every three Fort Worth workers were employed at one of some 1,000 businesses that were not Convair. Most were small concerns, ninety percent had fewer than fifty employees and only twenty-five employed 250 or more workers. A subsequent study in 1960 covering 1948 through 1959 suggested that Convair's impact on the Fort Worth economy, while substantial, was less than determinative. The 1960 analysis compared fluctuations in Convair's employment to bank debits between 1948 and 1959. In those twelve years, Convair's workforce ranged from a low of 11,300 in the first quarter of 1948 to a high of 30,800 in the last quarter of 1951 and ended with 19,200 in the last quarter of 1959. In the same period, Fort Worth bank deposits ranged from a low of $98 million recorded in the first quarter of 1948 to a high of $207.6 million in the third quarter of 1959, declining slightly to $194.6 million in the last quarter of 1959. The author suggested that the relatively stable rise in bank debits occurring while Convair underwent sizable employment swings indicated the factory's economic impact was muted, although he identified one economic indicator, real estate values in west Fort Worth, that was closely correlated with variations in Convair's employment. The analysis was interesting but may not have given sufficient weight to the significance of both debits and Convair employment hitting their lowest points in the first quarter of 1948 and the steady increase in Convair's employment recorded from 1955 to 1959 when Fort Worth experienced record deposits.[2]

The failings of Fort Worth's postwar commercial development outside Convair are clear. Chicago consultants analyzed issues limiting downtown Fort Worth's vitality as an economic and cultural civic center in the late 1950s. Their report cited lagging infrastructure growth as a major contributing problem, pointing out that between 1945 and 1958 downtown Dallas added thirty-two major buildings with 3.5 million square feet of office space, increasing its total office space to 8 million square feet, four times that of Fort Worth's downtown. Fort Worth's lack of available office space placed it at a major disadvantage in attracting businesses at a critical juncture during the 1950s when incipient commercial migration to the Southwest created demands for 2.05 million square feet of office space in Texas, approximately

Convair aerial view, 1957. Courtesy W. D. Smith Commercial Photography, Inc., Collection, Special Collections, University of Texas at Arlington Libraries.

equal to all of downtown Fort Worth's office area. Thanks to its large available office supply, Dallas outperformed all other cities in attracting new businesses, filling 1.4 million square feet, or 68 percent of the total new demand in Texas. Dallas's success dwarfed Fort Worth leasing of just 60,000 square feet or Oklahoma City's 50,000 square feet and was almost three times Houston's 540,000 square feet (San Antonio leased no new space). Houston's lackluster performance compared to Dallas was all the more amazing since Houston, unlike Fort Worth, had added 2.7 million square feet, less than Dallas but still significant. Dallas won the commercial competition of the 1950s by investing in excess office space just before the great commercial migration took off.

The report was even more critical of the poor state of amenities available for downtown convention business. Fort Worth's downtown, filled with cheap transient hotels, had only sixteen class A, B or C hotels with a mere 2,381 rooms, and the only large civic auditorium, Will Rogers Memorial, was four miles from the city center and functionally limited (lack of air conditioning). The report concluded that significant growth or improvements to revitalize downtown would require a new downtown auditorium and more first-rate hotel rooms. In addition, Fort Worth offered few cultural or entertainments magnets capable of drawing visitors and keeping them entertained. Downtown had no live theaters and only five movie houses, far fewer than the ten cinemas in downtown Dallas or eleven each in Houston and San Antonio.[3]

Many thought the answer lay in the Gruen Plan, an ambitious program developed by Victor Gruen, a Beverly Hills architect and city planner, that envisioned downtowns as self-sustaining communities of high-density housing surrounded by amenities within walking distance, eliminating the need for cars. Fort Worth formed a committee to study the plan, but the idea, although attractive, stalled in the face of many challenges, not the least of which was financing. Amon Carter Jr., a committee member, suggested a scaled-down initiative for a downtown auditorium and a loop around the city. The Tarrant County Convention Center, now the Fort Worth Convention Center, that opened in 1968 provided a large downtown auditorium.[4]

Fort Worth may not have developed economically as quickly as its neighbors, but it did not stagnate. The nonagricultural workforce increased from 139,000 in 1948 to 203,900 in 1959. Armour and Swift packinghouses remained major commercial concerns, although their relative importance declined, and oil continued to be a big business in Fort Worth despite having lost primacy to Houston and Midland. In 1958 the Fort Worth oil industry employed 16,500 workers earning $70 million in annual wages, about one-fourth of Fort Worth's total industrial wages of $283 million. In addition, 6,000 Fort Worthians received rents or royalties from petroleum production outside Tarrant County (no oil or gas wells were in Tarrant County at the time). In 1958 TCU's Bureau of Business Activity rated Fort Worth's business at 141 on a scale using 1947 to 1949 as a 100 base, implying a 41 percent increase between 1949 and 1958. Between 1947 and 1959, the number of manufacturing firms in Tarrant County increased 121 percent, the number employed in manufacturing grew 61 percent, and the value added by manufacturing rose an impressive 377 percent.[5]

Fort Worth achieved some major commercial advances in the end of the 1950s leading into the 1960s. In 1959 workers began draining eighty-five-acre Katy Lake near Seminary Drive, a preliminary step in the construction of Seminary South, Fort Worth's first shopping mall and one of the largest in Texas. Its construction helped Fort Worth building permits hit a then all-time high of $58.4 million in 1959. In 1960 Tarrant County bank deposits rose $64 million over 1959, to $829.5 million, and loans increased $17 million to $410.6 million, about one-sixth that of Dallas, which led the state with $2.7 billion in outstanding loans. In 1961 Carling Brewery announced plans for a $20 million brewery to begin production in 1963, employing up to 400 (now a Molson Coors Brewery).[6]

A comparative study of business activity between 1940 and 1962 for Fort Worth, Dallas, and Houston revealed no major shift in relative growth rates. All three grew at substantial but not wildly disproportionate rates. Focusing on value added by manufacturing, Fort Worth increased 2,009.8 percent between 1940 and 1962, Dallas 2,312.0 percent, and Houston 1,872.6 percent. Dallas clearly did the best, but Fort Worth edged out Houston for second in percentage growth. Houston had the largest total value added by manufacturing in both 1940 and 1964 despite trailing both Dallas and Fort Worth in percentage increases; in fact, the relative standing of all three remained constant despite the significant percentage difference. In 1940 Fort Worth's value added was 36.7 percent of Houston and 52.8 percent of Dallas; in 1962 it was 39.4 percent of Houston and 46.2 percent of Dallas—virtually unchanged but with a noticeable decline relative to Dallas. Dallas also performed well in a head-to-head comparison to Houston. In 1940 Dallas's value added was 70 percent of Houston's, and in 1962 it was 85 percent. The overall result was that all three did well, Dallas performing slightly better than Fort Worth and Houston but with no major shifts. That was not necessarily bad news for Fort Worth, but it did indicate that its position as Texas's third ranked economic urban center was becoming more firmly fixed, while the economic bonanza occurring between 1940 and 1960 widened the gap between Fort Worth and Dallas and Houston in absolute terms.

Chart 21.2 Business Activity for Texas's Four Largest Cities, 1940 (Dollar Values in Millions)

City	Businesses	Salaried	Salaries	Wage Earners	Wages	Value Produced	Value Added
Houston	589	2,586	$5	15,618	$19.3	$141.7	$69.3
Dallas	645	1,671	$2.9	13,709	$12.9	$126.8	$48.3
Fort Worth	284	954	$2	7,010	$7.2	$89.2	$25.5
San Antonio	328	772	$1.2	5,814	$5	$43.8	$18

Source: Manufactures, 1939, vol. 3, *Reports for States and Outlying Areas*, Sixteenth Census of the United States: 1940 (Washington, DC: Government Printing Office, 1942), 994–99.

Chart 21.3 Manufacturing Statistics for Fort Worth, Dallas, and Houston, 1962 (Dollar Values in Millions)

City	Factories	Employees	Payroll	Value Added	Capital Expenditures
Houston	1,750	92,000	$572	$1,367	$169
Dallas	1,756	107,000	$577	$1,165	$49
Fort Worth	784	52,000	$297	$538	$18

Source: "Manufactures," sec. 29 in *Statistical Abstract of the United States, 1964*, eighth ed. (Washington, DC: Government Printing Office, 1964), p. 781, chart 113.

Conclusion

Fort Worth's economic development between 1942 and 1960 was largely driven by defense spending related to World War II and the Cold War, a rising tide that lifted many American cities. The most important and obvious effect of that economy, Convair, began even before Pearl Harbor and remained (and remains, as Lockheed Martin) a major contributor to the Fort Worth economy. Convair, coupled with numerous commercial developments, allowed Fort Worth to maintain its relative ranking as Texas's third-ranked economy behind Houston and Dallas, with San Antonio fourth. The statistics suggest relative continuity in that no city significantly outperformed the rest in the way Houston had between 1920 and 1940. Dallas did solidify its position as the state's number two economy and narrow its gap with Houston, all thanks to its remarkable success in attracting new commercial development.

There is an interesting argument that Fort Worth's economic growth between 1942 and 1960 was remarkably different from its earlier growth, that the driving forces during World War II and the postwar lay largely outside local control. In its early development prior to 1917, Fort Worth survived and prospered thanks, in large measure, to the efforts of a few energetic boosters who were chiefly responsible for building a great railroad transportation center and bringing the two large packinghouses that formed the city's economic base. Boosters also played a role, albeit a diminished one, in securing the large military presence during World War I that helped push Fort Worth to economic supremacy in Texas. Fort Worth leaders lobbied for the bases and provided the infrastructure required to support Camp Bowie and the three airfields, but the final decision rested elsewhere. In the lead-up to World War II, Fort Worth donated land for construction and improved ground transportation and utilities, smoothing Convair's development, but the impetus behind the economy shifted from local to national centers.

Population growth for the four largest Texas cities between 1940 and 1960 indicate Fort Worth's growth lagged in the 1950s. All four cities recorded significant and uniform percentage increases between 1940 and 1950—47.4 percent for Dallas, 55 percent for Houston, and 60.9 percent for San Antonio, with Fort Worth actually recording the second-highest percentage growth, 56.9 percent, a remarkable feat that surely reflects Fort Worth's economic success in the 1940s. The results between 1950 and 1960 were not as favorable for Fort Worth. The growth rate in Houston edged up slightly to 57.3 percent, Dallas increased its rate of growth significantly to 56.4 percent, and San Antonio's rate declined significantly to 43.9 percent, but Fort Worth stalled, adding only 27.8 percent to its 1950 population, less than half its growth rate in the 1940s. Dallas probably grew faster because of its success attracting new businesses, and the oil industry is often credited for driving Houston's growth, but no easy answer explains Fort Worth's relatively slow growth in the 1950s.

Chart Conclusion.1 Population Increases in Fort Worth, Dallas, Houston, and San Antonio, 1940–1960

City	1940	1950	% Change over 1940	1960	% Change over 1950
Houston	384,514	596,163	+55	938,219	+55
Dallas	294,734	434,462	+47.4	679,684	+55
San Antonio	253,854	408,442	+60.9	587,718	+43.9

(Continued)

Chart Conclusion.1 Continued

City	1940	1950	% Change over 1940	1960	% Change over 1950
Fort Worth	177,662	278,778	+56.9	356,268	+27.8

Fort Worth's slower growth in the 1950s is evident comparing relative population increases between 1940 and 1960. In those two decades Houston added 144 percent to its population, San Antonio 131.5 percent, and Dallas 130.6 percent, while Fort Worth grew 100.5 percent, substantially less than its competition.

Little changed between 1940 and 1960 concerning vice in Fort Worth, but by the end of the 1950s law enforcement began to exert sustained enforcement pressure, with much of that change related to a decline in corruption. The lack of effective enforcement in the 1940s and most of the 1950s had allowed gambling and prostitution to remain readily available at known casinos and bordellos all over town. The available evidence suggests quite strongly that law enforcement was complicit at many levels in that arrangement. That was also true for most of the 1950s, but by the close of the decade signs appeared that a corner had been passed, that a change in attitudes was near, perhaps stimulated by public disclosures of economic ties between vice purveyors and police. Gambling and prostitution were the stocks in trade for most of Fort Worth's criminal underworld. Most, if not all, of the major members of that clique met violent ends during a series of gangland assassinations that began in the 1940s and ran through the 1950s. Their unsolved murders are the stuff of legends and unlikely to ever be repeated.

The use of illegal narcotics became a widespread public problem in the late 1940s and continued to grow throughout the 1950s. Marijuana, the most common drug, remained widespread and relatively cheap, while harder options like heroin and cocaine were scarcer and dearer. Alcohol enforcement, which had been so important in Prohibition, almost disappeared as a newsworthy item with the exception of the rise in DWI enforcement.

The postwar era was a time of significant development for policing. The Fort Worth Police Department expanded its traffic division, adding personnel and developing DWI enforcement capabilities and radar units. In the 1950s the department took a major step in professionalization, adding a dedicated crime lab and a polygraph section. Patrol and other police officers were given instant communication with headquarters and other officers via in-car two-way radios, a major advance for motorized patrol. In-car radios with two-way capability made it possible to dispatch assists, allowing the use of one-officer patrol cars. Drug enforcement highlighted the need for undercover officers who were initially borrowed from state and federal agencies. Their effectiveness stressed the need for local operatives. The job became professionalized with established training standards, civil service protection, and the formation of a Police Officer's Association.

Civil rights for African Americans entered a critical stage in which Blacks accelerated the attack on segregation through street-level action and in the courts. Few of those battles took place in Fort Worth, but Black citizens united to fight segregated municipal facilities and neighborhoods. There were few victories, but the battle had been joined and would reap rewards later.

All in all, it was a tumultuous period with lots of sound, fury, and promises for the future.

Endnotes

Notes for Chapter 1

1. *New York Times*, November 18, 1941, p. 5.
2. *Fort Worth Star Telegram*, July 7, 1946, Section 4, pp. 1–8.
3. Seth Shepard McKay, *Texas and the Fair Deal, 1945–1952* (San Antonio: Naylor, 1954), 1–3, 12–13; *Fort Worth Star Telegram*, July 7, 1946, Section 4, pp. 1–8.
4. *New York Times*, April 19, 1942, p. 32.
5. "Our Chamber in the War," *This Month in Fort Worth* 22, no. 1 (January 1945): 7–8; Oliver Knight, *Fort Worth: Outpost on the Trinity* (University of Oklahoma Press, 1953; repr., Fort Worth: Texas Christian University Press, 1990), 212; *Fort Worth Star Telegram*, June 23, 1942, p. 1; December 4, 1945, p. 1; December 7, 1945, pp. 1–2; February 24, 1946, Section 1, p. 9; September 29, 2024, pp. 3A–5A.
6. *Manufactures, 1939*, vol. 3, *Reports for States and Outlying Areas*, Sixteenth Census of the United States: 1940 (Washington, DC: Government Printing Office, 1942), 46; *Fort Worth Star Telegram*, January 14, 1943, p. 4; "National Defense Should Mean Big Business for Fort Worth," *This Month in Fort Worth* 14, no. 11 (November 1940): 4.
7. *Fort Worth Star Telegram*, January 24, 1943, p. 3.
8. *Fort Worth Star Telegram*, April 19, 1942, p. 118; August 10, 1942, p. 15.
9. *Fort Worth Star Telegram*, May 22, 1944, p. 13; November 16, 1942, p. 21.
10. J'Nell L. Pate, *Arsenal of Defense*: *Fort Worth's Military Legacy* (Denton: Texas State Historical Society, 2011), p. 73; Knight, *Outpost*, 212–13; Homer Cryer, "The President's Message," *This Month in Fort Worth* 22, no. 1 (January 1945): 2 and 8; "Economic Development," *This Month in Fort Worth* 22, no. 2 (February 1945): 9; *Fort Worth Star Telegram*, December 4, 1945, p. 1; December 7, 1945, pp. 1–2.
11. *New York Times*, March 12, 1941, p. 29; May 29, 1941, p. 32; May 29, 1942, p. 27.
12. *New York Times*, May 20, 1942, p. 15; April 18, 1942, p. 2.
13. *Fort Worth Star Telegram*, April 19, 1942; May 20, 1945, p. 15; December 7, 1945, pp. 1–2; May 26, 2024, p. 1C; *New York Times*, March 12, 1941, p. 29; "Economic Development," p. 9.
14. *New York Times*, May 6, 1942, p. 10.
15. *Fort Worth Star Telegram*, April 19, 1942, pp. 22 and 74.

16. *Fort Worth Star Telegram,* August 18, 1943, p. 3.
17. *Fort Worth Star Telegram,* December 17, 1942, p. 17.
18. Pate, *Arsenal of Defense*, 74; *New York Times*, February 16, 1941, p. 103; January 26, 1942, p. 27; April 27, 1943, pp. 29 and 34; May 2, 1943, p. 142.
19. *Fort Worth Star Telegram,* September 16, 1942, p. 1; October 8, 1942, p. 6; October 21, 1942, p.1; September 30, 1942, p. 2; August 18, 1943, p. 4.
20. *Fort Worth Star Telegram,* September 16, 1943, p. 1; October 1, 1944, p. 3; August 30, 1944, pp. 1 and 8; February 6, 1944, p. 11.
21. *Fort Worth Star Telegram,* December 28, 1941, pp. 1, 22–23; January 1, 1942, p. 10; January 2, 1942, p. 1; April 1, 1942, p. 1; January 1, 1943, pp. 1, 4, 21.
22. *Fort Worth Star Telegram,* May 14, 1942, p. 7 and 10; September 4, 1942, pp. 1 and 8; March 27, 1945, p. 2; Knight, *Outpost*, 212; *Population*, vol. 3, *The Labor Force: Part 5, Pennsylvania–Wyoming*, Sixteenth Census of the United States: 1940 (Washington, DC: Government Printing Office, 1943), 46.
23. "Council of Social Agencies of Fort Worth and Tarrant County, 1929–1956," R0068, Second Annual Report 1941, by Executive Secretary Margaret D. Yates, File: Annual Report 1941, Box 1, Local History Archives, Fort Worth Public Library (hereafter cited as "Local History Archives, FWPL").
24. *Fort Worth Star Telegram,* August 8, 1942, p. 1; April 10, 1942, pp. 1 and 6; October 29, 1943, p. 8; April 19, 1942, pp. 1 and 8.
25. *Fort Worth Star Telegram,* April 24, 1942, p. 8; May 6, 1943, p. 6; November 1, 1942, p. 1.
26. *Fort Worth Star Telegram,* January 2, 1944, p. 3; February 14, 1943, pp. 1 and 4.
27. *Fort Worth Star Telegram,* October 4, 1942, p. 6; October 8, 1942, p. 7; May 5, 1943, p. 16; June 29, 1944, p. 12; Harold Rich, *Fort Worth: Outpost, Cowtown, Boomtown* (Norman: University of Oklahoma Press, 2014), 197–98.
28. *Fort Worth Star Telegram,* February 10, 1944, p. 2.
29. *Fort Worth Star Telegram,* June 8, 2023, pp. C1–C2; September 24, 1942, p. 13.
30. *Fort Worth Star Telegram,* May 6, 1943, p. 30; September 2, 1943, p. 6; September 3, 1943, p. 1; May 13, 1943, p. 4.
31. *Fort Worth Star Telegram,* April 27, 1942, p. 17; January 3, 1945, p. 1; January 1, 1942, p. 10; January 2, 1942, p. 1; January 1, 1943, pp. 1, 4, 21; April 1, 1942, p. 1; September 1, 1942, p. 1; May 2, 1943, p. 10; December 31, 1943, p. 1; December 31, 1944, p. 2.

Notes for Chapter 2

1. *Fort Worth Star Telegram,* November 11, 1943, pp. 1 and 6.
2. *Fort Worth Star Telegram,* November 15, 1944, p. 10; February 9, 1942, pp. 1 and 4; *Fort Worth Press,* March 6, 1945, p. 1.
3. *Fort Worth Star Telegram,* March 7, 1942, p. 2; November 30, 1944, p. 12; September 22, 1944, p. 17.
4. *Fort Worth Star Telegram,* November 1, 1944, pp. 1 and 4; November 15, 1944, p. 10; September 22, 1943, p. 15.
5. *Fort Worth Star Telegram,* November 13, 1944, pp. 1–2; November 27, 1944, p. 1; Ann Arnold, *Gamblers & Gangsters: Fort Worth's Jacksboro Highway in the 1940s & 1950s* (Austin: Eakin Press, 1998), 123–24.
6. *Fort Worth Star Telegram,* November 15, 1944, p. 10; November 30, 1944, p. 12; *Fort Worth Press,* November 5, 1945, p. 1; November 6, 1945, p. 2; November 13, 1945, p. 16.
7. *Fort Worth Star Press,* November 1, 1945, p. 1; November 3, 1945, pp. 1 and 7; November 5, 1945, p. 1; November 6, 1945, p. 2; November 13, 1945, p. 16; February 18, 1946, p. 1.
8. Rich, *Outpost*, 193–97; *Fort Worth Star Telegram,* July 16, 1942, pp. 1 and 4; Robert Polito, *Savage Art: A Biography of Jim Thompson* (New York: Alfred A. Knopf, 1995), 105–7; "Council of Social Agencies of Fort Worth and Tarrant County, 1929–1956," R0068, File Annual Report 1943, Box 1, p. 9, Local History Archives, FWPL; "Council of Social Agencies of Fort Worth and Tarrant County, 1929–1956" R0068. File Annual Report 1942, p. 8, Local History Archives, FWPL.
9. *Fort Worth Star Telegram*, January 14, 1942, pp. 1–2; January 18, 1942, p. 4; January 22, 1942, pp. 1 and 4; January 23, 1942, p. 5.
10. Harold Rich, *Fort Worth Between the World Wars* (College Station: Texas A&M University Press, 2020), 195; *Fort Worth Star Telegram*, February 6, 1942, pp. 1 and 4; see Susan M. Reverby, *Examining Tuskegee: The Infamous Syphilis Study and Its Legacy*, The John Hope Franklin Series in African American History and Culture, ed. Waldo E. Martin Jr. and Patricia Sullivan (Chapel Hill: University of North Carolina Press, 2013).
11. *Fort Worth Star Telegram,* March 12, 1942, pp. 1 and 4; December 27, 1942, p. 2; February 11, 1943, p. 4.
12. *Fort Worth Star Telegram,* February 11, 1943, p. 4; July 27, 1943, pp. 1 and 4; April 21, 1944, p. 6.
13. *Fort Worth Star Telegram,* March 3, 1944, p. 8; February 21, 1944, p. 16; "Agenda Item 16171, February 3, 1944," p. 524, *Tarrant County Commissioners Court Minutes*, vol. 39, 1943–1944 (hereafter cited as TCCCM).
14. *Fort Worth Star Telegram,* September 5, 1943, p. 7.

15. *Fort Worth Star Telegram*, July 27, 1943, pp. 1 and 4; August 7, 1943, p. 9; October 11, 1943, p. 8; April 18, 1944, p. 6.
16. *Fort Worth Star Telegram*, November 3, 1943, p. 4; February 2, 1944, p. 6; September 21, 1944, p. 10.
17. *Fort Worth Star Telegram*, April 8, 1944, pp. 1–2; April 9, 1944, pp. 1 and 4; May 2, 2022, p. A2; Frank Jackson, "The Life and Legacy of Clarence Otto 'Big Boy' Kraft: A Baseball Journey," *Handbook of Texas Online*, April 4, 2024, https://www.tshaonline.org/handbook/entries/kraft-clarence-otto-big-boy; see Adam Cohen, *The Imbeciles: The Supreme Court, American Eugenics, and the Sterilization of Carrie Black* (New York: Penguin Press, 2016).
18. *Fort Worth Star Telegram*, April 8, 1944, pp. 1–2; April 9, 1944, pp. 1 and 4; "Agenda Item 16170, February 3, 1944," p. 524, TCCCM; "Agenda Item 16355, April 24, 1944," p. 607, TCCCM.
19. *Fort Worth Star Telegram*, April 9, 1944, pp. 1 and 4; April 8, 1944, pp. 1–2.
20. *Fort Worth Star Telegram*, April 9, 1944, pp. 1 and 4; April 8, 1944, pp. 1–2; April 10, 1944, pp. 1–2; *Fort Worth Press*, April 10, 1944, p. 1.
21. *Fort Worth Star Telegram*, April 17, 1944, p. 1; April 12, 1944, p. 9.
22. *Fort Worth Star Telegram*, January 1, 1944, p. 1; April 9, 1944, pp. 1 and 4; May 6, 1944, p. 2; August 3, 1944, p. 3.
23. *Fort Worth Star Telegram,* December 31, 1942, p. 8; March 22, 1944, p. 1; March 23, 1944, p. 1; *Fort Worth Press*, August 8, 1945, p. 1.
24. *Fort Worth Star Telegram,* September 22, 1943, p. 10; October 9, 1943, pp. 1 and 2; October 11, 1943, p. 1; *Fort Worth Press,* April 15, 1944, p. 1.
25. *Fort Worth Star Telegram,* April 10, 1944, pp. 1 and 2; April 11, 1944, p. 2.
26. *Fort Worth Star Telegram,* November 10, 1943, pp. 1 and 6.
27. *Fort Worth Star Telegram,* February 3, 1944, pp. 1 and 6; April 14, 1944, p. 1; April 17, 1944, pp. 1–2; April 18, 1944, p. 9; May 4, 1944, p. 1; November 8, 1956, p. 1; *Fort Worth Press,* April 17, 1944, p. 1; April 18, 1944, p. 1.
28. Rich, *Between the World Wars*, 179; *Fort Worth Press,* April 18, 1944, p. 1.

Notes for Chapter 3

1. *Fort Worth Star Telegram*, December 31, 1941, pp. 1 and 7; July 22, 1942, p. 1; April 8, 1943, p. 4; *Fort Worth Press,* June 26, 1946, p. 1.
2. *Fort Worth Star Telegram*, January 1, 1942, p. 2; January 4, 1942, p. 5; September 10, 1942, p. 4; November 4, 1942, p. 4.

3. *Fort Worth Star Telegram*, November 12, 1943, p. 12; *Fort Worth Press,* July 26, 1945, p. 1; March 28, 1945, p. 1; March 31, 1945, p. 3.
4. *Fort Worth Star Telegram*, January 22, 1942, p. 9; January 23, 1943, p. 1; February 24, 1943, pp. 1 and 6; April 8, 1943, p. 1; April 9, 1943, p. 31.
5. *Fort Worth Star Telegram*, May 26, 1942, p. 4; December 16, 1943, p. 29; June 24, 1942, p. 1; *Fort Worth Press,* February 13, 1946, p. 11.
6. *Fort Worth Star Telegram*, March 18, 1942, p. 9.
7. *Fort Worth Star Telegram*, November 3, 1943, p. 1; May 22, 1945, p. 9; December 15, 1943, p. 6.
8. *Fort Worth Star Telegram*, September 24, 1943, p. 20; April 20, 1945, p. 9; July 6, 1945, p. 1; *Fort Worth Press,* January 4, 1945, p. 1.
9. *Fort Worth Star Telegram*, January 1, 1942, p. 10; July 2, 1942, p. 13; July 2, 1944, p. 13; September 21, 1942, p. 5
10. *Fort Worth Star Telegram*, September 2, 1943, p. 1; February 13, 1942, p. 1.
11. *Fort Worth Star Telegram*, December 21, 1943, p. 11; November 10, 1944, pp. 1 and 10.
12. *Fort Worth Star Telegram*, January 19, 1942, pp. 1 and 4; October 14, 1942, pp. 1–2; *Fort Worth Press,* October 9, 1945, p. 1; November 2, 1945, p. 10.
13. "Council of Social Agencies of Fort Worth and Tarrant County, 1929–1956," R0068, File Annual Report 1941, p. 1, Local History Archives, FWPL; *Fort Worth Star Telegram*, September 10, 1944, p. 2; July 2, 1944, p. 13; July 29, 1943, p. 7; December 30, 1941, p. 2; January 1, 1942, p. 5; January 8, 1942, p. 22.
14. *Fort Worth Star Telegram*, October 3, 1944, p. 6; July 22, 1943, p. 24; June 15, 1943, p. 18; June 16, 1943, p. 1; June 17, 1943, p. 7; June 18, 1943, p. 10.
15. "Council of Social Agencies of Fort Worth and Tarrant County, 1929–1956," R0068, File Annual Report 1944, Sixth Annual Report 1945, p. 9, Local History Archives, FWPL; *Fort Worth Star Telegram*, October 16, 1944, p. 1; December 3, 1944, p. 11.
16. *Fort Worth Star Telegram*, February 20, 1942, pp. 1 and 4; March 26, 1942, p. 1; December 5, 1944, pp. 1 and 11.
17. *Fort Worth Star Telegram*, March 27, 1943, pp. 1–2.
18. *Fort Worth Star Telegram*, August 5, 1942, p. 1; March 23, 1943, p. 1; *Fort Worth Press,* April 4, 1945, p. 3.
19. *New York Times*, April 6, 1941, p. 199; *Fort Worth Star Telegram*, January 13, 1942, p. 5; January 8, 1943, p. 5; January 22, 1944, p. 1.
20. *Fort Worth Star Telegram*, February 24, 1943, pp. 1 and 6; April 10, 1953, p. 40; March 13, 1943, p. 2.

21. *Fort Worth Star Telegram*, February 26, 1943, pp. 1 and 8; May 31, 1943, pp. 1–2; June 2, 1943, p. 13; November 23, 1943, p. 8; November 25, 1943, p. 29; November 28, 1943, p. 13; December 1, 1943, p. 3.
22. *Fort Worth Star Telegram*, March 28, 1943, p. 3; December 15, 1960, p. 1; *Fort Worth Press,* February 28, 1945, pp. 1 and 8; December 25, 1945, p. 1; December 26, 1945, p. 1.
23. Arnold, *Gamblers & Gangsters*, 122–23; *Fort Worth Star Telegram*, October 9, 1943, p. 1; October 11, 1943, p. 1; December 2, 1943, p. 1; December 3, 1943, pp. 1 and 8; December 4, 1943, p. 1; March 4, 1950, p. 1.
24. Arnold, *Gamblers & Gangsters*, 109–13; *Fort Worth Star Telegram*, November 6, 1944, p. 4; June 7, 1944, pp. 1 and 3; November 18, 1944, p. 1.
25. *Fort Worth Star Telegram*, October 27, 1944, p. 1.
26. *Fort Worth Star Telegram*, October 30, 1944, p. 2.
27. *Fort Worth Press*, October 10, 1945, p. 6; *Fort Worth Star Telegram*, March 5, 1958, p. 1; March 6, 1958, p. 1; March 9, 1958, pp. 1 and 4.
28. *Fort Worth Star Telegram*, February 5, 1944, pp. 1–2; July 14, 1944, pp. 1 and 8; July 19, 1944, p. 4.
29. *Fort Worth Star Telegram*, March 29, 1943, pp. 1 and 4; October 20, 1943, p. 1; March 17, 1944, pp. 1 and 8; *New York Times*, March 27, 1943, p. 15; October 27, 1943, p. 23.

Notes for Chapter 4

1. *Manufactures, 1939*, 46; *Fort Worth Star Telegram*, June 14, 1942, p. 2B; February 27, 1942, p. 8; July 5, 1943, p. 8; August 4, 2024, p. 14A; *Fort Worth Press,* January 23, 1945, p. 3; Rich, *Between the World Wars*, 227.
2. *Fort Worth Star Telegram*, March 12, 1942, p. 4; December 13, 1943, p. 5; June 21, 1942, p. 13; May 31, 1944, p. 4.
3. *Fort Worth Star Telegram*, April 3, 1942, p. 1; November 27, 1942, p. 1; June 22, 1943, p. 1; January 4, 1943, p. 1; see Rachel Marie-Crane Williams, *Run Home If You Don't Want to Be Killed: The Detroit Uprising of 1943* (Chapel Hill: University of North Carolina Press, 2021).
4. *Fort Worth Star Telegram*, September 24, 1943, p. 23; July 2, 1944, p. 13; June 1, 1944, p. 10.
5. *Fort Worth Star Telegram*, July 23, 1944, p. 7; November 10, 1944, pp. 1 and 10; March 16, 1943, p. 10; January 21, 2025, Local Section, p. 5; *Fort Worth Press,* March 19, 1945, p. 8; Lady George Munchus-Forde, "History of the Negro in Fort Worth: Syllabus for a High School Course" (MA thesis, Fisk University, 1941), 57–59, 60; "Item 16092, January 3, 1944," p. 394, TCCCM.

6. To Walter White from Irma Brown, November 20, 1945, p. 5; to Irma Brown from Thurgood Marshall, September 11, 1945; to Walter White from Irma Brown, December 5, 1945, p. 1–4; to Walter White from Irma Brown, November 20, 1945, pp. 3–5; all found in Clark Brooks Burglary Charges and Ollie Brown Courts-Martial, NAACP Papers, Part 09: Discrimination in the U.S. Armed Forces, 1918–1955, Soldier Trouble, Folder "Brooks, Clark, 1945–1947," Library of Congress1945. NAACP via Special Collections, University of Texas at Arlington Library (hereafter cited as "Special Collections UTA").
7. *Fort Worth Star Telegram*, July 13, 1942, pp. 1–2; December 31, 1944, p. 6.
8. *Fort Worth Star Telegram*, January 25, 1944, p. 1; March 22, 1943, p. 1; *Fort Worth Press,* July 12, 1945, p. 1; June 25, 1946, p. 1; June 28, 1946, p. 1.
9. *Fort Worth Star Telegram*, July 30, 1943, p. 8; July 5, 1944, p. 17; July 6, 1944, p. 4; September 22, 1943, p. 12.
10. *Fort Worth Star Telegram*, August 30, 1943, p. 20; October 14, 1943, p. 14; May 2, 1944, p. 10; May 31, 1944, p. 6.
11. *Fort Worth Star Telegram*, June 19, 1942, p. 5; June 19, 1943, p. 3.
12. *Fort Worth Star Telegram*, December 29, 1944, p. 8; May 27, 1944, p. 3; June 2, 1944, p. 25; March 14, 1944, p. 2; *Fort Worth Press,* March 24, 1945, p. 8; April 5, 1945, p. 10; April 24, 1945, p. 8; September 1, 1945, p. 10; "Council of Social Agencies of Fort Worth and Tarrant County, 1929–1956," R0068, File Annual Report 1941, Local History Archives, FWPL; "Council of Social Agencies of Fort Worth and Tarrant County, 1929–1956," R0068, File Annual Report 1941, March 1941, p. 3, Local History Archives, FWPL.
13. Merline Pitre, "At the Crossroads: Black Texas Women in the Civil Rights Era, 1930–1954," in *Black Women in Texas History*, ed. Bruce Glasrud and Merline Pite (College Station: Texas A&M Press, 2008), 136; *Fort Worth Star Telegram*, October 5, 1942, p. 5; June 27, 1944, p. 5; June 21, 1943, p. 19.
14. Joseph Abel, "Sunbelt Civil Rights: Race, Labor and Politics in the Fort Worth Aircraft Industry, 1940–1980" (PhD diss., Rice University, 2011), 4 and 152; *Fort Worth Star Telegram*, December 22, 1942, p. 32; June 4, 1944, p. 5; December 25, 1942, p. 12.
15. *Fort Worth Star Telegram*, May 20, 1944, p. 2; May 16, 1944, p. 11; July 16, 1944, p. 22.
16. *Fort Worth Star Telegram*, July 23, 1943, p. 26; December 21, 1944, p. 28; *New York Times*, June 2, 1946, p. 9.
17. *Fort Worth Star Telegram*, November 10, 1942, p. 4; May 8, 1944, p. 1; May 17, 1944, p. 22; June 19, 1944, p. 1; July 16, 1944, p. 22; July 28,

1944, p. 14; *Fort Worth Press,* April 20, 1944, p. 1; March 5, 1945, p. 2; Charles L. Zelden, *The Battle for the Black Ballot: Smith v. Allwright and the Defeat of the Texas All-White Primary,* Landmark Law Cases and American Society (Lawrence: University Press of Kansas, 2004), *passim.*

18. *Fort Worth Star Telegram*, February 7, 1942, p. 10; *New York Times*, June 2, 1946, p. 9.
19. *Fort Worth Star Telegram*, June 29, 1944, p. 5; *Fort Worth Press*, September 26, 1945, p. 9.
20. *Fort Worth Star Telegram*, September 12, 1944, p. 3; September 15, 1944, p. 8; September 12, 2021, p. 2C; June 29, 1944, p. 5.
21. *Fort Worth Star Telegram*, July 15, 1943, p. 3; October 27, 1943, p. 2.
22. *New York Times*, August 30, 1942, p. 100.

Notes for Chapter 5

1. *Fort Worth Star Telegram*, August 4, 1947, p. 8; June 7, 1942, p. 5; August 14, 1942, p. 21; *New York Times*, October 15, 1943, p. 21; Rich, *Between the World Wars*, pp. 209-211; Diann Campbell, "Women in Combat: The World War II Experience in the United States, Great Britain, Germany and the Soviet Union," *Journal of Military History* 57, no. 2 (April 1993): 301–23.
2. *Fort Worth Star Telegram*, April 19, 1942, pp. 1 and 8; April 27, 1942, p. 14; March 8, 1942, p. 2; May 26, 1942, p. 13; October 5, 1942, p. 5; December 17, 1942, p. 10; July 28, 1943, p. 1; August 20, 1944, p. 9.
3. *Fort Worth Star Telegram*, June 16, 1943, p. 1; September 28, 1943, p. 1; December 15, 1944, p. 20; January 15, 1943, p. 1.
4. *Fort Worth Star Telegram*, August 17, 1942, p. 35; *New York Times*, April 30, 1942, p. 16.
5. *Fort Worth Star Telegram*, September 18, 1942, p. 30; December 20, 1942, p. 46; September 29, 1942, p. 22.
6. Pate, *Arsenal of Defense*, 79; *Fort Worth Star Telegram*, July 3, 1942, p. 9; January 21, 1943, p. 2; November 30, 1942, p. 22.
7. *Fort Worth Star Telegram*, July 12, 1942, p. 21; August 20, 1942, p. 6; September 4, 1942, p. 1; September 6, 1943, p. 4; October 29, 1943, p. 8.
8. *Fort Worth Star Telegram*, October 4, 1943, pp. 1 and 10; November 3, 1943, p. 1; November 22, 1943, pp. 1 and 4.
9. "Council of Social Agencies of Fort Worth and Tarrant County, 1929–1956," R0068, File Annual Report 1943, Box 1, p. 7, Local History Archives, FWPL; Harold L. Smith, "'All Good Things Start with the Women': The Origins of the Texas Birth Control Movement," *Southwestern Historical Quarterly* 14, no. 3 (January 2011): 260 and 265.

10. *Fort Worth Star Telegram*, February 2, 1947, p. 2; December 22, 1942, p. 32.
11. *Fort Worth Star Telegram*, July 14, 1943, p. 17; November 14, 1943, p. 35.
12. *Fort Worth Star Telegram*, May 22, 1951, p. 2; July 18, 1951, p. 1; June 11, 1956, p. 14; March 10, 1958, p. 15.
13. *Fort Worth Star Telegram*, January 12, 1953, p. 1; November 17, 1954, p. 1; April 24, 1951, p. 4; November 23, 1954, p. 1; January 7, 1955, p. 1; November 8, 1951, p. 60.
14. *Fort Worth Star Telegram*, March 31, 1952, pp. 1–2; July 7, 1953, pp. 1 and 4; July 8, 1953, p. 1; December 13, 1953, p. 23; December 14, 1953, p. 2; May 30, 1954, p. 14; June 10, 1958, p. 21; June 13, 1958, p. 1; September 23, 1947, p. 1.
15. *Fort Worth Star Telegram*, January 23, 1953, p. 15.
16. *Fort Worth Press,* December 16, 1946, p. 7; *New York Times*, July 5, 1948, p. 18; *Fort Worth Star Telegram*, March 7, 1949, pp. 1–2.
17. *Fort Worth Star Telegram*, July 11, 1944, pp. 1 and 4; July 17, 1944, pp. 5 and 22; July 23, 1944, pp. 1 and 4.
18. *New York Times*, November 23, 1947, p. 83; *Fort Worth Star Telegram*, May 7, 1947, p. 4; January 20, 1948, p. 19.
19. *New York Times*, March 6, 1944, p. 10; April 19, 1944, p. 25; June 24, 1944, p. 18; November 30, 1944, p. 25; *Fort Worth Star Telegram*, May 7, 2023, pp. 1C–2C.

Notes for Chapter 6

1. *Fort Worth Press,* April 10, 1945, p. 1; *Fort Worth Star Telegram*, January 1, 1945, pp. 1, 4–7; January 6, 1945, p. 1; April 13, 1945, p. 7; April 15, 1945, Section 2, p. 1; April 19, 1945, p. 16; *This Month in Fort Worth* 22, no. 5 (May 1945): 16.
2. *Fort Worth Star Telegram*, January 2, 1945, p. 6; January 6, 1945, p. 5; March 11, 1945, Section 3, p. 1; March 23, 1945, Section 2, p. 9; April 8, 1945, Section 1, p. 5; December 7, 1945, pp. 1–2.
3. *Fort Worth Star Telegram*, January 2, 1945, pp. 5–6; March 1, 1945, p. 8; March 7, 1945, p. 9; March 11, 1945, Section 1, p. 5; March 24, 1945, p. 3; March 30, 1945, p. 4; June 2, 1945, p. 1; *Fort Worth Press,* March 8, 1945, p. 1.
4. *New York Times*, June 22, 1943, pp. 1 and 13; November 24, 1943, pp. 1 and 12; January 29, 1945, p. 22; October 6, 1946, pp. 1 and 12; October 11, 1946, p. 16; October 16, 1946, p. 1; *Fort Worth Star Telegram*, January 1, 1945, p. 5; February 19, 1946, p. 8; March 24, 1945, p. 3; March 30, 1945, p. 4; November 10, 1945, p. 1; H. S. Foster; "City's Metropolitan Area Needs 13,000 Houses to Care for New Population," *This Month in Fort Worth* 22, no. 9 (September 1945): 8.

5. *Fort Worth Star Telegram*, March 24, 1945, p. 3; March 30, 1945, p. 4; April 18, 1946, p. 1; July 1, 1946, p. 1; July 2, 1946, p. 1; July 6, 1946, p. 1; July 8, 1946, pp. 1–2; August 16, 1946, p. 1; *New York Times*, October 6, 1946, pp. 1 and 12; October 11, 1946, p. 16; October 16, 1946, p. 1.
6. *New York Times*, October 15, 1944, p. 112; January 12, 1944, p. 11; January 13, 1944, p. 12; March 24, 1944, p. 23; *Fort Worth Star Telegram*, June 6, 1944, p. 7.
7. McKay, *Texas and the Fair Deal*, 1–3 and 12–13; *Fort Worth Press*, March 16, 1945, p. 20; *Fort Worth Star Telegram*, February 26, 2023, p. 14A; February 2, 1945, p. 3; February 25, 1945, Section 1, p. 6; March 2, 1945, p. 16; July 7, 1946, pp. 1–8; "Housing," *This Month in Fort Worth* 22, no. 1 (January 1945): 17.
8. "Our Chamber of Commerce in the War," *This Month in Fort Worth* 22, no. 1 (January 1945): 9; "Labor Shortage Looms for Area," *This Month in Fort Worth* 22, no. 2 (February 1945): 12; *Fort Worth Star Telegram*, January 7, 1945, Section 2, p. 1; January 29, 1945, Section 1, p. 1; May 5, 1945, p. 1; May 2, 1945, pp. 1 and 5.
9. *Fort Worth Star Telegram*, January 3, 1945, p. 1; January 7, 1945, Section 2, p. 2; January 19, 1945, Section 2, p. 9; "Our Chamber of Commerce in the War," *This Month in Fort Worth* 22, no. 1 (January 1945): 7–9.
10. *Fort Worth Star Telegram*, February 1, 1945, p. 5; July 6, 1945, p. 1; January 19, 1945, Section 2, p. 9; February 19, 1945, p. 3; April 4, 1945, p 1; *Fort Worth Press,* August 1, 1945, p. 2; September 12, 1945, p. 1 September 26, 1945, pp. 1 and 3; December 26, 1945, p. 9.
11. *Fort Worth Star Telegram*, February 19, 1945, p. 3; April 4, 1945, p. 1; *Fort Worth Press,* April 4, 1945, p. 1.
12. *Fort Worth Star Telegram*, February 16, 1945, p. 8; March 22, 1945, p. 22; March 27, 1945, p. 2; Grant Harward, "History of Camp Barkeley: A Key Military Training Facility in WWII," *Handbook of Texas Online*, updated January 16, 2019, https://www.tshaonline.org/handbook/entries/camp-barkeley.
13. *New York Times*, March 12, 1943, p. 18; May 6, 1945, p. 13; May 26, 1945, p. 1; *Fort Worth Press*, August 15, 1945, p. 1; *Fort Worth Star Telegram*, May 9, 1945, p. 1; May 10, 1945, p. 8; May 24, 1945, p. 1; May 25, 1945, p. 1; June 2, 1945, p. 1; June 4, 1945, p. 3; June 5, 1945, p. 2; July 4, 1945, p. 8.
14. *Fort Worth Press*, August 11, 1945, p. 2; January 1, 1946, p. 2; *New York Times*, August 16, 1945, p. 13; September 10, 1945, pp. 1 and 32; August 11, 1946, p. 69.

15. "Housing," *This Month in Fort Worth* 22, no. 2 (February 1945): 17; Foster; "City's Metropolitan Area Needs 13,000 Houses"; *Fort Worth Star Telegram*, January 2, 1945, p. 6; January 5, 1945, p. 5; January 13, 1945, p. 3; January 21, 1945, Section 2, p. 1; February 2, 1945, p. 3; March 11, 1945, Section 3, p. 1; March 23, 1945, Section 2, p. 9; April 8, 1945, Section 1, p. 5; December 7, 1945, pp. 1–2.
16. *Fort Worth Star Telegram*, December 31, 1944, p. 6; January 1, 1946, p. 11; *Fort Worth Press*, December 31, 1945, p. 1.

Notes for Chapter 7

1. *Fort Worth Star Telegram*, September 5, 1945, p. 5; October 24, 1945, p. 8; November 9, 1945, p. 6; November 19, 1945, p. 8; December 9, 1945, p. 1; January 13, 1946, section 1, p. 9; February 15, 1946, p. 1; February 28, 1948, p. 1; William L. O'Neil, *American High: The Years of Confidence, 1945–1960* (New York: Free Press, 1986), 10; "Housing," *This Month in Fort Worth* 22, no. 10 (October 1945): 13.
2. "Agenda Item 15975, November 12, 1943," p. 447, TCCCM; *Fort Worth Star Telegram*, August 9, 1953, p. 4; July 23, 1959, p. 4.
3. *Fort Worth Star Telegram*, November 14, 1945, p. 1; November 30, 1945, pp. 1–2; February 1, 1946, p. 1; January 13, 1946, Section 1, p. 9; February 15, 1946, p. 1; December 22, 1945, pp. 1–2.
4. *Fort Worth Star Telegram*, November 9, 1945, p. 6; November 29, 1945, p. 1.
5. *Fort Worth Star Telegram*, December 21, 1945, p. 1; February 19, 1946, p. 7; April 2, 1946, pp. 7–8; April 25, 1946, p. 10; November 10, 1945, p. 1; "United States Help in Housing Is Sought," *This Month in Fort Worth* 22, no. 11 (November 1945): 6; H. S. Foster, "City's Metropolitan Area needs 13,000 Homes to Care for New Population," *This Month in Fort Worth* 22, no.9 (September 1945): 8.
6. *Fort Worth Star Telegram*, April 18, 1946, p. 1; July 1, 1946, p. 1; July 2, 1946, p. 1; July 6, 1946, p. 1; July 8, 1946, pp. 1–2; July 20, 1946, p. 1; August 16, 1946, p. 1.
7. *Fort Worth Star Telegram*, November 10, 1945, p. 1; February 10, 1945, p. 8; August 26, 1946, p. 1; September 7, 1946, p. 1; September 17, 1946, p. 1; October 4, 1946, p. 1; October 10, 1946, p. 4; October 11, 1946, p. 1; October 14, 1946, p. 1; October 15, 1946, p. 1; October 18, 1946, p. 1; October 22, 1946, p. 1; *New York Times*, October 16, 1946, p. 1.
8. *Fort Worth Star Telegram*, October 20, 1946, p. 1; October 25, 1946, p. 1; October 26, 1946, p. 1; November 1, 1946, p. 1; November 10, 1946, p. 1; December 16, 1946, p. 1.
9. *Fort Worth Press*, December 11, 1946, p. 4.

10. *Fort Worth Star Telegram*, February 1, 1946, pp. 1 and 8; February 9, 1946, p. 1; February 11, 1946, p. 2; February 27, 1946, p. 2; April 1, 1946, p. 14.
11. *Fort Worth Star Telegram*, December 13, 1946, p. 2; January 1, 1947, p. 4; O'Neill, *American High*, 18–19.
12. *Fort Worth Star Telegram*, July 16, 1945, p. 1; January 1, 1946, p. 7; January 7, 1946, p. 1; January 11, 1946, p. 1; January 16, 1946, p. 1; January 18, 1946, p. 7; February 2, 1946, p. 1; May 9, 1946, p. 8.
13. *Fort Worth Star Telegram*, June 23, 1945, p. 1; July 22, 1945, Section 1, p. 1; August 5, 1945, Section 1, p. 4; September 20, 1945, p. 2; October 4, 1945, p. 1; October 5, 1945, p. 1; November 5, 1945, p. 1; June 30, 2024, pp. 1C and 3C; Homer Cryer, "The President's Message," *This Month in Fort Worth* 22, no. 1 (January 1945): 6.
14. *New York Times*, January 3, 1946, pp. 1 and 13; January 27, 1946, pp. 1 and 5; December 20, 1946, p. 6.
15. Maurice G. Lambert, *Memories of Liberator Village* (n.p.: Memorabiliacs Press, 2006), 13; *Fort Worth Press*, February 25, 1946, p. 1; *Fort Worth Star Telegram*, February 25, 1946, pp. 1–2; March 28, 1946, pp. 1–2; April 18, 1946, p. 4; May 2, 1946, p. 1; May 6, 1946, p. 1.
16. *Fort Worth Press*, May 1, 1946, p. 1; May 2, 1946, p. 1; *Fort Worth Star Telegram*, May 1, 1946, pp. 1 and 4; May 2, 1946, p. 1; October 20, 1946, Section 1, p. 3.
17. *Fort Worth Press*, May 2, 1946, p. 1; May 7, 1946, pp. 1–2; *Fort Worth Star Telegram*, May 2, 1946, p. 1; May 3, 1946, p. 1; May 4, 1946, p. 1; May 6, 1946, p. 1; May 7, 1946, p. 6.
18. *Fort Worth Press*, May 10, 1946, p. 1; May 18, 1946, p. 1; *Fort Worth Star Telegram*, May 10, 1946, p. 1; May 11, 1946, p. 1; May 13, 1946, p. 1; May 14, 1946, pp. 1 and 4; May 18, 1946, pp. 1–2; July 8, 1947, p. 1.
19. *Fort Worth Star Telegram*, October 13, 1948, p. 1.
20. *Fort Worth Press*, October 9, 1946, p. 1; December 18, 1946, p. 1; December 27, 1946, p. 1; Knight, *Outpost*, 213; *Fort Worth Star Telegram*, December 18, 1946, p. 1; January 4, 1947, p. 4; April 18, 1948, p. 1; April 9, 1947, p. 1; April 6, 1949, pp. 1 and 4.
21. *Fort Worth Star Telegram*, April 16, 1947, p. 8; April 30, 1947, p. 24; September 18, 1947, p. 1; *Fort Worth Press*, February 14, 1946, p. 1.
22. *Fort Worth Star Telegram*, May 7, 1947, p. 6; June 18, 1947, p. 1; June 4, 1947, p. 1; September 17, 1947, p. 1.
23. *Fort Worth Press*, April 11, 1946, p. 8; *Fort Worth Star Telegram*, September 17, 1947, p. 1; May 28, 1948, p. 2; June 24, 1948, p. 1; January 15, 1948, p. 7; April 14, 1948, p. 1.
24. *Fort Worth Star Telegram*, May 2, 1947, p. 1; October 10, 1948, p. 6.

25. *Fort Worth Star Telegram*, August 21, 1947, p. 2; July 23, 1947, p. 1.
26. *Fort Worth Press*, March 20, 1946, p. 1; *Fort Worth Star Telegram*, October 29, 1947, pp. 1 and 4; November 22, 1947, p. 1; March 5, 1948, p. 1; July 2, 1948, p. 1; July 10, 1948, p. 1; February 26, 1947, p. 11.
27. *Fort Worth Star Telegram*, February 8, 1947, p. 3; February 12, 1947, p. 1; October 8, 1947, p. 15; September 22, 1949, p. 1; August 21, 1947, pp. 1 and 6; September 20, 1949, p. 1.
28. *Fort Worth Star Telegram*, April 19, 1948, p. 2; March 29, 1950, p. 6; December 26, 1947, p. 9; September 30, 1948, p. 10; January 19, 1945, p. 5; February 19, 1945, p. 3; April 4, 1945, p. 1; *Fort Worth Press*, August 1, 1945, p. 2; September 12, 1945, pp. 1 and 2; December 26, 1947, p. 9; August 20, 1946, p. 16.
29. Rich, *Between the World Wars*, 22; *Fort Worth Star Telegram*, August 28, 1947, p. 1.
30. *Fort Worth Press*, August 30, 1946, p. 1; Rich, *Between the World Wars*, 22; *New York Times*, May 18, 1949, p. 21; *Fort Worth Star Telegram*, April 22, 1947, p. 23; May 16, 1949, p. 2; May 17, 1949, p. 1; May 18, 1949, p. 1; May 20, 1949, p. 1.
31. *Fort Worth Star Telegram*, December 28, 1948, p. 8; July 13, 1949, p. 1; July 24, 1949, p. 1; October 30, 1949, pp. 1–481; "Fort Worth Fiesta-cade" souvenir program, July 16–23, 1949. Local History Archives, FWPL.
32. *Fort Worth Star Telegram*, September 19, 1948, p. 11; September 19, 1942, p. 10; November 28, 1948, p. 14; *Fort Worth Press*, January 4, 1945, p. 1.
33. *Fort Worth Star Telegram*, May 7, 1945, p. 5; May 21, 1947, pp. 1 and 4.
34. *Fort Worth Star Telegram*, October 22, 1948, pp. 1 and 6.
35. *Fort Worth Star Telegram*, September 9, 1947, pp. 1 and 6; June 4, 1947, p. 1; June 5, 1947, p. 1; June 19, 1947, p. 1.
36. Daniel J. Haase, *Gateway to the West: A Historical Look at the Development of East Fort Worth and Its Neighborhoods* (Fort Worth: pub. by author, 2019), 29; *Fort Worth Star Telegram*, March 9, 1948, p. 15; September 23, 1948, pp. 2 and 26; September 30, 1948, pp. 1 and 10; September 29, 1949, p. 24; December 4, 1949, pp. 74–94.

Notes for Chapter 8

1. *Fort Worth Press*, January 10, 1946, p. 2; February 25, 1946, p. 19; *Fort Worth Star Telegram*, May 2, 1947, p. 1; December 12, 1950, p. 24; December 19, 1950, p. 1.
2. *Fort Worth Press*, January 12, 1946, pp. 1–2; *Fort Worth Star Telegram*, January 22, 1946, p. 1.

3. *Fort Worth Star Telegram*, March 10, 1949, p. 1; March 11, 1949, p. 1; March 12, 1949, p. 1; *New York Times*, March 11, 1949, p. 3; March 12, 1949, p. 14.
4. *Fort Worth Star Telegram*, April 28, 1949, pp. 1 and 10.
5. *Fort Worth Star Telegram*, April 29, 1949, pp. 1 and 4; April 30, 1949, pp. 1 and 4; May 2, 1949, p. 1; May 3, 1949, p. 1; June 22, 1949, p. 1; August 20, 1959, p. 1.
6. *Fort Worth Star Telegram*, November 23, 1950, p. 28; October 17, 1950, p. 2; February 24, 1950, p. 11; October 6, 1950, p. 6; November 10, 1950, p. 1; February 14, 1951, p. 11.
7. *Fort Worth Star Telegram*, March 14, 1950, p. 1; November 8, 1950, p. 2; December 16, 1950, p. 2.
8. *Fort Worth Star Telegram*, December 9, 1947, p. 1; January 14, 1948, pp. 1 and 8; January 31, 1948, p. 1; February 5, 1948, pp. 1 and 6.
9. *Fort Worth Star Telegram*, February 10, 1948, p. 10.
10. *Fort Worth Press*, January 5, 1946, p. 1.
11. *Fort Worth Star Telegram*, December 9, 1947, p. 6; October 30, 1947, p. 1; March 5, 1950, p. 5; April 14, 1950, p. 6.
12. *Fort Worth Star Telegram*, July 13, 1948, p. 1; March 15, 1948, p. 9; January 31, 1950, p. 30.
13. *Fort Worth Star Telegram*, February 15, 1947, p. 1.
14. *Fort Worth Star Telegram*, March 15, 1948, p. 1; July 16, 1948, p. 12; July 8, 1948, p. 8; July 13, 1948, p. 1; March 5, 1950, p. 5; January 25, 1950, p. 8; July 20, 1950, p. 22.
15. *Fort Worth Star Telegram*, September 10, 1948, p. 1; July 8, 1949, p. 8.
16. *Fort Worth Star Telegram*, August 4, 1947, p. 8.
17. Polito, *Savage Art*, 106.
18. *Fort Worth Star Telegram*, April 3, 1946, p. 1; April 8, 1946, p. 1; *Fort Worth Press*, June 14, 1946, p. 17; October 29, 1946, p. 14; December 3, 1946, p. 1.
19. *Fort Worth Star Telegram*, April 11, 1950, p. 1; January 8, 1947, p. 1; August 11, 1947, p. 1; Arnold, *Gamblers & Gangsters*, 85.
20. *Fort Worth Star Telegram*, August 14, 1947, pp. 1 and 4; August 25, 1947, p. 30; August 23, 1947, p. 1; August 29, 1947, p. 1; August 28, 1947, p. 1.
21. *Fort Worth Star Telegram*, September 29, 1948, p. 4; October 8, 1947, p. 1; January 7, 1949, p. 2.
22. *Fort Worth Star Telegram*, May 6, 1949, p. 1; May 7, 1949, p. 1; August 11, 1947, p. 1; May 13, 1949, pp. 1 and 4.
23. *Fort Worth Star Telegram*, May 16, 1949, p. 2; May 11, 1949, p. 1; May 12, 1949, pp. 1 and 10; May 14, 1949, p. 1; October 19, 1949, p. 1; May 13, 1949, pp. 1 and 4.

24. *Fort Worth Star Telegram*, May 13, 1949, pp. 1 and 4; May 15, 1949, p. 2; May 18, 1949, p. 1; May 23, 1949, p. 13; May 25, 1949, pp. 1–2; May 30, 1949, pp. 1–2; May 31, 1949, pp. 1 and 4; June 1, 1949, p. 4; July 8, 1949, p. 1.
25. *Fort Worth Star Telegram*, August 22, 1949, p. 1; August 9, 1949, p. 10.
26. *Morning Sentinel* (Waterville, ME), April 29, 1986, p. 23; *Dallas Morning News*, October 8, 1950, pp. 1 and 6; *Fort Worth Star Telegram*, September 20, 1949, p. 1; September 22, 1949, p. 1.
27. *Fort Worth Star Telegram*, October 2, 1950, p. 1; October 9, 1950, p. 1; October 13, 1950, p. 7; October 16, 1950, p. 1; October 20, 1950, p. 10; October 25, 1950, p. 2.
28. *Fort Worth Star Telegram*, October 21, 1950, p. 1; October 27, 1950, p. 12; November 25, 1950, pp. 1–2; August 23, 1950, p. 1.
29. Arnold, *Gamblers & Gangsters*, 122–32; Elston Brooks, *Don't Dry-Clean My Blackjack* (Fort Worth: Branch-Smith, 1979), 19–29.
30. Arnold, *Gamblers & Gangsters*, 10, 13, 33, 40, 43, 50–51; *Fort Worth Star Telegram*, January 21, 1948, pp. 1 and 6; January 22, 1948, pp. 1 and 6; January 24, 1948, p. 1.
31. *Fort Worth Star Telegram*, March 10, 1948, p. 1; March 8, 1948, pp. 1 and 4; March 9, 1948, p. 1; August 24, 1948, p. 1; August 13, 1948, p. 14; Arnold, *Gamblers & Gangsters*, 124–26.
32. *Fort Worth Star Telegram*, October 1, 1948, pp. 1 and 6; October 2, 1948, p. 1; November 23, 1950, pp. 1 and 10; Arnold, *Gamblers & Gangsters*, 125–26.
33. Rich, *Between the World Wars*, 179; *Fort Worth Star Telegram*, November 22, 1950, pp. 1–3.
34. *Fort Worth Star Telegram*, November 23, 1950, p. 1; November 25, 1950, pp. 1–2; December 6, 1950, pp. 1–2; December 8, 1950, pp. 1 and 4; December 9, 1950, p. 1; December 11, 1950, 1; Arnold, *Gamblers & Gangsters*, 24–31, 118–29.
35. *Fort Worth Star Telegram*, November 23, 1950, p.1; December 6, 1950, pp. 1–2; November 13, 1950, p. 10; July 24, 1950, p. 1; Arnold, *Gamblers & Gangsters*, 122–23; Brooks, *Don't Dry-Clean My Blackjack*, 19–29.

Notes for Chapter 9

1. *Fort Worth Press*, May 16, 1945, p. 1; January 3, 1946, p. 1; *Fort Worth Star Telegram*, May 23, 1945, p. 1; December 7, 1949, p. 1; August 27, 1950, p. 4.
2. *Fort Worth Star Telegram*, June 8, 1947, p. 8; April 15, 1947, p. 1; November 25, 1949, p. 6.

3. *Fort Worth Star Telegram*, January 1, 1947, pp. 1–2; January 1, 1948, pp. 1 and 8; April 12, 1947, p. 2; January 13, 1948, p. 4; January 2, 1950, p. 1; January 6, 1950, p. 14; January 12, 1950, p. 18; January 17, 1950, p. 1.
4. *Fort Worth Star Telegram*, January 1, 1947, p. 1; January 6, 1947, p. 1; October 24, 1947, p. 31; May 16, 1950, p. 16.
5. *Fort Worth Star Telegram*, May 8, 1947, p. 1; July 26, 1947, p. 1; May 12, 1947, p. 4; May 16, 1947, p. 1.
6. *Fort Worth Star Telegram*, January 16, 1948, p. 1; August 2, 1949, p. 1; October 14, 1949, p. 1; November 20, 1950, pp. 1–2; November 30, 1950, p. 6.
7. *Fort Worth Star Telegram*, August 22, 1950, p. 5.
8. *Fort Worth Star Telegram*, December 2, 1949, p. 10; December 9, 1949, p. 1; December 23, 1949, pp. 1–2.
9. *Fort Worth Star Telegram*, November 6, 1950, pp. 1 and 4; November 16, 1950, p. 1; October 11, 1950, p. 1; October 13, 1950, p. 1; October 26, 1950, p. 1.
10. *Fort Worth Star Telegram*, January 15, 1947, p. 1; January 26, 1947, p. 6; January 28, 1947, p. 8; December 12, 1947, p. 14; March 9, 1950, p. 1.
11. *Fort Worth Press*, April 30, 1946, p. 1; *Fort Worth Star Telegram*, December 13, 1947, pp. 1–2; February 28, 1950, pp. 1–2; April 24, 1950, p. 16.
12. *Fort Worth Press*, November 20, 1946, p. 1; April 11, 1946, p. 5; *Fort Worth Star Telegram*, February 18, 1947, p. 8.
13. *Fort Worth Star Telegram*, January 23, 1949, p. 77; January 11, 1947, p. 3; April 16, 1948, p. 8; April 21, 1948, p. 4.
14. *Fort Worth Star Telegram*, January 21, 1947, pp. 1 and 4; May 27, 1950, p. 2.
15. *Fort Worth Star Telegram*, January 19, 1945, Section 2, p. 9; May 8, 1947, p. 14; August 2, 1947, p. 1; September 19, 1947, p. 1; September 20, 1947, p. 1; October 3, 1947, p. 1.
16. *Fort Worth Star Telegram*, November 21, 1947, p. 13; November 13, 1947, p. 1; November 26, 1947, p. 2; December 3, 1947, p. 1; April 6, 1948, p. 14; June 11, 1948, p. 1; November 3, 1949, p. 39; February 11, 1950, p. 2; *Fort Worth Press*, December 11, 1945, p. 5.
17. *Fort Worth Star Telegram*, January 6, 1947, p. 8; December 3, 1948, p. 14.
18. *Fort Worth Star Telegram*, May 4, 1948, p. 14; May 5, 1948, pp. 1 and 10; June 26, 1948, p. 1; July 7, 1948, pp. 1 and 6; July 8, 1948, pp. 1 and 6; July 9, 1948, pp. 1 and 8; March 16, 1949, p. 1; April 3, 1949, p. 6; May 22, 1950, p. 1; June 9, 1950, pp. 1 and 4.
19. *Fort Worth Star Telegram*, November 6, 1948, pp. 1 and 4; November 19, 1948, pp. 1 and 6; November 20, 1948, pp. 1 and 4.

20. *Fort Worth Star Telegram*, November 30, 1948, pp. 1 and 4; December 1, 1948, pp. 1 and 6; December 2, 1948, pp. 1 and 8; December 3, 1948, p. 1; December 14, 1948, p. 1 and 4; August 8, 1949, p. 1.
21. *Fort Worth Star Telegram*, September 23, 1948, pp. 1 and 8; September 25, 1948, p. 1; September 27, 1948, p. 1; February 3, 1950, pp. 1 and 4.
22. *Fort Worth Star Telegram*, October 10, 1949, pp. 1–2; October 11, 1949, p. 1.
23. *Fort Worth Star Telegram*, January 24, 1947, p. 1; October 9, 1947, p. 1; April 11, 1947, pp. 1–2; April 19, 1947, p. 1.

Notes for Chapter 10

1. *Fort Worth Star Telegram*, January 20, 1947, p. 2; March 7, 1947, p. 15; September 15, 1947, p. 3; August 2, 1948, p. 4; December 22, 1950, p. 17.
2. *Fort Worth Press*, June 19, 1946, pp. 1–2; April 10, 1946, p. 11; *Fort Worth Star Telegram*, January 23, 1946, p. 20; February 6, 1948, p. 2; January 25, 1948, p. 24.
3. *New York Times*, July 25, 1949, p. 15.
4. Richard Selcer, *A History of Fort Worth in Black and White: 165 Years of African American Life* (Denton: University of North Texas Press, 2015), 376; Reby Cary Papers, Box 1, File 18, Local History Archives, FWPL; *Fort Worth Star Telegram*, August 19, 1948, p. 2; August 26, 1947, p. 8; August 28, 1947, p. 12; November 7, 1947, p. 4.
5. *Fort Worth Star Telegram*, April 22, 1948, p. 18; Merline Pitre, "At the Crossroads," in Glasrud and Pitre, *Black Women in Texas History*, 131.
6. *Fort Worth Star Telegram*, October 13, 1949, p. 1; April 18, 1950, p. 28; *Fort Worth Mind*, June 23, 1950, p. 1; Tina Cannon, "Cowtown and the Color Line: Desegregating Fort Worth's Public Schools" (PhD diss., Texas Christian University 2009), 70–71.
7. *Fort Worth Star Telegram*, September 5, 1950, p. 1; September 6, 1950, p. 1; "Mosier Valley Study," Planning Department, City of Fort Worth, 1985, p. 1; George N. Green, "The History of Mosier Valley: A Community of Resilience and Heritage," *Handbook of Texas Online*, updated December 8, 2020, https://www.tshaonline.org/handbook/entries/mosier-valley-tx.
8. *Fort Worth Star Telegram*, March 3, 1947, p. 1; September 4, 1950, p. 1.
9. "Council of Social Agencies of Fort Worth and Tarrant County, 1929–1956," R0068, Annual Report 1947, p. 6, Local History Archives, FWPL; *Fort Worth Star Telegram*, August 4, 1947, p. 17; April 8, 1949, p. 1; February 11, 2024, p. 1C–2C.

10. *Fort Worth Press,* March 19, 1946, p. 7; *Fort Worth Star Telegram,* October 21, 1947, p. 4; November 18, 1949, p. 14; April 9, 1949, p. 1; April 22, 1949, p. 1.
11. Letter to Stuart Symington, secretary of the Air Force, December 8, 1949, p. 1, and attached affidavit, pp. 1–3, "Wellington G. Valentine," NAACP Collection, 1949–1955, Legal File, Soldier Troubles, Special Collections, UTA.
12. *Fort Worth Star Telegram*, January 16, 1947, p. 10; November 12, 1949, p. 3; November 16, 1943, p. 1; February 20, 1950, p. 1; February 24, 1950, p. 1; March 13, 1950, p. 1.
13. *Fort Worth Star Telegram*, June 3, 1950, p. 2; June 14, 1950, pp. 1 and 4; June 15, 1950, p. 1; November 22, 1950, p. 11.
14. *New York Times*, June 2, 1946, p. 9; *Fort Worth Star Telegram*, June 30, 1949, p. 6; February 12, 1950, p. 15; February 25, 2023, pp. 1C-2C.
15. *Fort Worth Star Telegram*, July 30, 1950, p. 10.
16. Munchus-Forde, "History of the Negro," 45–47, 87–88.
17. *Fort Worth Press*, March 21, 1946, p. 1; *Fort Worth Star Telegram*, May 26, 1948, p. 6; July 1, 1948, p. 1; May 28, 1948, p. 1; June 9, 1948, p. 12.
18. *Fort Worth Press*, January 28, 1946, p. 5; *Fort Worth Star Telegram*, July 30, 1950, p. 10; January 16, 1947, p. 10; July 2, 1947, p. 1; June 7, 1950, pp. 1–2; Selcer, *Fort Worth in Black and White*, 395-400.
19. *Fort Worth Star Telegram*, September 28, 1950, p. 26; September 15, 1950, p. 16; February 19, 1950, p. 8; April 4, 1948, p. 37; *Fort Worth Mind*, January 18, 1947, p. 7; January 20, 1947, p. 1.
20. *Fort Worth Star Telegram*, January 14, 1947, p. 2; February 12, 1950, p. 15; June 2, 1947, p. 4; June 25, 1948, p. 4; September 27, 1950, p. 10.
21. *Fort Worth Star Telegram*, February 10, 1947, p. 1; February 13, 1947, p. 14; February 14, 1947, pp. 1 and 8; February 22, 1947, p. 1; February 27, 1947, p. 6; April 3, 1947, p. 14; June 22, 1947, p. 3.
22. *Fort Worth Star Telegram*, August 4, 1948, p. 2; August 3, 1948, p. 4; January 16, 1950, p. 1; July 6, 1949, p. 1.
23. *Fort Worth Star Telegram*, February 23, 1948, pp. 1–2; March 8, 1948, p. 4; March 9, 1948, p. 12; June 23, 1949, p. 14; *Fort Worth Press*, December 4, 1946, p. 9; *Fort Worth Mind*, October 28, 1951, p. 1; November 23, 1951, p. 7.
24. *Fort Worth Press*, October 1, 1945, p. 3; *Fort Worth Star Telegram*, September 13, 1945, pp. 1 and 6; August 16, 1948, pp. 1–2; August 17, 1948, p. 1; August 22, 1948, p. 1; August 24, 1948, p. 1; August 31, 1948, p. 1; June 22, 1949, p. 1.
25. *Fort Worth Star Telegram*, March 6, 1950, p. 1; September 30, 1950, p. 2; April 4, 1950, p. 16; April 20, 1950, p. 1.

26. *New York Times*, April 18, 1948, p. 112; October 28, 1949, p. 25; *Fort Worth Star Telegram*, April 27, 1948, p. 15.
27. *Fort Worth Star Telegram*, March 7, 1949, pp. 1–2; March 8, 1949, p. 28; March 26, 1949, p. 1; March 30, 1949, pp. 1 and 6; April 3, 1949, pp. 1–2.
28. *Fort Worth Mind*, July 7, 1950, p. 1; *Fort Worth Star Telegram*, July 5, 1950, pp. 1–2; July 12, 1950, p. 8; Reby Cary, *"The Apex." Beyond the Chaos: Unchained Aspirations of African-Americans in Fort Worth* (Fort Worth: pub. by author, 2017), 16–24; *New York Times*, July 16, 1948, p. 12.
29. *Fort Worth Star Telegram*, January 26, 1947, p. 2; June 22, 1947, p. 9.
30. Kenneth N. Hopkins, "The Early Development of the Hispanic Community in Fort Worth and Tarrant County, Texas, 1849–1949," *East Texas Historical Review* 38, no. 2 (October 2000): 64–65; *Fort Worth Star Telegram*, July 8, 1947, p. 8: May 9, 1950, p. 1; October 12, 1947, p. 9; January 9, 1948, p. 12; November 10, 1948, p. 14.
31. *New York Times*, November 10, 1948, p. 14.

Notes for Chapter 11

1. *Fort Worth Star Telegram*, February 16, 1945, p. 8; March 22, 1945 p. 2; March 27, 1945, p. 2.
2. *Fort Worth Star Telegram*, May 9, 1945, p. 1; August 1, 1945, p. 6; August 2, 1945, p. 1.
3. *Fort Worth Star Telegram*, February 26, 2023, p. 14A; May 10, 1945, p. 8, May 13, 1945, Section 1, p. 4; May 26, 1945, p. 1; May 30, 1945, p. 9; June 7, 1945, p. 5; February 18, 1946, p. 3; August 14, 1945, p. 1; August 15, 1945, p. 1; August 17, 1945, p. 5; August 18, 1945, p. 2; September 1, 1945, p. 1; September 28, 1945, p. 1.
4. *Fort Worth Star Telegram*, August 12, 1945, Section 1, p. 1; August 17, 1945, pp. 8–9; August 17, 1945, p. 2; August 21, 1945, p. 9; August 28, 1945, p. 16; August 31, 1945, p. 1; October 14, 1945, Section 1, p. 9.
5. *Fort Worth Star Telegram*, January 2, 1947, p. 5; May 3, 1946, p. 10; February 1, 1946, p. 1; February 24, 1946, Section 2, p. 9; December 3, 1946, p. 2; "Postwar Planning Underway at Globe Aircraft," *This Month in Fort Worth* 22, no. 1 (January 1945): 12.
6. *Fort Worth Star Telegram*, August 12, 1945, Section 1, p. 6; August 28, 1945, p. 16; October 26, 1945, p. 12; October 31, 1945, p. 1; November 19, 1945, p. 2; May 9, 1946, p. 8; August 18, 1945, p. 2; September 2, 1945, Section 1, p. 2; September 9, 1945, Section 1, p. 2; October 3, 1945, p. 2; November 11, 1945, pp. 1 and 4; December 2, 1945, p. 1; Knight, *Outpost*, 213; "Postwar Highway Plans Outlined," *This Month in Fort Worth* 22, no. 7 (July 1945): 7.

7. *Fort Worth Star Telegram*, May 25, 1945, p. 1; June 2, 1945, p. 1; June 6, 1945, p. 9; August 4, 1945, Section 1, p. 4; August 17, 1945, pp. 1 and 8; Homer Cryer, "The President's Message," *This Month in Fort Worth* 22, no. 1 (January 1945): 6; "Our Chamber of Commerce in the War," *This Month in Fort Worth* 22, no. 1 (January 1945): 8–9; Knight, *Outpost*, 213.
8. *Fort Worth Star Telegram*, February 2, 1945, p. 3; February 25, 1945, Section 1, p. 6; March 2, 1945, p. 16; "Housing," *This Month in Fort Worth* 22, no. 2 (February 1945): 17; February 16, 1946, p. 2; February 24, 1946, Section 1, p. 9.
9. *Fort Worth Star Telegram*, January 1, 1947, pp. 1, 9, 15; January 10, 1947, p. 10; January 26, 1947, p. 1; September 28, 1947, p. 11; "Fort Worth Plans for the Future," *Fort Worth Chamber of Commerce*, 1945, 5; *Fort Worth Magazine* 24, no. 5 (May 1950): 8; *Fort Worth Magazine* 25, no. 7 (July 1950): 7.
10. *Fort Worth Star Telegram*, January 6, 1947, p. 4; March 18, 1949, p. 1.
11. *Fort Worth Star Telegram*, July 29, 1949, p. 6; May 9, 1948, p. 34.
12. "Fort Worth: Hub of the Southwest," *Fort Worth Chamber of Commerce*, 1948, 7; *Fort Worth Star Telegram*, April 27, 1947, p. 10; April 11, 1948, p. 32; June 11, 1950, pp. 1–2; November 15, 1950, p. 42; *Fort Worth Magazine*, Vol. 25, no. 7 (July 1950), pp. 7 and 18.
13. *Fort Worth Star Telegram*, June 27, 1950, pp. 1–2; July 23, 1950, p. 2; January 1, 1947, p. 4; January 9, 1947, p. 1; January 13, 1947, p. 1; December 19, 1949, p. 1; January 1, 1949, p. 9; January 3, 1948, p. 1.
14. Knight, *Outpost*, 213; *Fort Worth Star Telegram*, February 4, 1945, Section 1, p. 2; March 2, 1945, p. 16; March 27, 1945, p. 2; May 3, 1946, p. 10; "Our Chamber of Commerce in the War," *This Month in Fort Worth* 22, no. 1 (January 1945): 11; "Fort Worth Leads in War Production," *This Month in Fort Worth* 22, no. 3 (March 1945): 11; Buckley B. Paddock, ed. *History of Texas: Fort Worth and the Texas Northwest Edition*, 4 vols. (Chicago: Lewis Publishing, 1922), 2:238.
15. Paddock, *History of Texas*, 2:238; Knight, *Outpost*, 212; "Fort Worth Plans for the Future," *Fort Worth Chamber of Commerce*, 1945, 3; *Fort Worth Star Telegram*, December 4, 1945, Section 1, p. 2; March 2, 1945, p. 16; March 27, 1945, p. 2; May 3, 1945, p. 10; "Our Chamber of Commerce in the War," *This Month in Fort Worth* 22, no. 3 (March 1945): 11.
16. *Fort Worth Star Telegram,* February 16, 1941, pp. 1 and 4; January 15, 1942, p. 1; February 12, 1947, p. 9; March 9, 1947, p. 4; May 11, 1947, p. 4; March 2, 1948, p. 7; *New York Times*, February 16, 1941, p. 103.
17. *Fort Worth Star Telegram*, December 20, 1949, p. 1.
18. *Fort Worth Press*, August 11, 1945, p. 7.

Notes for Chapter 13

1. *Fort Worth Star Telegram*, January 21, 1952, p. 2; April 1, 1951, pp. 1 and 6; February 28, 1951, p. 1; April 6, 1951, p. 1.
2. *Fort Worth Star Telegram*, December 19, 1952, pp. 1 and 16; December 28, 1952, p. 10; March 3, 1955, p. 1; February 25, 1953, p. 1; February 26, 1953, p. 1; April 7, 1953, pp. 1 and 4; April 8, 1953, pp. 1 and 4; April 17, 1953, p. 1; April 22, 1953, p. 1.
3. *Fort Worth Star Telegram*, September 26, 1953, pp. 1–2; December 13, 1953, pp. 1–2.
4. *Fort Worth Star Telegram*, March 21, 1955, p. 1; March 23, 1955, p. 40; April 6, 1955, p. 1.
5. *Fort Worth Star Telegram*, January 2, 1951, p. 6; September 8, 1952, p. 2; March 11, 1952, p. 3; August 5, 1952, p. 7; July 19, 1953, p. 6; November 14, 1954, p. 15.
6. *Fort Worth Star Telegram*, April 2, 1952, p. 1; September 19, 1953, p. 1.
7. *Fort Worth Star Telegram*, September 14, 1951, p. 1; October 8, 1951, p. 1; October 9, 1951, p. 1; October 10, 1951, p. 1; October 13, 1951, pp. 1–2.
8. *Fort Worth Star Telegram*, January 4, 1952, p. 1; September 16, 1952, pp. 1 and 4.
9. *Fort Worth Star Telegram*, September 17, 1952, p. 1; September 21, 1959, p. 2.
10. *New York Times*, June 18, 1955, p. 8; *Fort Worth Star Telegram*, August 7, 1951, p. 16; January 5, 1951, p. 14; January 14, 1951, p. 14; June 14, 1954, pp. 1–2.
11. Brooks, *Don't Dry-Clean My Blackjack*, 32–34; *Fort Worth Star Telegram*, June 22, 1953, p. 1; March 4, 1954, p. 1; April 17, 1953, p. 8.
12. *Fort Worth Star Telegram*, July 11, 1951, p. 20; May 16, 1954, p. 1; September 10, 1951, p. 10; September 13, 1954, p. 10.
13. *Fort Worth Star Telegram*, May 10, 1949, p. 16; November 8, 1953, p. 12; July 31, 1952, p. 24; August 3, 1952, p. 15; August 6, 1952, p. 30; August 7, 1952, p. 1; August 8, 1952, p. 8; April 12, 1958, p. 1.
14. *Fort Worth Star Telegram*, August 14, 1952, p. 20; August 2, 1955, p. 1; August 3, 1955, p. 1; August 4, 1955, p. 1; August 6, 1955, p. 1; August 21, 1952, p. 10.
15. *Fort Worth Star Telegram*, June 16, 1951, pp. 1–2; June 17, 1951, pp. 1–2, 4.
16. *Fort Worth Star Telegram*, August 20, 1952, pp. 1–2; February 18, 1955, pp. 1 and 14; June 24, 1955, p. 1; May 23, 1952, p. 1; *New York Times*, June 24, 1955, p. 24.
17. *Fort Worth Star Telegram*, June 27, 1951, p. 6; January 15, 1953, p. 13.

18. *Fort Worth Star Telegram*, July 18, 1951, p. 1; September 21, 1951, p. 1; April 15, 1951, p. 27; December 30, 1951, p. 10; January 3, 1952, p. 1; August 3, 1952, p. 15; March 7, 1954, p. 8; January 3, 1956, p. 1.
19. *Fort Worth Star Telegram*, July 17, 1952, p. 1; December 23, 1952, p. 5; December 28, 1952, p. 1; May 12, 1953, p. 21; July 23, 1952, p. 21; August 17, 1952, p. 9.
20. *Fort Worth Star Telegram*, March 27, 1951, p. 1; October 25, 1951, p. 1.
21. *Fort Worth Star Telegram*, April 25, 1953, p. 1; April 26, 1953, p. 1; November 14, 1954, p. 1; November 22, 1954, p. 1; November 29, 1954, p. 1; April 28, 1958, p. 4; *New York Times*, December 20, 1953, p. 78.
22. *Fort Worth Star Telegram*, August 5, 1951, p. 1; January 23, 1954, p. 3; June 25, 1952, p. 1; July 15, 1951, p. 22; *New York Times*, August 22, 1953, p. 23.
23. *Fort Worth Star Telegram*, February 5, 1954, p. 1; February 14, 1955, p. 1.
24. *Fort Worth Star Telegram*, September 19, 1954, p. 1; September 20, 1954, p. 1; September 23, 1954, p. 2; October 4, 1954, pp. 1–2; December 31, 1957, p. 1; February 24, 1958, p. 1; *New York Times*, October 4, 1954, p. 29.

Notes for Chapter 14

1. *Fort Worth Star Telegram*, January 10, 1951, p. 1; April 4, 1951, p. 1; July 17, 1951, p. 26; June 5, 1952, p. 13.
2. *Fort Worth Star Telegram*, April 22, 1951, p. 1; January 19, 1951, p. 1.
3. *Fort Worth Star Telegram*, February 7, 1951, pp. 1 and 4; February 10, 1951, pp. 1–2; February 13, 1951, p. 1; February 16, 1951, p. 1; Brooks, *Don't Dry-Clean My Blackjack*, 19; Arnold, *Gamblers & Gangsters*, pp. 29–38.
4. *Fort Worth Star Telegram*, February 15, 1951, pp. 1 and 16; February 19, 1951, p. 1; February 22, 1951, p. 1; Arnold, *Gamblers & Gangsters*, 32–38.
5. *Fort Worth Star Telegram*, February 14, 1951, p. 1; February 17, 1951, pp. 1and 2; Arnold, *Gamblers & Gangsters*, 33–36.
6. *Fort Worth Star Telegram*, March 3, 1951, p. 1; March 8, 1951, p. 1; March 5, 1951, pp. 1–2; March 17, 1951, p. 1; Arnold, *Gamblers & Gangsters*, 40.
7. *Fort Worth Star Telegram*, February 22, 1951, pp. 1–2; February 23, 1951, p. 6; January 3, 1951, p. 1; March 28, 1951, p. 1; April 18, 1951, p. 1; May 5, 1951, p. 1.
8. Arnold, *Gamblers & Gangsters*, 41–45; *Fort Worth Star Telegram*, June 19, 1951, p. 1; February 24, 1951, p. 1; February 25, 1951, p. 1; May 10, 1951, p. 1; May 29, 1951, pp. 1 and 4.
9. *Fort Worth Star Telegram*, July 3, 1951, p. 1; December 11, 1951, p. 1.

10. Arnold, *Gamblers & Gangsters*, 45–47; *Fort Worth Star Telegram*, October 30, 1951, p. 1; February 2, 1952, p. 1; August 19, 1952, p. 32.
11. *Fort Worth Star Telegram*, March 17, 1952, p. 1; March 20, 1952, p. 1; May 23, 1952, pp. 1 and 12; March 28, 1952, p. 1.
12. Arnold, *Gamblers & Gangsters*, 22, 40, 58, 114, 142, 147–50; *Fort Worth Star Telegram*, May 8, 1952, pp. 1 and 10; May 11, 1952, p. 1; May 13, 1952, p. 1.
13. *Fort Worth Star Telegram*, May 15, 1952, p. 1; May 16, 1952, pp. 1 and 6; May 21, 1952, pp. 1–2; May 22, 1952, p. 1.
14. *Fort Worth Star Telegram*, April 16, 1953, p. 1; January 30, 1954, p. 1; February 7, 1954, p. 1.
15. *Fort Worth Star Telegram*, March 31, 1951, p. 1; December 22, 1953, p. 1; July 1, 1953, p. 4; September 23, 1954, p. 1.
16. *Fort Worth Star Telegram*, July 19, 1952, p. 32; November 5, 1954, p. 1.
17. *Fort Worth Star Telegram*, March 4, 1953, p. 1; May 13, 1956, p. 5; February 14, 1952, pp. 1 and 10; October 30, 1953, p. 8; December 18, 1953, p. 1.
18. *Fort Worth Star Telegram*, June 28, 1955, pp. 1 and 10; June 29, 1955, p. 1.
19. *Fort Worth Star Telegram*, April 15, 1954, p. 1; August 24, 1954, p. 1.
20. *Fort Worth Star Telegram*, March 25, 1951, p. 1; August 8, 1951, pp. 1 and 4; Brooks, *Don't Dry-Clean My Blackjack*, 20.
21. *Fort Worth Star Telegram*, August 23, 1951, pp. 1 and 10; Arnold, *Gamblers & Gangsters*, 26, 31, 126–28, 130–31.
22. *Fort Worth Star Telegram*, June 30, 1952, p. 1; December 20, 1953, p. 1; Arnold, *Gamblers & Gangsters*, 80 and 100; *Austin American Statesman*, December 8, 1953, p. 1.
23. *Tampa (FL) Tribune*, April 9, 1955, p. 3; *Fort Worth Star Telegram*, April 7, 1955, pp. 1 and 10; April 8, 1955, p. 1; April 9, 1955, p. 1; April 16, 1955, pp. 1–2; May 24, 1955, p. 1; April 13, 1956, p. 5; Arnold, *Gamblers & Gangsters*, 73–78, 101.
24. *Fort Worth Star Telegram*, November 20, 1955, pp. 1 and 10; November 22, 1955, pp. 1–2; November 23, 1955, p. 1; November 28, 1955, p. 1; March 20, 1956, p. 1.
25. *Fort Worth Star Telegram*, November 10, 1955, p. 1.
26. *Fort Worth Star Telegram*, February 16, 1955, p. 1.
27. *Fort Worth Star Telegram*, March 5, 1955, p. 1; November 1, 1955, pp. 1 and 12; November 2, 1955, p. 1; Brooks, *Don't Dry-Clean My Blackjack*, 20–22.
28. *Fort Worth Star Telegram*, April 14, 1958, p. 1; April 16, 1958, p. 1; August 29, 1958, p. 8.
29. *Fort Worth Star Telegram*, May 3, 1955, pp. 1 and 10; May 4, 1955, p. 1; May 27, 1955, p. 1; Arnold, *Gamblers & Gangsters*, 101.

30. *Fort Worth Star Telegram*, May 5, 1955, p. 1; Richard Selcer, *Fort Worth: A Texas Original* (Austin: Texas State Historical Association, 2004), 98.
31. *Fort Worth Star Telegram*, August 27, 1955, pp. 1–2; Arnold, *Gamblers & Gangsters*, 103–6.
32. *Fort Worth Star Telegram*, August 27, 1955, pp. 1–2; August 31, 1955, pp. 1 and 5; September 1, 1955, pp. 1 and 4; December 11, 1955, pp. 1 and 14; December 21, 1956, p. 1.
33. *Fort Worth Star Telegram*, March 15, 1956, p. 1.
34. *Fort Worth Star Telegram*, May 16, 1955, pp. 1–2; August 18, 1956, p. 1; January 6, 1960, p. 14.
35. *Fort Worth Star Telegram*, April 14, 1951, pp. 1–2; April 15, 1951, p. 7; April 16, 1951, pp. 1 and 4; April 23, 1951, p. 1; June 2, 1951, p. 1; June 12, 1951, p. 21.
36. *Fort Worth Star Telegram*, November 14, 1953, p. 1.
37. *Fort Worth Star Telegram*, December 2, 1951, p. 20; August 27, 1951, p. 19; December 10, 1954, p. 23.
38. *Fort Worth Star Telegram*, October 5, 1954, p. 15; November 21, 1951, p. 22; August 22, 1952, p. 12; Polito, *Savage Art*, 105.
39. *Fort Worth Star Telegram*, January 14, 1955, p. 1; *New York Times*, July 8, 1956, p. 161; January 17, 1954, p. 53.
40. *Fort Worth Star Telegram*, July 2, 1951, p. 8; December 4, 1953, p. 7; December 3, 1953, p. 18.
41. *Fort Worth Star Telegram*, November 22, 1951, p. 1.
42. *Fort Worth Star Telegram*, October 21, 1955, pp. 1 and 10; October 19, 1955, p. 1; October 20, 1955, p. 1; October 22, 1955, p. 1; *New York Times*, January 8, 1956, p. 54.
43. *Fort Worth Star Telegram*, January 1, 1953, p. 10; February 11, 1957, p. 1.
44. *Fort Worth Star Telegram*, June 7, 1953, p. 2; March 15, 1955, p. 34; March 16, 1955, p. 6.
45. *Fort Worth Star Telegram*, April 29, 1954, pp. 15 and 48; August 10, 1954, p. 9.
46. *Fort Worth Star Telegram*, December 8, 1953, p. 16.
47. *Fort Worth Star Telegram*, November 18, 1954, p. 32; January 21, 1955, p. 28; March 22, 1955, p. 6; July 11, 1957, p. 19; August 31, 1957, p. 2; December 2, 1957, p. 1.
48. "Warden's Notebook: Charles Louis Beland, Alcatraz Number 618," NAID 236759950, Record Group 129, Bureau of Prisons, Department of Justice, Washington, DC; *Fort Worth Star Telegram*, August 21, 1951, pp. 1 and 4; September 15, 1951, p. 3; November 26, 1955, p. 1; May 4, 1956, p. 1; Rich, *Between the World Wars*, 178; *New York Times*, April 20, 1956, p. 16.

49. *Fort Worth Star Telegram*, January 30, 1952, p. 1; March 16, 1954, p. 12.
50. *Fort Worth Star Telegram*, March 2, 1951, p. 1; November 5, 1954, p. 1; "Crime Commission," *Fort Worth: Official Publication of the Chamber of Commerce*, October 1952, 18 and 42.
51. *Fort Worth Star Telegram,* March 2, 1951, p. 1; November 5, 1954, p. 1.
52. *Fort Worth Star Telegram*, April 3, 1953, pp. 1 and 6; April 16, 1954, p. 1; July 27, 1954, p. 12; August 24, 1954, p. 1.

Notes for Chapter 15

1. *Fort Worth Star Telegram*, April 25, 1951, p. 1; April 30, 1951, p. 1; September 15, 1951, p. 2.
2. *Fort Worth Star Telegram*, August 14, 1951, p. 1; October 2, 1953, p. 1; March 3, 1954, p. 1.
3. *Fort Worth Star Telegram*, June 18, 1952, p. 1; June 29, 1952, p. 1; September 21, 1953, p. 1.
4. *Fort Worth Star Telegram*, April 4, 1952, p. 38; April 10, 1952, p. 2; March 29, 1955, p. 1.
5. *Fort Worth Star Telegram*, August 14, 1951, p. 1; October 17, 1951, p. 1; October 20, 1951, p. 1; August 27, 1952, p. 32.
6. *Fort Worth Star Telegram*, August 14, 1952, p. 1; June 29, 1952, p. 2; June 30, 1952, p. 14; May 31, 1953, p. 1.
7. *Fort Worth Star Telegram*, September 15, 1951, p. 1; September 20, 1951, p. 16; October 20, 1951, p. 1.
8. *Fort Worth Star Telegram*, August 31, 1951, p. 1; July 3, 1952, p. 1.
9. *Fort Worth Star Telegram*, February 8, 1952, pp. 1 and 4.
10. *Fort Worth Star Telegram*, February 18, 1952, p. 1; April 14, 1952, p. 1; July 11, 1952, p. 1.
11. *Fort Worth Star Telegram*, June 17, 1952, p. 1; June 21, 1952, p. 1.
12. *Fort Worth Star Telegram*, December 26, 1955, pp. 1 and 10; October 1, 1956, p. 4.
13. *Fort Worth Star Telegram*, April 28, 1953, p. 1; May 5, 1953, pp. 1 and 10; May 30, 1953, p. 1; *Fort Worth Mind*, May 8, 1953, p. 1.
14. *Fort Worth Star Telegram*, May 15, 1953, p. 1; May 22, 1953, p. 48.
15. *Fort Worth Star Telegram*, September 23, 1953, pp. 1–2; October 2, 1953, p. 1.
16. *Fort Worth Star Telegram*, October 22, 1953, p. 1; October 25, 1953, p. 1; Brooks, *Don't Dry-Clean My Blackjack*, 2.
17. *Fort Worth Star Telegram*, July 9, 1954, p. 8.
18. *Fort Worth Star Telegram*, April 1, 1954, p. 1; January 1, 1952, p. 1; April 15, 1954, p. 9; January 28, 1955, p. 10; February 7, 1955, p. 1; January 2, 1956, p. 11.

19. *Fort Worth Star Telegram*, June 26, 1951, p. 4; October 8, 1954, p. 1; November 9, 1954, pp. 1 and 12; July 17, 1952, p. 2.
20. *Fort Worth Star Telegram*, September 26, 1952, p. 17; January 2, 1956, p. 11.
21. *Fort Worth Star Telegram*, July 2, 1952, p. 1; February 21, 1955, p. 2.
22. *Fort Worth Star Telegram*, September 3, 1951, p. 24; April 10, 1953, p. 1.
23. *Fort Worth Star Telegram*, September 26, 1951, p. 1; November 8, 1953, p. 1; February 20, 1952, p. 3; May 26, 1954, p. 1.
24. *Fort Worth Star Telegram*, June 7, 1952, p. 2; October 1, 1952, pp. 15 and 23.
25. *Fort Worth Star Telegram*, September 19, 1953, p. 1; June 3, 1954, p. 9; December 26, 1954, p. 16; May 13, 1955, p. 1.
26. *Fort Worth Star Telegram*, October 4, 1952, pp. 1–2; October 5, 1952, pp. 1 and 8; October 6, 1952, pp. 1 and 6; October 25, 1952, p. 1.
27. *Fort Worth Star Telegram*, November 3, 1952, pp. 1–2; February 26, 1958, pp. 1–2.
28. *Fort Worth Star Telegram*, March 4, 1953, p. 20; April 10, 1953, p. 1; January 13, 1954, pp. 1–2; January 4, 1956, p. 1.
29. *Fort Worth Star Telegram*, March 15, 1952, p. 1; March 17, 1952, p. 1.
30. *Fort Worth Star Telegram*, December 10, 1954, pp. 1 and 10; January 14, 1955, p. 1; April 21, 1956, p. 1.
31. *Fort Worth Star Telegram*, February 19, 1953, pp. 1–2; February 20, 1953, p. 1; March 18, 1953, p. 25; March 30, 1953, p. 1; *New York Times*, March 23, 1953, p. 45.
32. *Fort Worth Star Telegram*, February 23, 1953, pp. 1–2; March 24, 1953, p. 1; *New York Times*, March 23, 1953, p. 45.
33. *Fort Worth Star Telegram*, February 28, 1952, p. 41; July 17, 1951, p. 1; March 16, 1955, p. 6.
34. *Fort Worth Star Telegram*, August 5, 1953, p. 1.

Notes for Chapter 16

1. *Fort Worth Star Telegram*, October 30, 1951, p. 11; "Table B-35," *Population*, vol. 2, *Characteristics of the Population*, Sixteenth Census of the United States: 1940 (Washington, DC: Government Printing Office, 1942), p. 1035; "Table I," *Census Tract Statistics*, part 2, *Denver–Nashville*, vol. 3 of Seventeenth Census of the United States: 1950 (Washington, DC: Government Printing Office, 1951), 7.
2. *Fort Worth Star Telegram*, January 11, 1951, pp. 1–2; January 16, 1951, p. 1; January 18, 1952, p. 3; December 28, 1953, p. 14; August 13, 1952, p. 6.
3. *Fort Worth Star Telegram*, May 10, 1951, p. 56; Cannon, "Cowtown and the Color Line," 72.

4. *Fort Worth Star Telegram*, June 2, 1951, pp. 1–2; July 13, 1951, p. 1; June 9, 1951, p. 4; July 25, 1953, p. 2.
5. *Fort Worth Star Telegram*, June 12, 1951, p. 4; *New York Times*, September 5, 1956, p. 17.
6. *Fort Worth Star Telegram*, January 30, 1951, p. 14; May 1, 1951, p. 5; August 23, 1951, p. 48; October 1, 1951, p. 14; January 16, 1951, p. 2.
7. *Fort Worth Star Telegram*, July 27, 1952, p. 16; August 3, 1952, p. 5; February 8, 1953, p. 8; April 19, 1954, p. 28.
8. *Fort Worth Star Telegram*, January 18, 1953, p. 5; October 7, 1954, p. 10.
9. *Fort Worth Star Telegram*, December 23, 1952, p. 5; December 21, 1957, p. 22; May 6, 1954, p. 68; April 24, 1951, p. 8; February 19, 1952, p. 6.
10. *Fort Worth Star Telegram*, April 18, 1955, p. 24; October 8, 1958, p. 4.
11. *Fort Worth Star Telegram*, June 20, 1951, p. 17; July 13, 1951, p. 1; June 14, 1951, p. 1; June 16, 1951, p. 3; July 19, 1951, p. 3.
12. *Fort Worth Star Telegram*, January 19, 1952, pp. 1–2; February 21, 1952, p. 1; July 3, 1953, p. 5.
13. *Fort Worth Star Telegram*, June 16, 1954, p. 1; November 10, 1955, pp. 1–2.
14. *Fort Worth Star Telegram*, May 2, 1952, p. 1; May 5, 1952, p. 26; December 15, 1955, p. 1; Susan A. Kline and the Fort Worth Parks and Community Services Department, *Fort Worth Parks* (Charleston, SC: Arcadia, 2010), 61.
15. *Fort Worth Star Telegram*, May 5, 1951, p. 1; February 1, 1954, p. 17.
16. *Fort Worth Star Telegram*, June 27, 1953, p. 7; March 17, 1952, p. 1.
17. *Fort Worth Star Telegram*, May 17, 1954, p. 1; June 8, 1954, p. 1; July 5, 1954, p. 1; July 14, 1955, p. 1; *New York Times*, September 26, 1954, p. 172; December 30, 1955, pp. 1 and 12.
18. *New York Times*, January 8, 1955, p. 19; Cannon, "Cowtown and the Color line," 113 and 117–19.
19. *Fort Worth Star Telegram*, August 23, 1953, p. 62; August 26, 1953, p. 1; August 27, 1953, p. 1; August 29, 1953, p. 1; November 30, 2019, pp. A1 and A5; Cannon, "Cowtown and the Color Line," 73–74; Selcer, *Fort Worth in Black and White*, 438–48; *Fort Worth Weekly*, Vol. 10, No. 30; November 15, 2023, pp. 4-7.
20. *Fort Worth Star Telegram*, October 7, 1953, p. 1; September 27, 1953, pp. 1–2; September 28, 1953, p. 7.
21. *Fort Worth Star Telegram*, October 12, 1953, pp. 1 and 7; November 2, 1953, pp. 1–2; November 4, 1953, pp. 1 and 4; November 5, 1953, p. 1; November 17, 1953, p. 1; *Fort Worth Weekly,* November 15, 2023, pp. 4–7.
22. *Fort Worth Star Telegram*, September 11, 1954, p. 1; September 12, 1954, p. 8; September 16, 1954, p. 1; October 6, 1954, p. 1; November 14, 1954, p. 1; *Lake Como Weekly* (Fort Worth), October 8, 1954, p. 1; October 22, 1954, p. 2.

23. *Fort Worth Star Telegram*, August 19, 1855, p. 1; September 23, 1955, p. 24; September 15, 1955, p. 1; August 18, 1955, p. 64; August 20, 1955, p. 1; Rich, *Between the World Wars*, 67–68.
24. *Fort Worth Star Telegram*, November 17, 1952, p. 1; December 11, 1952, p. 1; December 17, 1952, p. 1; April 23, 1954, p. 40; April 15, 1953, p. 1; April 20, 1954, p. 14.
25. *Fort Worth Star Telegram*, August 16, 1952, p. 1; October 2, 1952, p. 1; October 7, 1952, p. 3; October 16, 1952, p. 46.
26. *Fort Worth Star Telegram*, October 21, 1952, p. 3; December 30, 1952, p. 2; February 13, 1953, p. 1; April 1, 1953, p. 9; May 6, 1953, p. 1; September 20, 1953, p. 22; January 27, 2011, Obituaries; Selcer, *Fort Worth in Black and White*, 405–8.
27. *Fort Worth Star Telegram*, March 12, 1951, p. 3; June 6, 1952, p. 1; *New York Times*, July 15, 1954, p. 12.
28. *Fort Worth Star Telegram*, March 12, 1951, p. 3; March 2, 1952, p. 9; "Council of Social Agencies of Fort Worth and Tarrant County, 1929–1956," R0068, File Survey of Findings of the Fort Worth Workshop: Service to Latin Americans, 1952, pp. 1–7, Local History Archives, FWPL.
29. *Fort Worth Star Telegram,* October 2, 1952, p. 32; September 16, 1953, p. 9; February 28, 1954, p. 10; September 19, 1955, p. 1.

Notes for Chapter 17

1. *Fort Worth Star Telegram*, June 19, 1957, p. 6; November 3, 1957, p. 1; December 7, 1957, p. 1; November 21, 1960, p. 1.
2. *Fort Worth Star Telegram*, August 28, 1957, p. 1; December 22, 1957, p. 24; November 9, 1958, p. 1; September 2, 1960, pp. 1 and 8.
3. *Fort Worth Star Telegram*, March 20, 1958, p. 1; October 7, 1959, p. 1; August 23, 1960, p. 1; "Arlington: After 80 Years of Progress, 1876–1956," July 1, 1956, pp. 1–16.
4. *New York Times*, July 1, 1956, p. 198; *Fort Worth Star Telegram*, August 2, 1954, p. 1; February 27, 1959, p. 1.
5. *Fort Worth Star Telegram*, November 13, 1957, p. 1; January 24, 1960, pp. 1 and 7; June 28, 1958, p. 1.
6. *Fort Worth Star Telegram*, March 30, 1958, p. 1; March 31, 1958, pp. 1–2; April 2, 1958, pp. 1–2.
7. *Fort Worth Star Telegram*, September 18, 1958, pp. 1 and 6; September 19, 1958, pp. 1 and 8; September 20, 1958, p. 1; September 21, 1958, p. 1; September 22, 1958, pp. 1 and 4; September 23, 1958, p. 1; September 24, 1958, pp. 1 and 4; November 26, 1958, p. 1; December 11, 1959, p. 1.

8. *Fort Worth Star Telegram*, November 13, 1957, pp. 1 and 8; July 6, 1958, p. 1; February 27, 1959, p. 1; October 8, 1959, p. 1; January 22, 1961, p. 1; Brian A. Cervantez, *Amon Carter: A Lone Star Life* (Norman: University of Oklahoma Press, 2019), 209.
9. *Fort Worth Star Telegram*, August 14, 1958, p. 1; August 15, 1958, p. 1; November 19, 1958, p. 1.
10. *Fort Worth Star Telegram*, December 18, 1959, p. 1; December 2, 1960, p. 6.
11. *Fort Worth Star Telegram*, February 5, 1959, p. 1; April 25, 1959, p. 1; April 27, 1959, pp. 1–2; May 22, 1959, p. 1; *New York Times*, June 14, 1959, p. 61.
12. *Fort Worth Star Telegram*, April 2, 1959, pp. 1 and 16; April 8, 1959, p. 1; January 23, 1959, p. 1; May 27, 1960, p. 4.
13. *Fort Worth Star Telegram*, March 19, 1960, p. 5.
14. *Fort Worth Star Telegram*, May 12, 1960, pp. 1 and 3; August 25, 1960, p. 1.
15. *Fort Worth Star Telegram*, April 10, 1956, p. 31; April 19, 1956, p. 54; April 21, 1956, p. 1.
16. *Fort Worth Star Telegram*, February 24, 1956, pp. 1 and 6; November 20, 1958, pp. 1 and 6.
17. *Fort Worth Star Telegram*, September 22, 1959, p. 1; September 23, 1959, pp. 1 and 8; December 2, 1958, p. 5.
18. *Fort Worth Star Telegram*, October 28, 1959, p. 21; January 15, 1960, p. 36; January 28, 1960, p. 1; March 28, 1960, p. 19; Charles Bickley, "The Cellar: A Unique Music Club in Texas History," *Handbook of Texas Online*, updated September 18, 2023, https://www.tshaonline.org/handbook/entries/cellar.
19. *Fort Worth Star Telegram*, October 31, 1959, pp. 1–2; November 1, 1959, pp. 1–2; November 15, 1959, p. 1; September 13, 1960, p. 1.
20. *Fort Worth Star Telegram*, May 30, 1956, p. 14; July 7, 1960, p. 40; December 30, 1959, p. 4.
21. Cervantez, *Amon Carter*, 3; *New York Times*, February 5, 1957, p. 23; November 3, 1957, p. 169; October 1, 1959, p. 35; October 7, 1959, p. 68; *Fort Worth Star Telegram*, March 28, 1957, p. 56; October 1, 1959, pp. 1–2.
22. *Fort Worth Star Telegram*, January 22, 1959, p. 1.
23. *Fort Worth Star Telegram*, July 28, 1957, p. 1.
24. *Preliminary Reports: Population Counts for Standard Metropolitan Statistics*, Eighteenth Census of the United States: 1960 (Washington, DC: Government Printing Office, 1960), 57.
25. *Fort Worth Star Telegram*, June 20, 1960, p. 1; August 4, 1960, p. 1.

Notes for Chapter 18

1. *New York Times*, February 22, 1956, p. 18; February 23, 1956, p. 28; *Fort Worth Star Telegram*, February 22, 1956, p. 1; February 23, 1956, p. 1; April 1, 1956, p. 1.
2. *Fort Worth Star Telegram*, February 28, 1956, p. 28; March 5, 1956, p. 1; May 19, 1956, p. 1; January 29, 1958, p. 8; December 19, 1958, p. 25; *Daily News Texan* (Grand Prairie), July 26, 1962, p. 1.
3. *Fort Worth Star Telegram*, August 2, 1956, pp. 1–2; August 3, 1956, pp. 1 and 4.
4. Brooks, *Don't Dry-Clean My Blackjack*, 22–26; Arnold, *Gamblers & Gangsters*, 117–21; *Fort Worth Star Telegram*, October 9, 1956, pp. 1 and 6; February 3, 1957, p. 1.
5. *Fort Worth Star Telegram*, February 3, 1957, pp. 1 and 4; February 6, 1957, p. 2; February 10, 1957, p. 1; "Solution of Foley Death May Be Near," script of WBAP-TV newscast, February 5, 1957, pp. 1–3, KXAS-NBC-5 News Collection, UNT Library Digital Collections, University of North Texas, Denton; Brooks, *Don't Dry-Clean My Blackjack*, 23; Arnold, *Gamblers & Gangsters*, 130; Selcer, *Texas Original*, 98.
6. Arnold, *Gamblers & Gangsters*, 153–54; *Fort Worth Star Telegram*, September 20, 1958, pp. 1–2; September 23, 1958, p. 3; September 29, 1958, p. 1; September 30, 1958, pp. 1–2; October 1, 1958, p. 1; March 21, 1965, p. 1.
7. *Fort Worth Star Telegram*, June 4, 1958, p. 1.
8. *Fort Worth Star Telegram*, August 22, 1958, pp. 1 and 4; August 27, 1958, pp. 1 and 4; May 15, 1959, p. 1; August 27, 2005, p. 1B and 10B.
9. *Fort Worth Star Telegram*, September 23, 1958, p. 1; September 28, 1958, pp. 1 and 8; January 1, 1959, p. 1; January 20, 1959, p. 6; June 18, 1960, pp. 1–2; June 21, 1960, p. 1; August 27, 2005, p. 23.
10. *Fort Worth Star Telegram*, July 17, 1956, p. 1; August 10, 1956, p. 14; September 2, 1956, p. 1; September 28, 1956, p. 16; August 8, 1983, p. 14.
11. *Fort Worth Star Telegram*, March 8, 1956, p. 1; June 26, 1956, p. 1.
12. *Fort Worth Star Telegram*, April 30, 1957, pp. 1 and 6; *New York Times*, April 30, 1957, p. 17.
13. *Fort Worth Star Telegram*, May 1, 1957, pp. 1–2; May 2, 1957, p. 1; September 15, 1957, pp. 1 and 22.
14. *Fort Worth Star Telegram*, September 23, 1957, p. 17; September 24, 1957, pp. 1 and 8; September 26, 1957, p. 14.
15. *Fort Worth Star Telegram*, April 30, 1957, pp. 1 and 6; May 2, 1957, pp. 1–2; Arnold, *Gamblers & Gangsters*, 159–60.

16. *Fort Worth Star Telegram*, May 22, 1957, pp. 1 and 4; Arnold, *Gamblers & Gangsters*, 26 and 131.
17. *Fort Worth Star Telegram*, January 4, 1959, pp. 1–2; January 5, 1959, p. 3; Arnold, *Gamblers & Gangsters*, 131–32.
18. *Fort Worth Star Telegram*, September 28, 1959, p. 1; March 21, 1960, p. 1; March 22, 1960, pp. 1 and 4; March 23, 1960, p. 1; March 24, 1960, p. 1; April 1, 1960, pp. 1 and 10; April 7, 1960, p. 1.
19. *Fort Worth Star Telegram*, March 4, 1960, pp. 1 and 4; March 9, 1960, pp. 1 and 6.
20. *Fort Worth Star Telegram*, April 1, 1960, pp. 1 and 10.
21. *Fort Worth Star Telegram*, April 5, 1960, p. 1; April 7, 1960, p. 1; April 8, 1960, pp. 1 and 8; June 5, 1960, p. 1.
22. *Fort Worth Star Telegram*, March 9, 1960, p. 6; April 20, 1956, p. 1; April 28, 1960, p. 1; September 4, 1960, p. 1; *New York Times*, April 20, 1956, p. 16; April 20, 1960, p. 16; April 28, 1960, pp. 1 and 28; November 19, 1960, p. 11.
23. *Fort Worth Star Telegram*, September 18, 1956, p. 5; December 12, 1957, p. 18; December 31, 1957, p. 1; March 2, 1959, p. 1; Arnold, *Gamblers & Gangsters*, 131; *New York Times*, September 3, 1956, p. 1; September 4, 1956, p. 14.
24. *Fort Worth Star Telegram*, February 21, 1958, p. 1; September 18, 1960, pp. 1–2.
25. *Fort Worth Star Telegram*, September 19, 1960, pp. 1 and 6; September 2, 1960, p. 1; September 22, 1960, pp. 1–2.
26. *Fort Worth Star Telegram*, October 13, 1960, p. 1.
27. *Fort Worth Star Telegram*, March 27, 1958, p.1.
28. *Fort Worth Star Telegram*, May 22, 1956, p. 5; September 28, 1956, p. 1; July 21, 1956, pp. 1–2; July 22, 1956, pp. 1 and 6.
29. *Fort Worth Star Telegram*, February 11, 1957, p. 1; February 24, 1957, pp. 1 and 4; *Fort Worth Mind*, March 1, 1957, p. 1.
30. *Fort Worth Star Telegram*, June 11, 1957, p. 40; July 16, 1957, p. 1; April 7, 1960, p. 17; July 24, 1957, p. 1; January 24, 1960, p. 2.
31. *Fort Worth Star Telegram*, December 13, 1957, p. 1; April 4, 1958, p. 6; November 6, 1958, p. 65.
32. *Fort Worth Star Telegram*, July 10, 1958, p. 20; April 1, 1959, p. 2; January 14, 1959, p. 1; August 13, 1958, p. 8.
33. *Fort Worth Star Telegram*, September 27, 1958, p. 1; September 29, 1958, p. 32; July 22, 1958, p. 1.
34. *Fort Worth Star Telegram*, June 12, 1959, pp. 1 and 4; June 14, 1959, p. 6.
35. *Fort Worth Star Telegram*, February 28, 1959, p. 9; May 4, 1959, p. 1; October 30, 1959, p. 4; March 18, 1959, p. 3.

36. *Fort Worth Star Telegram*, July 8, 1958, p. 1.
37. *Fort Worth Star Telegram*, May 18, 1959, p. 23; May 27, 1959, p. 13; May 29, 1959, p. 1; January 23, 1958, pp. 1 and 6.
38. *Fort Worth Star Telegram*, June 6, 1959, p. 1; June 7, 1959, p. 1; June 17, 1959, p. 1; November 3, 1960, p. 1.
39. *Fort Worth Star Telegram*, August 10, 1957, p. 2; March 25, 1959, p. 1; March 19, 1959, p. 1; June 22, 1960, p. 1.
40. *New York Times*, June 26, 1958, p. 24; August 2, 1958, p. 19; February 11, 1959, p. 48; January 24, 1961, pp. 1 and 20; *Fort Worth Star Telegram*, December 15, 1959, p. 1.

Notes for Chapter 19

1. *Fort Worth Star Telegram*, March 27, 1957, p. 1; December 20, 1957, p. 22; November 14, 1958, p. 1; November 19, 1958, p. 1.
2. *Fort Worth Star Telegram*, June 2, 1959, p. 1; July 31, 1959, p. 1; September 1, 1959, p. 17; April 11, 1960, p. 13; November 29, 1959, p. 14.
3. *Fort Worth Star Telegram*, August 29, 1960, p. 1; January 5, 1961, p. 60.
4. *Fort Worth Star Telegram*, March 9, 1960, p. 15; April 26, 1960, p. 6.
5. *Fort Worth Star Telegram*, October 25, 1960, pp. 1 and 4.
6. *Fort Worth Star Telegram*, October 31, 1960, p. 1; February 26, 1961, p. 1.
7. *Fort Worth Star Telegram*, April 6, 1958, p. 71; August 27, 1958, pp. 1 and 4; February 5, 1959, p. 1; May 15, 1959, p. 1; February 28, 1959, p. 9.
8. *Fort Worth Star Telegram*, June 18, 1956, p. 1; June 20, 1956, p. 1; July 26, 1956, p. 10; October 6, 1957, p. 1; May 21, 1959, p. 1.
9. *Fort Worth Star Telegram*, November 10, 1956, p. 1; December 9, 1956, p. 1; November 23, 1957, p. 1; January 19, 1958, p. 1; January 22, 1958, p. 7.
10. *Fort Worth Star Telegram*, February 5, 1957, p. 1; December 24, 1957, pp. 1–2; April 10, 1959, pp. 1 and 8; July 22, 1960, p. 1.
11. A. D. Marshall, oral Interview by Harold Rich, conducted at the Fort Worth Jail Office, mid-1990s.
12. *Fort Worth Star Telegram*, August 15, 1957, p. 1; March 21, 1958, p. 1; June 20, 1958, p. 12.
13. *Fort Worth Star Telegram*, August 1, 1957, p. 29; August 26, 1959, p. 4; April 16, 1958, pp. 1 and 5; June 11, 1958, p. 1.
14. *Fort Worth Star Telegram*, March 20, 1959, pp. 1–2; March 21, 1959, pp. 1–2; March 22, 1959, pp. 1–2.
15. *Fort Worth Star Telegram*, March 29, 1959, pp. 1–2; March 31, 1959, p. 1; April 13, 1959, p. 1; April 22, 1959, p. 1; April 15, 1959, pp. 1 and 8; April 26, 1959, p. 1; May 4, 1959, p. 1; June 2, 1959, p. 1.
16. *Fort Worth Star Telegram*, March 5, 1958, p. 1; March 6, 1958, p. 1; March 9, 1958, pp. 1 and 4.

17. *Fort Worth Star Telegram*, October 23, 1959, pp. 1 and 6; October 28, 1959, p. 1; November 2, 1959, p. 1.
18. *Fort Worth Star Telegram*, August 11, 1958, p. 4; April 28, 1959, p. 36; June 22, 1959, p. 1; June 26, 1959, p. 7.
19. *Fort Worth Star Telegram*, October 15, 1959, p. 21.
20. *Fort Worth Star Telegram*, July 29, 1960, p. 1; August 5, 1960, p. 1; December 25, 1959, p. 1; *The Panther Scream*, Fort Worth Police Newsletter 14, No. 11 (November 1966), Miscellaneous Records, Fort Worth Police 1955–1968, Box 1, Local History Archives, FWPL.

Notes for Chapter 20

1. *Fort Worth Star Telegram*, January 17, 1956, p. 1; March 18, 1956, Section 4, p. 7.
2. *Fort Worth Star Telegram*, March 22, 1957, p. 1; May 29, 1957, p. 17; July 19, 1957, p. 7.
3. *Fort Worth Star Telegram*, July 19, 1957, p. 12; October 2, 1957, pp. 1 and 4; June 29, 1957, p. 7; *Fort Worth Mind*, October 4, 1957, p. 1.
4. *Fort Worth Star Telegram*, June 13, 1956, p. 1; October 5, 1956, p. 22; January 9, 1959, p. 1; August 18, 2019, pp. 1B and 3B; May 23, 1959, p. 1.
5. *Fort Worth Star Telegram*, May 29, 1956, p. 3; May 31, 1956, p. 1; January 1, 1959, p. 1; March 26, 1957, p. 1.
6. *Fort Worth Star Telegram*, March 24, 1956, p. 1; August 17, 1956, p. 12.
7. Lacie Ballinger, "Ku Klux Klan in Fort Worth," Seminar Paper (unidentified school, 1997), 16, Local History Archives, FWPL; *Fort Worth Star Telegram*, March 17, 1957, pp. 1 and 8; June 14, 1957, p. 37.
8. *Fort Worth Star Telegram*, May 10, 1956, p. 1; June 1, 1956, p. 1; June 6, 1956, p. 1; June 21, 1958, p. 1.
9. Stefanie Decker, "African-American Women in the Civil Rights Era, 1954–1974," in Glasrud and Pite, *Black Women in Texas History*, 163; *Fort Worth Star Telegram*, July 14, 1955, p. 1; September 9, 1956, pp. 1 and 6; August 23, 1956, p. 1; September 4, 1956, p. 1; September 8, 1959, pp. 1 and 7; October 1, 1959, pp. 1–2.
10. *Fort Worth Star Telegram*, October 9, 1955, p. 3; August 27, 1956, p. 1; August 29, 1956, p. 1; August 31, 1956, pp. 1 and 6; September 4, 1956, p. 1; January 1, 2024, pp. 1 and 7; *New York Times*, September 2, 1956, p. 74; Robyn D. Ladino, *Desegregation in Texas: Eisenhower, Shivers, and the Crisis at Mansfield High* (Austin: University of Texas Press, 1996), 6–8; John P. DeFelice, *History of Segregated I. M. Terrell High School, Fort Worth, Texas* (published by the author, 2022), 29; Selcer, *Fort Worth in Black and White*, 414–17; Samuel A. Wilson, "Vanished Legacies and Lost Culture of I. M. Terrell High School in Segregated Fort Worth. (MA thesis, University of Texas at Arlington, 2012), 31–41.

11. *New York Times*, September 1, 1956, pp. 1 and 6; September 5, 1956, p. 16; September 6, 1956, p. 11; Cannon, "Cowtown and the Color Line," 110–13; Ladino, *Crisis at Mansfield High*, 82–144.
12. *New York Times*, September 1, 1956, pp. 1 and 6; September 2, 1956, p. 40; September 3, 1956, p. 74; September 4, 1956, p. 26; September 5, 1956, p. 16; September 22, 1956, p. 17; September 26, 1956, p. 16; *Fort Worth Star Telegram,* August 30, 1956, pp. 1–2; December 4, 1956, p. 1; C. L. Douglas and Francis Miller, *The Life Story of W. Lee O'Daniel* (Whitefish, MT: Kessinger, 2010), *passim*.
13. *New York Times*, September 4, 1957, p. 36.
14. *New York Times*, October 4, 1959, p. 76.
15. *New York Times*, January 10, 1960, p. 64.
16. *New York Times*, December 27, 1959, p. 35; November 16, 1959, pp. 1 and 39; December 27, 1959, p. 35.
17. *Fort Worth Star Telegram,* May 3, 1956, p. 29; November 27, 1958, p. 12.
18. *Fort Worth Star Telegram,* September 3, 1956, p. 10; September 28, 1956, p. 8; October 6, 1956, p. 1; October 9, 1956, p. 16; November 7, 1958, p. 1.
19. *Fort Worth Star Telegram,* May 13, 1959, p. 1; May 16, 1959, p. 1; August 26, 1960, p. 12; March 2, 1960, p. 6.
20. *Fort Worth Star Telegram,* September 2, 1956, p. 1; September 4, 1956, p. 23; September 5, 1956, p. 1; November 30, 2019, pp. A1 and A5; *New York Times*, September 3, 1956, p. 9; September 4, 1956, p. 26.
21. *Fort Worth Star Telegram,* July 13, 1960, p. 14.
22. Pitre, "At the Crossroads," in Glasrud and Pitre, *Black Women in Texas History*, 144; *Fort Worth Star Telegram,* August 20, 1959, p. 18.
23. *Fort Worth Star Telegram,* August 27, 1959, p. 1; September 25, 1959, p. 32; February 5, 1960, p. 1; December 29, 1960, p. 2; March 3, 1957, p. 1.
24. *Fort Worth Star Telegram,* April 7, 1960 p. 1; October 18, 1960, p. 13; December 16, 1960, pp. 1 and 4.
25. Jamie McIlvain, "History of Hispanic Fort Worth" (Honors Paper, Texas Christian University, 1993), 24; *Fort Worth Star Telegram,* April 27, 1958, p. 8; September 16, 1960, p. 2.
26. *Fort Worth Star Telegram,* September 17, 1956, p. 1; June 2, 1958, p. 1; August 25, 1957, p. 16; September 11, 1959, p. 21,

Notes for Chapter 21

1. *Fort Worth Star Telegram*, December 23, 1956, p. 1.
2. Warren Johnson, "A Study of the Effect of Convair Employment Fluctuations on Fort Worth Business Activity" (MA thesis, Texas Christian University, 1960), 2, 9, 10, 18, 23.

3. *Fort Worth Star Telegram*, February 25, 1958, p. 1; February 26, 1958, p. 1; February 27, 1958, p. 1.
4. *Fort Worth Star Telegram*, March 6, 1958, p. 1; May 17, 1958, p. 1.
5. Johnson, "Convair Employment Fluctuations," 15; *Fort Worth Star Telegram*, January 11, 1959, Section 5, Part 2, p. 25; July 9, 1958, p. 1; *Fort Worth Magazine* 36, no. 1 (January 1960): 24.
6. "Big Shopping Center Going Up at Kay Lake," *Fort Worth Magazine* 36, no. 4 (April 1960): 42; "Carling Eyes Fort Worth," *Fort Worth Magazine* 36, no. 7 (July 1960): 20; *Fort Worth Magazine* 36, no. 8 (August 1960): 7; *Fort Worth Star Telegram*, January 11, 1959, p. 7; January 27, 1961, p. 1; January 6, 1961, p. 1; January 7, 1961, p. 2.

Bibliography

Newspapers and Magazines

Austin American Statesman
Daily News Texan (Grand Prairie)
Dallas Morning News
Fort Worth Chamber of Commerce
Fort Worth Magazine
Fort Worth Mind
Fort Worth Press
Fort Worth Star Telegram
Fort Worth Weekly
Lake Como Weekly (Fort Worth)
Morning Sentinel (Waterville, ME)
New York Times
The Panther Scream (Fort Worth Police Department Newsletter)
Tampa (FL) Tribune
This Month in Fort Worth

Archives and Collections

Bureau of Prisons. Department of Justice, Washington, DC.
Fort Worth Public Library.
  Local History Archives
  Reby Carey Papers
Special Collections, University of Texas at Arlington Library.
  Fort Worth Star Telegram Collection
  Margaret B. Carter Papers
W. D. Smith Commercial Photography, Inc., Collection
Tarrant County Commissioners Court, Fort Worth, Texas.
UNT Library Digital Collections. University of North Texas, Denton.
  KXAS-NBC-5 News Collection
  Texas History Collection

Government Records/Census

Census Tract Statistics. Part 2, *Denver–Nashville*. Vol. 3 of Seventeenth Census of the United States: 1950. Washington, DC: Government Printing Office, 1951.

"Manufactures." Sec. 29 in *Statistical Abstract of the United States 1964*. Eighth Edition. Washington, DC: Government Printing Office, 1964.

"Manufactures." Sec. 30 in *Statistical Abstract of the United States 1950*. Seventh Edition. Washington, DC: Government Printing Office, 1950.

Manufactures, 1939. Vol. 3, *Reports for States and Outlying Areas*. Sixteenth Census of the United States: 1940. Washington, DC: Government Printing Office, 1942.

Population. Vol. 2, *Characteristics of the Population*. Sixteenth Census of the United States: 1940. Washington, DC: Government Printing Office, 1942.

Population. Vol. 3, *The Labor Force: Part 5, Pennsylvania–Wyoming*. Sixteenth Census of the United States: 1940. Washington, DC: Government Printing Office, 1943.

Preliminary Reports: Population Counts for Standard Metropolitan Statistics. Eighteenth Census of the United States: 1960. Washington, DC: Government Printing Office, 1960.

Other Sources

Abel, Joseph. "Sunbelt Civil Rights: Race, Labor and Politics in the Fort Worth Aircraft Industry, 1940–1980." PhD dissertation, Rice University, 2011.

Arnold, Ann. *Gamblers & Gangsters: Fort Worth's Jacksboro Highway in the 1940s & 1950s*. Austin: Eakin Press, 1998.

Bickley, Charles. "The Cellar: A Unique Music Club in Texas History." *Handbook of Texas Online*, updated September 18, 2023. https://www.tshaonline.org/handbook/entries/cellar.

Black Men and Women in Texas: A Biographical Dictionary of Notable Living Texas Men and Women. Vol. 1. Fort Worth: National Black Heritage Museum, 1973.

Brooks, Elston. *Don't Dry-Clean My Blackjack.* Fort Worth: Branch-Smith, 1979.

Campbell, Diann. "Women in Combat: The World War II Experience in the United States, Great Britain, Germany and the Soviet Union." *Journal of Military History* 57, no. 2 (April 1993): 301–23.

Cannon, Tina N. "Cowtown and the Color Line: Desegregating Fort Worth's Public Schools." PhD diss., Texas Christian University, 2009.

Cary, Reby. *"The Apex." Beyond the Chaos: Unchained Aspirations of African-Americans in Fort Worth.* Fort Worth: published by the author, 2017.

Cary, Reby. *Pavers of the Way: The Panorama of Black Progress.* Fort Worth: published by the author, 2012.

Cervantez, Brian A. *Amon Carter: A Lone Star Life.* Norman: University of Oklahoma Press, 2019.

Cohen, Adam. *The Imbeciles: The Supreme Court, American Eugenics, and the Sterilization of Carrie Buck.* New York: Penguin Press, 2016.

"Crime Commission." *Fort Worth: Official Publication of the Chamber of Commerce*, October 1952, 1–48.

Cuellar, Carlos. *Stories from the Barrio: A History of Mexican Fort Worth.* Fort Worth: Texas Christian University Press, 2003.

Decker, Stephanie. "African-American Women in the Civil Rights Era, 1954–1974." In Glasrud and Pitre, *Black Women in Texas History*, 159–76.

DeFelice, John P. *History of Segregated I. M. Terrell High School, Fort Worth, Texas.* Published by the author, 2022.

Douglas, C. L., and Francis Miller. *The Life Story of W. Lee O'Daniel.* Whitefish, MT: Kessinger, 2010.

Glasrud, Bruce. "William M. McDonald: Businessman and Fraternal Leader." In *Black Leaders: Texans for Their Times*, edited by Alwyn Barr and Robert A. Calvert. Austin: Texas State Historical Association, 1981.

Glasrud, Bruce A., and Merlene Pitre, eds. *Black Women in Texas History.* Centennial Series of the Association of Former Student, Number 108. College Station: Texas A&M Press, 2008.

Gonzales, Richard. *Raza Rising: Chicanos in the North Texas.* Al Filo Mexican American Studies Series 10, edited by Roberto R. Calderón. Denton: University of North Texas Press, 2016.

Green, George N. "The History of Mosier Valley: A Community of Resilience and Heritage." *Handbook of Texas Online*, updated December 8, 2020. https://www.tshaonline.org/handbook/entries/mosier-valley-tx.

Haase, Daniel J. *Gateway to the West: A Historical Look at the Development of East Fort Worth and Its Neighborhoods*. Fort Worth: published by the author, 2019.

Hill, Cecilia N. Sanchez. "Mi Tierra, Tambien?" MA thesis, University of Texas at Arlington, 2018.

Holden, Glen M. "A Partial History of Education in Tarrant County." MA thesis, Texas Christian University, 1931.

Hopkins, Kenneth N. "The Early Development of the Hispanic Community in Fort Worth and Tarrant County, Texas, 1849–1949." *East Texas Historical Review* 38, no. 2 (October 2000): 54–67.

Jackson, Frank. "The Life and Legacy of Clarence Otto 'Big Boy' Kraft: A Baseball Journey." *Handbook of Texas Online*, April 4, 2024. https://www.tshaonline.org/handbook/entries/kraft-clarence-otto-big-boy.

Johnson, Warren. "A Study of the Effect of Convair Employment Fluctuations on Fort Worth Business Activity." MA thesis, Texas Christian University, 1960.

Kirkland, Melanie. "Fort Worth and the War Effort in World War II." Seminar, Texas Christian University, 1998.

Kline, Susan A., and the Fort Worth Parks and Community Services Department. *Fort Worth Parks*. Charleston, SC: Arcadia, 2010.

Knight, Oliver. *Fort Worth: Outpost on the Trinity*. University of Oklahoma Press: 1953. Reprint, Fort Worth: Texas Christian University Press, 1990.

Ladino, Robyn D. *Desegregation in Texas: Eisenhower, Shivers, and the Crisis at Mansfield High*. Austin: University of Texas Press, 1996.

Lambert, Maurice G. *Memories of Liberator Village*. Memorabiliacs Press, 2006.

McIlvain, Jamie. "History of Hispanic Fort Worth." Honors Paper, Texas Christian University, 1993.

McKay, Seth Shepard. *Texas and the Fair Deal, 1945–1952*. San Antonio: Naylor, 1954.

Mize, Ronald, and Alicia Swords. *Consuming Mexican Labor: From the Bracero Program to NAFTA.* 3rd ed. Toronto: University of Toronto Press, 2010.

Mullins, Marion Day. *A History of the Women's Clubs of Fort Worth, 1923–1973.* Fort Worth: Evans Press, 1973.

Munchus-Forde, Lady George. "History of the Negro in Fort Worth: Syllabus for a High School Course." MA thesis, Fisk University, 1941.

O'Neill, William L. *American High: The Years of Confidence, 1945–1960.* New York: Free Press, 1986.

Paddock, Buckley B., ed. *History of Texas: Fort Worth and the Texas Northwest Edition.* 4 vols. Chicago: Lewis Publishing, 1922.

Pate, J'Nell L. *Arsenal of Defense: Fort Worth's Military Legacy.* Denton: Texas State Historical Society, 2011.

Pate, J'Nell L. *Livestock Legacy: The Fort Worth Stockyards, 1887–1987.* Centennial Series of the Association of Former Students 27. College Station: Texas A&M Press, 1988.

Pate, J'Nell L. *North of the River: A Brief History of North Fort Worth.* Chisholm Trail Series 11. College Station: Texas A&M Press, 1994.

Pitre, Merline. "At the Crossroads: Black Texas Women, 1930–1954." In Glasrud and Pitre, *Black Women in Texas History*, 129–58.

Polito, Robert. *Savage Art: A Biography of Jim Thompson.* New York: Alfred A. Knopf, 1995.

Reverby, Susan M. *Examining Tuskegee: The Infamous Syphilis Study and Its Legacy.* John Hope Franklin Series in African American History and Culture, edited by Waldo E. Martin Jr. and Patricia Sullivan. Chapel Hill: University of North Carolina Press, 2013.

Rich, Harold. "A Distinctive Legacy: Settlement Patterns of Fort Worth's Hispanic Community." *West Texas Historical Journal* 82 (2006): 35–51.

Rich, Harold. *Fort Worth Between the World Wars.* College Station: Texas A&M University Press, 2020.

Rich, Harold. *Fort Worth: Outpost, Cowtown, Boomtown.* Norman: University of Oklahoma Press, 2014.

Selcer, Richard. *Fort Worth: A Texas Original.* Austin: Texas State Historical Association, 2004.

Selcer, Richard. *A History of Fort Worth in Black and White: 165 Years of African American Life*. Denton: University of North Texas, 2015.

Sherrod, Katie, ed. *Grace & Gumption: Stories of Fort Worth Women*. Fort Worth: Texas Christian University Press, 2007.

Smith, Harold L. "'All Good Things Start with the Women': The Origins of the Texas Birth Control Movement." *Southwestern Historical Quarterly* 14, no. 3 (January 2011): 253–85.

Sohmer, Rebecca R. "Fort Worth's Rock Island Bottom: A Social Geography of an African-American Neighborhood." MA thesis, Syracuse University, 1997.

Williams, Rachel Marie-Crane. *Run Home If You Don't Want to Be Killed: The Detroit Uprising of 1943*. Chapel Hill: University of North Carolina Press, 2021.

Wilson, Samuel A. "Vanished Legacies and Lost Culture of I. M. Terrell High School in Segregated Fort Worth." MA thesis, University of Texas at Arlington, 2012.

Zelden, Charles L. *The Battle for the Black Ballot: Smith v. Allwright and the Defeat of the Texas All-White Primary*. Landmark Law Cases and American Society. Lawrence: University Press of Kansas, 2004.

Index

D

E

F

G

H

N

R

T

Y

Z